Fundamentals
of
International
Business
Management

Fundamentals of International Business Management

Steven Globerman
Simon Fraser University

Prentice-Hall, Englewood Cliffs, New Jersey 07632

Library of Congress Cataloging-in-Publication Data

Globerman, Steven, (date)
  Fundamentals of international business management.

  Bibliography: p.
  Includes index.
  1. International business enterprises—Management.
  I. Title.
  HD62.4.G56 1986   658'.049   85-28164
  ISBN 0-13-340100-6

Editorial/production supervision and
  interior design: Joe O'Donnell Jr.
Cover design: Wanda Lubelska
Manufacturing buyer: Ed O'Dougherty

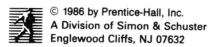 © 1986 by Prentice-Hall, Inc.
A Division of Simon & Schuster
Englewood Cliffs, NJ 07632

Printed in the United States of America

10 9 8 7 6 5 4 3

ISBN 0-13-340100-6   01

PRENTICE-HALL INTERNATIONAL (UK) LIMITED, *London*
PRENTICE-HALL OF AUSTRALIA PTY. LIMITED, *Sydney*
PRENTICE-HALL CANADA INC., *Toronto*
PRENTICE-HALL HISPANOAMERICANA, S. A., *Mexico*
PRENTICE-HALL OF INDIA PRIVATE LIMITED, *New Delhi*
PRENTICE-HALL OF JAPAN, INC., *Tokyo*
PRENTICE-HALL OF SOUTHEAST ASIA PTE. LTD., *Singapore*
EDITORA PRENTICE-HALL DO BRASIL, LTDA., *Rio de Janeiro*
WHITEHALL BOOKS LIMITED, *Wellington, New Zealand*

Contents

CHAPTER FIVE
Scanning the Political Environment, 115

CHAPTER SIX
Scanning the Sociocultural Environment, 141

CHAPTER FIFTEEN
Structuring and Controlling the International Firm, 383

Index, 409

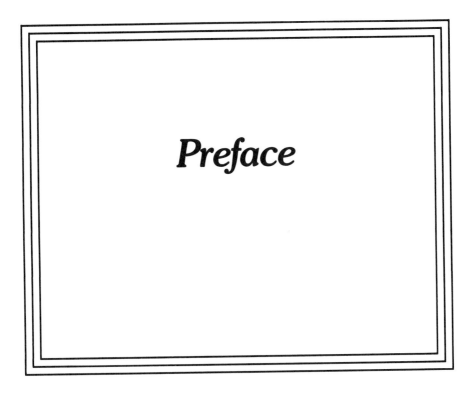

Preface

As a formal discipline in management education curricula, international business is a relatively new topic. Prior to the last ten to fifteen years international business was taught (if at all) as an adjunct to courses in international trade and economics. The post-World War II explosion in the volume of international trade, and especially in the magnitude of international investment by large, multinational companies, elevated the status of management-oriented approaches to the study of international business, and distinct courses geared to students hoping to manage in international organizations began to appear in the course offerings of business schools.

Not surprisingly for a relatively new subject, there is no clear consensus among educators concerning the appropriate content of a management course in international business. A survey of reading lists used in international business courses in different North American universities reveals the disparate approaches taken by experts in the field.* Many continue to emphasize the study of international trade theory and international economic institutions as the proper basis for management courses in international business. Others have begun to emphasize theories of the multinational enterprise that incorporate research done in economics and behavioral science on contracting, conflict, and the "inter-

*See James Dean and Richard Schwindt, *Business Administration Reading Lists and Course Outlines: International Business* (Durham, N. C.: Eno River Press, July 1981).

nalization'' of a company's competitive advantages. This latter approach often involves a consideration of the economic, political, and social effects of foreign direct investment on both the host and home economies.

A third approach—and the one adopted in this text—concentrates on the strategic decisions and operational activities that managers of international businesses must undertake in formulating and implementing their business plans. While knowledge of the international economic environment and global financial institutions is an important background element in the formulation of business plans, practical techniques for dealing with any organization's major problems—for example, how to finance, produce, and market its goods and services—constitute the manager's "toolkit." The underlying premise of this third approach to international business is that managers should be exposed to the basic tools of international management and that the finer points of economic theory and details about the world monetary system should be dealt with in economics courses.

While the tools of the international manager are not altogether different from those of the domestic manager, there are important differences that justify a separate treatment of management practices in international organizations. An important goal of this book is to identify and discuss the implications of the salient differences between international and domestic management practices.

To be sure, most textbooks that emphasize management decision-making issues and techniques also provide an overview of the major institutions and government agencies involved (directly or indirectly) with international trade and commerce. The degree of emphasis varies with the individual author's preference. I prefer to keep discussions of background institutional material fairly restricted. Necessary background is integrated directly into the discussion of management issues where relevant. For example, the role of central banks in the exchange-rate determination process is discussed in the section dealing with exchange rate forecasting. The nature and relevance of GATT and other agreements and laws affecting international trade and investment are discussed in sections that deal with international marketing and international investment. And so forth.

A recent conference of management educators stressed that international business training involves a lifetime process—with self-teaching, initiative, and work experience beyond the business school. Furthermore, besides economics, functional fields, and organization and management strategy, international business education might include the study of foreign languages, comparative governments, comparative commercial law, comparative sociology, international labor relations, history, and comparative literature.*

While such a rich menu of topics cannot be offered in a single text, I have tried to emphasize material that is acknowledged to be important by interna-

---

*See William Dymsza, "The Education and Development of Managers for Future Decades," *Journal of International Business Studies*, 18 (Winter 1982), 9–18.

tional business educators but that has not (in their view) been adequately covered in existing books to date. One such area is environmental scanning and analysis. Relevant techniques to accomplish these activities are covered extensively in this text. Another is the problems managers face in dealing with foreign constituencies, including labor unions and sovereign governments. Developing methods for identifying and resolving conflicts in overseas markets is a major responsibility of management that hitherto has received fairly cursory treatment in international business texts.

In all of the chapters dealing with strategic or tactical decision making in the international organization, I try to emphasize the particular relevance of the organization's international exposure to the management issues being addressed. In almost all cases issues and problems facing international managers resemble those confronting managers of purely domestic companies. However, the decision-making environment surrounding international companies is usually more complex than the environment in which purely domestic companies operate.

As an example, exchange-rate changes can be expected to affect the international competitiveness of most companies, including those that produce and sell their output within a single country. But the impacts of exchange-rate changes on the purely domestic organization are indirect. That is, they are related to increases or decreases in the competitiveness of foreign rivals resulting from decreases or increases in the values of foreign currencies relative to the home currency of the purely domestic business. The international business not only experiences these indirect impacts for each of its affiliates but may also realize balance-sheet (or wealth) changes as a result of exchange-rate changes against which it failed to ''hedge.'' International managers must therefore contend with questions of whether and how to hedge foreign-exchange risk on a more active basis than do managers of purely domestic companies.

Other aspects of the broader political and cultural environment are also more heterogeneous in the case of the international organization compared to the purely domestic company. Not only do legal and accounting rules surrounding business practices differ, but (perhaps more important) the unwritten codes of business behavior differ across countries. If a manager ignores salient differences in these unwritten codes, the consequences for his or her business may be far more severe than if he or she violates a formal legal requirement. The varied and unfamiliar international, political, and cultural environments put a greater burden on the international manager than on the purely domestic manager.

The material presented in the book presumes that the student is in an undergraduate business program and has passing familiarity with basic economic and algebraic principles. Prior courses in accounting, finance, marketing, and other business disciplines would be useful but are not at all essential. Indeed, an effort is made to incorporate brief overviews of basic ideas in these various management areas into the relevant chapters. Hence, what is most essential in approaching this book is an intellectual curiosity about how a successful international business organization is managed.

In preparing to write this book, I was struck by the preponderance of international business texts that had been written by two or more authors. Almost immediately after commencing my own research and writing, the reason for multiple authorship became apparent to me. The field of international business, as an academic discipline, is broad and diffuse. Therefore, the benefits from specialization of labor—achievable with several authors possessing different specialized areas of expertise—are potentially quite substantial.

While having managed to complete this text as a sole author, I cannot claim autonomy in its creation. Abundant help was received from numerous colleagues. My colleagues at Simon Fraser University were especially generous in reading and critiquing sample chapters. I am especially indebted to Professors Pao Cheng, John Herzog, Moustafa Magid, Lindsay Meredith, Barry Schacter, Carolyne Smart, William Wedley, and Mark Wexler. Constructive suggestions were also received from George Jacobs of British Columbia Institute of Technology, I. A. Litvak of York University, and David Rutenberg of Queen's University. Several outside reviewers made extensive and extremely useful comments for several versions of the manuscript. I would like to especially acknowledge the thorough review provided by Professor James McConnell of the University of Buffalo. To all of the above, as well as others too numerous to mention, I express my gratitude. I also extend absolution for any remaining weaknesses or shortcomings of the text.

I must also express a debt of gratitude to my research assistant, Larry Olson, who besides being diligent in finding appropriate references and case studies, was also extremely conscientious in coordinating numerous administrative tasks associated with preparing the manuscript for publication. Anita Mahoney's cheerful and efficient word processing substantially expedited the production of this book. Errors in various versions of the manuscript were identified by students in my international business course, who served as enthusiastic, if somewhat captive, audiences.

CHAPTER ONE

Background to Studying International Business

The primary objective of this text is to provide the reader with a solid understanding of the short-run and long-run decisions that managers of international businesses must make in the course of formulating and implementing specific business plans, along with an in-depth exposure to the techniques and tools that are available for use by international managers. If this sounds like a frighteningly austere and somewhat theoretical statement of purpose, we hasten to note an additional objective: to provide the reader with a lively survey of contemporary issues in the international business environment. The basic importance of the material covered in this book will probably be readily apparent to both actual and aspiring international business managers. We hope that the book also conveys a sense of the excitement and fun associated with international business.

THE JOB OF MANAGING

A recurring theme throughout this book is the claim that managing in an international business is ordinarily more complex and uncertain than managing in companies that restrict their activities to a single country. But this does not mean that international and domestic managers would have little to talk to each other about at cocktail parties. On the contrary, many aspects of the management function are qualitatively similar, even within business organizations as diverse as a local phar-

1

macy in Mount Vernon, Washington (population 8,000), and the giant conglomerate International Telephone and Telegraph, which has operating subsidiaries in many different countries around the world.

For example, senior management in any business organization must establish overall objectives for the organization as well as identify and choose strategies to realize those objectives. The implementation of an overall corporate strategy, in turn, involves formulating and activating specific plans and tactics for ongoing functional activities in the organization, including finance, purchasing, production, and marketing. Since these activities are the subject matter for the "bread and butter" courses in most management schools, one should expect international managers to be at least as familiar with the basic principles in those areas as their domestic management counterparts.

The existence of a fundamental core to the practice of management ensures that many of the basic issues confronting managers in both line and staff positions are similar from business to business. Nevertheless, specific problems and challenges confront both line and staff managers of international businesses that do not confront (at least to the same extent) managers of purely domestic enterprises. The identification and analysis of these challenges constitute the basis for the study of the field known as international business, or international management. We will shortly consider some salient differences between managing an international and a purely domestic firm. But first it would be useful to be more explicit about what we mean by international business.

A DEFINITION OF INTERNATIONAL BUSINESS

No simple or universally accepted definition exists for the term *international business.* Indeed, one can find a number of definitions in the business literature. At one end of the definitional spectrum, international businesses are defined as organizations that buy and/or sell goods and services across two or more national boundaries, even if management is located in a single country.[1] At the other end of the spectrum, international businesses are equated only with the four or five hundred biggest enterprises with operating units outside their own country.[2] In the middle are institutional arrangements that provide for some managerial direction of economic activity taking place abroad but stop short of controlling ownership of the businesses carrying on the activity, for example, joint ventures with locally owned businesses or with foreign governments.

---

[1] See John Fayerweather, *International Business Management: A Conceptual Framework* (New York: McGraw-Hill, 1969), p. 5.

[2] See Raymond Vernon and Louis T. Wells, Jr., *Manager in the International Economy,* 4th ed. (Englewood Cliffs, N.J.: Prentice-Hall, 1981), pp. 3–4.

For our purposes, any organization that does business in or with two or more countries can be considered an international business. Thus our definition would admit a relatively small, family-owned, import–export business as well as giant multinationals such as IBM and Nestlé. On the surface, it may seem illogical to group companies whose managers and productive assets are located in a single country with companies whose subsidiaries literally span the globe and whose managers are located in dozens of countries. Certainly the complexities associated with managing an international giant such as IBM dwarf those associated with managing a souvenir shop on the border between the United States and Canada, although the manager of the souvenir shop might not concede this point. But many of the special problems and issues that arise from doing business in two or more national political jurisdictions are relevant to both companies. Hence, while it is often necessary to distinguish between companies whose assets are located entirely in a single country but whose outputs and/or inputs cross national borders and those with affiliates operating in foreign countries, many of the basic tools and techniques that managers in the latter set of companies would fine useful, managers in the former set would find useful as well.

PERSPECTIVES ON INTERNATIONAL BUSINESS ACTIVITIES

There is no single measure akin to gross national product that summarizes the overall scope and magnitude of international business activity. One perspective on the dynamics of international business activity is provided by changing patterns of exports and imports. Table 1.1 adopts this perspective in reporting imports and exports for different parts of the world for selected years. The difference in the reported worldwide values of imports and exports represents a statistical discrepancy since an export from one part of the world is obviously an import by another part of the world. However, there is no necessary matching of imports and exports at the level of the individual country or region. For example, a country can import more than it exports for a considerable period of time as long as its trusting trade partners provide it with the wherewithal to make its payments, say in the form of loans.

Table 1.1 indicates that world trade in commodities and manufactured goods increased a remarkable tenfold over the period 1965 to 1980. The growth in U.S. imports exceeded this average, while U.S. exports grew at a somewhat slower rate. Not surprisingly, given the size of the U.S. economy, exports from and imports into the U.S. constitute a significant share of world exports and imports. But the largest single trading bloc is made up of countries that comprise the European Economic Community (EEC). Exports from EEC countries comprised almost 33 percent of world exports in 1980, while EEC imports were almost 36 percent of world imports. The remarkable growth of the Japanese economy in in-

TABLE 1.1 Imports and Exports for Selected Years and Regions (values in $ millions U.S.)

	IMPORTS				EXPORTS			
	1965	1975	1980	1983	1965	1975	1980	1983
World	197,326	901,299	2,046,159	1,910,051	185,616	871,234	1,993,335	1,816,377
U.S.	21,348	103,843	256,984	269,878	27,003	106,157	212,887	200,538
EEC[1]	69,758	304,407	729,276	587,981	64,014	295,768	657,251	570,666
EFTA[2]	15,117	62,331	137,638	109,901	12,111	52,928	116,105	104,330
CPEs[3]	20,658	92,063	161,634	191,690	21,779	84,616	175,074	198,938
Japan	8,169	47,880	140,523	146,992	8,452	55,754	129,542	146,676

Sources: United Nations, *Statistical Yearbook*, 32nd ed., tables 178–179, New York, 1983; and United Nations, *Monthly Bulletin of Statistics*, November, table 52, New York, 1984.

[1] Belgium–Luxembourg, Denmark, France, Germany, Greece, Ireland, Italy, Netherlands, U.K.
[2] Austria, Finland, Iceland, Norway, Portugal, Sweden, Switzerland.
[3] Centrally planned economies.

4

ternational trade activity is also highlighted in table 1.1. Over the period shown, Japanese exports increased by a factor of 15, while Japanese imports increased by a factor of 17.

Table 1.1 understates the magnitude of total international trade since it excludes trade in services. Examples of internationally traded services include banking, transportation, tourism, consulting, insurance, and the like. A recent report puts the value of world trade in services at more than $350 billion (U.S.) in 1980, or approximately 17 percent of total world trade in commodities and manufactured goods. The U.S. is the largest single exporter of services with an export value of close to $35 billion. It is followed closely by Britain ($34 billion), France ($33 billion), and West Germany ($32 billion). Taken as a unit, the EEC had service exports valued at close to $165 billion, almost half the world total. Japan's service exports were placed at approximately $19 billion.[3]

While absolute dollar values of international trade are interesting statistics in their own right, they are more meaningful measures of the significance of international business when put in the context of overall economic activity. In table 1.2 I have attempted to do that by showing the ratio of exports to total gross domestic product for 1981 for a selected group of countries. Those of you who have studied macroeconomics will recall that gross domestic product is the value of all final goods and services produced by residents of a country. The countries selected for inclusion in the table represent the major trading economies in the non-Communist world.

One can see that the relative importance of international trade varies extensively across countries. For the relatively small economies of Singapore, Hong Kong, and (to a lesser extent) Belgium, international business is the life blood of the economy. For large economies, such as those of the U.S. and Japan, it is

TABLE 1.2   Ratio of Exports to Gross Domestic Product, 1981 (1982)

SELECTED COUNTRIES

Australia	= 12.8 (13.5)	Austria	= 23.8 (23.4)	Belgium	= 58.4 (60.7)
Canada	= 24.6 (23.0)	Denmark	= 28.0 (27.7)	France	= 17.6 (17.1)
West Germany	= 25.7 (26.7)	Hong Kong	= 73.5 (69.1)	Indonesia	= 26.2 (–)
Italy	= 21.6 (21.1)	Ireland	= 46.2 (45.8)	Japan	= 13.4 (13.0)
Korea	= 32.3 (–)	Norway	= 31.8 (31.2)	Netherlands	= 48.3 (48.1)
Singapore	= 156.1 (139.2)	Sweden	= 25.4 (27.0)	United Kingdom	= 20.6 (20.3)
United States	= 8.0 (6.95)	Thailand	= – (18.9)		
Spain	= – (11.3)	Malaysia	= – (45.7)		

Sources: United Nations, *Statistical Yearbook*, 32nd ed., table 184, New York, 1983; United Nations, *Monthly Bulletin of Statistics*, July and November, tables E and 53, New York, 1984.

[3] "U.S. Arms for Reduced Barriers in International Service Trade," *Toronto Globe and Mail*, December 29, 1983, p. B3.

relatively much less important.[4] But international trade is becoming an increasingly important feature of U.S. business activity, as witnessed by the fact that the ratio of exports to gross domestic product approximately doubled from 1970 to 1981.

MULTINATIONAL ENTERPRISES

American readers of this book, after studying table 1.2, might be contemplating asking for a refund given the seemingly small role that exports and imports play in the American economy. Before doing so, however, the role of the multinational enterprise in international trade should also be considered. Specifically, the data in table 1.2 understate the involvement of American companies in international business since they fail to explicitly identify the exports and imports of American companies that are located outside the U.S. These companies are affiliates of companies headquartered in the U.S. An example would be General Motors of Canada. General Motors is the largest privately owned company in Canada, with substantial exports to the U.S. and other countries. If one were to include the value of output produced by the foreign affiliates of U.S. companies in a measure of U.S. international business activity, the relevance of studying international business would be quite persuasive indeed.

By way of amplification, table 1.3 reports the total worldwide sales of the twenty-five largest U.S. multinational enterprises (MNEs) for 1983, with their foreign sales broken out (stated) separately. The list is a veritable *Who's Who* of corporate America. The companies listed in table 1.3 all have subsidiaries located in countries outside the U.S. For our purposes, we shall identify any company that has a controlling interest in one or more companies outside its home country as an MNE. For reasons we will discuss in chapter 2, many MNEs are relatively large companies. Indeed, nine of the first ten companies listed in table 1.3 (with the exception of Phibro–Salomon) were among the twenty-five largest companies in the world.

MNEs are not found exclusively in the United States. Many large MNEs are headquartered elsewhere, as suggested by table 1.4. Specifically, table 1.4 lists the twenty-five non-U.S. companies that held the largest dollar value of investments in U.S.-located companies in 1983. In some of the cases listed, the ownership share in the U.S. company is a minority one. Hence, it is unclear whether the ownership was a controlling one in accordance with our definition of MNE. But in most cases the ownership share exceeds 50 percent, which assures a controlling interest for the non-U.S. firm. It is interesting to compare the nature

---

[4] It should be noted that the ratios for Singapore and Hong Kong are 1975 estimates, the latest year for which the ratios are reported. Given the rapid growth of the consumer sector in the two economies over the past decade, more recent estimates would undoubtedly be lower.

TABLE 1.3   The Twenty-Five Largest U.S. Multinationals, 1983

COMPANY	INDUSTRY	FOREIGN REVENUE ($ MILLIONS)	TOTAL REVENUE ($ MILLIONS)
1. Exxon	Petroleum	61,815	88,651
2. Mobil	Petroleum	32,629	55,609
3. Texaco	Petroleum	25,157	40,068
4. Phibro-Salomon	Financial services	20,100	29,757
5. IBM	Computers	17,058	40,180
6. Ford Motor	Motor vehicles	16,080	44,455
7. General Motors	Motor vehicles	14,913	74,582
8. Gulf	Petroleum	11,535	26,581
9. Standard Oil Calif.	Petroleum	10,952	27,342
10. Du Pont	Chemicals	10,816	35,173
11. Citicorp	Financial services	9,650	17,037
12. ITT	Conglomerate	7,808	20,249
13. BankAmerica	Financial services	5,943	13,299
14. Dow Chemical	Chemicals	5,726	10,951
15. Standard Oil Indiana	Petroleum	5,363	27,937
16. Chase Manhattan	Financial services	4,943	8,523
17. General Electric	Aircraft engines/ generating equipment	4,758	27,681
18. Occidental Petroleum	Petroleum	4,544	19,709
19. Safeway Stores	Retailing	4,528	18,585
20. Sun Co.	Petroleum	4,282	14,928
21. Proctor and Gamble	Consumer goods	3,685	12,452
22. J.P. Morgan	Financial services	3,446	5,764
23. Xerox	Copy/office equipment	3,393	8,464
24. Eastman Kodak	Photo equipment	3,270	10,170
25. Sears Roebuck	Retailing	3,246	35,883

Source: *Forbes*, July 2, 1984, pp. 114–15.

of the companies listed in tables 1.3 and 1.4. Petroleum and chemical companies are prominent in both lists. Consumer goods, including autos, and banks are also well represented. In the next chapter, we will consider some explanations of why MNEs tend to be clustered in specific industries.

While the companies listed in tables 1.3 and 1.4 also do a substantial amount of exporting from their home countries, they are far from being the most intensive group of exporters. This point is illustrated by table 1.5, which lists the twenty-five top exporting companies in the United States in 1983 as measured by exports as a percentage of sales. It is interesting to note that only General Electric and Eastman Kodak appear in both tables 1.3 and 1.5. Furthermore, there is, if anything, an inverse relationship between the ratio of exports to sales and total sales across the twenty-five firms listed in table 1.5. The point made here is that it is not just the giant MNEs that are involved in international business.

TABLE 1.4 The Twenty-Five Largest Foreign Investors in the U.S., 1983

FOREIGN INVESTOR	HOME COUNTRY	U.S. COMPANY	INDUSTRY	REVENUE ($ MILLIONS)
1. Seagram Co. Ltd.	Canada	J.E. Seagram, Du Pont	Spirits/chemicals	36,653
2. Anglo American of S. Africa	South Africa	Numerous	Metals/financial services	32,417
3. Royal Dutch/Shell	Netherlands/U.K.	Shell Oil	Petroleum	20,978
4. British Petroleum	U.K.	Standard Oil of Ohio	Petroleum	11,599
5. Mitsui & Co.	Japan	Mitsui	Conglomerate	9,545
6. B.A.T. Industries	U.K./Canada	BATUS	Paper/retailing	7,122
7. Flick Group	Germany	W.R. Grace	Conglomerate	6,219
8. Tengelmann Group	Germany	Great A&P Tea	Retailing	5,222
9. Régre Nationale des Usines Renault	France	American Motors	Motor vehicles	4,489
10. Brascan Ltd.	Canada	Scott Paper, Noranda	Paper/metals	4,251
11. Beneficiaries of U.S. Philips Trust	Netherlands	North American Philips	Electronics	4,250
12. Generale Occidentale	France	Grand Union	Retailing	3,519

13. Volkswagenwerk	Germany	Volkswagen of America	Motor vehicles	3,492
14. Bayer A.G.	Germany	Numerous	Chemicals	3,445
15. Mitsubishi	Japan	Mitsubishi International Corp.	Trading company	3,165
16. Unilever	Netherlands	Lever Brothers/ Thomas J. Lipton	Household products/food	3,119
17. Nestlé	Switzerland	Numerous	Household products/food	2,700
18. Midland Bank	U.K.	Crocker National	Banking	2,560
19. Hanson Trust	U.K.	Numerous	Conglomerate	2,361
20. Bell Canada	Canada	Northern Telecom	Tele-communications	2,195
21. Hongkong and Shanghai Banking Corp.	Hong Kong	Marine Midland Bank	Banking	2,156
22. CIBA-GEIGY	Switzerland	CIBA-GEIGY Corp.	Chemicals/drugs	2,104
23. Petrofina SA	Belgium	American Petrofina	Petroleum	2,069
24. Française des Pétroles	France/Canada	Total Petroleum	Petroleum	2,034
25. George Weston	Canada	Numerous	Food products	2,033

Source: *Forbes*, July 2, 1984, pp. 101–03.

9

TABLE 1.5   The Twenty-Five Leading U.S. Exporters, 1983

COMPANY	INDUSTRY	TOTAL REVENUE ($ MILLIONS)	EXPORTS/ SALES x 100
1. Boeing	Aircraft	11,129	43.30
2. Caterpillar Tractor	Construction equipment	5,424	29.20
3. International Minerals and Chemicals	Industrial minerals	1,462	26.90
4. McDonnell Douglas	Aircraft	8,111	25.95
5. Northrop	Aircraft	3,261	25.38
6. Hewlett-Packard	Computers	4,710	23.46
7. A. E. Staley	Feeds and grain products	1,679	21.50
8. Archer Daniels Midland	Grain products	4,292	20.99
9. Digital Equipment	Computers	4,272	19.12
10. Dresser Industries	Oil field equipment	3,473	18.52
11. Engelhard	Chemical and metal products	2,099	18.40
12. Weyerhaeuser	Wood products	4,883	17.82
13. Eastman Kodak	Photo equipment	10,170	17.36
14. Ingersoll Rand	Drills/compressors	2,274	17.02
15. Signal Companies	Engines	6,151	16.66
16. United Technologies	Aircraft engines	14,669	16.25
17. General Electric	Aircraft engines/ generating equipment	26,797	15.78
18. Chrysler	Motor vehicles	13,240	15.70
19. Celanese	Chemicals/fibers	3,498	15.03
20. Westinghouse	Generating equipment	1,389	14.57
21. Emerson Electric	Electronic components	3,476	14.44
22. Textron	Helicopters/ aerospace products	2,980	14.16
23. Monsanto	Chemicals/fibers	6,299	13.95
24. FMC	Defense/petroleum and farm equipment	3,498	13.80
25. Raytheon	Electronic defense systems	5,937	13.19

Source: *Fortune*, August 6, 1984, p. 65. © Time, Inc. All rights reserved.

OTHER INTERNATIONAL BUSINESS STRUCTURES

There are a number of other ways in which international business takes place that are not covered in the preceding tables. These cover a variety of collaborative efforts between the extremes of a pure export/import business and fully owned or majority-owned subsidiaries abroad.[5]

[5] The following descriptions of these various structures are taken from Richard W. Wright, "Evolving International Business Arrangements," in K. C. Dhawan, Hamid Etemad, and Richard W. Wright, *International Business: A Canadian Perspective* (Don Mills, Ontario: Addison-Wesley Publishing Co., 1981), pp. 490–505.

Franchising

In a franchise agreement, the international company grants the use of some asset to a franchisee in a foreign country. The former agrees to supply the latter on a continuous basis some important ingredient—perhaps a critical component or service—for the end product. The latter, in turn, obtains the right to conduct business using the trade name or trademark of the franchisor. For this the franchisee pays fees or royalties to the franchisor.

The reader who has done any foreign traveling is undoubtedly quite familiar with a number of well-known franchise arrangements. The ubiquitous McDonald's fast-food restaurants are franchised businesses, as are Holiday Inn hotels. The arrangements between McDonald's Corporation and its franchisees illustrates fairly well the essential nature of the franchising arrangement. McDonald's provides its local franchisees with management and technical training and assists in locating, equipping, and decorating the premises. In return, the franchisee pays McDonald's a purchase fee plus royalties on sales.

Management Contracts

In this type of arrangement the international company sells a particular corporate resource—management skills—to a foreign company or government. A contract is signed for a given number of years over which time the international company may undertake to manage (for a fee) anything from an entire company or project to a specified, limited management function. As well, most management contracts provide for the training of local personnel. An example is Saudi Arabia's decision to hire Bell Canada to manage the installation of modern switching and transmission equipment in Saudi Arabia's telephone system.

Contractual Joint Ventures

A contractual joint venture is typically a partnership arrangement in which two or more companies (or a company and a government agency) share the costs of an investment, along with the long-term profits (that it is hoped will materialize). The contractual joint venture is usually formed for a particular project of limited duration and terminates once the project is completed. An example of this type of international business structure is provided by Boeing's 767 passenger aircraft. Like most other commercial airplane developments the 767 was an international effort. Boeing itself had primary responsibility for most of the wings, the cockpit, and the final assembly. The design and construction of the rest of the airplane were put out to other companies both inside and outside the U.S. In Italy, for example, Alitalia SAI had responsibility for the rudder and fins. In Japan a consortium of the Civil Transport Development Corporation, Mitsubishi Heavy Industries Ltd., Kawasaki Heavy Industries Ltd., and Fuji Heavy Industries Ltd. built the main body of the aircraft.[6]

---

[6] This joint-venture arrangement is described in David Clutterbuck, ''The Jigsaw with Bits in Three Countries,'' *International Management,* August 1981, pp. 16–18.

Equity Joint Ventures

An equity joint venture is a company owned by more than one organization. It is generally a separate company formed as a subsidiary by two or more corporations or by a corporation and a governmental agency. Each partner holds stock in the subsidiary and shares in the profits (or losses) in relation to its ownership share. There are many examples of equity joint ventures. A number have recently been undertaken in the rapidly growing telecommunications industry. For example, the Finnish Company Nahia Group recently teamed up with the American Tandy Corporation to establish a jointly owned Asian facility to manufacture mobile telephones. Nahia is primarily providing the technical and manufacturing expertise, while Tandy provides the marketing capacity for the joint venture.[7]

Although comprehensive statistical data are unavailable, it is widely acknowledged that joint ventures are a prominent international business structure. Most large U.S. companies are involved in at least one international joint venture, and the limited available evidence suggests that large firms headquartered in other countries are relatively more inclined to participate in international business through joint ventures. Furthermore, sovereign governments (especially in developing countries) have been increasing pressure on foreign companies to establish joint ventures with local companies rather than pursue other forms of international business.

One expert on international joint ventures—J. Peter Killing of the University of Western Ontario—has identified the special difficulties associated with managing this type of business structure. See reference list at end of chapter. In particular, differences in the priorities and objectives of joint-venture partners can create dissension and a lack of cohesion in the organization. Killing suggests that joint ventures will generally work out better when all of the venture's operating and strategic decisions are made by one of the joint-venture partners. The more equally shared the responsibility for management decisions, the greater the likelihood that the venture will end in failure. Of course, foreign governments may be reluctant to see their local businesses cast in the role of a ''passive'' investor.

In the next chapter we will discuss the advantages and disadvantages of these various forms of international business from the firm's perspective. We will also consider several theories that attempt to explain which particular structure will be chosen under a given set of circumstances. But first we should motivate the reader's interest a bit more by elaborating on the unique features of international business management.

THE UNIQUE ASPECTS OF INTERNATIONAL BUSINESS

The unique challenges and problems faced by international business management can perhaps best be identified within the context of a discussion of how firms for-

---

[7] See ''A Mobile Phone Maker Finds a Hookup in the U.S.,'' *Business Week*, July 2, 1984, p. 40.

mulate and implement business plans. Since all firms, both international and purely domestic, go through essentially the same procedural stages in formulating and implementing business strategies, an overview of this process offers a nicely structured framework for comparing and contrasting management functions in the two types of organizations.

Ultimately, the distinguishing feature of international business is that international firms operate in environments that are highly uncertain and where the rules of the game are often ambiguous, contradictory, and subject to rapid change, as compared to the domestic environment. As one expert has put it: "Conducting international business is really not like playing a whole new ball game; however, it is like playing in a different ball park, where you have to learn the factors unique to the playing field."[8]

The dynamic nature of the international business environment can be illustrated with several examples from the past decade. While the following examples are only a few that might be cited, they illustrate the theme that doing business on an international basis is a highly complex and challenging undertaking. For example, the rapid economic growth of the Asia–Pacific region has opened up major new markets for foreign suppliers and has spawned a host of new competitors for North American and European firms. While Japan is the major economy in this region, smaller Pacific Rim countries have also enjoyed remarkable rates of economic growth. Two relatively small economies—Hong Kong and Singapore—enjoyed growth rates in their real gross national products of close to 10 percent per year over the period 1977–1982, while only slightly less rapid growth was experienced by China, Taiwan, Indonesia, Malaysia, and South Korea. Obviously, managers who are able to exploit the opportunities presented by the emergence of this growth area have a substantial edge on their counterparts who are unwilling or unable to do business in the Asia–Pacific region.

Another noteworthy change in the international business environment is the emergence of countertrade (or barter-type) arrangements for international trade. By some estimates, countertrade is employed in upwards of 20 percent of international transactions. In part, this growth in countertrade, where payment is made in goods and services rather than foreign exchange, reflects a shortage of "hard currencies" (especially U.S. dollars) held by Eastern European and Third World countries. It also reflects a growing propensity of many governments to directly regulate the quantity and nature of imports into their countries. Obviously, managers who are unfamiliar with the mechanics of countertrade will be at a significant disadvantage in the international business environment compared to their more enlightened counterparts.

Along similar lines, an increasing number of governments in recent years have attempted to blunt the economic power of large multinational companies. In particular, they have sought to control the inflow of foreign direct investment into

---

[8] James M. Higgins, *Organizational Policy and Strategic Management*, 2nd ed. (New York: Dryden, 1983), p. 28.

their countries. For example, Canada and Australia established agencies to screen incoming direct investments by foreign-owned companies. Other countries have also taken steps to assure greater local control over domestic economic activity, such as encouraging foreign investors to establish joint ventures with local businesses instead of setting up wholly owned subsidiaries. Managers who are astute in identifying new ways of doing business that satisfy the changing priorities of foreign governments have an obvious and major competitive advantage over their competitors who cannot—or will not—adapt to these changing priorities.

It must be stressed that the impacts of these dynamic ''factors unique to the playing field'' for international business are felt in all relevant stages of evolving and implementing business plans. To illustrate, let us consider the first broad stage of the process: formulating a corporate-mission statement.[9]

THE MISSION STATEMENT

As outlined in figure 1.1, the first step in formulating and implementing a set of business plans is to define the firm's mission (or guiding principles) in the marketplace. The mission statement should, among other things, provide a long-term view of what the company is striving to become and provide direction to divisional and subsidiary managers in their efforts to develop their own business plans. Strategic-planning experts Benjamin Tregoe and John Zimmerman suggest that a firm's mission principles can be defined in terms of three broad categories: products offered/markets served, capabilities, and results (see table 1.6). For example, Hewlett–Packard represents a company that defines its corporate mission in terms of a technological imperative. Specifically, its business plans and operating strategies emanate from the principle that it must remain in the forefront of computing technology. As another example, Imperial Oil, the Canadian subsidiary of Exxon, develops corporate strategy based on its underlying mission to be an integrated natural resource.

Whatever other components of table 1.6 management chooses as its mission statement, the mission statement of a firm engaged in (or commencing) international business activities should incorporate a global perspective. That is, the firm's senior management should explicitly define the company's mission in terms of an international mandate (for example, to be a supplier of accounting software in English-speaking countries) rather than allow the company's international activities to develop as an incidental adjunct to its domestic activities. Incorporating an international outlook into the firm's basic statement of purpose will help focus the attention of managers (at all levels of the organization) on the opportunities (and hazards) outside the domestic economy. A succinct example of one company's international mandate is provided by Black and Decker's vision of be-

---

[9] Much of the following discussion is taken from Steven Globerman and Carolyne Smart, ''Strategic Planning in International Businesses,'' Simon Fraser University, mimeographed, 1984.

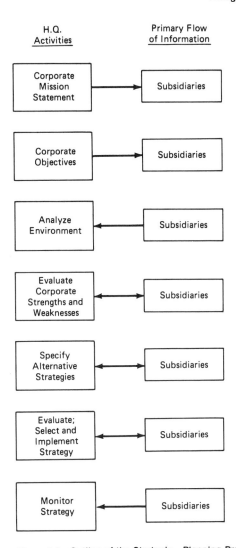

H.Q. Activities	Primary Flow of Information

Figure 1.1   Outline of the Strategic—Planning Process

ing a worldwide, broad-based marketer of consumer products. Another example, somewhat less tightly drawn, is the vision expressed by Franz Tyaack, president and chief executive officer of Westinghouse Canada, of world trade winning out in the long run. In Tyaack's own words: "Our strategy, in the long term, is based on world trade winning out. If that is a wrong assumption, then I'm leading this organization down the tubes."[10]

[10] As cited in Robert English, "Westinghouse Pins Hopes on Exports," *Financial Post* (Toronto), May 26, 1984, p. 1.

TABLE 1.6   Principles for Defining Mission Statement

CATEGORY	STRATEGIC AREA
Products/markets	Products offered
	Market needs
Capabilities	Technology
	Production capability
	Method of sale
	Method of distribution
	Natural resources
Results	Size/growth
	Return/profit

Source: Benjamin W. Tregoe and John W. Zimmerman, *Top Management Strategy* (New York: Simon & Schuster, 1980), p. 43. Copyright
© 1980 by Kepner-Tregoe, Inc. Reprinted by permission of Simon &
Schuster, Inc.

Establishing Organizational Objectives

Objectives are the specific results that managers seek to achieve in pursuing
a firm's mission. They are typically formulated in all areas upon which the survival or success of a firm depends. For example, objectives may encompass financial and marketing targets such as minimum rates of return on invested capital
and minimum market shares for a firm's product line. Both international and
purely domestic companies require an explicit statement of corporate objectives in
order to guide managers in their decision making and to facilitate performance
evaluation at all levels of an organization. International businesses, however,
must set their objectives on a global basis and with a view to environmental differences, requirements that add a dimension of complexity to the objective-setting
exercise.

This added complexity is illustrated in the case of rate-of-return objectives.
Typically, required rates of return on capital investments will depend upon a
firm's cost of capital, that is, the cost of the capital acquired to finance the firm's
investments. A firm's cost of capital may in turn depend in complex ways upon
the international distribution of the firm's business activities. For example, it can
be argued that internationalization lowers a firm's cost of capital by increasing its
access to foreign capital markets. Furthermore, where economic activity is less
than perfectly synchronized across countries, doing business in two or more national markets will reduce the volatility of a firm's sales and profits associated with
the business cycle. By itself (as we shall discuss in a later chapter) this diversification could also lower the firm's cost of capital; however, there may be certain
unique risks attached to international ventures (e.g., expropriation of assets by
foreign governments) that lead to higher costs of capital for the international firm.
By contrast, the purely domestic firm has a substantially easier job in identifying

its capital costs since the risks it faces are usually related to business-cycle considerations that are fairly well known and geographically contained.

The consequences of adopting specific financial and nonfinancial objectives also may depend upon the geographical domain of a firm's business activities, not only for economic reasons but for cultural and political reasons as well. As a result, objectives that are appropriate for certain international firms may be inappropriate for others. As an illustration, Higgins notes that product quality is often of less concern in countries like England that have internal markets that are protected by government from competition. In contrast, a firm selling in the Japanese market probably would have high quality as a very important objective. Japan stresses quality more than other countries, in part because the Japanese see it as the means to be highly competitive in the international marketplace. Consequently, Japanese consumers have come to expect (and demand) a very high level of product quality.[11]

Analyzing the Environment

If a firm is to realize its specific objectives, it must choose and implement strategies that take advantage of opportunities in the environment in which it operates, while dealing with threats posed by the environment. All of a firm's functional strategies, including how it produces and markets its output as well as how it finances its activities and staffs its organization, will be influenced by specific aspects of the environments in which it does business. And herein lies the source of most differences between international and domestic business management: managers of international businesses confront a much more heterogeneous environment compared to managers of purely domestic businesses.

Some of the salient differences between the international and domestic business environments are summarized in table 1.7. First and perhaps foremost is the fact that international managers must anticipate and cope with changes in exchange rates. For an individual company earning income and incurring expenses denominated in different currencies, changes in the value of foreign currencies relative to its home (or domestic) currency can have substantial impacts on the company's cash flow as well as on its reported profitability. As a result, exchange-rate forecasting and foreign-exchange management are especially prominent activities in most international businesses of any substantial size.

Secondly, while all businesses must be concerned not only with forecasting demand conditions for their goods and services but also with the behavior of cost factors, such as wages and interest rates, the forecasting job for international managers is complicated by the multiplicity of economic environments in which their firms operate. Since changes in wages, interest rates, and other prices are imperfectly synchronized across national economies, management cannot simply assume that profit margins will move in a consistent fashion in all countries in

[11] Higgins, *Organizational Policy,* p. 28.

TABLE 1.7   Differences between the Domestic and International Environments

DOMESTIC	INTERNATIONAL
1. Single currency.	1. Currencies differing in stability and value.
2. Uniform financial and business climate.	2. Variety of economic climates.
3. Relatively homogeneous market.	3. Fragmented and diverse markets.
4. Uniform legal and accounting framework.	4. Diverse legal and accounting framework.
5. Relatively stable political climate.	5. Political change is often discontinuous.
6. Cultural mores and values are relatively well understood.	6. Cultural values and mores must be identified and understood.
7. Data are available and collection is relatively easy.	7. Collection of accurate data is a formidable task.

Source: Adapted from William W. Cain, "International Planning: Mission Impossible," *Columbia Journal of World Business*, (Vol. 5, No. 4) July–August 1970, p. 58.

which their firm does business. But as one manager put it to us, exploiting differences in demand and cost conditions across countries is the fun of international business.

A multiplicity of tastes and preferences toward given products also confronts international management. As an illustration of this point, while American consumers tend to favor shopping in supermarkets and department stores, Japanese consumers favor small retail shops. In particular, Japanese homemakers prefer to buy fresh food on a daily basis at the local store within walking distance. The shopping habits of the Japanese have strongly favored the business prospects of convenience stores such as 7-Eleven and fast-food places such as McDonald's and Kentucky Fried Chicken.[12] An understanding of important differences in consumers' tastes and preferences across geographic boundaries can (among other things) prevent a firm from transferring marketing practices that are appropriate in one region to other markets in which they would be costly mistakes.

Legal and accounting practices also differ from country to country, putting a burden on these overhead activities in international businesses that most often can be avoided by purely domestic companies. The burden is particularly acute for multinational enterprises, which must obey the financial-reporting requirements and corporate-taxation statutes of different sovereign governments. Other forms of legislation that have an important impact on international businesses include tariff and nontariff barriers to trade, product labeling requirements and product standards, and labor-practices codes.

---

[12] See "Frustrating Foreign Businessmen," *Far Eastern Economic Review*, December 3, 1982. The advantage of small shops is enhanced by legal restraints against large firms usurping the markets of small firms under certain conditions.

It is certainly true that political actions abroad can affect purely domestic firms. One dramatic example was the sharp rise in the price of oil following the overthrow of the Shah of Iran. Another is the decline in South American tourism to Miami as a result of the restrictions that various South American governments have placed on foreign travel by their citizens. In the latter case many shops, restaurants, and hotels in the Miami area have suffered sharp decreases in their revenues and profits. But the group of businesses most vulnerable to political change in foreign markets are multinational companies whose assets may be confiscated, or held hostage, by hostile foreign governments. The variety of political environments in which international firms operate complicates the task of anticipating significant political changes, and the complex international legal environment makes it far more difficult for the international firm to redress an unfavorable action taken against it by a foreign government than would be true for a purely domestic firm challenging a domestic government agency.

Perhaps the most difficult (and important) aspect of the international business environment for managers to understand and cope with is the variety of sociocultural attributes they confront in the various societies in which their firms do business. For example, attitudes toward different forms of advertising and promotion may differ markedly between countries, and such differences may not be restricted to consumer goods. This latter point is illustrated by the case of the Danish chemical company Novo Industries. Because Danish investors tend to favor bonds rather than equities, the reports of brokerage firms are not very influential in Denmark. In contrast, U.S. and English investors apparently put a good deal of stock in such reports. Hence, observers credit the very enthusiastic recommendations of a major British stockbroker and (subsequently) a large U.S. investment dealer as stimulating enthusiastic buying of Novo's shares in North America. At the same time, Danish investors virtually ignored the brokerage company reports.[13]

Attitudes in the work place on the part of both labor and management will also differ across countries. The following example is relayed by a Ford executive, an American, who helped set up Ford of Europe. "It was easy to get our British people to agree [to a plan], but five minutes later they were always back questioning it," the American recalls. "It seemed almost impossible to get the German Ford people to agree to anything; but once they did they just kept marching even if they were marching right off the end of the earth."[14]

The greater complexity of the international environment is accentuated by the less accessible sources of international (as opposed to domestic) information. Frequently an adequate understanding of the cultural, economic, and political characteristics of nations can be gained only through the experience of doing business in those countries. The inadequacy of "arms-length" research is made

---

[13] See A. I. Stonehill and K. B. Dullum, *Internationalizing the Cost of Capital* (Chichester, England: John Wiley & Sons, 1982).

[14] As cited in David P. Rutenberg, *Multinational Management* (Boston: Little, Brown, 1982), p. 177.

worse by the fact that accurate data on the relationships of interest in foreign economies are often unavailable, especially for newly industrialized countries, or (worse) they are distorted for political purposes by foreign governments.

Evaluating Corporate Strengths and Weaknesses

The uncertainties and complexities of international operations are such that firms require a synergistic advantage to offset the higher costs of operating multiculturally. Put more simply, firms should seek to identify and exploit those opportunities that draw upon their particular skills and experiences. While this advice might seem to be a fairly trivial insight, there are numerous examples of firms that have come to financial grief by venturing outside their core areas of expertise without laying the proper groundwork in terms of acquiring the skills necessary to carry out the planned international activities.

Firms can also fail when they mistakenly assume that the strengths required for success at home are appropriate and necessary in the foreign milieus they enter. Indeed, the special requirements of operating in some cultures may negate carefully cultivated internal advantages. Conversely, characteristics of the firm that seem to offer no significant advantage in the home market may be of substantial benefit in foreign markets. This point may be illustrated again with reference to Novo Industries. During 1979 the term *biotechnology* became fashionable among financial analysts and journalists, especially in North America. While initially Novo's management was reluctant to identify the company as a biotechnology firm, for fear that exaggerated optimism about the promise of biotechnology could backfire on the firm, it soon came to position itself publicly relative to the biotechnology industry. Novo's management felt that a failure to do so could lead the company's customers in the U.S. to the faulty conclusion that Novo neither understood the profound interest taken in the U.S. toward biotechnology nor had the ability or intent to defend its position.

The growing perception among American investors that Novo was a world leader in biological technology led to substantial interest in the company's shares among both analysts and investors. On the other hand, Danish investors continued to view Novo as a producer of starch enzymes, albeit a progressive one. They were not as enamored of the company's potential in biotechnical research and were net sellers of the company's shares at the same time that Americans were enthusiastic buyers.[15]

The identification of corporate strengths and weaknesses essentially amounts to an internal appraisal of the firm's competitive advantages and disadvantages in the marketplace. It represents a process whereby management tries to identify, in a structured way, the skills and resources with which it is essentially well endowed and those that are in relatively short internal supply. The Novo example illustrates well the point that strengths and weaknesses are relevant to specific national markets. Given the greater number and diversity of markets in

---

[15] See Stonehill and Dullum, *Internationalizing the Cost of Capital, p. 51.*

which the international firm operates, it is evident that the process of internal appraisal is more complex for international managers than for managers of purely domestic firms. The complexity associated with evaluating strengths and weaknesses in the international firm may obscure certain advantages from management's view. For example, an international firm may have access to sources of financial capital that the purely domestic firm does not have owing to better international banking connections or to an enhanced ability to raise debt or equity capital on foreign bond and stock markets. Novo's experience is instructive in this respect. Observers argue that by tapping the international capital markets, Novo reduced its costs of both debt and equity and increased the liquidity of the firm's shares.

International firms also may enjoy superior access to skilled labor through the activities of their foreign affiliates. These foreign affiliates constitute an "internal" labor market that can efficiently mobilize skilled workers in one geographic area to work in other geographic areas. In addition, training programs that have been successfully implemented in one affiliate can (where appropriate) be implemented in other affiliates, giving the multinational company a great deal of flexibility in expanding specific segments of its work place.

On the other hand, internationalization can embody hidden costs. For example, the (ordinarily) larger size of a multinational company may introduce bureaucratic rigidities into its decision-making processes that put the firm at a decided strategic disadvantage. A highly centralized company may be relatively inflexible and less able to function in rapidly changing environments than some of its smaller or more flexible competitors. Also, the high profile, which companies such as IBM or Coca Cola cultivate as a strategic strength, can become a weakness in some situations. The management of well-known companies, for example, might be less free to reallocate resources across countries or across different product lines, particularly when reallocation involves shutting down production facilities in specific countries. In short, when one thinks (in broad terms) about an organization's strengths and weaknesses, including the ability of its management to respond quickly and flexibly to changing opportunities and threats in the environment, an international firm's strategic internal appraisal can become quite complicated in comparison to similar evaluations undertaken by purely domestic companies.

Evolving an International Strategy

Formulating a comprehensive business plan is the most critical factor in the strategic-management process. The purpose of strategic choice is to select from an array of possible alternatives a course of action that will accomplish organizational objectives within the context of a firm's mission. The future is always uncertain; consequently, there are usually a number of feasible alternatives that would be appropriate to the needs of a firm at any time. Managers must make calculated judgments about the future and then select a strategy that will enhance a firm's competitive position. Obviously, risk is always involved in such a process, and the risks are often greater for international firms than for purely domestic firms.

Managers in an international firm will find the process of evaluating alternative strategies complicated by the need to reconcile their organization's strengths and weaknesses with a far more heterogeneous environment than confronts the domestic firm. Environmental heterogeneity complicates the strategic-choice process in at least two broad ways. First, strategies that may appear to be optimal for implementation in certain geographic markets may be wholly inappropriate for other markets. Where marketing approaches—and other aspects of corporate strategy—can be uniquely tailored to specific geographic areas, the complexity introduced by environmental heterogeneity might be fairly modest. On the other hand, where actions taken in one geographic market spill over to affect a firm's activities in other markets, the search for a "globally optimal" business plan can be an extremely difficult process.

Furthermore, as noted in the preceding section, environmental heterogeneity also complicates the identification of a firm's strengths and weaknesses. For example, the possession of a modern, capital-intensive production facility would ordinarily be thought of as a competitive strength. If the plant, however, is located in a region where the threat of expropriation has become substantial or where the exchange rate is drifting up over time, the plant may actually represent a significant operating risk to the firm, especially where that plant's output is used to source production activities in other plants operated by that firm.

The actual process of strategic choice also may be different for international firms. Business and cultural environments vary so widely around the world that the internal decision-making processes may be quite different from those employed in purely domestic firms. For example, in some countries, such as West Germany, labor interests may have legal claims to participation in strategic choices. The Japanese style of management, which requires extensive consultation and consensus, also illustrates the impact of culture on the strategic-choice process. One expert notes that while a multinational's decision processes are essentially similar to other organizations, "the number of strategists is often greater, the incrementation is more pronounced, the usages of power are more frequent, coalitions abound, and the time taken for making decisions is often much greater than in the United States and Canada."[16]

Numerous techniques, both quantitative and qualitative, have been developed and used for evaluating alternative business strategies. Since most international firms manufacture and sell a range of products, the various techniques must take into account country attractiveness as well as product strength during strategic evaluation. This necessity to consider country attractiveness along with product strength in formulating and choosing a business plan adds an additional dimension of complexity not encountered by purely domestic firms.

---

[16] Higgins, *Organizational Policy*, p. 179.

Implementing and Evaluating Strategy

Once a business plan has been formulated, appropriate actions must be taken to bring about its implementation. In particular, head-office management must ensure that managers in different geographic areas and hierarchical levels of the organization do not attempt to subvert the global corporate objectives of the firm in pursuit of their own local self-interest. Every firm with multiple operations faces the problem of preventing subgoal optimization by subsidiary managers; however, this problem is particularly acute in international firms, especially when divisions and subsidiaries are located abroad. This condition arises in part from the fact that head-office management ordinarily has less information about the local environment than the managers of the foreign subsidiaries. This characteristic of unbalanced information (or "information impactedness," as some economists have termed it) supports the wisdom of allowing managers of foreign affiliates a good deal of authority to formulate their own operating and investment strategies. Many local managers, intentionally or unintentionally, subvert corporate strategy because they recognize the need (where head office does not) to develop appropriate local strategies.

On the other hand, unbalanced information also promotes the ability of subsidiary managers to expend corporate resources in the pursuit of strategies that enhance their own personal objectives at the expense of overall corporate objectives. Thus, head-office management is involved in a delicate balancing act between giving either too much or too little decision-making autonomy to divisional and subsidiary managers. Some firms solve the problem of making appropriate tradeoffs between decentralization and centralization (or standardization) by treating functional areas differently. For example, a function such as marketing may be relatively decentralized since it is often critical for this activity to be adapted to local conditions. On the other hand, activities relating to production may be relatively centralized since the firm often tries to present a consistent image worldwide (with respect to quality, for example).

Problems in reconciling the objectives of headquarters and affiliate management can be alleviated to some extent by involving affiliate managers in the corporate-planning process from the outset. In this way information concerning the critical idiosyncrasies of foreign markets can be incorporated more directly into head office's strategic-planning exercise. Nevertheless, changes in the environment between planning periods ordinarily will still necessitate flexibility at the implementation stage. Moreover, the incentives and opportunities for affiliate managers to pursue their own objectives will remain. This dilemma can also be addressed by designing a control system (that is, a system of rewards and penalties), such that managers of divisions and subsidiaries have more to gain by acting in the interest of the global organization than in their own immediate self-interest.

Geographical distances, cultural and national differences, variations in business practices, and other environmental idiosyncrasies can make communications between head office and international divisions very difficult. Consequently, a reliable and effective control system is critical. A good system can help break down communication barriers and promote coordination among diverse groups. It is also vital to the effective functioning of the corporate incentive system.

The core of the control system in any relatively large organization is the capital and operating budgets for the company. In most companies, divisional and subsidiary management are given an upper limit for capital expenditures that can be made on their own authority. Requests for capital funding above that amount will be evaluated (by head office) in terms of a coordinated projection of the overall company's future activities. The operating budget, on the other hand, is usually short-term and quite detailed, covering expected sales, expenses, and cash flow. Domestic divisions and foreign subsidiaries of the firm set sales and profit targets, which are forwarded to head office for incorporation into detailed plans for overall financial and personnel requirements. The division and subsidiaries are assigned profit goals attached to their operating plans, which form a basis for evaluating the performance of divisional and subsidiary management.

The financial and marketing performances reported, however, for divisions or subsidiaries of an organization, may provide a misleading picture of the contribution of any individual affiliate to the global objectives of the organization, where the affiliate directly or indirectly contributes to the improved profit performances of other affiliates in the global organization. For example, head-office management may deliberately choose to source profits in low-tax jurisdictions, while ''loading'' costs on high-tax affiliates. Given substantial international differences in corporate tax rates, interaffiliate ''cross-subsidies'' are more prevalent in the international firm than in the purely domestic firm. Reported performances may also be misleading when idiosyncratic environmental conditions have an impact on certain affiliates but not on others. For example, Ford's German affiliate has frequently suffered production ''downtime'' because the British plant that supplied required parts and components experienced recurring labor problems that disrupted production.

The design of an effective management-control system should acknowledge the interdependencies among divisions and subsidiaries in their financial performances. Failure to explicitly acknowledge these interdependencies will lead to misallocation of resources within the organization as well as to disaffection among employees and the potential loss of talented managers. These factors will have a negative impact on a firm's ability to implement its chosen strategies.

Implementation of a business plan should also acknowledge differences in management practices and attitudes. For example, the tendency in France is to move decisions as far up the company hierarchy as they can go. By contrast, North American companies have relatively decentralized decision-making structures. As a consequence, attempts to implement techniques (such as management by objectives) that are well suited to decentralized organizations have failed in France.

As a final complication, the concepts of control and evaluation are neither

understood nor accepted in all countries, primarily for cultural reasons. For example, in some cultures, business relationships are closely entwined in kinship,
friendship, and reciprocal relationships. Consequently, the concept of objective
appraisal is not acceptable, nor is it practiced. In such situations, it is very difficult
for headquarters management to apply the same criteria to all divisions and affiliates and implement common control mechanisms. The burden on management is, again, to be flexible in adapting to the idiosyncrasies of specific regions
while retaining the integrity of centralized management direction.

THE PLAN OF THIS BOOK

Our intention is to organize the study of international business management
around the business-planning framework outlined in figure 1.1. While the
various line and staff activities considered in this book are not necessarily watertight compartments of each major stage of the planning process, they can be
usefully analyzed within the context of that framework. We hasten to add,
however, that this book is not concerned, per se, with the details and complexities
of strategic planning, either in domestic or in international companies. Rather, it
is concerned with identifying and evaluating important analytic and strategic
issues that confront international managers in the various stages of the planning
process. The planning process described in figure 1.1 therefore provides an
organizing focus for the text.

The foregoing discussion suggests that international managers require a
fairly broad background to succeed in the dynamic and complex international
business environment. Most scholars agree that international business is a multidisciplinary field that draws upon many fields of study. From the social sciences
the field draws upon economics, political science, sociology, psychology, history,
and anthropology. A knowledge of foreign languages and international law is also
quite useful. Of course, functional fields of business administration form the basis
of any international business curriculum. The latter include finance, marketing,
production, personnel management, and accounting.[17] However, the application
of techniques in these and other functional business activities must be adapted to
the unique needs of the international manager. In particular, strategic and functional decisions must be consistent with the unique economic, political, and
cultural characteristics of given market areas.

Thus, the second chapter examines several fundamental issues related to incorporating an international outlook into the firm's basic statement of purpose
and into its objectives. Namely, why should a firm consider expanding its business
activities beyond its domestic borders? And (presuming there is a satisfactory
answer to this question) how might the expansion be accomplished? In addressing

[17] See William Dymsza, "The Education and Development of Managers for Future Decades," *Journal of International Business Studies,* 13 (Winter 1982), 9–18.

these issues, we will be concerned with identifying the advantages and disadvantages of international diversification along with the various institutional arrangements that can be employed to maximize the benefits of international business activity.

Another important aspect of the objective-setting exercise is whether and to what extent an organization's statement of objectives should include explicit recognition of the goals of foreigners who may be affected by the organization's activities. For example, should the organization explicitly recognize the social and economic goals of foreign governments in setting its objectives? What should management do if it appears that the firm's internal and external objectives are incompatible?

Chapters 3 through 6 are broadly concerned with the international business environment and with managerial approaches to identifying potential advantages and risks in that environment. Specifically, chapter 3 provides a brief overview of a critical and unique feature of the international firm's environment: the international financial system. It also discusses the basic mechanism of exchange-rate determination and the approaches to forecasting changes in exchange rates. The dramatic appreciation in the price of the U.S. dollar relative to other foreign currencies in the past few years has made the topic of foreign-exchange rates front-page news. If nothing else, therefore, a basic understanding of the international financial system should enhance the reader's popularity at cocktail parties enormously.

Chapter 4 discusses approaches to evaluating the international economic environment with a view toward identifying business opportunities and competitive threats. Chapter 5 deals with how the international political climate can be assessed and monitored to ensure that potentially favorable economic factors are not offset by unfavorable political and legal developments. And chapter 6 confronts the difficult issue of how dominant social and cultural values can be identified in overseas markets and be incorporated into an evaluation of the firm's international business prospects.

The focus of chapters 7 and 8 is on the relationship between a firm's international business activity and two critical resources: financial capital and skilled personnel. Specifically, the two chapters evaluate the competitive advantages or disadvantages that might be conferred on the firm in these two key areas as a result of its international business activities. Hence, chapter 7 considers how a firm's international expansion can affect its financing capacity, while chapter 8 looks at the impact of internationalization on the firm's personnel costs and on the need for new human resource management practices.

Chapters 9 through 13 discuss various ongoing functional activities in the international firm for which tactical business strategies must be developed. While strategies in all functional areas will reflect the unique challenges and complexities posed by the firm's foreign business activities, the measurement and management of foreign-exchange risk are of special concern to the international firm. Chapter 9 therefore discusses issues related to measuring foreign-exchange risk, while chapter 10 evaluates alternative approaches to managing such risk. Chapter 11 is concerned with international business-government relations with particular attention devoted to alternative strategies for negotiating with foreign governments. Emphasis is also placed on understanding the special demands that tactical decision makers in this staff function face as a result of their firm's international involvement. In a similar manner, chapter 12 focuses on marketing strategies for international business, and chapter 13 considers the issues surrounding production strategies.

The last two chapters of the book deal with aspects of implementing and monitoring a firm's international business plans. Chapter 14 is concerned with budgeting and capital-management activities in the international firm. Included in this context is the management of working capital used to finance international business activities. Finally, chapter 15 considers how the ongoing activities of the international business are coordinated and made consistent with the organization's global objectives. The formal (and informal) organizational structure is one such coordinating mechanism. Another is the financial reporting system of the international company. Included in chapter 15 is a discussion of the accounting problems created by multinational investment as well as a brief overview of computerized information systems in international business.

CONCLUDING COMMENTS

The danger inherent in any introductory textbook is that the author will try to cover too much material and (to coin a metaphor) leave the reader lost in a forest of detail, unable to see the trees. It is hoped that by focusing (in a comprehensive way) on the salient differences between international and domestic business, in the context of different aspects of the corporate planning process, this book will present no such problem for the reader.

But the reader deserves to be warned that a good deal more study and training lie ahead of a successful career in international business. Indeed, a recent conference of management educators stressed that international business training involves a lifetime process—with self-teaching, initiative, and work experience beyond the business school. Furthermore, besides economics, functional (business) fields, and organization and management strategy, international business education might include the study of foreign languages, comparative governments, comparative commercial law, comparative sociology, international labor relations, history, and comparative literature.[18]

Leonardo da Vinci, were he alive today, might find the aforementioned international business curriculum more than a match for his Renaissance talents. But as most students of business and economics are quick to learn, where entry

[18] For a more extensive discussion of these points, see William Dymsza, "Future International Business Research and Multidisciplinary Studies," *Journal of International Business Studies* (Spring/Summer 1984), pp. 9–13.

into a business is easy and the risks of failure are low, the rewards are commensurately low. For those looking for exceptionally challenging and rewarding careers, the training requirements of international business signal magnificent opportunities.

DISCUSSION QUESTIONS

1. What major managerial issues are addressed in the strategic-planning exercise?
2. How do a firm's mission statements differ from its statement of objectives?
3. How does the existence of once-for-all transactions costs associated with establishing foreign affiliates abroad help to explain our finding that the export/sales ratio tends to decline as a firm's absolute size increases, other things constant?
4. In what specific ways are the problems of managing business activities spread across different regions of the United States similar to the problems of managing business activities spread across different countries? In what ways are they different?
5. As the head of strategic planning for the Federated Jellybean Company, you must prepare an evaluation of a plan to establish jellybean factories in Britain and Germany. One aspect of the plan that remains unclear is how this expansion would affect Federated's cost of capital. As head of strategic planning for Federated, how would you evaluate the likely impact of the planned expansion on Federated's overall cost of capital?
6. In what specific ways is the management of subsidiaries located abroad likely to differ from the management of exporting and importing activities centralized in a single country? In what ways is it likely to be similar?
7. Looking at the industrial distribution of America's leading exporters and largest MNEs, does it appear that exporting and establishing subsidiaries abroad are substitutes or complements?

REFERENCES

BROOKE, MICHAEL Z., and H. LEE REMMERS, *The Strategy of Multinational Enterprise,* 2nd ed. London: Pitman Publishing, 1978.

HAFSTEDE, G., "Maturation, Leadership and Organization: Do American Theories Apply Abroad?" *Organizational Dynamics,* 9 (Summer 1980), 42–63.

HARRELL, G. D., and R. O. KEEFER, "Multinational Strategic Market Portfolios," *MS Business Topics,* 2 (Winter 1981), 5–15.

KILLING, J. PETER, *Strategies for Joint Venture Success.* New York: Praeger Publishers, 1983.

PEARCE, JOHN, and RICHARD ROBINSON, JR., *Strategic Management.* Homewood, Ill.: Richard D. Irwin, 1982.

SETHI, NARENDRA K., "Strategic Planning Systems for Multinational Companies." *Long Range Planning,* 15 (1982), 80–89.

CHAPTER TWO

Theories of International Business

In the previous chapter we described a variety of ways in which international business is conducted. We also emphasized that if a firm expects to be successful in international business, it must incorporate a global view into its mission statement (or its corporate statement of purpose). This point is further underscored by an observation of Jacques Maisonrouge, a senior international executive of the IBM corporation for many years. On the basis of his business experience, Maisonrouge considers a "truly global perspective" to be one of the two most essential qualities to a manager's success in today's business world. The other is the ability to manage human resources.[1] But why should management even consider expanding its firm's activities beyond the firm's domestic boundaries? What advantages can be gained by "going international"? And does the way the firm carries on international business affect the benefits realized? These are the major issues considered in this chapter.

MOTIVES FOR "GOING INTERNATIONAL"

Ultimately, the rationale for any business strategy must be that it benefits the owners of the company. In this regard, there are two broad ways in which a com-

---

[1] Jacques Maisonrouge, "The Education of a Modern International Manager," *Journal of International Business Studies,* 14 (Spring/Summer 1983), 145.

mitment to international business can benefit shareholders: (1) improved net earnings (profits) for the company and (2) reduced risk. Existing explanations of international business, in one way or another, all elaborate on why "going international" can promote one or both of these sources of benefit.

Cash-Flow Considerations

As we will discuss in more detail in a later chapter, the wealth of a firm's shareholders is related to the value of the firm's net cash inflows minus net cash outflows over time. Net cash inflows will be heavily influenced by the value of sales revenues earned by the firm, while net cash outflows will largely reflect the costs of producing and distributing the firm's output. Thus, undertaking international business activities may be beneficial to a firm's shareholders because it enhances the value of sales revenues and/or because it contributes to lower costs.

Surveys indicate that a main reason cited by firms for expanding their international activities is that their domestic markets are relatively saturated and significant further domestic growth would require taking substantial market share away from their rivals.[2] This action, in turn, would threaten the stability of the domestic price structure and might, in extreme cases, touch off ruinous industry price wars. International expansion might, therefore, promote increased sales revenues over time by allowing companies in mature, developed economies to increase their volume of sales without suffering a significant reduction in the average price(s) received for their product(s).

Even when there is ample scope for expansion within the domestic economy, international expansion might be a preferred strategy if the expected increase in profit on incremental sales abroad exceeds the expected increase in profit on additional domestic sales. This condition might arise if higher average sales prices were obtainable in foreign markets and these higher average prices were not offset by correspondingly higher average costs.

Higher net selling prices might be attainable in certain foreign markets because of a weaker degree of competition in those markets. Lower levels of competition abroad may, in turn, be related to higher levels of concentration in foreign industries or to formal or informal agreements among firms in foreign markets to avoid vigorous price competition.[3] Studies have shown that overseas expansion by a few U.S. firms can touch off a bandwagon effect among other U.S. firms to enter the same markets, in order to prevent the early entrants from

---

[2] For a fairly recent and comprehensive survey of why specific firms chose to invest in foreign countries, see I. A. Litvak and C. J. Maule, *The Canadian Multinationals* (Toronto: Butterworths, 1981).

[3] Concentration is a measure of the percentage of sales or employment accounted for by the largest firms in an industry. The relevant notion is that the higher the concentration in an industry, the weaker the extent of competition, all other things constant. Studies have shown that the entry of U.S. and Japanese firms into European markets led to an intensification of competitive pressures in those markets.

preempting the markets entered.[4] More recently, Japanese companies have been exhibiting bandwagon behavior toward establishing affiliates in the U.S. For example, in May of 1984 Nissan Motor Company announced plans to begin producing automobiles in the U.S. Its decision came more rapidly than most analysts had expected. The swift growth in Honda's U.S. output and a joint-venture agreement between General Motors and Toyota were seen as factors influencing the speed of the move.[5] And within days of Nissan's announcement, Mazda Corporation, Japan's third largest auto maker, announced plans to start manufacturing passenger cars in Dearborn, Michigan.

Firms surveyed about their reasons for expanding internationally also indicate that reducing costs is an important motive for international expansion, especially expansion taking the form of establishing subsidiaries abroad. The primary consideration in this regard usually is access to lower cost factors of production. This motive figured prominently, for example, in Warner Communication's decision to move its Atari video games manufacturing division from the United States to Hong Kong in order to take advantage of lower labor costs in Southeast Asia. Other relevant factors of production for which firms often seek lower costs abroad include raw materials, energy inputs, and technological knowledge. In the case of the last factor, many foreign firms have (over the years) established subsidiaries in the "Silicon Valley" of California in order to act as listening posts for the latest developments in microprocessing technology. In addition, a physical presence in the area is seen as necessary to identify skilled personnel that might be hired to fill niches in the foreign firm's labor force at home.[6]

In some cases, a bandwagon effect may develop among vertically related activities if one firm in the vertical chain expands internationally. For example, a number of Japanese auto-parts makers have followed Honda's recent move to Ohio. By the summer of 1984, Honda and its overseas suppliers had plans for a nine-plant production and distribution network in Ohio that would employ thirty-six hundred workers. Honda finds it cheaper to buy components for its assembly operation from nearby plants, including U.S.-owned plants, than to import them. In addition, having suppliers nearby lets Honda adopt the just-in-time delivery system that it has used in Japan. Under this system, suppliers send components to an assembly when they are needed, thus eliminating big stockpiles, which are expensive to finance at today's high interest rates.[7] A clustering of nearby suppliers also cuts shipping costs.

[4] Jurek Martin, "Nissan's U.S. Move Is Part of Global Goal," *Toronto Globe and Mail*, May 28, 1984, p. IB7.

[5] F. T. Knickerbocker, *Oligopolistic Reaction and Multinational Enterprise* (Boston: Division of Research, Graduate School of Business Administration, Harvard University, 1975). This process also apparently characterizes European and Canadian direct investment in the United States.

[6] In an unknown number of cases these listening posts have undoubtedly served as a base from which to conduct industrial espionage.

[7] See "Japanese Autoparts Makers Follow Honda Plant to Ohio," *Toronto Globe and Mail*, July 7, 1984, p. B3.

Finally, international expansion may allow large firms to spread overhead costs (such as advertising) over a larger volume of output. In effect, international business may allow the firm to fully exploit available economies of scale. In this regard, Meredith found that American advertising in magazines and other publications "spills over" into Canada through U.S.-Canadian border stations or the mail, and this process in turn stimulates U.S. business expansion into Canada. Parenthetically, it has also stimulated attempts by the Canadian government to block easy access by Canadians to the American media.[8]

Where internationalization increases a firm's revenues or decreases its costs, international expansion obviously can be a profitable decision for the firm and should be undertaken, all other things constant. But there are other potential justifications for going international that should also be considered.

Risk Diversification

The notion that risk-averse investors should diversify their investments is a well-accepted principle of portfolio management. In a somewhat similar manner, it has been argued that the owners of a firm will benefit if that firm spreads its sources of income over a set of activities that are diversified internationally. The basic notion here is that the firm's income stream will be rendered less volatile by doing business in a variety of countries rather than putting all of its business eggs in a single geographic basket. More formally, the overall variance of the firm's cash flow will be reduced if the cash-flow streams from its various international business activities are less than perfectly correlated. A statistical discussion of this proposition is provided in appendix 2A.

There are a variety of reasons to conjecture that the income streams from business activities carried on in different parts of the world will be imperfectly correlated. One is related to differences in economic conditions across countries that, in turn, are related to differences in resource endowments, demographic conditions, government policies, and attitudes toward working and saving. For example, countries rich in natural resources, such as Australia, tend to perform relatively well in periods of worldwide economic expansion accompanied by rapid inflation, since natural-resource prices tend to move up more rapidly than prices of manufactured goods do during periods of inflation. On the other hand, a country like Japan, which is a large net importer of natural resources, including crude oil, tends to do relatively well economically in periods of stable natural-resource prices, all other things constant. By doing business in both Australia and Japan, a firm is somewhat "hedged" against abrupt changes in economic conditions related to swings in natural-resource prices.

Geographic diversification can also help smooth out the variance in a firm's earnings owing to unexpected political events, including war and other hostilities. Even North American firms face the prospect of adverse political events. For ex-

---

[8] Lindsay Meredith, "U.S. Multinational Investment in Canadian Manufacturing Industries," *Review of Economics and Statistics,* 66 (February 1984), 111-19.

ample, privately owned utility companies in several Canadian provinces were nationalized in the past by provincial governments. If a firm does business in a variety of political jurisdictions, there is a better chance that the bulk of its earnings will escape the influence of relatively isolated and random occurrences of this sort.

The risk-diversification motive for international business has been questioned by a number of scholars. The basic argument here is that the diversification benefits that can be achieved through a firm's expansion of international business activities can be realized even more efficiently if the owners of the firm make portfolio investments (i.e., minority shareholder investments) in companies located in foreign countries. Foreign stocks can be purchased in a variety of ways. For example, they can be bought directly from foreign brokers. Alternatively, investors may purchase American depository receipts (ADRs) through U.S. brokers. ADRs are receipts for shares rather than the actual shares themselves, although most can be bought and sold as readily as any other U.S. securities. Furthermore, they usually pay dividends denominated in U.S. dollars, which is a further convenience for many investors. Moreover, an increasing number of foreign companies are listing their shares for trading on North American stock exchanges.

Detractors of this line of argument point out a variety of shortfalls to international portfolio diversification. For example, changes in currency values can cut into stock gains. Commission charges and other countries' taxes on dividends also reduce the returns to foreign portfolio investments. And in some cases, annual reports and information bearing on a foreign company's performance may be difficult to obtain, making it hard to monitor the foreign investment.[9] A way to overcome some of these pitfalls is to invest in one of a growing number of mutual funds that specialize in foreign stocks. Table 2.1 lists a number of funds located in the U.S. that specialize in investments on foreign stock markets. By investing in a mutual fund, the investor—especially the small one—obtains the benefits of expert advice, diversification across different currency units, and relatively low transactions costs.

The debate surrounding the diversification benefits of international business is not purely an obsession of academics with no practical relevance to managers. On the contrary, it is an extremely relevant debate. For if the owners of a company can as easily diversify risk through their own portfolio investments, managers of that company are offering no additional diversification benefits to owners by internationalizing the firm's business activities. Indeed, specific overseas activities may impose additional risk on the owners if those activities are especially prone to unfavorable actions taken by foreign governments or to other unique hazards.[10] In the end result, unwanted diversification will lower (rather than increase) the value of a company to current and prospective owners.

[9] Imagine how you would feel as an owner of a company if management informed you that the company had purchased some land in Beirut to develop into rental apartment buildings.

[10] A summary of the arguments made on either side of this issue is provided in Richard E. Caves, *Multinational Enterprise and Economic Analysis* (Cambridge: Cambridge University Press, 1982), pp. 24-29.

TABLE 2.1   Some International Mutual Funds Located in the U.S.

FUND	LOCATION OF INVESTMENTS
Canadian Fund	Canada
First Investors International	Worldwide
G. T. Pacific	Far East
Kemper International	Worldwide
Merrill Lynch Pacific	Far East
Putnam International	Worldwide
Scudder International	Worldwide
T. Rowe Price International	Worldwide
Templeton Foreign	Worldwide
Transatlantic	Worldwide
United International Growth	Worldwide

Source: Patricia O'Toole, "Shopping Abroad for Foreign Stocks," *Money*, December 1983, p. 170.

The risk-diversification benefits of international business have consequently been an important subject for empirical analysis. Unfortunately, the evidence is not unambiguous. For example, some studies find that multinational enterprises have more stable earnings streams than their purely domestic counterparts, all other things constant. Others find little difference in earnings variability across the two sets of companies.[11] On balance, it seems fair to conclude that the diversification benefits to the owners of a company that is "going international" may depend very much on the background of the company and the nature of the international activities being undertaken. We shall have more to say on this issue in chapter 7.

Fortunately, the evidence regarding the cash-flow and profitability impacts of internationalization is somewhat more conclusive. Specifically, studies tend to show that multinational enterprises are more profitable than similar (in other respects) domestic companies. Furthermore, the importance of servicing a global market has emerged as a strong factor in the profile of successful, start-up ventures.[12] It is often the case, however, that profitable international business ventures only materialize after fundamental changes occur in the policies of governments. A potentially dramatic illustration of this claim may be emerging in the case of Japan. Until recently an American or European industrialist looking for a factory site in Japan would most likely be shown the door. Now the Ministry of International Trade and Industry (MITI) appears to be helping foreign businesses enter the Japanese market.[13]

---

[11] For a review of some evidence, see Alan Rugman, *International Diversification and the Multinational Enterprise* (Lexington, Mass.: Lexington Books, 1979).

[12] Lisa Stephens, "Staying with Niche Key to Growth Firms' Success," *Toronto Globe and Mail*, June 18, 1984, p. B8.

[13] A description of the changing attitude toward foreign investors on the part of Japanese authorities is found in Lee Smith, "Japan Hustles for Foreign Investment," *Fortune*, May 28, 1984, p. 152.

Part of the explanation for this apparent change in attitude on the part of Japanese officials is an increasing emphasis on domestic consumption, which is leaving smaller amounts of domestic savings available to finance capital investment and the creation of jobs. Hence, importing foreign capital, some of it in the form of affiliates established by multinational enterprises, is becoming a more attractive option to Japanese policymakers. Another part of the explanation may be pressure from the U.S. government to loosen restrictions on the flow of money into and out of Japan. The U.S. government has long maintained that the Japanese have kept their currency (the yen) artificially weak, thereby stimulating Japanese exports while discouraging imports from the U.S., by isolating Japan from world financial markets. As we shall see in chapter 3, preventing foreigners from buying yen in order to make investments in Japan would indeed depress the value of the yen relative to the U.S. dollar.

Exchange-Rate-Generated Capital Gains

A rationale for one form of international business—establishing subsidiaries abroad—has been linked to fluctuating exchange rates. Specifically, it has been suggested that managers can benefit their shareholders by investing in countries whose currencies are likely to increase in value against the company's home currency. Thus, if a company is headquartered in the U.S., its managers should presumably look to make overseas investments in countries whose currencies are expected to increase in value against the U.S. dollar.

A simple example will serve to illustrate this potential rationale for establishing foreign subsidiaries. Assume that the current exchange rate between the U.S. dollar and the British pound is £1.00 = $1.75 U.S. That is, holders of U.S. dollars would need to give up 1.75 units of that currency to obtain 1 unit of the British currency. Thus, if the U.S.-based company planned to buy a British company for £50 million, it would need to sell $87.5 million in order to buy the requisite amount of British currency. Assume that the value of the British company (as denominated in British pounds) remains constant over the ensuing year but the value of the pound goes up against the U.S. dollar so that £1.00 = $2.00 U.S. If the U.S.-based parent sells the British subsidiary for £50 million and converts the proceeds into dollars, it will receive (ignoring transactions costs) $100 million, thereby providing a nominal gain of approximately 14.3 percent on the transaction. Depending upon the firm's cost of capital, this might represent an attractive rate of return.

For reasons we will develop later on in this book, while management should be concerned about the likely direction of exchange-rate changes, most experts agree that establishing subsidiaries abroad merely to realize capital gains from exchange-rate changes is an ill-advised strategy. For one thing, there are less costly ways to speculate on an appreciation of any specific foreign currency, including the use of currency futures markets for short-term speculating and the bond market for longer-term speculating. The costs of speculating using these alternatives are ordinarily much lower than those involved in buying and operating a collection of tangible assets, such as a going business. For another, unless management has reason to believe that it is particularly adept at forecasting foreign-exchange-rate changes (in which case it probably should be in the business of managing other firms' foreign-exchange positions), it should not employ shareholders' money to engage in currency speculation. More specifically, if investing abroad provides an inadequate expected rate of return, assuming exchange rates do not change, the investment should probably not be undertaken in any case.

In summary, a firm might consider initiating or expanding its international business activities if it expects geographic diversification to increase its discounted net cash flow, either by increasing revenues and/or by decreasing costs, or to reduce the variance of its expected net cash flow. Underlying management's decision to do business outside of the firm's domestic market is a conviction that the firm possesses some competitive advantage vis-à-vis its foreign rivals. This competitive advantage might derive from the firm's ownership of a unique asset, such as a patent on a specific machine, or a trademark, such as the name Coca Cola. It might derive from lower costs of production, which in turn are a consequence of lower wage rates or access to lower-cost sources of energy in the domestic economy. It might derive from superior management that is better able to identify the needs of the marketplace and better able to motivate workers to produce high-quality products at competitive prices. As an empirical matter, the international competitiveness of U.S. firms often rests upon their technological superiority, while the competitive advantages of Canadian and Scandinavian firms often lie in resource-based activities.

The successful penetration of foreign markets requires management to identify the firm's competitive advantages as well as markets in which those advantages can be effectively exploited. It also requires management to identify the most cost-effective way to exploit the firm's competitive advantages in the target markets.

THE THEORY OF INTERNATIONAL TRADE

Economists have long been concerned with explaining why certain geographic locations are particularly favorable for specific economic activities but not for others. One early puzzle for international trade economists was to explain why Portugal tended to export wine to England while England exported textile goods to Portugal. Anyone who has spent a cloudy and cold spring day in England might consider the puzzle to be trivial. But in fact, part of the obvious nature of international trade flows is a result of models developed by early trade theorists.

The Principle of Comparative Advantage

The underlying basis for international trade rests upon the principle of comparative advantage. And it is the worldwide pattern of comparative advantage that determines why firms located in specific geographic regions will be more competitive in a given economic activity than firms located elsewhere.

The principle of comparative advantage can perhaps be most simply illustrated by reference to the earliest exposition of the concept: the Ricardo model.[14] This model, developed by the eighteenty-century economist and businessman David Ricardo, rests on the simplistic notion that labor is the sole source of value in the production of goods and services. As a result, a country will produce and export products that use the lowest amount of labor time relative to foreign countries and import those products that use the highest amount of labor time in production relative to foreign countries. In Ricardo's model, only relative amounts of labor time matter.

The essence of Ricardo's comparative-advantage concept can be illustrated with reference to table 2.2. This table reports a hypothetical distribution of worker-years required to produce a single car or a single truck in either the U.S. or Canada. For example, it shows that two worker-years are required to produce a car in the U.S., while in Canada four worker-years are required. Equivalently, half a car can be produced in the U.S. per worker-year, while one-quarter of a car can be produced in Canada. The table also shows that six worker-years are required to produce a truck in the U.S., while eight worker-years are required to produce a truck in Canada.

An important point to note with reference to this example is that the U.S. has an absolute advantage in the production of both cars and trucks. That is, the U.S. can produce both cars and trucks with less labor than Canada can. Nevertheless, since the U.S. is relatively more efficient in the production of cars, it can be shown that both Canadians and Americans can benefit from trade in these two products.

The important deduction from table 2.2 is that in the U.S. three times the number of worker-years is required to produce a truck compared to a car, while in Canada only twice the number of worker-years is required. According to the labor theory of value, therefore, the price of trucks should be three times as high as the

TABLE 2.2 Worker-Years Required for Production (output per worker-year)

	UNITED STATES	CANADA
1 car	2 (.5/year)	4 (.25/year)
1 truck	6 (.17/year)	8 (.125/year)
Price of truck/price of car	3/1	2/1

Source: Stephen P. Magee, *International Trade*, © 1980, Addison-Wesley, Reading, Ma. Reprinted with permission.

[14]The following discussion is taken from Stephen P. Magee, ''Theories of Comparative Advantage,'' in K. C. Dhawan, Hamid Etemad, and Richard W. Wright, *International Business: A Canadian Perspective* (Reading, Mass.: Addison-Wesley Publishing Co., 1981).

price of cars in the U.S. but only two times as high in Canada. Under these circumstances, trucks will be exported from Canada and cars will be exported from the U.S. To see this point, consider the following. Each truck produced in the U.S. costs American workers the equivalent (in foregone output) of three cars. Trucks could be imported from Canada at the effective cost of two cars per truck, given the relative cost of trucks in Canada. Clearly, American workers would benefit by producing cars and leaving truck production to the Canadians. Conversely, the "opportunity cost" of a car produced in Canada is half a truck. By contrast, cars can be imported from the U.S. at an effective cost of at most one-third of a truck per imported car. Thus, it pays Canadian workers to specialize in the production of trucks while importing cars from the U.S.

What should be emphasized in discussing this example is that even though U.S. workers are more efficient in producing both cars and trucks, it pays them to specialize in producing cars, while it pays Canadians to specialize in producing trucks. Ricardo's important insight into the relevance of comparative advantage would lead one to predict that countries should export products in which their unit labor costs are relatively low and import those with relatively high unit labor costs. While there is some empirical support for this prediction, the Ricardian model is recognized by economists as being overly simplistic in that it relies on a single factor of production—labor—to explain international trade patterns.

A more realistic model, known as the Heckscher-Ohlin model (henceforth H-O model), suggests that countries will export products that use more of the country's abundant factor of production. Specifically, countries that enjoy low costs of capital relative to labor will export goods that are relatively capital-intensive to produce. Conversely, countries where labor costs are low relative to the cost of capital equipment should export labor-intensive products.

Although eminently plausible, the H-O model did not receive much support from empirical tests. One explanation for its relatively poor empirical performance is that the H-O model fails to distinguish between different types of labor and capital. For example, it fails to distinguish between skilled and unskilled labor.

The basic H-O model also ignores the influence of technology and economies of scale on locational advantage. With respect to the first factor, the availability of new technology and the speed at which new technology is implemented ordinarily vary across countries. To the extent that countries differ in their ability to create and implement new technology, trade patterns may reflect such differences. Where production processes are characterized by economies of scale, that is, a negative relationship between unit production costs and output volume, one might want to further qualify the basic H-O model. Specifically, one would expect large countries to export products requiring relatively large plant sizes for efficient production, while small countries would specialize in the production of products for which the optimum plant size is small, all other things the same.

The H-O model, when qualified along the lines indicated above, does a reasonably impressive job in "explaining" the competitive advantages of specific regions in different economic activities. In particular, recent studies have found that differences in skill levels of the work force are an especially important determinant of trade patterns for any time period, with technology playing a prominent role in determining the competitive positions of different countries in the early stages of a product's life cycle. To be sure, government intervention is often a powerful influence offsetting geographic patterns of comparative advantage. In particular, tariffs and quotas may encourage certain economic activities to be undertaken in regions that do not enjoy a comparative advantage in those activities. Tariffs are taxes on imports levied by the government of the importing country. The tax can be a flat rate or, more typically, a percentage of the value of the imported goods—that is, an ad valorum tariff. The tax—when passed on in part or in full to host country consumers—raises the price of foreign goods relative to their domestically produced alternatives, thereby encouraging a shift away from foreign-produced goods on the part of consumers. Quotas are a more direct trade barrier in that the host government restricts the quantity of foreign-made goods of a specific type that can be imported regardless of price. It is a combination of tariffs and quotas that explains why lower-priced shoes and garments are still being produced in North America rather than being entirely imported from low-wage countries such as Malaysia.

MODES OF INTERNATIONAL BUSINESS

The Ricardian and H-O models were meant to explain geographical patterns of comparative advantage. The presumption of the models was that differences in comparative advantage would be reflected in patterns of exports and imports. But in the preceding chapter we noted that exporting and importing are only one method of carrying out international business. Thus, some additional explanation is needed to account for the various modes of international business.

We can think of this issue in more concrete terms by considering the choices facing U.S.-owned computer-hardware companies, such as Apple Computer, Inc. As is the case for many U.S.-owned, technology-oriented companies, Apple enjoys a strong competitive position in world markets. Fairly recently Apple opened a plant in Mexico to produce Spanish-language computers for sale throughout Latin America and in the United States. Apple Mexico is 51 percent owned by a Mexican holding company and private investors, with 49 percent controlled by Apple Computer. Why would Apple Computer have chosen this joint-venture mode of international business rather than continue to export computers from the U.S.? Given a decision to relocate production to Mexico, perhaps because of the lower wages there, why did it not simply license its proprietary firmware and its trademark to local investors?

The Life-Cycle Model of International Business

One early attempt to explain observed modes of international business was the so-called life-cycle model. Consistent with early studies of international business, this model suggests that firms expand into foreign markets on an incremental basis and, furthermore, that until management becomes reasonably familiar with the economic, political, and cultural environment abroad, the firm's international business activities should be restricted to exporting and importing or to licensing the production and sale of its products abroad to other companies with facilities in foreign markets.

The costs of gathering and processing information about the prospects for investing abroad can be quite high in comparison to the costs of evaluating domestic investments or assessing export or import opportunities. A substantial portion of these costs can be thought of as being "fixed." That is, they will be relatively constant regardless of the size of the firm's investment abroad. This high fixed-cost component constitutes an important reason for expecting that foreign investment will be mainly an activity of large firms that are able to contemplate making a large capital commitment to foreign investment.

The implications of these characteristics of foreign investment for a firm's choice of international business mode have been summarized by Richard E. Caves:

> . . . firm's foreign subsidiaries perform better when they initially choose sites with low information costs and gather information roundabout by first exporting or licensing independent foreign producers than when they proceed ''cold turkey'' with the foreign-investment decision. Because the firm's previous stock of knowledge holds little value for the foreign-investment process itself, an incremental investigation of foreign markets clearly is likely to be an efficient procedure.[15]

Consistent with early postwar studies of international trade and investment patterns, earlier versions of the life-cycle model assumed that the introduction of new products generally took place in the U.S. This assumption, which was consistent with factual observation, reflected the large absolute size and the high per capita income level of the U.S. economy, both of which would encourage the introduction of new products by U.S.-based businesses. These incentives on the "demand side" of the market were reinforced by advances in basic science and technology, which stemmed from the U.S. government's large expenditures on defense and space-exploration programs.

Of course, the fact that a large and wealthy market for new products exists in the U.S. does not necessarily explain why production of those products should initially be located there rather than produced somewhere else and imported into the U.S. One plausible explanation is that minimizing production costs may not be a firm's most important consideration during the uncertain and risky initial stage of

---

[15] Caves, *Multinational Enterprise*, p. 72.

launching a new product. Rather, proximity to the customer base in order to monitor reactions to the product and also an emphasis on controlling quality and making quick adaptations to the product may be dominant influences that encourage the innovator to concentrate the product launch close to the decision-making center of the innovating enterprise.

In early life-cycle models, exports of U.S.-based innovations grow as incomes abroad rise. And as time progresses the demand in some developed non-U.S. markets grows sufficiently to support one or more local production facilities that fully exploit extant economies of scale. Furthermore, the product becomes sufficiently standardized so that price competition begins to emerge as an important consideration, and, consequently, cost considerations start to play a more prominent role in locational decisions. As lower labor costs and savings on transportation costs and (perhaps) tariffs provide increasing cost advantages to locating the underlying economic activities elsewhere, the innovator begins to establish affiliates abroad or enter into licensing or joint-venture agreements with foreign firms. The incentive to transfer production activity abroad is accelerated by the emergence of competitors in the host markets, who may be successful in convincing host governments to block the entry of foreign goods and foreign competitors once they have established their own facilities.

The cycle by which U.S.-based producers lose their competitive advantage to producers in other developed economies (which may include affiliates of U.S.-owned companies) is repeated again as the newly industrialized countries eventually acquire a production-cost advantage over the mature developed economies. In this stage of the international life cycle of a product, location is dictated almost exclusively by cost considerations. In particular, since the production process is fairly well standardized by that late date, production tends to be relocated in areas where unskilled labor is plentiful and therefore relatively cheap.[16]

Recently economists have begun to draw attention to a fourth stage in the product life cycle, the so-called dematuring stage. The idea here is that for some products the degree of standardization breaks down as increasingly sophisticated markets demand more and more variants of the product. The dematuring product is likely to be manufactured relatively close to the market to which it is sold, since information about new market preferences can more quickly be passed back and acted upon by local producers. In addition, the automation of production processes also reduces the labor content required, further eroding the comparative advantage of countries with low labor costs.

A suggested example of a product that has gone through all four life-cycle stages (see figure 2–1) is the television set, which was first produced on a large scale in the U.S. Production in other advanced countries followed as the market

---

[16] The foregoing description of the product life-cycle model is taken from Raymond Vernon and Louis T. Wells, Jr., *Manager in the International Economy,* 4th ed. (Englewood Cliffs, N.J.: Prentice-Hall, 1981), pp. 93–95.

FIGURE 2.1   Stages of the Product Life Cycle

STAGE ONE:	NEW PRODUCT

Characteristics:	1. Consumption concentrated in the U.S.; limited consumption in other developed countries. 2. Production concentrated in the U.S.; foreign markets served by exports. 3. Quality and reliability are main attributes sought by consumers; price is a secondary consideration. 4. Production is complex and marked by short lengths of run.

STAGE TWO:	MATURING PRODUCT

Characteristics:	1. Consumption becomes substantial in other developed countries. 2. Production shifts to other developed countries, primarily through the activities of multinational companies. 3. Price becomes increasingly important to purchasers. 4. Production runs begin to lengthen.

STAGE THREE:	STANDARDIZED (MATURE) PRODUCT

Characteristics:	1. Worldwide consumption of the product. 2. Production shifts to low-wage, industrializing countries. 3. Price becomes most important attribute to purchasers. 4. Production techniques are standardized and emphasize long lengths of run.

STAGE FOUR:	DEMATURING STAGE

Characteristics:	1. New developments in technology and/or consumer tastes break down product standardization. 2. Production of specialized versions of the basic product is concentrated in technologically advanced, high-income countries.

developed in those countries and as the price fell and technology became more standardized. Production became concentrated in Japan in particular, since it enjoyed low labor costs. But increasingly, production is moving away from Japan to Southeast Asian countries with much lower labor costs. At the same time, there are indications of dematuring in this sector. Specifically, demand is emerging for television sets that embody state-of-the-art digital-transmission technology, such as high-density television (HDTV) and stereo sets, as well as for pocket television sets. These new vintages of television receivers are being developed and produced primarily in the U.S. and Japan.[17]

[17] This description of dematuring is taken from Michael Williams, "Lease of Life for Old Industries," *Chief Executive,* November 1983, pp. 93–94. The various stages of the life-cycle model are summarized in figure 2.1.

Extensions of the Life-Cycle Model

The basic life-cycle model suggests a number of underlying influences on the choice of international business mode and the likelihood of one or another mode being chosen at different stages of the cycle. In particular, it suggests that exporting and importing will generally precede licensing, joint venturing, and/or establishing overseas affiliates as a mode of international business. However, the life-cycle model has come in for criticism in recent years. One criticism is related to the model's focus on the U.S. as the locus of product innovation. An "updated" version of the model would presumably acknowledge the increase in new products emanating from Japan and Europe—a trend consistent with the emergence of these markets as high-income economies.

Perhaps more fundamental criticisms of the basic life-cycle model relate to its vagueness about the nature of the tradeoffs between licensing, joint venturing, and direct investment (i.e., establishing affiliates abroad) and its imprecision regarding the precise timing of mode switches. The life-cycle model also seems inconsistent with occasional examples of companies that do not expand incrementally into foreign markets but, rather, establish overseas subsidiaries as their first international business venture. In recent years, international-business scholars have attempted to extend the basic life-cycle model to remedy these perceived shortcomings. One important extension is associated with the work of Peter Buckley and Mark Casson of the University of Reading.[18]

Buckley and Casson distinguish three types of costs associated with a particular mode of market servicing:

1. A nonrecoverable (sunk) set-up cost, which is a once-for-all cost incurred as soon as the mode is adopted.
2. A recurrent fixed cost (i.e., independent of the rate of output), which is due to indivisibilities in the factor inputs hired in connection with the market-servicing activity (e.g., the salary of the local manager).
3. Recurrent variable cost (e.g., the output-related costs of labor, materials, and so forth).

Given any number of modes or arrangements for servicing (or being serviced from) a foreign market, the firm will presumably choose the most efficient mode given the volume of business that the firm plans to do.

Where the target volume of output was expected to remain constant over time, there would presumably be no switching of modes unless changes took place in the environment (independent of planned output) that altered the relative costs of employing the alternative modes. While such changes can and do take place, as we shall describe below, Buckley and Casson consider the interesting and more typical case to be where the relative cost of one or another mode of international business varies with the volume of business the firm undertakes and where that

---

[18] The following discussion is taken from Peter J. Buckley and Mark Casson, "The Optimal Timing of a Foreign Direct Investment," *Economic Journal*, 91 (March 1981), 75–87.

volume is expected to grow over time. They allow for the possibility that some modes may have higher fixed costs and lower incremental (or variable) costs than other modes. If a given mode has both higher fixed and higher variable costs than another mode, it would never be economical to use at any planned volume of output. Intuitively, therefore, we would expect that as the planned volume of business increases, modes characterized by relatively high fixed costs and relatively low incremental costs would become more economical to implement.

This intuitive notion is formalized in figure 2.2, which is adapted from Buckley and Casson's article. The first quadrant of the diagram shows the assumed behavior of the cost functions associated with three possible modes for undertaking a specific set of international transactions.[19] The functions are specified as being time dependent since the volume of transactions are anticipated to grow over time in the pattern shown by the reverse S-shaped curve in the second quadrant. For purposes of illustration, it is assumed that the first mode has the lowest fixed costs and the highest incremental costs, while the third mode has the highest fixed costs and the lowest incremental costs. This relationship can be seen by the fact that curve $C_1(t)$ has the lowest intercept on the $C(t)$ axis while it has the

Figure 2.2   Choice of Mode for International Business
Peter Buckly and Mark Casson, "The Optimal Timing of a Foreign Direct Investment,"
Economic Journal, Vol. 91, June 1981, p. 78.

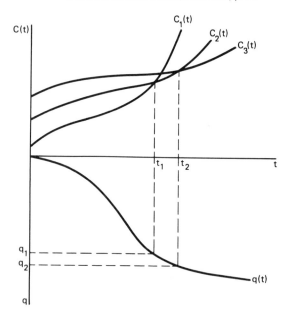

---

[19] We assume, as do Buckley and Casson, that the alternative modes are mutually exclusive. That is, only one mode can be used at a time.

steepest slope. On the other hand, $C_3(t)$ has the highest intercept on the $C(t)$ axis while it has the shallowest slope.

The growth curve drawn in the second quadrant implicitly assumes that the volume of output (q) will initially grow at an increasing rate with respect to time (t), but will then grow at a decreasing rate, eventually reaching some limiting upper value. If we read up from the growth curve in quadrant 2 to the cost functions in quadrant 1, we can determine the most cost-efficient mode to use at all times as well as the specific time at which it pays to switch modes. For example, given the assumed curves in the two quadrants, the firm should plan on using mode 1 up until time t, when it should switch to mode 2. Given the projected growth path for the product, it should switch to mode 3 at time t^2.

Application of the Buckley-Casson Model

Buckley and Casson apply this simple model to three possible modes of market servicing: exporting, licensing, and establishing foreign subsidiaries. Exporting can be expected to have the lowest fixed costs as long as the exports are produced by increasing the utilization of existing plants in the source country. Some fixed costs may be incurred in establishing a distribution network in the importing country. On the other hand, incremental costs are likely to be high under exporting since they include not only production costs that vary with output but transportation costs and tariff payments as well.

In the case of international licensing, a firm sells or rents the right to use a valuable property right that it possesses, such as a trademark or a patent, to a foreign firm. The foreign firm most likely to become a licensee is one that possesses assets complementary to the property right in question, for example, a distribution and retail network suitable for a product offered under license. Typically, a license will oblige the licensee to hire new fixed assets (for production) and to increase the utilization of existing fixed assets (for distribution). To these fixed costs (which will be borne at least in part by the licensor in the form of a lower payment or fee for licensing the use of the property right) must be added the costs of monitoring the license and insuring against default. These latter, so-called transactions costs, when added to the other fixed costs of licensing make it likely that the total fixed costs associated with the licensing mode will exceed the fixed costs of exporting. On the other hand, because licensing avoids international transport and tariff costs, the variable costs of licensing are likely to be correspondingly lower than for exporting.

With foreign direct investment (that is, establishing a subsidiary abroad), the firm will need to buy new production equipment as well as to establish an independent distribution system. It will also need to incur costs associated with familiarizing itself with the economic, social, and political environment in the region where it is contemplating setting up a subsidiary. While costly information will also need to be collected when evaluating the exporting and licensing modes, the information-gathering and processing efforts are unlikely to be as substantial as in the case of direct investment abroad, since many aspects of the foreign business environment will have only an indirect impact on a firm that restricts its involvement in foreign markets to exporting or licensing. For example, management would not need to be as familiar with foreign tax laws or with labor practices as would be the case for the direct investment mode.

On the other hand, a firm exploiting its international competitive advantage via the direct-investment mode can avoid certain transactions costs that affect firms choosing the licensing mode. In particular, costs associated with negotiating terms of a license and monitoring the use of that license will presumably be minimal for the parent firm "renting" a valuable property right to its subsidiaries abroad, since the parent retains fiat control over the way in which the property right is exploited.

While Buckley and Casson do not explicitly treat the joint-venture mode, it might be argued that joint ventures are similar (in terms of their cost structure) to the licensing option. Specifically, the costs associated with setting up production and distribution facilities are shared among the joint-venture partners, thereby lowering the front-end costs of doing business abroad as compared to the direct investment mode. Also, market data, political intelligence, and other information needs can be partially (or wholly) supplied by partners in the host economies, further reducing the required fixed costs of this international business mode. As in the case of licensing, however, there will be costs associated with negotiating terms of the joint-venture agreement, monitoring the behavior and performance of the partners, and renegotiating terms of agreement in the event of disputes. As noted above, these transactions costs are likely to be lowest in the direct investment option.

A key consideration in "fixing" the position of the cost curves in figure 2.2 is therefore the cost of negotiating and monitoring "arms-length" agreements in licensing and joint-venture arrangements. While some authors argue that the costs of specifying, implementing, and monitoring economic transactions between independently owned firms can be quite substantial under a wide range of circumstances, others believe that these costs tend to be exaggerated.[20] The available evidence suggests that the magnitude of these costs is sensitive to the nature of the economic activity involved. In particular, costs are likely to be more substantial when the transacting firms are dealing with new technologies, with state-of-the-art technologies, and/or when the environment in which the firms operate is subject to change in unpredictable ways. Such conditions are likely to characterize industries such as chemicals, pharmaceuticals, electronics, and aircraft. They are less characteristic of manufacturing industries, such as textiles, food and beverages, and paper products.

Where there are substantial incremental costs associated with transferring resources (including knowledge about the production process) from the licensor to

---

[20] For several views on the relevance of transactions costs to theories of international business, see Kiyoshi Kojima, "Macroeconomic versus International Business Approach to Direct Foreign Investment," *Hitotsubashi Journal of Economics*, 23 (June 1982), 1–19.

the licensee or across joint-venture partners, it is likely that the variable costs associated with these intermediary modes will be higher than those associated with establishing and operating foreign affiliates. To some extent, incremental costs related to physical transactions (such as transferring skilled employees) can be expected. More generally, incremental costs will be the result of a need for the licensing (or joint-venture) partner to monitor the behavior of the licensee (or the other joint-venture partners) to ensure that the latter are not acting in ways that violate formal and informal agreements among the various participants. Effective use of new information may also require periodic renegotiation of the original licensing (or joint-venture) agreement, which imposes additional, ongoing costs on these modes of international business. Again, these costs are likely to be of greatest significance in high-technology industries.

In summary, combining presumptions about the cost relationships characterizing various modes of international business with a model of the type suggested by Buckley and Casson gives a more precise (if not profound) insight into the choice of international business mode. It is a useful way for managers to structure their decision making about the mode(s) of international business that might be most appropriate for implementing a global (or international) business plan. It also provides useful insight into the forces that shape and change the way international business is undertaken in the world economy.

CHANGES INFLUENCING CHOICE OF MODE

Available data do not permit the researcher to describe with any precision the relative importance of different international business modes over time. However, one point worth noting is that (in relative terms) the direct investment mode has probably enjoyed the fastest growth in this century. One scholar has estimated that by 1914 around $14 billion had been invested in enterprises or branch plants in which either a single or a group of nonresident investors owned a majority or substantial minority equity interest or that were owned or controlled by first-generation expatriates who had emigrated earlier. By 1978 the figure had grown to around $393 billion. The bulk of this growth took place in the period following 1960, when the total value of accumulated foreign direct investment was approximately $67 billion. Furthermore, whereas direct investment prior to 1960 was largely U.S. based and resource oriented, more recent patterns reflect greater overseas investment by European and Japanese firms in a variety of manufacturing and even service industries.[21]

Recent evidence suggests that the direct investment mode is losing some of its attraction. In particular, U.S. firms are increasingly willing to consider licensing as a substitute for direct investment, and corporate licensing departments are

[21] See John H. Dunning, "Changes in the Level and Structure of International Production: The Last One Hundred Years," in Mark Casson, ed., *The Growth of International Business* (London: George Allen & Unwin, 1983), pp. 84–139.

being upgraded.[22] In part, this seems to be due to increasingly restrictive government policies regarding direct investment. For example, the Andean Pact's "fade-out" rules (introduced in 1971) require foreign affiliates to sell shares to local investors and increase the local content of their products. In addition, the creation of new technology is probably more extensive (geographically) than ever before, thereby increasing the number of companies capable of participating in the licensing market. Other factors that may be shifting the emphasis of firms away from the direct investment mode to the licensing mode are the intensified political risks and economic uncertainties of overseas capital investments in plant and equipment and the shifting emphasis in certain firms from production to marketing and R&D functions.

The growing preference of host governments for cooperative international business modes, such as licensing or joint-venturing agreements, highlights the important influence that government policy exerts on international business decisions. As a further illustration, numerous studies have documented that tariffs and other barriers to imports have encouraged foreign direct investment. In effect, international firms are encouraged to exploit their competitive advantage by "hopping over" tariff walls and, in the process, making job-creating investments in the host economy. The prominent role that governments play in the international economy raises a fundamental issue for international managers; namely, should management incorporate the objectives of foreign governments (and other foreign stakeholders) into the firm's statement of objectives?

TOWARD AN INTEGRATED THEORY
OF INTERNATIONAL BUSINESS

The discussion to this point has identified various theories that, on the one hand, explain why certain activities are carried out in specific regions and, on the other hand, explain why specific business modes are used to carry out given international business activities. The obvious challenge for scholars of international business is to develop an integrated theory that simultaneously explains the location of specific international business activities and the structure used to carry out each activity.

A major contribution toward developing such an integrated theory has been made by Professor John Dunning of the University of Reading. Dunning calls his model an "eclectic theory" of international production.[23] This theory basically posits that the configuration of international business activity will be determined

[22] F. Contractor and T. Sagafi-Nejad, "International Technology Transfer: Major Issues and Policy Responses," *Journal of International Business Studies,* 12 (Fall 1981), 113–35.

[23] See John Dunning, "Toward an Eclectic Theory of International Production: Some Empirical Tests," *Journal of International Business Studies,* 11 (Spring/Summer 1980), 9–31; and George Norman and John Dunning, "Intra-Industry Foreign Direct Investment: Its Rationale and Trade Effects," *Weltwirtschaftliches Archiv,* 120 no. 3 (1984), 522–39.

by three groups of factors: (1) firm-specific factors, which confer a competitive advantage in any given business activity on specific firms; (2) location-specific factors, which make it more advantageous to carry out a given activity in one country rather than another; and (3) "internalization" advantages, which make the international transfer of labor, capital, technology, and other factors through the internal market of the multinational enterprise more efficient than "arms-length" transfers in the open market, where the latter include both direct exporting and importing as well as licensing and franchising.

The eclectic theory posits several specific conditions that underlie foreign direct investment. Specifically, it suggests that such investment will take place when three conditions are satisfied. First, the international firm enjoys specific advantages (often termed ownership advantages) in operating in particular foreign markets that enable it to compete against local firms. Second, the firm believes that these ownership advantages can best be exploited internally. Third, there are locational advantages of a foreign as compared to a domestic production base. Ownership advantages may be related to the country of origin of the foreign direct investor or to proprietary resources possessed by the investor. To illustrate this distinction, the financial industry in Great Britain developed sooner than in most other countries, reflecting Great Britain's prominent position as an industrial and commercial power in the nineteenth and early twentieth centuries. As a result, British financial organizations enjoyed the benefits of experiential learning and ties to international commerce that their would-be foreign competitors were lacking. It is therefore no surprise that British banks and insurance companies are prominent multinational companies. On the other hand, Britain's chemical industry enjoyed no such obvious competitive head start on foreign competitors. And, indeed, there are relatively few British-based multinational chemical companies compared to, say, Germany or Switzerland. Yet Imperial Chemical Industries is a leading multinational company headquartered in Great Britain.

Empirical research indicates that firms from different parts of the world tend to possess different firm-specific advantages. For example, companies headquartered in the developed economies (and especially in the United States) tend to enjoy a competitive advantage in developing and marketing new consumer and industrial products. Large North American firms also frequently enjoy easier access to financial capital than their foreign rivals.

The former advantage (in particular) tends to be best exploited by developing new technology in (although not necessarily for) the home market, while utilizing the technology in foreign markets by establishing overseas subsidiaries. Easier access to capital is also frequently best exploited by internalizing production and marketing activities within a single-ownership structure like the multinational enterprise, especially in such activities as resource extraction. Since it is often extremely difficult to rent or sell new technology, foreign direct investment is often chosen as the business mode to capture the benefits of the firm's research and development in international markets. In the case of natural-resource extraction, end-to-end control of the relevant activity assures greater security of supply.

For North American- and European-based firms, therefore, the key consideration in choosing to establish overseas subsidiaries is (in many cases) the ease or difficulty with which underlying production and marketing knowledge can be sold in the marketplace. Whether or not technical and marketing resources are actually transferred abroad to be used by overseas subsidiaries depends upon the relative costs of producing at home versus the costs of producing overseas.

In contrast to European- and (especially) North American-based companies, the competitive advantage of businesses based in developing countries rests in their experience gained from operating in countries characterized by low wages, volatile political climates, and underdeveloped social infrastructures, e.g., poor transportation facilities, few schools, and so forth. Moreover, because of their smaller size and Third World political affiliations, multinationals from developing countries frequently enjoy a special goodwill among host governments of other developing countries. Their familiarity with economic and cultural conditions in low-income countries also enables them to produce more suitable products for Third World markets.[24]

Since in most cases multinational enterprises from developing countries operate in foreign countries using "standard" technologies, it is not obvious why they find it most beneficial to exploit their firm-specific advantages by establishing overseas subsidiaries. Perhaps the answer is that whether or not a technology is standard depends upon technical sophistication of the country in question. For example, a seemingly standard technology in Korea may be relatively complex in Malaysia.

OBJECTIVES OF THE INTERNATIONAL FIRM

Once management has made a commitment to a "global perspective" and has made the decision to explore strategies to expand the scope of its international business activities, it must establish objectives against which it can evaluate the likely success of specific alternative strategies as well as measure the success or failure of the alternative(s) chosen. As noted earlier, privately owned firms are ordinarily concerned with long-run profitability and with the stability of profit growth over time. Many firms also incorporate rate-of-return and market-share criteria into their statement of objectives. Besides being generally consistent with long-run profitability, the latter objectives provide management with a more explicit set of targets by which to evaluate and monitor policies.

Explicit concern with the welfare of other corporate "stakeholders" besides the shareholder, especially with the welfare of residents in the foreign countries in which the firm does business, is less obviously complementary to the firm's profit objective. Indeed, the objectives of foreign governments may conflict with those of

---

[24]Krishna Kumar and Kee Young Kim, "The Korean Manufacturing Multinationals," *Journal of International Business Studies*, 15 (Spring/Summer 1984), 45–51.

management in corporate headquarters and pose a threat to the international firm's ability to operate profitably in the host economy, at least in the short run. To be sure, management in any large organization—purely domestic or international—faces pressures from a number of different constituencies, including labor, local suppliers, domestic consumers, and governments, and the goals of these broader constituencies may conflict, from time to time, with the objectives of shareholders. However, there is an important qualitative difference between the conflicts raised by external groups in the domestic economy and those raised by foreigners. Namely, whereas domestic stakeholders will share an underlying national allegiance to shareholders and managers of locally owned companies, stakeholders in foreign economies may find the presence of foreign-owned businesses or foreign imports a threat to broad national objectives, including political sovereignty. Thus, while managers must always be concerned with preserving the social legitimacy of their corporate activities, this is an especially challenging task for managers of international companies.

Can International Firms Be Profitable and Socially Legitimate?

A decision to adopt a global (or international) corporate mission challenges management to reconcile the profit objectives of home-country shareholders with the goals and objectives of foreign-interest groups, especially foreign governments. Whether and how this balancing act can be accomplished will depend upon the specific company, and a definitive answer can be obtained only after management does a thorough evaluation of the economic, political, and social environments of the foreign markets being considered. However, there are certain general principles that are relevant in addressing the question on a preliminary basis.

In particular, there are certain objectives that tend to be widely held by foreign governments, and in many cases these objectives are codified either in rules of behavior for international companies or in criteria that are applied by agencies responsible for approving investments by foreigners in the host economy.

A good example of the general objectives that foreign governments hold for multinational companies is provided by the screening criteria of Canada's Foreign Investment Review Agency (FIRA). Under the Foreign Investment Review Act, FIRA is responsible for evaluating specific foreign direct investments with respect to whether or not they constitute a significant benefit for Canada. In this regard, five broad criteria are consulted:

1. The effect of the investment on the level and nature of economic activity in Canada, including the effect on employment, on resource processing, on the utilization of parts, components, and services produced in Canada, and on exports from Canada;
2. The degree and significance of participation by Canadians in the business enterprise or new business associated with the investment and in any industry or industries in Canada of which the business enterprise or new business forms would form a part;

3. The effect of the investment on productivity, industrial efficiency, technological development, product innovation, and product variety in Canada;
4. The effect of the investment on competition within any industry or industries in Canada; and
5. The compatibility of the investment with national industrial and economic policies, taking into consideration industrial- and economic-policy objectives enunciated by the government or legislature of any province likely to be significantly affected by the investment.[25]

Given the broad objectives most national governments (including the Canadian government) hold out for foreign investors, some conflict between management and international stakeholders is inevitable. In particular, disagreements may arise over the distribution of income created by the activities of multinational firms. For example, foreign-owned firms and host governments may disagree about the ''fairness'' of the prices that resident foreign affiliates pay to (or receive from) their parent firms for inputs and services purchased from (or sold to) the parent. We shall have more to say about this transfer-pricing issue in a later chapter.

Conflict may also arise when the multinational company disagrees with the host government as to how the national interests of a country will best be served. Frequently the source of the disagreement will be related to the short-run sacrifices that the multinational firm will need to make in order to promote what public policymakers see as the long-run interests of their economy. An example of this is the insistence by many governments that more research and development be done by foreign affiliates, even though it would be much less costly for those affiliates to tap into the research and development efforts of their parent organizations. While there may be long-run benefits to the host economy from developing an indigenous capacity to produce new products, the near-term costs to the affiliate that is ''encouraged'' to undertake indigenous innovation may far exceed the future benefits that the affiliate itself can expect to capture from the host economy's elevated capacity to innovate.

It is imperative that management understand the objectives of foreign governments as well as the economic demands that might follow from pursuit of those objectives, since it is extremely unlikely that a firm will operate profitably in the international business environment when its actions are inconsistent with the objectives of important foreign stakeholders. Identification of the objectives of foreign stakeholders and the potential political actions that might be taken by foreign governments is (in part) the subject of political-risk analysis, a topic we will take up in detail in chapter 5.

[25] These criteria are discussed in detail in Richard Schultz, Frank Swedlove, and Katherine Swinton, *The Cabinet as a Regulatory Body: The Case of the Foreign Investment Review Act,* Economic Council of Canada, working paper no. 6, September 1980. In spring 1985, the Foreign Investment Review Agency was replaced by a new government agency called Investment Canada. While the criteria for evaluating foreign direct investment in Canada are still in effect, the Canadian government has indicated that Investment Canada will be more receptive to most forms of foreign direct investment than was the Foreign Investment Review Agency.

TABLE 2.3   A Partial List of Responsibilities of Multinational Companies under the OECD Declaration of June 21, 1976

1. Industrial and regional development.
2. Protection of the environment.
3. Creation of employment opportunities.
4. Promotion of innovation and the transfer of technology.
5. Cooperation with the local community and business interests.
6. Promotion of equal opportunity employment.
7. No solicitation or rendering of bribes or other improper benefit, direct or indirect, to any public servant or official.
8. Abstention from any improper involvement in local political activities.
9. Publication of sufficient factual information on the structure, activities, and policies of the enterprise.

Source: Raymond Waldmann, *Regulating International Business Through Codes of Conduct* (Washington: American Enterprise Institute for Public Policy Research, 1980), pp. 93–95.

What is important to note at this point is that the objectives of foreign stakeholders may be at least partially influenced by negotiation or through other legitimate channels of influence. In this regard, international management should seek to reduce the extent of misconceptions about the likely benefits and costs of the various objectives held by foreign stakeholders. In particular, it should attempt to identify and expose those objectives that promote the economic interests of narrowly defined interest groups in the host economy at the expense of the country's broader social interests.

A good basis for coming to grips with the issues that are important to foreign stakeholders is provided in the guidelines for multinational enterprises recommended by the Organization for Economic Cooperation and Development. A partial list of the responsibilities of multinational companies under the OECD Declaration of June 21, 1976, is provided in table 2.3. It can be seen that while the items in table 2.3 overlap some of the concerns of Canada's Foreign Investment Review Agency (described above), there are a number of novel items that reflect the particular concerns of governments of underdeveloped and newly industrialized countries. The point we are stressing here is that before management makes a significant commitment to a specific international business strategy, it should be well aware of the objectives of foreign stakeholders. Furthermore, the chosen strategy should be able to accommodate the ''nonnegotiable'' objectives of foreign stakeholders while promoting the firm's profitability and other ''internal'' objectives.

SUMMARY AND CONCLUSIONS

International business can potentially enhance the welfare of a company's shareholders in two important ways: (1) net cash flow can be increased over time as a result of higher revenues and (or) lower costs, and (2) earnings variability can be reduced as a result of geographic diversification of the firm's economic activities. Higher net revenues could materialize from international expansion if a company has excess capacity in its organization, and if expansion in overseas markets poses less of a disruptive threat to the industry's pricing structure than does domestic expansion. Higher net revenues could also materialize from international expansion if the firm obtained access to lower-cost factors of production.

The potential risk-reduction benefits of internationalization depend upon whether the geographical diversification undertaken within the firm provides superior risk-pooling possibilities compared to opportunities for geographical diversification provided by financial markets. It has been argued that internationalization undertaken by management is a preferred form of diversification for shareholders either because portfolio investments in specific geographic markets are restricted or because they are more costly to identify and transact than the expansion activities identified and implemented by international management. While the relevant evidence is not unequivocal, it supports, on balance, the existence of diversification gains to international business.

The extent to which the latent benefits of international business are actually realized will depend, in part, upon the mode of international business chosen by management. Most studies of international business suggest that firms expand into foreign markets on an incremental basis, starting first with exporting and importing and then moving on to licensing and establishing subsidiaries abroad. The cost structures of the various modes, the expected volume of international business, and the policies of governments all have a major combined influence on the preferred mode at different times.

An important consideration in a firm's decision to expand internationally is whether it can accommodate the objectives of foreign stakeholders. Management must identify the important objectives of foreign governments and other foreign stakeholders and determine the implications of these objectives for the corporation's shareholders and other important ''domestic'' stakeholders. Where conflict exists, negotiation might be attempted to modify specific goals of foreign governments. It would be distinctly unwise of management to ignore important objectives of foreign governments in formulating its own international-business plans.

DISCUSSION QUESTIONS

1. How can existing theories of international business help explain why the OPEC countries have largely restricted their international business activities to exporting and importing (both goods and financial capital) rather than establishing subsidiaries abroad to market their oil and to access goods and services produced abroad?

2. Would you as a potential shareholder in a U.S.-based company be willing to pay a higher price for the shares of that company contingent on the company's establishing a subsidiary in Canada, all other things the

same? Explain your answer. What if the subsidiary was to be established in Hong Kong?

3. Distinguish among the following concepts: fixed costs, incremental costs, transactions costs. How is each relevant to the firm's choice of international-business mode?

4. Would you expect attitudes regarding the responsibilities of multinational companies to differ among government policymakers depending upon their country's stage of economic development?

5. How can existing theories of international business help explain why such a substantial percentage of the largest U.S. multinationals are oil companies? Would you expect U.S. petroleum companies to be displaced (over time) as the leading multinationals by some other group(s) of firms? In which sectors of the economy would you expect the latter group(s) to be located?

6. Consider a situation in your country where the objectives of a multinational company came into conflict with those of a national government. Outline what causes led up to this dispute. What remedies were applied? Who won? Compare your answer with others in the class and, if possible, calculate a frequency distribution of winners and losers.

REFERENCES

CALVET, A. L., "A Synthesis of Foreign Direct Investment Theories and Theories of the Multinational Firm," *Journal of International Business Studies,* 12 (Spring/Summer 1981), 43–59.

DAVIDSON, W. H., and D. G. MCFETRIDGE, "International Technology Transactions and the Theory of the Firm," *Journal of Industrial Economics,* 32 (March 1984), 253–64.

DEARDORF, A. V., "The General Validity of the Heckscher-Ohlin Theorem," *American Economic Review,* 72 (1982), 683–94.

FAIR, RAY, "Estimated Output, Price, Interest Rate, and Exchange Rate Linkages among Countries," *Journal of Political Economy,* 90 (1982), 507–35.

HAMILTON, CARL, and LARS E. O. SVENSSON, "Do Countries' Factor Endowments Correspond to the Factor Contents in Their Bilateral Trade Flows?" *Scandinavian Journal of Economics,* 86 (1984), 84–97.

TEECE, DAVID J., "Technological and Organizational Factors in the Theory of the Multinational Enterprise," in MARK CASSON, ED., *The Growth of International Business,* pp. 63–83. London: George Allen & Unwin Ltd., 1983.

WALMSLEY, JOHN, *Handbook of International Joint Ventures.* London: Graham & Trotman, 1982.

WELLS, J. T., ED., *The Product Life Cycle and International Trade.* Boston: Division of Research, Graduate School of Business Administration, Harvard University, 1972.

WILKINS, M., *The Emergence of Multinational Enterprise: American Business Abroad from the Colonial Era to 1914.* Cambridge, Mass.: Harvard University Press, 1970.

WOLF, B. N., "Industrial Diversification and Internationalization: Some Empirical Evidence," *Journal of Industrial Economics,* 26 (December 1977), 177–91.

APPENDIX 2A: A MORE FORMAL DISCUSSION
OF RISK DIVERSIFICATION

The notion that risk-averse investors should diversify their portfolio of securities is a well-accepted principle of portfolio management. The benefit of diversification is illustrated by the following relationships.

Let $E(\widetilde{R}_X)$ and $E(\widetilde{R}_Y)$ be the expected returns on two assets, X and Y, and let $\mathrm{Var}(\widetilde{R}_X)$ and $\mathrm{Var}(\widetilde{R}_Y)$ be the variances of the expected returns on the two assets. Then the expected return of the two-asset portfolio $E(\overline{R}_P)$ is the weighted average of the expected returns of the two-assets, where the weights (P_X and P_Y) are the proportions of the investors' portfolio invested in assets X and Y respectively:

(2.1) $E(\overline{R}_P) = P_X E(\widetilde{R}_X) + P_Y E(\widetilde{R}_Y)$

The variance of returns on the portfolio is given as:

(2.2) $\mathrm{Var}(\overline{R}_P) = P_X^2 \mathrm{Var}(\widetilde{R}_X) + P_Y^2 \mathrm{Var}(\widetilde{R}_Y)$
$+ 2P_X P_Y SD(\widetilde{R}_X)SD(\widetilde{R}_Y)p(\widetilde{R}_X\widetilde{R}_Y)$

where Var denotes variance and SD denotes standard deviation. The correlation coefficient between the two asset return streams is given as $p(\widetilde{R}_X\widetilde{R}_Y)$. Thus, if X and Y were identical assets, and $p = 1$, $\mathrm{Var}(\overline{R}_P)$ would be given as equation 2.3:

(2.3) $\mathrm{Var}(\overline{R}_P) = P_X^2 \mathrm{Var}(\widetilde{R}_X) + P_Y^2 \mathrm{Var}(\widetilde{R}_Y)$
$+ 2P_X P_Y SD(\widetilde{R}_X)SD(\widetilde{R}_Y)$

On the other hand, when $p < 1$, the value of the last term in the general expression for $\mathrm{Var}(\overline{R}_P)$, i.e., equation 2.2, would be less than the value in equation 2.3. Indeed, when $p = -1$, the last expression in equation 2.2 would have a negative sign. Thus, the variance of the expected returns on a portfolio declines as the correlation between the income streams of the pooled assets decreases. International diversification that reduces $\mathrm{Var}(\overline{R}_P)$ might therefore have value to investors concerned with reducing investment risk, since it can effectively pool imperfectly correlated income streams from geographically distinct markets.

Some observers, including many managers, argue that expanding the international scope of a firm's business activities will therefore reduce the variance of the expected returns on a firm's pool of assets and thereby benefit shareholders. The notion that revenue and cost streams will be imperfectly correlated across countries seems quite plausible given that the timing of business-cycle movements across countries is not fully synchronized. Therefore the expected income streams associated with facilities producing output for a number of distinct national economies will likely be imperfectly correlated. That is, $p < 1$. All else constant, the variance of the expected returns on the international firm's portfolio of assets should be lower than if all of the firm's activities were concentrated in a single country.

As noted in chapter 1, there are at least two important qualifications to the argument that diversification is an appropriate motive for international expansion. One is that investors may be able to realize an equivalent degree of diversification by holding shares in companies located in different national economies. For example, a U.S. investor could diversify away risk that is systematically related to U.S. business-cycle conditions by investing in a mutual fund that specializes in acquiring shares of non-U.S. companies. Where this form of diversification is available at low cost to most investors, it is unlikely that internationalization per se will benefit the shareholders of individual companies.

A second qualification is that investing in fixed assets located in foreign countries will impose certain risks on the international firm that would not be borne at all, or at least not to the same extent, by the purely domestic firm, including the risk of expropriation. The implication of this observation can be expanded upon by returning to equation 2.2. Imagine that Y, a domestic asset, has an expected income stream that is identical to X, a second domestic asset. Management has an opportunity to sell asset Y and invest the proceeds in an asset (Z) located in a less developed country. The expected rate of return to asset Z exceeds the expected return to asset Y and is also imperfectly correlated with asset X's income stream.

Thus $E(\tilde{R}_Z) > E(\tilde{R}_Y)$ and $p(\tilde{R}_X\tilde{R}_Z) < 1$. Therefore the last term in equation 2.2 will decrease if asset Z displaces asset Y in the firm's portfolio. However, if the variance of the expected income stream attached to asset Z (Var $\tilde{R}_Z$) exceeds (Var $\tilde{R}_Y$), the impact of international diversification on Var ($\tilde{R}_P$) is ambiguous. Indeed, one can easily imagine an increase in the variance term (Var $\tilde{R}_Z$) that more than offsets the decrease in the cross-product standard deviation term.

CHAPTER THREE

The International Monetary Framework and Exchange Rates

Once the corporate-mission statement has been defined to include a global perspective, management must seek to determine whether there are international business opportunities that promise to help the company realize its objectives. It must also evolve a set of strategies to take advantage of opportunities in the international business environment. In turn, if successful international business strategies are to evolve over time, responsible decision makers in the organization must understand the major features of the international economic, political, and cultural environments.

In chapter 1, we indicated a number of ways in which the international and domestic business environments differ. In this chapter we focus on what is perhaps the single most prominent distinction: the use of more than one currency to accomplish international business transactions. A variety of institutions and markets have evolved to facilitate international payments, and a familiarity with these institutions and markets is vital for effective international management. Furthermore, some of the most vexing decisions that confront international managers are related to the workings of international money markets. It seems appropriate, therefore, that we first consider the international monetary framework in our Cook's tour of the international business environment.

THE BASIS FOR A SYSTEM
OF INTERNATIONAL EXCHANGE

In any transaction that is undertaken voluntarily by both parties, some payment must be made when goods and services are transferred from seller to buyer, or when capital funds are exchanged between borrower and lender. The complicating factor in the case of international transactions is that often different currencies are involved. Thus, when an American sells goods to another American, settlement can be made simply by the transfer of money balances from one domestic banking account to another. When the American sells goods to a Canadian, the former will again expect to be paid in U.S. dollars, while the latter will ordinarily be holding Canadian dollars in his or her bank account. To bridge this mismatch between the currency of the buyer and the seller, there must be a market where the Canadian can sell Canadian dollars and obtain U.S. dollars.

In fact, there is a complex and interconnected network of markets in which various currencies are exchanged for both present and future delivery. There is also a broad set of legal instruments that can be used for settling international financial obligations, with different risks and costs attached to the use of each.

Definition of Foreign Exchange

Before describing the participants that collectively comprise the international money markets, we should first make explicit the notion of "foreign exchange." Transacting in foreign exchange is generally considered to be the mechanism by which international payments obligations are settled. These transactions require, for example, the conversion of the currency of one country into the equivalent currency of another country. The term *foreign exchange* actually covers all media of international exchange and not just currency. Other media of exchange include bank notes, drafts, and bills.

Perhaps the most common instruments of payment used to settle foreign-exchange transactions are bank drafts and money orders. These are instruments drawn by the issuing bank on its branch or agency or on its account with a correspondent bank in the country concerned. They are recognized by negotiating banks as commitments of the issuing bank and therefore as secure as that bank. As an example, a Canadian importer might go to his or her branch of the Bank of Nova Scotia to have a bank draft or money order drawn up in U.S. dollars in order to pay an American exporter for goods shipped from the United States. The bank draft or money order will ordinarily identify the name of the party to whom payment is to be made (the exporter) and the correspondent bank on whose account initial payment will be drawn, say the Bank of New York.

Upon making payment to the exporter's bank (when the draft or money order is cashed), the Bank of New York will debit the Bank of Nova Scotia's account for the equivalent amount of U.S. dollars. The Bank of Nova Scotia will, in turn, have charged the Canadian importer an amount in Canadian dollars suffi-

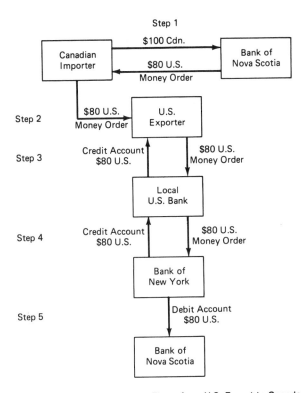

Figure 3.1 Foreign-Exchange Flows for a U.S. Export to Canada

cient to cover the anticipated debit in its account at the Bank of New York plus any other costs associated with preparing and processing the draft.

The mechanics of this transaction are illustrated in figure 3.1. For simplicity of exposition, we will assume (somewhat unrealistically) that final settlement of liabilities is done by cash rather than by debiting a checking account balance. Thus, in the first sequence a Canadian importer goes to his branch of the Bank of Nova Scotia (Scotiabank) to buy a money order for $80 U.S. To keep matters simple, let's assume that the cost of the money order is $100 Canadian, which the importer pays in cash. We note that nothing fundamentally changes in the analysis if we assume that the importer pays by writing a check against his account at the bank.

The importer then mails the money order to the U.S. exporter, who deposits it in his local bank.[1] The local bank therefore acquires the $80 money order as an asset by crediting the exporter's bank account for $80. The local bank, in turn, will attempt to liquidate the money order since it bears no interest. Since the order

---

[1] More typically, large amounts of money would be "wired" directly into the exporter's bank account, but (again) nothing is sacrificed by developing the story in a somewhat stylized fashion.

is drawn on the Bank of New York, the local bank will present the Bank of New York with the money order, which will be negotiated for cash, either wired to the local bank or deposited in the local bank's account at the Bank of New York if the two have a correspondent banking relationship.

At this stage, the Bank of New York and the Scotiabank must "settle up." Specifically, the Scotiabank must make good the money order drawn against its account at the Bank of New York. If the Scotiabank has sufficient funds on deposit ($80), the Bank of New York can debit the former's account and the transaction will be closed. If it does not, Scotiabank will need to raise $80 U.S. to mail or (more realistically) to wire to the Bank of New York in order to close out the transaction. Through this chain of transactions, a debit incurred by a Canadian importer, denominated in U.S. dollars, is settled without the need for the importer to hold working capital in U.S. dollars. Intermediation by international banks accomplished the necessary currency transformations.

The example presented above is highly stylized in that a very small transaction was used for purposes of illustration. In fact, since bank drafts or money orders sent through the mail may get lost, or at the least will be slow to reach their destination, telex and other forms of electronic funds transfer are the most commonly used method for transferring large remittances and for the settlement of interbank foreign-exchange trading. Also, it is highly unlikely that Scotiabank would react to such a small draw-down in its inventory of U.S. dollars. However, if the required payment to Bank of New York constituted a significant portion of Scotiabank's inventory of U.S. dollars held on deposit at the Bank of New York—or elsewhere—it would probably seek to offset the inventory draw-down by going into the market to buy U.S. dollars. Scotiabank would pay for the U.S. dollars purchased either with Canadian dollars or with other foreign currencies for which Scotiabank's management feels the bank is holding excess inventory.

Through its actions in buying U.S. dollars, the Canadian importer became an indirect participant in the international foreign-exchange market, while Scotiabank became a direct participant. Typically, there will be many nonbank firms and commercial banks around the world buying and selling foreign exchange. The third major participant in foreign-exchange markets is national governments, normally represented by their central banks. We will discuss the participation of central banks in these markets in a later section.

THE FOREIGN-EXCHANGE MARKET

It is tempting to think of the foreign-exchange market as a giant department store, where specific currencies are bought and sold at particular locations in the store. In fact, the foreign-exchange market is not located in one geographic area but is dispersed throughout major financial centers around the world. In these various centers, including New York, London, Tokyo, Milan, Zurich, Toronto, and Hong Kong, banks—on behalf of their clients—are continually buying and selling foreign exchange as required. A significant proportion of the transactions are done by bank traders dealing directly with banks in other financial centers throughout the world by telephone and (to a lesser extent) by telex. Foreign-exchange brokers perform the role of a central coordinating point for foreign-exchange trading. Specifically, by acting as agents for banks in buying and selling foreign exchange, they keep bank traders advised of the latest prices and completed deals.

The amount of trading done worldwide in foreign exchange is enormous. On any given day the dealings of the foreign-exchange trading room of a major North American bank can run to hundreds of millions of dollars. While accurate statistics are difficult to compile, one scholar estimates that the average daily foreign-exchange trading volume in 1979 equaled $120 billion, with about 95 percent of that total being interbank trades.[2] Most direct interbank trading involves an exchange of the U.S. dollar for some other currency. Indeed, foreign-exchange traders claim that 99 percent of the value of foreign-exchange transactions involve the U.S. dollar.[3]

There are several reasons why the U.S. dollar—over time—supplanted gold and the pound sterling as the medium of exchange for international financial transactions. One is that the large absolute size of the U.S. economy assures that a substantial volume of U.S. dollars will be available to international banks and corporations for use as a medium of exchange. One can easily imagine how international trade would be stymied if traders relied instead upon the Swiss franc as a medium of exchange. The Swiss economy is relatively small, and consequently the value of Swiss francs outstanding in banks and corporations around the world is well below what would be required to finance international trade and investment. A second reason for the dollar's role as the international medium of exchange is its relatively stable purchasing power in international markets. This in turn reflects, as we shall see, the fact that inflation rates in the U.S. are generally below those in other countries. It is true, of course, that Switzerland and Germany have had superior inflation performances in the postwar period, but their relatively small economies mitigate against the possibility that their currencies will take on roles as international media of exchange. Finally, the U.S. dollar is an eminently convertible one, meaning that individuals, corporations, and private banks around the world can buy, sell, or hold dollars generally free of restrictions by the Federal Reserve System—the U.S. central bank.[4]

The role of the U.S. dollar as the primary international medium of exchange

---

[2] See Ian Giddy, ''Measuring the World Foreign Exchange Market,'' *Columbia Journal of World Business,* 14 (Winter 1979), 39. Daily volume on the New York foreign-exchange markets alone in 1985 ran to about $25 billion, according to surveys by the Federal Reserve Board.

[3] Ibid.

[4] An exception to this statement is provided by the case of the U.S. government's ''freezing'' the dollar deposits of the Iranian government held in U.S. banks during the Iranian hostage crisis of 1980. Interestingly, and not surprisingly, the U.S. action led to a number of other countries switching their dollar deposits into assets denominated in British pounds or German marks.

can be illustrated by considering how Australian imports from Greece would be paid for. In the international money markets, banks—acting as intermediaries for Australian importers—would first buy U.S. dollars with Australian dollars and then use the U.S. dollars to buy Greek drachma. Therefore, when the Australian bank quotes a retail price for the Greek drachma to the Australian importer of olive oil, the quote includes the costs of accomplishing two transactions in the interbank market, each using the U.S. dollar, as shown in equation 3.1:[5]

(3.1) Aussie dollars/U.S. dollars x U.S. dollars/Greek drachma

= Aussie dollars/Greek drachma

It is a relevant question to ask why any single currency (or commodity for that matter) should be used as a medium of exchange. The answer is relatively straightforward. There are great efficiencies in having a common standard for quoting prices and in having a medium of exchange whose value is known and accepted by all participants in the market. By analogy, imagine the chaos that would ensue in your local supermarket if prices of some items were quoted in Italian lira, some in Japanese yen, some in Mexican pesos, and so forth, even if current rates of exchange were posted in the store for all to see. And very little business might be transacted in the store if purchasers were unsure what form of payment the store owner would accept from day to day.

COUNTERTRADE

Notwithstanding the widespread use of the U.S. dollar as an international medium of exchange and the widespread advantages of employing such a medium, a significant portion of world trade takes place by what might be considered a form of barter. In its simplest form, the seller of a good or service receives payment in the form of some other good or service. In one such recently announced arrangement, Saudi Arabia would get ten Boeing 747 airliners and fifty Rolls-Royce RB-211 engines in exchange for Saudi crude oil. Having no intention of getting into the oil-refining business, Boeing did not intend to take possession of the crude oil. Rather, the crude was to be delivered to several oil traders who would pay cash to Boeing and Rolls-Royce.[6] It is not unusual for trading companies to act as intermediaries in a barter agreement. The trading companies pay cash to take unwanted merchandise off the hands of one or the other party to barter. Of course, the price paid will be less than the full market value of the goods involved.

---

[5] This example along with an accompanying discussion of the U.S. dollar's role as a reserve currency is found in Ronald I. McKinnon, *Money in International Exchange* (Oxford: Oxford University Press, 1979).

[6] "Boeing, Rolls-Royce Set Saudi Oil-Plane Swap," *Toronto Globe and Mail*, July 19, 1984, p. B2.

Barter is the simplest form of the set of arrangements known as counter-trade. Counterpurchase is another. In this case, a purchase by one party is linked explicitly to a reciprocating purchase by the other party. For example, when Canadair Ltd. of Canada sold a fleet of water bombers to Yugoslavia a few years ago, it agreed to take part payment in Yugoslavian goods in a parallel deal. In effect, Canadair implicitly agreed to buy a certain amount of Yugoslavian goods with the cash it was entitled to receive from the sale of water bombers.[7]

One of the fastest growing forms of countertrade is compensation trade, or buy-back. In this arrangement, an exporter sells equipment, plant, or technology and agrees either to take payment in, or to purchase, all or part of the goods produced by the exported equipment and technology. The period of the agreement in these cases often exceeds ten years, and the value of the products "bought back" often exceeds the value of the original exports. In a related form of countertrade, the seller agrees to "offset" a portion of exports with purchases of inputs produced in the importing country.

One other form of countertrade, called a switch, covers cases where goods sent from one country to a second country are actually paid for by a third country or by a trading company. The third country or the trading company would then enjoy a claim on goods produced by the first country, and this claim will presumably be pressed at some future date in compensation for the original payment. In effect, the third country or trading company is acting again as an intermediary.

The U.S. Department of Commerce estimates that countertrade accounted for more than 20 percent of world trade in 1984, up from 3 percent in 1976.[8] Having just given a succinct yet, we trust, persuasive discussion of why the use of a single currency is an efficient way to finance international trade, we are faced with explaining why upwards of 20 percent of world trade apparently does not rely directly on the foreign-exchange markets. Unfortunately, it is not possible to give a simple explanation of the seeming anomaly of countertrade. But it is possible to say that the underlying motivation for countertrade is the widespread existence of non-convertible currencies. In an increasing number of countries, national governments have taken to rationing foreign exchange, especially the U.S. dollar. The inability of many LDC countries to borrow dollars needed to finance their international trade further accentuated their reliance on barter-type trade.[9]

Since we shall be quite preoccupied with the managerial implications of the current international monetary system, it is appropriate to consider briefly the managerial implications of the apparently growing trend toward countertrade.

---

[7] For a description of a variety of countertrade arrangements, see Albert Sigurdson, "Canada's Partners Seek Countertrade," *Toronto Globe and Mail,* December 17, 1983, p. IB6.

[8] Ibid. The U.S. Department of Commerce projects that by the year 2000, one-half of all international trade might be undertaken through countertrade.

[9] A more detailed description of the countertrade phenomenon can be found in Irene Lange and James F. Elliot, "East-West Trade and Barter," in Hans Thorelli, ed., *International Marketing Strategy,* rev. ed. (New York: Pergamon Press, 1982).

One implication is that management should have access to expert advice in negotiating countertrade agreements. Specifically, it should be able to call on experts for help in establishing the value of unfamiliar goods that are offered in exchange for the firm's exports. As noted above, commercial banks and trading companies can often fill this role successfully. It is also recommended that management establish the degree of demand for the firm's product as a prerequisite to determining whether countertrade demands are genuine or are being used as a negotiating tactic. The negotiating process will obviously be more complex when bargaining encompasses terms of exchange for a range of goods and services rather than a single price expressed in units of a single currency.

EXCHANGE RATES

For the bulk of international business that is financed through purchases and sales of foreign exchange (primarily involving the U.S. dollar), the trading of foreign exchange follows a number of conventions. In particular, all traded (or convertible) world currencies are quoted by traders in U.S. dollars. Currency values are conventionally quoted to four significant digits. In the United States, it is customary to quote the value of a unit of foreign currency in U.S. dollars; for example, $1.00 Cdn. = $.7600 U.S. In other markets, it is the custom to quote the number of units of the foreign currency equivalent to one U.S. dollar; for example, $1.3158 Cdn. = $1.00 U.S.

The quotation of foreign-exchange rates can be a confusing business if it is not kept clear which currency is being used as the basis of comparison. But confusion can be kept to a minimum by recognizing the reciprocal nature of foreign-exchange quotations. For example, the exchange rate quoted for the U.S. dollar in Toronto on August 1, 1984, was $1.3085 Cdn. = $1.00 U.S. This was equivalent to the rate quoted for the Canadian dollar in New York on that same date, which was $1.00 Cdn. = $.7642 U.S. as shown by equation 3.2:

(3.2) $ Cdn./U.S. = 1.3085 = 1/$U.S./$Cdn. = 1/.7642 = 1.3085

Foreign exchange is traded on either a spot or forward basis.[10] In the North American interbank market, the U.S. dollar spot rate in terms of the Canadian dollar is for delivery of both currencies the following business day. The Mexican peso is also quoted for next-day delivery in North America, but currencies other than the Canadian dollar and Mexican peso are quoted for spot delivery two days hence. In virtually every other currency market in the world, the spot rate for all currencies is for delivery two days in the future. This two-day delay is for uni-

---

[10] The following description of the spot and forward exchange markets follows the discussion in the Royal Bank of Canada, "Foreign Exchange, The Money Market and International Trade," Montreal, mimeographed, 1977. A so-called swap involves simultaneously buying spot and selling forward or vice versa and hence can be broken down into these two basic categories.

formity and to allow time for the preparation and dispatch of instructions to banks in different countries and time zones to make appropriate entry accounts. While the occasional spot market currency transaction takes place that does not involve the American dollar, all forward transacting in the interbank market utilizes the American dollar as an intermediary-vehicle currency. Thus, commercial banks make forward quotes only in terms of the American dollar. The rate of exchange in forward transactions is fixed for settlement at some specific date or optional period beyond the usual spot term of one or two days. This rate is a combination of the spot rate, plus or minus the premium or discount for the particular term from the spot date to the delivery date of the relevant foreign exchange. In a following section we will discuss the determinants of the forward premium or discount on a currency.

Forward markets exist for most major currencies. Quotations are usually for fixed periods such as one, two, three, six, and up to twelve months, although odd periods and terms beyond twelve months can often be negotiated from commercial banks on an individual basis. Transactions in forward contracts between banks are normally for fixed dates, but transactions done by banks with their clients are usually on the basis of delivery at any time during the last fifteen or last thirty days before the maturity date.

Forward Market versus Futures Market

Before considering the basic determinants of spot and forward exchange rates, it is useful to distinguish between the interbank forward market and the organized futures market, since the two are quite distinct in organization and operation.[11] The interbank forward market is the currency-trading arena primarily for large banks and their multinational corporate customers. Contracts are individually tailored to suit the customer's requirements, including amounts and maturity dates. Bank dealers obtain their compensation for writing forward contracts from the difference between their buying and selling rates, called the spread. The interbank forward market is a true delivery market in that over 90 percent of all forward contracts that are written culminate in the delivery of the actual currency specified by the contract.

The major organized futures market is the International Monetary Market (the IMM), which opened for trading in January 1972 as an adjunct to the Chicago Mercantile Exchange. In contrast to the interbank forward market, transactions on the futures markets are of a standard size. The standard contract sizes for the major currencies traded on the IMM are given in table 3.1. The purpose of having different contract sizes is to make all contracts roughly comparable in terms of their aggregate dollar value.

Maturity dates are also standardized for futures contracts. For contracts traded on the IMM, these dates fall on the third Wednesday of March, June,

---

[11] Our description of the two markets is taken from Allan M. Loosigian, *Foreign Exchange Futures: A Guide to International Currency Trading* (Homewood, Ill.: Dow Jones-Richard D. Irwin, 1981).

TABLE 3.1   Standard Contract Sizes on the International
Monetary Market

CURRENCY	SIZE (UNITS)
Swiss francs	125,000
Canadian dollars	100,000
British pounds	25,000
German marks	125,000
Japanese yen	12.5 million

September, and December. In fact, delivery of the contracted-for currencies rarely takes place in the futures market. Rather, exchange contracts are nearly always settled by a liquidating sale or purchase prior to the delivery date. Several other relevant distinctions between the two markets might be briefly noted. Foreign-exchange brokers dealing in the futures market charge their customers a set commission for each contract they buy and sell rather than quote a bid and ask price as the banks do. Exchange-market traders must post with their brokers a good-faith deposit, known as margin, to guarantee their performance on each contract, whereas no such requirement exists on forward contracts. But notwithstanding these differences, international businesses use both markets for essentially the same purpose: to lock in exchange rates for currencies in which they do business. That is, both markets are vehicles for hedging against changes in exchange-rate relationships.

Having coped with a rather abstract discussion of the elements of the forward market, the reader might appreciate some concrete details. For example, if one had called the foreign-exchange desk at the Chase Manhattan Bank on August 1, 1984, and asked for quotes on the one-, three-, and six-month forward contracts on the Canadian dollar, as well as the spot rate of exchange, one would have been quoted the rates given in table 3.2. Since differentials among banks in forward-rate quotations could not persist for long given the highly integrated North American banking structure, we may take it that all North American banks would have quoted virtually identical rates to those in table 3.2.

Arbitrage

Our confident assertion that exchange-rate differentials across markets would not persist for any length of time that is meaningful for the typical corporate participant demands some justification. The underlying explanation can be indicated by imagining that one North American bank quotes a dollar/mark spread of $0.4997–99, while another quotes a spread of $0.5001–03. This means that the first bank stands ready to buy German marks at a rate of $0.4997 U.S. to the mark and to sell marks at a rate of $0.4999 U.S. to the mark. The bid and ask prices of the second bank are correspondingly $0.0004 higher. In this case a professional foreign-exchange trader could buy marks from the first bank (at a price of $0.4999

TABLE 3.2 Spot Rate and Selected Forward Rates for the Canadian Dollar, August 1, 1984

TERM	RATE
Spot	$.7642
1 month forward	.7637
3 months forward	.7624
6 months forward	.7611

per mark) and sell them to the second bank (at a rate of $0.5001) making a riskless profit of $0.0002 per mark for the price of two telephone calls. Clearly, differentials in quoted exchange rates that exceed the very nominal costs of communication are unsustainable. The process by which exchange rates quoted in different markets are kept from exceeding the costs of communicating between those markets is known as arbitrage.

Forward Premiums and Discounts

The forward-rate structure reported in table 3.2 gives specific information to a prospective buyer (or seller) of Canadian dollars.[12] For example, if an individual wishes to buy Canadian dollars for delivery one month hence, he or she will need to pay $.7637 U.S. for each Canadian dollar to be delivered. Similarly (and ignoring the spread between bid and ask prices), the individual would receive $.7637 U.S. for each Canadian dollar sold to the bank for delivery one month hence. Similar interpretations can be given to the three- and six-month forward rates cited in table 3.2.

Given the rates cited in table 3.2, the Canadian dollar is said to be at a discount in the forward market, since a progressively smaller amount of U.S. dollars is required to buy a given amount of Canadian dollars the more distant the contract date. The percentage of premium (+) or discount (–) in a forward quote is computed by the formula given in equation 3.3:

(3.3) Forward (+) or (–)
= Forward rate-spot rate/Spot rate X 12 X 1/#months forward X 100

Using the formula in equation 3.2, we can calculate the one-month forward discount on the Canadian dollar as equal to .79 percent. The three- and six-month forward discounts equal .94 and .81 percent, respectively. Note that the forward premium or discount must be expressed as a per annum percentage in order to provide for a common basis of comparison across forward contracts of different maturities as well as to facilitate comparisons to interest rates. The relevance of the

---

[12] For purposes of convenience in the following discussion we have used the asking prices of the Canadian dollar, thereby ignoring the existence of a spread between bid and ask prices.

latter comparisons will be made clear when we discuss the concept of covered-interest arbitrage.

THE BEHAVIOR OF EXCHANGE RATES

An important and recurring theme of this book is that the profitability of an international business is affected both directly and indirectly by changes in exchange rates. Moreover, uncertainty about future exchange rates poses unique problems and challenges for international managers. Therefore, it is not so much the value of exchange rates at a given time that concerns managers as it is the volatility of exchange rates over time.[13]

Prior to the early 1970s most exchange rates were pegged to the U.S. dollar, and central banks in the major developed countries assumed the responsibility for maintaining the values of their currencies within a 1 percent band of the official rate. This is not to say that the official rate never changed. On the contrary, in cases where it was apparent that a given exchange ratio was becoming unrealistic in light of international competitive trends, a central bank would be permitted by agreement with other central banks to engineer a discrete adjustment in its currency value and then resume its official support at a new official rate of exchange against the U.S. dollar. Under this fixed-rate regime, foreign-exchange markets were characterized by periods of relative stability disrupted by periodic periods of extreme turbulence.

Since March 1973 the values of major industrial currencies have been determined primarily by free-market forces of supply and demand. That is, central banks in the major western economies are no longer committed to pegging the values of their currencies to an official rate of exchange against the U.S. dollar, although central banks do intervene in foreign-exchange markets from time to time, ostensibly to ensure ''orderly'' market conditions. The movement from a pegged to a floating exchange-rate regime has resulted in exchange rates becoming more volatile, although the foreign-exchange markets could never be characterized as a ''sleepy hollow.''

An indication of how volatile the foreign-exchange markets have been in the post-1970 period is provided in figure 3.2. This figure shows the nominal values of six major convertible currencies against the U.S. dollar expressed in the form of an index number, with the base period taken to be March 1973. It can be seen that the volatility of these markets became especially pronounced after 1975, perhaps as a result of the growing sophistication and boldness of foreign-exchange traders. Note also that a number of strong trends emerged in the foreign-exchange markets over the period 1973–1981. Specifically, the values of the Swiss franc, German

---

[13] An excellent discussion of the behavior of foreign-exchange rates over time is contained in Richard Levich, ''Empirical Studies of Exchange Rates: Price Behavior, Rate Determination and Market Efficiency,'' in Ronald W. Jones and Peter B. Kenen, eds., *Handbook of International Economics* (Amsterdam: North-Holland Publishing Company, 1982).

Nominal Exchange Rates

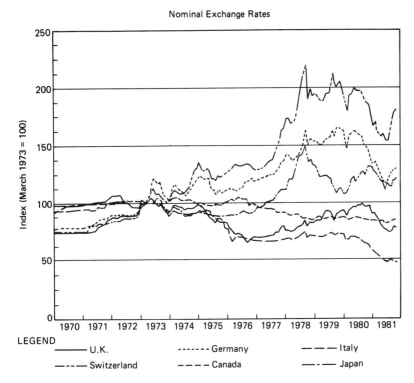

LEGEND

——— U.K.   ------- Germany   — — — Italy

—--— Switzerland   — — — Canada   —-— Japan

Figure 3.2 Nominal Exchange Rates
Richard Levich, "Empirical Studies of Exchange Rates: Price Behavior, Rate Determi-
nation, and Market Efficiency," chapter 19 in *Handbook of International Economics*,
Ronald Jones and Peter Kenen, eds., North-Holland Publishing Co., Amsterdam, 1982.
Reprinted by permission of the author and North-Holland Publishing Co.

mark, and Japanese yen increased markedly over the period, while the values of
the British pound, Canadian dollar, and (especially) the Italian lira declined
substantially.

The emergence of the Swiss, German, and Japanese currencies as "safe
havens" against the ravages of inflation was the major foreign-exchange news
story of the 1970s. Many speculators who continued to buy forward contracts in
those currencies enjoyed "windfall" capital gains, while companies and governments that borrowed funds denominated in those currencies saw their effective
cost of debt, that is, interest and principal payments, adjusted for exchange-rate
changes, skyrocket. The woeful experience of this latter group led to a growing
conventional wisdom among international managers to store working capital in
the so-called hard-currency countries, such as Germany and Switzerland, while
avoiding borrowing funds denominated in those currencies.

But as if to confirm the principle that convenient rules of thumb do not work
for long in the foreign-exchange markets, the experience of the 1980s has been

almost a mirror image of that of the 1970s. Specifically, the value of the U.S. dollar has soared against all currencies, including the vaunted German mark and Swiss franc. This pattern is described in table 3.3. In 1981 it took approximately 2.26 marks to purchase one U.S. dollar. By April 1984 about 2.65 marks were required. This 17 percent decline in the value of the mark exceeded the approximate 10 percent decline in the value of the Swiss franc; however, it is modest compared to the 30 percent decline in the value of the British pound.

To the extent that management can predict the gyrations in exchange rates exhibited in figure 3.2 and table 3.3, or even sharp reversals in trend such as the one that took place in 1981, fluctuating exchange rates would have no major significance for international managers since their impact could be fully anticipated and integrated into the company's planning activities. The next issue to consider, therefore, is whether exchange-rate changes are amenable to accurate and relatively economical forecasting.

EXCHANGE-RATE DETERMINATION

The basis of any forecast of price change—and exchange rates can be seen as prices—is the familiar economic model of supply and demand. The basic model as applied to the foreign-exchange market is developed in figure 3.3. The market is assumed to be that for the buying and selling of Canadian dollars. Thus, the horizontal axis measures the quantity of Canadian dollars sold in the foreign-exchange markets for some given period of time. The vertical axis measures the price of the Canadian dollar as a ratio of the quantity of U.S. dollars required to obtain one Canadian dollar. Note that if a greater number of U.S. dollars are required to purchase a Canadian dollar, the Canadian dollar would be appreciating in value against the U.S. dollar; that is, its price would be going up.

The (upward) slope of the supply curve and the (downward) slope of the de-

TABLE 3.3   Foreign-Exchange Rates (currency units per dollar)

CURRENCY	1981	1982	1983	1984			
				JANUARY	FEBRUARY	MARCH	APRIL
1. Canadian dollar	1.1990	1.2344	1.2325	1.2484	1.2480	1.2697	1.279
2. French franc	5.4396	6.5793	7.6203	8.5948	8.3051	8.0022	8.141
3. German mark	2.2631	2.4280	2.5539	2.8110	2.6994	2.5993	2.647
4. Italian lira	1138	1354	1519	1707	1666	1614	1638
5. Japanese yen	220.6	249.1	237.6	233.8	233.6	225.3	225.2
6. Swiss franc	1.9674	2.0327	2.1006	2.2380	2.2050	2.1490	2.191
7. British pound[a]	202.4	174.8	151.6	140.8	144.2	145.6	142.1

Source: Board of Governors of the Federal Reserve System, *Federal Reserve Bulletin,* 70 (May 1984), A64 table 3.28.

[a]Value in U.S. cents.

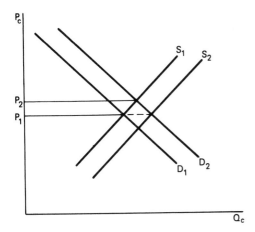

P_c = Quantity of U.S. Dollars/Quantity of Canadian Dollars

Q_c = Quantity of Canadian Dollars

Figure 3.3   Determinants of the Spot Price of the Canadian Dollar

mand curve embody certain assumptions about economic behavior. To appreciate these assumptions, we should briefly consider the underlying motivations for buying and selling a foreign currency. Considering the Canadian dollar in terms of the U.S. dollar, we can conjecture a number of sources of demand. For example, individuals and corporations currently holding U.S. dollars might want to purchase Canadian-made goods and services. This would require them to purchase Canadian dollars through their banks or foreign-exchange brokers. The latter, in turn, would need to enter the foreign-exchange market to buy the Canadian dollars needed. Presumably, the cheaper the price of the Canadian dollar, the more attractive Canadian goods and services will be to Americans. In stepping up their purchases of Canadian goods and services, they will also demand a greater quantity of Canadian dollars from their bankers and brokers, hence the inverse relationship between price and quantity demanded.

Conversely, Canadians interested in buying American goods and services will need to buy U.S. dollars. They will do so primarily by selling Canadian dollars at their banks. The banks, in turn, will need to replenish their inventories of U.S. dollars. They will do so by going into the foreign-exchange markets to buy American dollars with the Canadian dollars they acquire from their customers. The supply of Canadian dollars therefore reflects a mirror-image demand for U.S. dollars. Now if the Canadian dollar goes up in price against the U.S. dollar, it is equivalent to the U.S. dollar declining in value against the Canadian dollar. And just as a declining Canadian dollar would stimulate greater purchases of Canadian goods and services, a declining U.S. dollar would encourage Canadians to buy more U.S. goods and services—and more American dollars. This is the underlying rationale for an assumed upward-sloping supply curve in figure 3.3.

Given an initial supply curve (*S*1) and an initial demand curve (*D*1), the equilibrium price for the Canadian dollar is *P*1. This simply means that at price *P*1, supply and demand equilibrate, and there is no pressure exerted in the market for further price adjustments. By contrast, imagine that the supply curve was given as *S*2, while the demand curve remained at *D*1. In this case, *P*1 would not be the equilibrium exchange rate since at this price the supply of Canadian dollars would exceed the demand for Canadian dollars. In a free market the price of the Canadian dollar would decline to the level at which *D*1 and *S*2 intersected.

The role of the central bank in today's floating-rate market can be illustrated by reference to the preceding discussion. That is, imagine that the Canadian dollar at *P*1 was overpriced and that the equilibrium price corresponded to the intersection between *S*2 and *D*1. If the drop from the old exchange rate to the equilibrium rate was steep, it is most likely that the Bank of Canada would intercede to assure a gradual decline rather than risk a sharp and sudden decline that might occur in a completely free market. In this case the Bank of Canada would intervene by buying Canadian dollars in the foreign-exchange markets and selling U.S. dollars to pay for its purchases. In this way the bank's actions would dampen the downward pressure on the Canadian dollar. Conversely, in periods of intense upward pressure on the price of the Canadian dollar (a rare occurrence in the last decade), the Bank of Canada would intervene by buying U.S. dollars and selling Canadian dollars on the foreign-exchange markets.

In considering figure 3.3, it is apparent that the sources of upward or downward pressure on a currency correspond to factors that encourage shifts in the supply and demand curves for that currency. If those factors were easy to identify and readily predictable, one would have the makings of a promising foreign-exchange forecasting model. Unfortunately for international managers, matters are not so straightforward. Notwithstanding an enormous expenditure of time, skill, and money, no theory (as Levich notes) has been accepted as a complete explanation for exchange-rate behavior. However, a number of theories offer at least a partial explanation of exchange-rate movements.

Purchasing-Power Parity

One venerable model of exchange-rate behavior is known as the purchasing-power parity (PPP) model. In its most popular formulation, the model rests on the presumption that exchange rates are set so as to preserve the relative purchasing power of currencies over time. This notion is captured in the formulation of the model given in equation 3.4:

$$(3.4) \quad R^* = PI^1/PI^2 \times R^0$$

where R^* is the equilibrium exchange rate measured as the number of units of currency 1 required to purchase a unit of currency 2; R^0 is the base-period rate of exchange; PI^1 is some general price index in country 1 and PI^2 is the corresponding price index in country 2. The PPP model therefore suggests that if prices increase in country 1 to twice what they are in country 2, country 1's currency should decline to half its nominal value against currency 2.

On the surface the PPP model seems eminently sensible and elegantly simple. It rests on the notion that exchange-rate adjusted prices in two countries must increase at the same rate, or else changes in export/import patterns will take place—with corresponding changes in exchange-rate relationships—so as to restore equivalency in purchasing power between the two currencies. By way of elaboration, assume that the initial supply and demand curves for the Canadian dollar are given as $S1$ and $D1$ in figure 3.3. That is, the equilibrium exchange rate is assumed to be $P1$. If the rate of inflation in the U.S. begins to exceed the rate of inflation in Canada, Canadian goods and services will start to become relatively cheaper than U.S.-produced goods and services at the $P1$ exchange rate. This should encourage an increase in the demand for Canadian goods and services as manifested in a shift of the demand curve for Canadian dollars, say, to $D2$. The price of the Canadian dollar should increase so that, in equilibrium, Canadian goods are essentially equivalent in price to U.S. goods when the comparison is made in a common currency.

Unfortunately for international managers, the PPP model has not proven to be a very useful forecasting tool, since purchasing-parity relationships tend to be restored only over relatively long periods of time. The observation of the legendary British economist John Maynard Keynes that we are all dead in the long run may be especially appropriate when applied to international businesses that "guess" incorrectly about the direction of exchange rates in the short run.

Capital Flows

Other models of exchange-rate determination build on the PPP model by acknowledging that foreign-exchange transactions reflect not only international demand patterns for goods and services, but also international investment patterns. For example, if investors can earn a higher rate of return in Canada than in the U.S. when appropriate adjustments are made for the risks associated with the alternative investments, it can be expected that a shift of investment capital will take place from the U.S. to Canada. This in turn should be reflected in an increase in the demand for Canadian dollars and upward pressure on the value of the Canadian dollar. In fact, many observers argue that the dramatic *decline* in the value of foreign currencies against the U.S. dollar illustrated in table 3.3 is primarily due to relatively high interest rates in the United States, along with the relatively low rate of inflation in the U.S.

In effect, more elaborate models of exchange-rate determination recognize that currency relationships will reflect patterns of trade in goods and services as well as in capital investment. A variety of variables (besides relative inflation rates) that are theoretically linked to these patterns are usually included in exchange-rate forecasting models. It is not essential for our purposes to go into further detail on the precise nature of contemporary exchange-rate forecasting models. Suffice it to say that most international managers will probably not want to undertake the development of a model in-house. Consulting services are available (usually at a fairly hefty fee) that employ elaborate statistical forecasting models. Whether these services are worth the money is an open question. In particular, many financial economists would agree that a virtually costless—and no less accurate—forecasting tool is available to international business managers.

USING FORWARD RATES AS A FORECASTING TOOL

Return to table 3.2. The forward structure for the Canadian dollar reported in the table implicitly embodies a "market" forecast about the future spot rate for the Canadian currency. For example, it embodies the estimate of currency traders that the Canadian dollar—on September 1, 1984—would be worth $.7637 U.S. The relevant issue for international managers is whether forward exchange rates provide reasonably reliable forecasts of future spot exchange rates. If they do, it becomes less likely that management or the consultants that might be hired will be able to "outguess" the forward market.

There are two attributes of the exchange-rate forecasts embodied in the forward-rate structure that financial economists consider relevant: unbiasedness and efficiency. The forward rate is considered an unbiased estimator of the future spot rate if, on average, there is no systematic tendency of the forward rate to overestimate or underestimate the future spot rate.[14] The concept of efficiency is not quite as straightforward. Essentially, the efficient-market hypothesis suggests that economic agents act upon information available to them such that exchange rates reflect all available information that could be potentially useful in developing trading rules to earn profits net of transaction costs.

Recent writings on the subject argue that market efficiency can be discussed only with reference to specified information sets. For example, Caves and Feige talk about two levels of information. The first is the past history of the price (or exchange rate) under consideration. If the past history of the price is of no value in forecasting, then the market is deemed to be weak-form efficient. The second level of information includes those variables other than the past history of the price itself that might provide useful information. To characterize the notion of market efficiency with respect to the second level of information, Caves and Feige introduce the concept of incremental efficiency. A variable is considered incrementally useful for forecasting if it improves upon the forecasts yielded by the past history of the price itself. If a market is both incrementally efficient and weak-form efficient,

---

[14] In a more elaborate definition of the unbiasedness property, the forward rate equals the expected future spot rate plus a risk premium term. This definition is explained and evaluated in Jean-Claude Cosset, "Forward Rates as Predictors of Future Interest Rates in the Eurocurrency Market," *Journal of International Business Studies*, 13 (Winter 1982), 71–84. Cosset finds no evidence that the risk premium for a variety of currencies is different from zero.

then there is no information at either level that is useful for forecasting. Conventional terminology refers to such a market as semistrong-form efficient.[15]

In fact, a convincing empirical test of efficiency in the foreign-exchange market is rendered extremely difficult by the fact that there is no general agreement on a model of the exchange-rate-determination process that might be used in such a test. Nevertheless, a large number of studies have, in one way or another, examined the efficiency properties of foreign-exchange markets. These studies broadly support both the weak and semi-strong forms of the market efficiency hypothesis. However, for individual currencies during specific time periods, there is evidence that past price movements can help predict future spot exchange rates. For example, one recent study examined the relationship between the forward exchange rate for the U.S. dollar against sixteen major currencies and the subsequent spot exchange rates, on a monthly basis for the period September 1978 to September 1983. The authors of this study found that a simple model embodying past price changes outperformed the forward rate as a predictor of future spot rates.[16] Notwithstanding this evidence, most economists continue to believe that foreign-exchange markets are, on the whole, efficient.

Available evidence also indicates that the forward rate is not an especially accurate forecaster of the future spot rate. For example, one study found that changes in forward rates explained, on average, less than 10 percent of the changes in future spot rates over time.[17] By itself, the rather poor predictive ability of the forward-rate structure suggests that management should not rely very heavily upon the forecasts embodied in forward rates. Unfortunately, as poor as the forecasts are from the forward-rate structure, there is no evidence that so-called currency experts are consistently more accurate forecasters of future exchange rates.

Loosigian summarizes a number of studies evaluating the performance of forecasting services. He identifies three broad forecasting approaches: econometric, judgmental, and technical. The econometric approach involves specifying a theoretical model of how exchange rates are determined and then estimating the relevant coefficients of the model through statistical techniques. The judgmental approach is more subjective. Here the forecaster melds statistical data with interpretation of other evidence to produce a more qualitative forecast. The technical approach involves strict statistical extrapolation of past trends, untempered by judgment or by theoretical considerations.

Loosigian concludes that over short-time horizons, the judgmental

[15] Douglas W. Caves and Edgar L. Feige, "Efficient Foreign Exchange Markets and the Monetary Approach to Exchange-Rate Determination," *American Economic Review*, 70 (March 1980), 120–34.

[16] See Andy Murfin and Paul Ormerod, "The Forward Rate for the U.S. Dollar and the Efficient Markets Hypothesis, 1978–1983," *Manchester School of Economics and Social Studies*, 53 (September 1984), 292–99. But a number of recent studies supporting the efficient markets hypothesis are discussed in Levich, "Empirical Studies."

[17] See J. A. Frenkel, "Tests of Rational Expectations in the Forward Exchange Market," *Southern Economic Journal*, 46 (April 1980), 1083–1101.

forecasters performed better than those who are econometrics-oriented, with the reverse being true for periods of one year or longer. However, most advisory firms failed to outperform the forward rates as predictors of the future spot rate. While following some advisory recommendations would have been profitable over the short run, blindly following most of the services (especially the econometric services) would have bankrupted most individual speculators for specific periods of time.

MANAGERIAL IMPLICATIONS
OF FORWARD-MARKET EFFICIENCY

The forecasting properties of forward exchange rates are not merely curiosities for academic researchers. On the contrary, the evidence we have described has a number of potentially important implications for international managers. For example, unless management believes it has some special insight into the future behavior of exchange rates, it is as well off to use the forecasts implied in the forward-rate structure as any other. It is true that forward rates are rarely quoted beyond two years into the future. On the surface, this would seem to require the use of special models to forecast the longer-run behavior of exchange rates. In fact, the concept of covered-interest arbitrage, which we will discuss below, offers an alternative way to use available market information to forecast future exchange rates.

The high degree of uncertainty about the future behavior of exchange rates also suggests that international managers recognize the potentially substantial impacts that exchange-rate changes can have on corporate profitability and (indeed) on corporate survival. For example, management should consider hedging against the risks of exchange-rate changes when relatively low-cost hedging techniques are available. In assessing the economic merits of different international ventures, management is well advised to use a range of potential future exchange rates, since the unanticipated variance in exchange rates is likely to be substantial. And projects that require exceptionally favorable changes in exchange rates in order to be profitable probably ought not be undertaken.

THE COVERED-INTEREST-ARBITRAGE PROCESS

In table 3.2 we reported the forward-rate structure for the Canadian dollar as at August 1, 1984. We went on to discuss the sorts of market forces that influence general movements in exchange rates, including changes in the value of the Canadian dollar; however, we were not explicit about what determines the forward-rate structure for a currency. In this section we want to consider this issue, as well as its managerial implications.

Consider the following hypothetical situation. Imagine that individuals can invest in a Canadian-dollar-denominated asset—such as a Canadian government note—for one year and receive a yield of 15 percent, while an investment in a U.S.-dollar-denominated asset (of comparable maturity and risk) promises a yield of 10 percent. For investors living either in Canada or the U.S., or anywhere else for that matter, the higher yield obtainable in Canada would dictate, all other things the same, liquidating some portion of their U.S.-dollar-denominated investments and reinvesting the proceeds in a Canadian-dollar-denominated asset of comparable risk and maturity. By itself, this switching process would lead to the prices of U.S.-dollar-denominated assets being bid down (i.e., thereby increasing the yield on those assets) while the price of Canadian-dollar-denominated assets would be bid up (i.e., the yields on those assets would decline). If there were no other relevant considerations, this process of reinvestment would eventually lead to a convergence of yields on comparable assets on both sides of the border.

In fact, matters are not so simple. In particular, non-Canadian investors, who ultimately will want to restore their asset holdings to U.S. dollars, will be concerned about the value of the Canadian dollar when the Canadian-dollar-denominated asset finally matures. That is, U.S. investors who liquidate their dollar-denominated asset in order to buy the higher yielding Canadian asset will be concerned about what that Canadian asset will be worth in *U.S. dollar terms* when the asset matures. For the maturity of the investment, U.S. investors will be exposed to potential declines in the value of the Canadian dollar relative to the U.S. dollar. However, risk-averse investors can lock in a future conversion rate by selling forward Canadian dollars. These adjustments in the capital and currency markets simultaneously establish the forward-rate structure in the currency markets and the relative yields in the capital markets.

The adjustments briefly outlined in the preceding paragraph have been elaborated in a model of what is referred to as the covered-interest-arbitrage process. To elaborate on this process, while keeping the associated arithmetic simple, let us assume that the spot rate of exchange between the U.S. and Canadian dollars is at parity; that is, $1 U.S. = $1 Cdn. However, the one-year forward rate is assumed to be $1 U.S. = $1.0500 Cdn. Thus, the U.S. dollar is assumed to be at a 5 percent premium to the Canadian dollar in the one-year forward market. Assuming that a 15 percent return can be earned on a Canadian government note due to mature in one year, while only a 10 percent yield can be earned on a U.S. government note of one-year maturity, do holders of the U.S. government note have an incentive to switch into the equivalent Canadian government note?

Ignoring transactions costs (which typically run to about .50 percent of the value of foreign-exchange transactions), the ''per dollar'' return associated with making the switch would be given by the following sequence of cash flows:

(3.5) $1 U.S. → $1 Cdn. → $1.15 Cdn. → $1.0953 U.S. = 9.53% < 10%

The first arrow reflects the investor's purchase of Canadian dollars with U.S. dollars at a par exchange rate. The second arrow reflects the anticipated (risk-adjusted) principal plus yield on the one-year Canadian government note. The third arrow represents the anticipated value of the proceeds of the Canadian investment (in equivalent U.S. dollars) presuming the investor sells forward (for one-year delivery) the full amount of the anticipated Canadian dollar proceeds.[18] Note that the forward sale of the Canadian dollar proceeds will be made at the same time as the investment is made in the Canadian asset. In this way the investor will have hedged against an unfavorable change in the value of the Canadian dollar relative to the U.S. dollar over the holding period of the investment.

Barring unforeseen and unlikely contingencies, such as the expropriation or "freezing" of foreign-owned assets by the Canadian government, U.S. investors can realize an approximate 9.5 percent yield on a "covered" investment in Canada. This compares unfavorably to the 10 percent yield obtainable in the U.S., especially when the relevant transactions costs are reckoned into the calculations. Thus, given our initial assumed yield differentials and forward-rate structure, there is no incentive for short-term capital to flow north. Nor is there a realistic incentive for capital to flow south, since the transactions costs (including the bid-and-ask spread) associated with selling Canadian government notes and buying U.S. government notes and (at the same time) buying Canadian dollars foward are likely to exceed the yield differential of less than ½ of 1 percent.

Now consider what might happen if all the data in the preceding example remained unchanged except the one-year forward rate, which we now assume to be $1 U.S. = $1.02 Cdn. Ignoring transactions costs, the "per dollar" return associated with switching from the U.S. asset to the Canadian asset would be given by the following cash-flow sequence:

$$(3.6) \quad \$1 \text{ U.S.} \rightarrow \$1 \text{ Cdn.} \rightarrow \$1.15 \text{ Cdn.} \rightarrow \$1.128 \text{ U.S.}[19]$$
$$= 12.8\% > 10.0\%$$

Given the result of equation 3.6, investors can anticipate a "hedged" return on the Canadian-dollar-denominated investment that exceeds the expected return on an equivalent U.S.-dollar-denominated investment. This will encourage investors holding the U.S. asset to switch into the Canadian asset, while at the same time selling forward Canadian dollars for delivery one year hence. Adjustments will be felt in both the foreign-exchange markets and the Canadian capital markets. Specifically, the combination of increased spot purchases and forward sales of Canadian dollars will contribute to an increase in the forward discount on the Canadian dollar. This follows since the spot price of the Canadian dollar will come under upward pressure, while the forward price of the Canadian dollar will come under downward pressure.

At the same time, the increased demand for the Canadian asset will put up-

---

[18]Thus, $1.095 U.S. = $1.15 Cdn. × 1/1.05 = $1.15 Cdn. × .9524 U.S./Cdn. = $1.0953 U.S.

[19]Note: $1.15 Cdn. × $1 U.S./$1.02 Cdn. = $1.1275.

ward pressure on the price of that asset or (equivalently) downward pressure on the asset's yield. In fact, given the smaller size of the foreign-exchange market relative to the market for government securities, the former market will be affected proportionately more than the latter. These combined processes should drive the one-year forward discount on the Canadian dollar approximately into equality with the yield differential on the equivalent Canadian and U.S. assets, and the process should proceed so rapidly as to leave little scope for nonprofessionals to profit (in a riskless way) from international differences in interest rates.

Equilibrium Relationships

The key implication of the covered-interest-arbitrage concept is that the forward-rate structure of a currency is determined by the interest-rate differentials between assets denominated in that currency and U.S.-dollar-denominated assets. This relationship is expressed more precisely as:

$$(3.7) \quad ((X_F - X_S)/X_S) \times 12/\# \text{ months forward} \times 100 = R_F - R_D$$

where X_F is the appropriate forward exchange rate, X_S is the appropriate spot exchange rate, R_F is the yield on a foreign-currency-denominated asset, and R_D is the yield on a risk-equivalent domestic asset.

In the immediately preceding example, investors holding U.S.-dollar-denominated assets would (prior to arbitrage) perceive relationship 3.7 as follows:

$$(3.8) \quad (1.02 - 1.00)/1.00 \times 12/12 \times 100 \neq 15 - 10$$

It is this inequality that encourages arbitrage to take place. Using equation 3.7, we can solve for the equilibrium forward exchange rate (X'_F); that is, the value of X_F for which no incentive for arbitrage would exist:

$$(3.9) \quad X_F = (15 - 10)/100 + 1 = 1.05$$

At this point, the reader might be somewhat dismayed that relative inflation rates have not somehow figured in the determination of the forward-rate structure. After all, forward rates are acknowledged to be a forecast of future spot-exchange rates. And in an earlier section, we noted that most economists accord a role for inflation rates in the exchange-rate-determination process through the PPP process. But by making one further assumption, we can bring inflation rates back into the picture. Specifically, we assume that the nominal interest rate increases to reflect the anticipated rate of inflation. That is, the rate of interest in a country (R) will consist of a so-called real component (R'), plus an adjustment for the anticipated rate of inflation (R^i). Thus, if investors expect a 5 percent rate of inflation over the next year and would be happy with a 4 percent return after inflation, they will demand a total return of 9 percent on an asset.

This relationship between nominal interest rates and inflation is known as the Fisher effect, after the economist who first proposed it. For our purposes it allows us to postulate that:

$$(3.10) \quad R_F - R_D = PI^f - PI^d$$

where PI^f and PI^d are the anticipated rates of foreign and domestic inflation, respectively.[20]

By substitution back into equation 3.7, we can see that the interest-arbitrage model is theoretically consistent with the purchasing-parity model.[21] As in the case of the PPP model, the interest-arbitrage model has been subject to extensive empirical testing. Unfortunately, as in the former case, methodological problems plague reliable testing of the interest-arbitrage model. As well, the model will hold only if capital markets are perfectly free of government intervention. Yet in many cases governments will impose controls on the flow of financial capital across their borders. Differences in tax rates and threats of foreign-exchange controls also distort the workings of covered-interest arbitrage. Nevertheless, there is some empirical support for the interest-parity theory of the forward exchange rate. Before the cry of "so what?" leaps from the lips, let us consider the implications of this empirical support.

MANAGERIAL IMPLICATIONS
OF INTEREST ARBITRAGE

Recall our claim that the forward-rate structure for convertible currencies may be as accurate an exchange-rate forecasting tool as management will find. But forward rates are rarely quoted more than two years into the future. Does this mean that special and elaborate forecasting models are needed for predicting long-run exchange-rate movements? The interest-parity model suggests that the answer is no. Specifically, the model suggests that a "market" forecast of long-run exchange-rate relationships can be obtained by comparing interest-rate differentials on assets of comparable risk and with a maturity corresponding to the forecast period. Since interest-rate differentials reflect expectations about differences in inflation rates, and since the latter—in the long run—should underlie exchange-rate changes, the former offer a relatively cheap forecast of long-run exchange-rate movements.

Another important implication to managers of the interest-parity model is that international differences in borrowing and lending terms may not be

---

[20] The formulation expressed in equation 3.10 presumes that the real component of interest rates in the two countries remains constant over time.

[21] That is, the forward premium or discount on a currency will equal the inflation-rate differential between that country and the U.S.

significantly different, once the forward discount (or premium) on foreign exchange is taken into account. At a minimum, management should not simply look at differences in international interest rates when considering borrowing funds or investing surplus cash. The relevant interest rate is the "covered" rate, that is, the yield paid (or received) when exchange-rate differences are incorporated into the comparison between interest rates.

If management chooses to disagree with the implied prediction of the future spot-exchange rate embodied in the forward-rate structure or in longer-term interest-rate differentials, it may find specific overseas borrowing and lending opportunities attractive. For example, management may be attracted by the prospect of floating twenty-year bonds in Japan at an average annual interest rate of 7.5 percent, when comparable bonds in the U.S. must provide a yield of 12 percent per annum. But it should be explicit about why it does not believe the appreciation in the Japanese yen over the twenty-year period will not more than offset the interest differential.

SUMMARY AND CONCLUSIONS

A fundamental feature of the international business environment is the use of foreign exchange to effect business transactions. Firms involved in international business will find the need to buy or sell currencies other than their own domestic medium of exchange in order to pay bills or liquidate receivables denominated in foreign currencies. This raises at least two issues of fundamental importance to management: (1) how can the buying and selling of foreign exchange be carried out efficiently, and (2) how can future movements in specific currencies be anticipated?

The bulk of foreign-exchange transactions are executed by large commercial banks either for their customers or for their own accounts. Foreign exchange can be bought or sold on either a spot or forward basis. Spot purchases involve payment essentially for immediate delivery, while forward purchases involve deferred delivery and payment. An analogous interpretation can be given to spot and forward sales of a currency. While most corporations undertake foreign-exchange transactions through their banks, an increasing percentage of foreign-exchange trading is done through futures markets. While a number of differences exist between the interbank forward market and the futures market, perhaps the most salient difference is that the interbank forward market usually involves actual delivery of foreign exchange, while final delivery is rarely taken in the futures market.

Exchange rates are simply ratios of currency prices that are determined in interlinked markets that (for practical purposes) consist of the leading financial centers in North America, Europe, and the Far East. These markets are linked electronically, and arbitrage ensures that exchange rates established in one market do not differ from rates established in other markets by more than the costs of communicating between those markets. Basic forces of supply and demand determine currency prices, as in the case of other goods and services.

The supply of a currency and the demand for it will reflect a variety of transactions involving that currency, The transactions include imports and exports of goods and services into and out of the country as well as inflows and outflows of investment capital. There are a variety of models that purport to explain and predict exchange-rate changes. Most models embody the notion of purchasing-power parity, which holds that the price of currency A relative to currency B will change in proportion to the difference in the inflation rates between the two countries. Thus, if prices in country A double relative to prices in country B, currency A will lose half its value relative to currency B.

While the purchasing-power parity theory tends to hold in the long run, it does not provide a basis for particularly accurate forecasts over time periods that are relevant for managers. Indeed, the available evidence indicates that the forward-rate structure provides management with efficient and unbiased estimates of future exchange rates that, on average, are no less accurate than those provided by relatively expensive forecasting services. However, exchange-rate changes are notoriously difficult to forecast, which suggests that international managers should incorporate a variety of exchange rate assumptions in their evaluations of alternative international business strategies. It further suggests that managers concerned about adverse exchange-rate changes should actively consider the use of hedging techniques. Different approaches toward hedging exchange-rate risks are discussed in a later chapter.

To the extent that the foreign-exchange markets and financial-capital markets are relatively free from government restrictions and threats of intervention, the forward discount or premium on a currency with respect to the U.S. dollar should reflect interest-rate differentials between assets denominated in that currency and assets denominated in the U.S. currency. The process by which this equilibration takes place is known as covered-interest arbitrage. Under certain assumptions, the interest-arbitrage process is directly linked to the notion of purchasing-power parity. Thus, observed interest-rate differentials between currencies are often used as low-cost exchange-rate forecasts by managers.

DISCUSSION QUESTIONS

1. What are the major differences between the forward market and the futures market for foreign exchange?

2. The table below gives the forward prices for the British pound as quoted in Toronto on August 10, 1984. Calculate the forward premium (or discount) for the British pound relative to the Canadian dollar for each month shown. Then calculate the forward premium (or discount) for the Canadian dollar relative to the British pound. What is the relationship between the two calculations?

BRITISH POUND
($ Cdn./ £)

Spot	$1.7171
1 month forward	1.7194
2 months forward	1.7220
3 months forward	1.7250
6 months forward	1.7347
12 months forward	1.7443

3. If on that date (August 10, 1984), the annualized yield on ninety-one-day treasury bills in Canada was approximately 12.10 percent, what would be the expected yield on a British government Treasury bill of comparable maturity to assure covered interest-rate parity?

4. If the yield on three-month British government bills equaled the yield on ninety-one day Treasury bills in Canada, would capital flow from Britain to Canada, or vice versa, given the forward-rate structure in question 2? Explain the process by which interest-rate parity might be restored?

5. What explanations could you provide for persistent departures from covered-interest-rate parity? Is covered-interest parity more likely to exist in the case of actively traded currencies?

6. The table below gives the forward prices for the U.S. dollar as quoted in Toronto on August 10, 1984. Calculate the forward premium (or discount) for the British pound relative to the U.S. dollar using the data in question 2.

U.S. DOLLAR
($ Cdn./$ U.S.)

Spot	$1.3078
1 month forward	1.3087
2 months forward	1.3092
3 months forward	1.3096
6 months forward	1.3107
12 months forward	1.3113

REFERENCES

BALLIE, R. T., R. E. LIPPENS, and P.C. MACMAHON, "Testing Rational Expectations and Efficiency in the Foreign Exchange Market," *Econometrica*, 51 (1983), 553–63.

BILSON, JOHN, "Leading Indicators of Currency Devaluation," *Columbia Journal of World Business*, 14 (Winter 1979), 62–76.

BROWNSTEIN, VIVIAN, "Why the World Loves the Dollar," *Fortune*, February 18, 1985, pp. 54–55.

DORNBUSCH, R., "Exchange Rate Risk and the Macroeconomics of Exchange Rate Relationships," in R. Hawkins, R. Levich, and C. Wihlborg, eds., *Internationalization of Financial Markets and National Economic Policy*. Greenwich, Conn.: JAI Press, 1982.

DUFEY, GUNTER, and ROLF MIRUS, "Forecasting Foreign Exchange Rates: A Pedagogical Note," *Columbia Journal of World Business*, 16 (Summer 1981), 53–61.

HILLEY, JOHN, ET AL., "Does Covered Interest Arbitrage Dominate in Foreign Exchange Markets?" *Columbia Journal of World Business*, 14 (Winter 1979), 99–107.

ISARD, PETER, *Exchange Rate Determination: A Survey of Popular Views and Recent Models*. Princeton Studies in International Finance, No. 42, 1978.

CHAPTER FOUR

Scanning
the Overseas
Economic Environment

As discussed in chapter 1, a critical aspect of evolving an overall international business strategy, including the formulation of specific plans in functional areas of the firm such as marketing and production, is an ongoing assessment of the firm's environment. There are four elements of the environment that are encompassed by most scanning systems employed by businesses: the economic, technological, political, and social characteristics of geographic markets. An identification of the main features of the international business environment, combined with an evaluation of the firm's major strengths and weaknesses, provides the basis for formulating and modifying business strategies. This point is succinctly made by one expert in strategic planning for international business who notes: "The effectiveness of strategic planning is directly related to the capacity for environmental scanning." [1] It is further underscored by findings that competitive strategies that are successful in some regions of the world are failures in other regions. For example, strategies toward the introduction and marketing of new products that have proven to be highly profitable in Britain and Europe tend to be much less successful in North America and vice versa. [2]

[1] Subhash C. Jain, "Environmental Scanning in U.S. Corporations," *Long Range Planning*, 17 (1984), 117.
[2] See Thomas Scheeweis, "Determinant of Profitability: An International Perspective," *Management International Review*, 23 (1983), 15–21.

It should be stressed at the outset that environmental scanning and assessment is an ongoing activity in the firm that is undertaken at varying levels of detail. For example, at the early stages of a firm's planning cycle, environmental analysis tends to be relatively broad, focusing on the main factors potentially influencing the demand for a firm's output as well as on the primary economic, political, and cultural factors influencing the costs and risks of doing business in different countries. In effect, environmental analysis at the early stages of a firm's planning cycle amounts to a scanning of the international environment in order to identify major new business opportunities and also threats to a firm's ongoing businesses. The outcome of this scanning exercise should be a preliminary identification of markets that offer potentially favorable prospects for international expansion and those that do not. Whether business should be pursued in one or more specific markets, as well as the particular competitive strategies that might be employed, is the subject of more intensive analysis at the strategy-evaluation stage of the overall corporate-planning process.

In this chapter, we review and discuss various approaches to scanning the broad economic and technological aspects of a firm's environment. Surveys have shown that the economic environment tends to receive the greatest degree of attention on the part of corporate planners. This is because firms assume (in some cases incorrectly) that economic variables have the greatest influence on corporate profits. It also undoubtedly reflects the fact that economic variables are generally measurable and amenable to statistical analysis. Usually ranked next in importance is the technological environment.[3] Since technological change can ultimately be expected to influence either the demand for a firm's products or the costs of producing and marketing its output, we consider both the economic and technological scanning activities in the same chapter.

ATTRIBUTES OF THE ECONOMIC ENVIRONMENT

One can quite quickly list several dozen economic variables that, in theory, affect the overall attractiveness of a particular geographic region. Clearly the scanning exercise needs to be bounded by considerations of what is relevant and what is not especially relevant. For example, a natural-resources firm is especially interested in the availability of specific resources in different parts of the world as well as in the costs and taxes associated with extracting and transporting those resources from one region to another. It is not likely to be especially interested in the economic characteristics of a country that influence the demand for specific consumer products, such as the current level and prospective future growth rate of per capita income.

On the other hand, a manufacturer or distributor of consumer goods is likely to be very interested in current and prospective income levels in different parts of

[3]For one such survey, see Jain, "Environmental Scanning."

the world as well as in demographic characteristics such as the age distribution of the population, the relative size of the middle class, and household-formation rates. While natural resources (especially energy resources) will probably be used in the production and distribution of all types of consumer goods, their availability and cost are not likely to be critical screening factors for firms primarily concerned about marketing consumer products abroad.

As a practical matter, therefore, it is impossible for us to consider in this chapter all of the individual variables that might be relevant to firms involved in scanning their economic environments. Rather, we must aim for generality by focusing on the factors that are typically included in what economists call the firm's revenue (or demand) and cost functions. The demand function describes the relationship between the quantity of output demanded in the marketplace and the variables that determine that quantity. The cost function describes the relationship between the costs of producing output and the factors that influence production costs. With a knowledge of the underlying demand and cost relationships, management can formulate some preliminary evaluations of the potential profitability of alternative international business ventures. That is because profit is simply the difference between revenues and costs. Revenue, in turn, equals the quantity of output sold (q) times average selling price (p), while cost equals the quantity of output produced (also q) times per unit cost (c). Thus profit (II) is given by equation 4.1:

$$(4.1) \ \text{II} = pxq - cxq$$

where pxq is total revenue and cxq is total cost. Management might therefore approach the scanning exercise by considering the factors that influence total revenue and total cost.

REAL INCOME

The broad factors traditionally considered when screening the ''demand side'' of a market are listed in table 4.1. For consumer goods perhaps the most important factor influencing the per capita demand for a product in a given region is real disposable income per capita. By real income we mean the monetary value of income adjusted for inflation. Disposable income nets out tax liabilities from the gross income of individuals. Presumably, the higher the per capita income in a region, the greater the potential demand for goods and services in that region, all other things being constant. Equivalently, at any set of prices charged, firms can expect to sell more in high-income markets than in low-income markets, other things being equal.

While the existing level of per capita income influences the current potential size of a market, management will also be quite interested in the potential growth prospects for that market. After all, it will take time for the firm to formulate and

TABLE 4.1   Attributes of the Economic Environment

DEMAND-RELATED FACTORS

---

1. Average income
2. Expected growth in income
3. Availability and prices of substitute and complementary products
4. Government barriers and incentives to international business
5. Demographic factors
   (a) Population size
   (b) Age distribution of population
   (c) Income distribution in the population
   (d) Literacy of the population

COST-RELATED FACTORS

---

1. Average wage rates
2. Labor productivity
   (a) Capital/labor ratios
   (b) Natural resources/labor ratios
   (c) Technological change
   (d) Education and scale economies
3. Taxation and government regulation

---

implement plans to enter a foreign market. Furthermore, given the (usually) substantial costs of commencing international business, management should think of a commitment to international business as being long run in nature. Hence, a prognosis for income growth is important. It is also useful to have some understanding of what economists call the income elasticity of demand. The latter statistic captures the relationship between growth in the income level of a market and growth in demand for a product. More formally, the income elasticity of demand (E_y) is defined in equation 4.2:

$$(4.2) \quad E_y = \frac{\Delta Q_{x,t}}{Q_{x,t}} \cdot \frac{Y_t}{\Delta Y_t} = \frac{\Delta Q_{x,t}}{Q_t} \div \frac{\Delta Y_t}{Y_t}$$

where $Q_{x,t}$ is the quantity demanded of good x in time t, and Y_t is real per capita disposable income in time t. Hence, E_y measures the proportionate change in quantity demanded relative to the proportionate change in real disposable income.

The relevance of the income-elasticity statistic for management is quite evident. Potential demand for a product will increase more substantially in growing markets if the product is characterized by a relatively high income elasticity of demand. Conversely, stagnant or declining markets may prove especially unfavorable for products with high income elasticities.

To elaborate on this concept, if product X were characterized by an income elasticity of demand equal to 2.00, it would imply that a 10 percent increase in real disposable income would increase quantity demanded of product X by 20 percent, all other things constant. On the other hand, if product Y were characterized by an income elasticity of demand equal to 0.50, the same 10 percent increase in real disposable income would lead to only a 5 percent increase in the quantity demanded of product Y.

As an empirical matter, goods that fulfill basic needs, such as foodstuffs, have relatively low income elasticities of demand (typically less than one), while highly discretionary items, such as high-performance sports cars, have relatively high income-elasticity coefficients. However, the income elasticity of demand will itself vary with an economy's real income level. For example, in an economy where per capita income equals $1,000 per year, even a doubling in income will leave the potential market for Mercedes Benzes relatively unchanged. On the other hand, potential demand could increase quite substantially if the doubling took place from a per capita income base of $30,000 per year.

An illustrative set of income-elasticity coefficients is reported in table 4.2. The estimates are drawn from two broad types of statistical studies: cross-section and time series. In a cross-section study, observations on consumption and income are drawn from a sample of countries at a given time. In a time-series study, observations on these variables are drawn from a sample of different years for a given country. Differences in the estimated income-elasticity measures reported

TABLE 4.2 Income-Elasticity Measurements

COMMODITY	CROSS-SECTION	TIME SERIES
1. Food and beverages (excluding alcoholic beverages)	.54	.80
2. Alcoholic beverages	.77	
3. Tobacco	.88	
4. Clothing	.80–.90	.70–.80
5. Textiles	.50	.80
6. Household and personal services	1.19	.80
7. Communication services	2.03	
8. Recreation	1.15	
9. Health	1.80	
10. Durable consumer goods		2.7
11. Furniture	1.61	
12. Appliances	1.40	
13. Metals	1.52	
14. Chemicals		2.1
15. Machinery and transportation equipment (excluding passenger cars)		1.5–2.0

Source: Reed Moyer, "International Market Analysis," *Journal of Marketing Research*, 5, no. 4 (November 1968), 356. Reprinted by permission of the American Marketing Association.

in table 4.2 are therefore partly the result of methodological differences in the way the estimates were derived.

The results shown in table 4.2 confirm our earlier assertion. Namely, necessities, such as food and clothing, tend to be income inelastic. That is, the income-elasticity coefficient is less than 1. On the other hand, the demand for consumer durables, such as furniture and appliances, tends to have elasticity coefficients greater than 1. Capital goods, such as machinery and transportation equipment and chemicals, also tend to be income-elastic. It should be pointed out that the estimates in table 4.2 are averages and may not apply equally to all income groups. Another qualification is that no price-change adjustments were made to the time-series calculations. As a consequence, the corresponding income-elasticity statistics reflect the influence of both income and price changes. In a short while we will describe a method for estimating the separate influences of income and price on market demand.

The income-elasticity coefficient combined with estimates of current and prospective income levels offers a relatively economical screening mechanism for international managers. As many management authorities have noted, it is prohibitive for most companies to examine all possible countries and markets throughout the world. However, focusing on only a limited number of countries may result in bypassing some of the most promising international market opportunities. They suggest the solution lies in the adoption of a screening procedure of secondary data to determine which countries to investigate in depth.[4] In this regard, current per capita income levels serve as a potentially effective screen. For example, in countries with relatively low per capita incomes, the demand for luxury goods is likely to be quite limited over the foreseeable future, even if economic growth proceeds quite rapidly. On the other hand, potential demand for household staples could increase quite dramatically in rapidly growing low-income countries.

A variety of publications provide estimates of current income levels in different countries and regions. For example, the United Nations' *Statistical Yearbook* is a rich source of international economic and demographic data. Table 4.3 reports recent per capita income estimates provided by this source for a sample of countries. The results exhibit the wide range of income levels encountered in international business. Statistics on income levels and the state of economic development in various regions of the world are often reported in business periodicals such as *The Far Eastern Economic Review*, *The Economist*, and *Business International*. If management has some insight into the income elasticity of demand for the product or set of products it is contemplating marketing on an international basis, data such as those provided in table 4.3 can help weed out unpromising marketing opportunities early on in the environmental-assessment process.[5]

---

[4]See, for example, Susan P. Douglas, C. Samuel Craig, and Warren J. Keegan, "Approaches to Assessing International Marketing Opportunities for Small and Medium-Sized Companies," *Columbia Journal of World Business*, 17 (Fall 1982), 26–31.

[5]There are complications associated with making income comparisons across countries. For a comprehensive, if somewhat technical, overview of the relevant restrictions and qualifications, see

TABLE 4.3   Per Capita National Income—Selected Countries, 1980

COUNTRY	PER CAPITA NATIONAL INCOME (IN $ U.S.)
1. Brazil	1,860
2. Belgium	10,956
3. Canada	9,133
4. Colombia	1,115
5. France	10,824
6. West Germany	11,759
7. India	226
8. Israel	4,473
9. Japan	7,672
10. Korea	1,355
11. Norway	11,529
12. Philippines	655
13. Tunisia	1,246
14. U.S.	10,094
15. U.K.	8,222

Source: United Nations, *Statistical Yearbook*, 1980, table 34.

One caution—and it is becoming increasingly relevant—is that there is a tendency for published income statistics to understate true per capita income levels. This is due to the widespread practice of unreported economic transactions that takes place in both developed and developing countries. In many cases the existence of this so-called underground economy is motivated by the incentive to avoid paying taxes. Furthermore, in developing countries an efficient bureaucracy dedicated to collecting and processing national income statistics often does not exist. As a result, several economists have suggested that total manufacturing output produced in a country be used as a measure of the purchasing power of consumers. Unfortunately, serious statistical biases may plague this variable as well.

COMPETITIVE AND COMPLEMENTARY PRODUCTS

The current size and future growth of a potential market can be meaningfully evaluated only with reference to the share of the market that management can reasonably hope to attain. This in turn requires an assessment of both existing competitors in the marketplace and potential competitors. The strategic analysis of competition requires a focus on a number of structural and behavioral determinants of competition, including barriers to entry and exit, the number of com-

---

Irving B. Kravis, "Comparative Studies of National Income and Prices," *Journal of Economic Literature*, 22 (March 1984), 1–39.

petitors, the goals and capabilities of competitors, and the stage of the industry's evolution.[6]

All other things equal, high costs of entry into an industry contribute to higher profits for firms that are financially and technically able to enter that industry. Exit costs, which may be thought of as writedowns on assets that are employed by firms in an industry when those firms discontinue operations, are an effective barrier to entry, since they increase the risks associated with doing business in the relevant industry.

The lower the costs of entry and exit, the larger the number of firms that can be expected to compete in a market and (ordinarily) the lower the market share the firm can expect to capture. Of course, this latter assertion must be qualified by a number of other relevant considerations. In particular, in a relatively young and rapidly growing industry, the competition generated by the existence of any given number of firms will ordinarily be less severe than in a mature, slow-growing industry.

The size distribution of firms will also have an important bearing on competitive conditions in an industry. For example, competition in an industry made up of a number of large, well-financed firms and a fringe of smaller firms will likely be different from the competition existing in an industry made up of dozens of medium-sized, expansion-minded firms. The main point here is that the goals and objectives of competitors as well as their competitive strengths and weaknesses must be considered in evaluating potential rivalry from substitute products. Large but relatively complacent firms may offer less competition than smaller, expansion-minded firms. Since the international firm is often operating (or contemplating operating) in unfamiliar markets, the task of identifying the likely strategies of its overseas competitors may be a particularly difficult one.

The nature of competition in an industry will also influence the prices a firm can hope to receive on its goods and services, given any share of the market it can successfully capture. For example, the widespread availability of substitute products will make consumers quite sensitive to price differences in the marketplace. This heightened price sensitivity, in turn, puts a tight lid on the prices the firm can charge without losing a large share of its market. On the other hand, a scarcity of good substitutes will provide a firm with leeway to charge higher prices without suffering a significant drop in market share.

While it is sometimes overlooked, the availability of complements also enhances the economic outlook for a given product. A complement is a good or service used in conjunction with the product that management is contemplating introducing in overseas markets. For example, golf courses are complements to golfing equipment, and videocassette recordings are complements to videocassette recorders. All other things being equal, the widespread availability of complementary products makes the introduction of any new product in overseas markets a

---

[6]An extensive treatment of competitive analysis can be found in Michael E. Porter, *Competitive Strategy* (New York: Free Press, 1980).

more attractive business opportunity. Indeed, the availability of complementary goods may be essential to the successful launch of a product, as makers of videotex equipment have learned. The growth of the market for videotex hardware has, to date, fallen below expectations primarily because of a scarcity of useful software.

Barriers to Trade

The policies of foreign governments toward international trade and investment constitute one of the single most important influences on competitive conditions in foreign markets. Many foreign governments, especially in less developed countries, protect local producers with a combination of tariff and nontariff barriers. This often enables firms already established in the domestic industry to maintain their shares of the local market while charging prices substantially above costs of production.

In principle, there are limitations on the extent to which foreign governments can protect established domestic producers, at least for those governments that are signatories to the General Agreement on Tariffs and Trade. In 1947 the U.S. and twenty-two other nations signed the General Agreement on Tariffs and Trade (GATT), which called for participating countries to meet periodically to negotiate on tariff cuts. Major rounds of multilateral tariff reductions subsequently took place. GATT today is a comprehensive international agreement (numbering some ninety signatory countries) that covers a number of areas of international trade. The four primary areas are (1) nondiscrimination, (2) elimination of quantitative restrictions, (3) fair-trading rules, and (4) dispute settlements.[7]

Under the nondiscrimination provision of GATT, governments must treat all foreign goods equally. And, in principle, equal treatment means that imported goods are to be accorded the same treatment as goods of local origin. In fact, however, there is ample scope under GATT for discrimination against foreign goods. For example, a country whose products are not competitive against imports could alter its tax rates to improve the competitiveness of local producers. Exceptions to the principle of equal treatment also exist in the area of government procurement and in the case of trading blocs such as the European Economic Community, whose member governments are permitted to discriminate in favor of member countries and against nonmembers. The freedom of sovereign governments to establish standards and regulations governing the sale of products also provides an opportunity for discrimination. For example, Japanese videocassette recorders have (at times) been held up at French ports of entry for months while inspectors assured themselves that the recorders met acceptable "safety" regulations and other standards.

Notwithstanding the opportunities for slippage, GATT has been quite suc-

---

[7]Much of the following discussion is taken from Wilson E. Schmidt and Tracy Murray, "International Economic Institutions and Negotiations," in I. Walter and T. Murray, eds., *Handbook of International Business* (New York: Ronald Press, 1982), pp. 5.18–5.26.

cessful in encouraging a substantial worldwide reduction in tariffs over the postwar period. Unfortunately, it has been less successful in preventing the establishment and eliminating the existence of so-called nontariff barriers, such as quotas. For purposes of clarification, a tariff is essentially a tax levied by a government on imported goods. Tariffs effectively make foreign goods more expensive than domestically produced goods, since the prices of foreign goods must increase to cover the tax. Quantitative restrictions, such as quotas, directly limit the quantity of foreign goods that can be imported into a country.

Under GATT, quotas can be used in restricted cases. For example, trade in agricultural products is exempt from quota prohibitions. Furthermore, countries whose domestic markets for textiles and apparel are disrupted by imports can negotiate "orderly marketing agreements" with specific exporting countries. Under such agreements, the exporting country limits its exports to the importing country. In recent years, there has been a proliferation of orderly marketing agreements, mostly involving exports from Pacific-rim countries such as Japan and Taiwan. Perhaps the most notable agreements involve restrictions on the quantity of automobiles shipped to the United States and Canada that were "voluntarily" adopted by Japanese auto makers. In fact, agreements affecting Japanese autos as well as those covering footwear from Taiwan and color televisions from Korea were essentially undertaken outside GATT.

Fair-trading rules are designed to prevent a variety of unfair practices that give products from one country a competitive advantage over products from another country. The practices of greatest concern are government subsidies and "dumping." Subsidies granted to domestic producers may give those producers a competitive advantage over imports, while subsidies granted to exporters may enable the latter to gain a competitive advantage over domestic producers in other countries, or over other exporters from nonsubsidizing countries. Subsidy practices are not illegal per se under GATT, but they are prohibited if they cause injury to competing firms located in the importing country. In this case the importing country is allowed to levy a countervailing duty sufficient to offset the effect of the subsidy.

Dumping is defined to be selling in foreign markets at prices below fair value. There can be substantial difficulties in determining what constitutes fair value, but generally it is taken to be the firm's average cost of production in its home market. Under GATT the importing country can introduce an offsetting antidumping duty, although frequently the alleged dumping behavior is terminated after consultations between the countries involved.

Finally, GATT is concerned with how to resolve disputes among signatories. Since GATT is written in general terms, some disputes arise as a result of differences in national interpretations of GATT rules. Other disputes arise when national governments are pressured by domestic interest groups into implementing trade policies that clearly violate the rules. In fact, successfully resolved disputes are almost always achieved through bilateral discussions between the disputing parties. GATT officials have no power to enforce the agreement, and they can only apply moral pressure against violators by publicly exposing their actions. This is sometimes done in the form of a panel report. For example, at the behest of the U.S. government, a GATT panel reviewed Canada's Foreign Investment Review Act and ruled that certain features of the act were in violation of GATT. Although under no legal obligation to do so, the Canadian government agreed to modify those features.

There is obviously a good deal more that might be said about government influences on the international economic environment. We pursue this subject a bit more in a later chapter dealing with government relations in the international firm. The main point we wish to make here is that, notwithstanding an effort to ''standardize'' the international trade environment through GATT, the degree to which foreign markets are open to outside competition often depends very much on the specific products and markets involved. For example, there are over ten thousand different product categories in the U.S. tariff schedules. And to add to the complexity, most developing countries do not belong to GATT. Hence, while American cigarettes are readily available in Great Britain, business people caught selling American cigarettes in South Korea are liable to imprisonment.

While international rules governing trade in goods are relatively clear under GATT, the international trade machinery governing services is less well developed. As a result, disparate protectionist practices have emerged, and many foreign governments have erected barriers to trade in services. In particular, the international firm's ability to set up overseas franchises may be threatened by the failure of foreign governments to protect the firm's trademark, or by a foreign government's insistence that the firm divulge trade secrets to local businesses.

As an example, Coca-Cola has experienced persistent difficulty in establishing local bottling plants in India as a result of the Indian government's insistence that Coca-Cola make its syrup recipe available to local bottlers. As another example, McDonald's Corporation was successful in its lawsuit to restrain its former French franchisee from using the McDonald's name and logo; however, the former franchisee continues to run the restaurants under their new name of O'Kitsch with essentially an identical menu to the one they used when they were McDonald's, including wine, without which no self-respecting French person would be seen eating anything.[8]

The point again to bear in mind is that opportunities to exploit a competitive advantage in international markets, as well as the associated risks, may be strongly influenced by the policies of foreign governments toward international business. A major problem for management is that these policies are not uniform across foreign countries. This implies that management may need to rely on the services of international trade consultants and lawyers to evaluate the legal and policy environments for international business in specific geographic regions. By contrast, there are relatively few restrictions on the flow of goods and services between geographic regions within a national economy, although local and state

---

[8] "Paris Sees the Golden Arches," *Toronto Globe and Mail*, March 19, 1984, p. B7.

governments do occasionally protect indigenous producers through discriminatory purchasing policies, tax concessions, and other subsidies to local businesses.

DEMOGRAPHIC FACTORS

The demography of a region includes population size and its composition, along with key socioeconomic attributes such as literacy rates in the population and wide or narrow disparities in a society's distribution of income. It is obvious that the larger the total population in a region, the larger the potential market, all other things constant. And just as there is a wide variation in per capita income levels across countries, there is also a substantial diversity in population sizes, as indicated in table 4.4.

While not as obvious, the age and sex composition of a population will also influence the potential demand for specific products. For example, if the product in question is a pacemaker for people with heart conditions, the relevant potential market consists of all people who have heart conditions or who are in high-risk categories for heart attacks. As another example, if the product in question is disposable baby diapers, the number of women in the population of child-bearing age is an important influence on potential demand for the product.

Other demographic attributes may be even more relevant than age and sex distributions depending upon the product or service involved. As a case in point, the potential demand for books, magazines, and newspapers will probably depend most heavily on literacy rates in the population.

In effect, demographic factors such as literacy rates stratify the total population into segments that are likely potential consumers and those that are not. An overall increase in population size is therefore relevant to potential demand, inasmuch as the segment of likely potential consumers increases concomitantly with the growth of the population. Stratification of the overall market by demographic characteristics also helps to identify significant changes in potential marketing opportunities. For example, the aging of the postwar "baby boomers" is creating a growing worldwide market for products and services geared to affluent and middle-income families.

THE DEMAND FUNCTION

For purposes of forecasting potential future sales and revenues, the various factors influencing demand for a product must be brought together in an integrated fashion. In business economics, this is typically accomplished by estimating a demand function. One such function is specified (in a general form) in equation 4.3:

$$(4.3) \quad Q = \infty \, Z_1^{\beta_1} \, Z_2^{\beta_2} \ldots Z_n^{\beta_n}$$

**TABLE 4.4   Total Population—Selected Countries,
1980 (in thousands)**

COUNTRY	TOTAL POPULATION
1. Brazil	123,032
2. Belgium	9,857
3. Canada	23,941
4. Colombia	27,093
5. France	53,713
6. West Germany	61,561
7. India	663,596
8. Israel	3,871
9. Japan	116,782
10. Korea	38,124
11. Norway	4,086
12. Philippines	48,400
13. Tunisia	6,369
14. U.S.	227,658
15. U.K.	55,945

Source: United Nations, *Statistical Yearbook*, 1980, table 19.

The Z's are the independent variables that are expected to influence (in a substantive way) the quantity of sales of a particular product (Q_i). The set of independent variables would ordinarily include real per capita disposable income, prices of substitutes and complements, and demographic variables, including total population.

The β coefficients represent statistical "weights" attached to each independent variable. Technically, they measure the proportionate change in Q for a given proportionate change in each Z variable, holding the value of all other Z variables constant. Hence, if Z_1 is real disposable income, β_1 is the income-elasticity coefficient, since its value represents the proportionate change in quantity relative to the proportionate change in income.

The use of equation 4.3 (or some variant) as a sales forecasting tool obviously requires management to have a good deal of information. For one thing, it requires management to know the variables (the Zs) that influence the demand for its products. It also obliges management to have estimates of the β coefficients, as well as estimates of the future values of the Z variables. Once all this information is available, it is a relatively straightforward procedure to insert the estimated future values of the Z variables into equation 4.3, and evaluate the equation to obtain forecast values of Q.

In practice, it is ordinarily much easier to describe how to go about estimating a demand-forecasting model than to actually carry out the exercise. The most difficult aspect of demand modeling, especially for overseas markets, is the lack of data on the relevant Z_i variables. In particular, it is often quite difficult to get information on the availability of competitive products and the key dimensions along which competition takes place in foreign markets. In addition, there are sometimes quite serious statistical problems associated with estimating the β coefficients. Nevertheless, organizing the demand-forecasting exercise around the "building" of a demand-function model forces management to articulate explicitly the critical assumptions underlying its overseas-sales-growth scenario. The availability of a demand-function model also facilitates testing the sensitivity of management's sales-growth scenarios to alternative assumptions about the · economic environment.

As a matter of fact, the overwhelming majority of small and medium-sized firms use relatively unsophisticated demand-analysis techniques. Often such techniques consist of nothing more than scanning business newspapers, periodicals, and industry publications for information about current and prospective overseas market conditions.[9] Others implement formal statistical analysis but restrict their attention to the relationship between demand and per capita income levels. That is, by multiplying the estimated income-elasticity coefficient by the expected growth in income for a region, management obtains a rough estimate of the demand growth potential for a product in that region. The reliability of the resulting estimate will depend upon how confident management is that other influences on demand (besides real income) will remain relatively constant over the forecast period.

INPUT-OUTPUT ANALYSIS

Current and prospective income levels in overseas markets are relevant not only to the potential demand for consumer goods but also for producer goods, that is, goods purchased by businesses as inputs to production processes. Since the demand for producer goods is derived from the demand for household goods, an economy's real income level and the growth in real income over time will ultimately influence current and future levels of demand for producer goods in a region.

While estimating income-elasticity coefficients for producer goods is conceptually possible, a more direct approach is to derive the demand for producer goods from input-output relationships in the economy. For example, if the largest users of fabricated copper are the housing and auto industries, forecasts of housing and auto demand will indirectly generate a forecast of the demand for fabricated copper, presuming that the quantity of fabricated copper per housing or auto unit is fairly stable.

The technique suggested in the preceding paragraph has been incorporated in input-output forecasting models. For example, if the management of a copper-

---

[9]See Jain, "Environmental Scanning."

products company is able to express the per unit requirements of fabricated copper for a variety of major final uses, such as housing, office buildings, and automobiles, and it has forecasts of future output levels in these usage sectors, the overall demand for fabricated copper could be forecast through the input-output relationship given as equation 4.4:

$$(4.4) \quad [I_1 \ I_2 \ \ldots \ I_n] \begin{bmatrix} Q_1 \\ Q_2 \\ \cdot \\ \cdot \\ \cdot \\ Q_n \end{bmatrix} = [F]$$

While somewhat unwholesome looking at first glance, equation 4.4 is really quite straightforward. The first expression shows n observations that report the unit input requirements for fabricated copper associated with n major final end uses. For example, I_1 might be the physical units of fabricated copper required to produce an automobile in a given weight class (say less than three tons). The other I's would provide similar information for other end uses of copper. The second expression would therefore consist of estimated output levels for the various end-use segments. Hence, Q_1 would represent the estimated number of cars of less than three tons expected to be produced in the market being evaluated. The other Qs would represent estimates of output levels for other end-use segments. When the first term is multiplied by the second term, one obtains the sum:

$$(4.5) \quad I_1 Q_1 + I_2 Q_2 + \ldots + I_n Q_n = F$$

Hence, the sum (F) is merely a numerical estimate of the overall demand for fabricated copper.

Typically, management will have reasonably reliable estimates of copper input requirements in various end uses, although the estimates may need to be revised from time to time to reflect changes in underlying production technologies and in the price of copper relative to copper substitutes, such as aluminum. Reliable estimates of the Q values will ordinarily be more difficult to obtain. Nevertheless, planned production levels are often provided formally or informally by major producers to their suppliers. And in many developing and centrally planned economies, government agencies are the largest purchasers of producer goods. Since these public-sector agencies frequently announce formal development plans, estimates of Q values may be more accessible and more meaningful than underlying data on income levels and other variables included in demand functions.

MACROECONOMIC SCANNING

As noted above, the economic-scanning activity will vary from company to company both in the degree of detail pursued and in the sophistication of the techniques employed. In many cases, management may be content with obtaining information about broad economic trends in overseas markets without necessarily relating those trends to the potential demand for specific products or groups of products. In some cases this focus on broad macroeconomic variables, such as national income, inflation, and interest rates, may reflect management's underlying belief that substantial demand will exist for the firm's specific products in economically healthy markets. In other cases it may reflect management's perception that one or two key economic variables will have a dominant influence on the profitability of doing business in a given region.

In cases where management's primary focus is on broad, economy-wide measures of the health and state of development of foreign markets, including tax levels and the extent of government regulation, the scanning system functions as a way to feed in perspectives on the external world for internal review. A wide variety of information sources are available to assist in this exercise, as suggested by table 4.5. Specifically, the table lists various sources of information about business conditions in foreign markets that are utilized by managers, according to a survey sample of Fortune 500 companies. The sources are listed in descending order of importance in accordance with rankings assigned by managers.

THE COST FUNCTION

Given forecasts of the quantity of output the firm might expect to sell in various international markets, along with the average prices it might hope to charge for the output sold, management can develop estimates of total revenue obtainable in specific markets. The other component of the firm's cash-flow stream, its expenditures, should also be evaluated. The basis for this evaluation is the anticipated cost function.

A cost function describes the relationship between a firm's planned output and its total costs. In the case of the international firm or the firm contemplating international expansion, a relevant consideration is whether cost functions in foreign markets lie below the cost function in the firm's domestic market for the output rates contemplated. Where they do, a firm can increase its net cash flow by undertaking production and distribution abroad. An important aspect, therefore, of the economic-scanning exercise is a consideration of the factors that determine cost-output relationships in different national markets.

Since wages are the most important component of costs in the majority of economic activities, comparing wage rates in different countries is an important part of the economic-scanning process. The question that naturally arises is how to compare wage rates denominated in different currencies. The general approach is

TABLE 4.5   Importance Rankings Assigned to Different Sources of Information (percentages)

	RANKINGS					
	FIRST (HIGHEST)	SECOND	THIRD	FOURTH	FIFTH (LOWEST)	TOTAL 100%
Daily newspapers, i.e., *New York Times, Wall Street Journal*, etc.	44	47	5	5	21	100
Publications of industry groups such as Conference Board, Brookings Inst., etc.	30	29	11	8	23	100
Business periodicals, i.e., *Fortune, Business Week, Forbes*	29	23	20	5	23	100
Futures consultants such as Hudson Institute, Stanford Research Institute, Data Research Inc., etc.	26	16	10	5	43	100
Government publications	22	20	21	8	29	100
Seminars and conferences	12	18	17	12	41	100
Publications or newsletters issued by private organizations such as *Futurist, Kiplinger Letter*, etc.	8	9	16	17	50	100
Academic journals, i.e., *Harvard Business Review, California Management Review, Business Horizons*, etc.	6	16	15	10	44	100
Information from professional associations such as the World Future Society	6	10	17	11	56	100
Universities	1	5	11	10	72	100
Literary publications such as *Atlantic, Harpers, New Yorker*	1	2	4	5	88	100

to convert reported wage rates to a common currency. For example, if the average wage rate in Canada's steel industry is $20 per hour, and the Canadian dollar is worth $.82 U.S. in the spot market, the exchange rate-adjusted wage rate in the Canadian steel industry is $16.40 U.S. per hour. This method of standardizing comparisons to a common currency effectively assumes that purchasing-power parity holds in foreign-exchange markets. As noted in chapter 3, this assumption is a tenuous one except as a limited tendency.

Another difficulty in comparing wage rates across countries is that payment practices may differ substantially. That is, reported wage rates may be only one component of overall cost per worker-hour, once social contributions such as employer contributions to employee pensions and health care and insurance plans are included in the calculation. The fact that required social contributions may differ substantially across countries makes simple international comparisons of wage rates of dubious value.

Fortunately for international managers, comprehensive surveys of costs per worker-hour in different countries and different industries are periodically undertaken by consulting companies and international banks. The partial results of a recent study undertaken by the Union Bank of Switzerland are reported in table 4.6. Specifically, the table shows the calculated cost per worker-hour in six developed countries, where cost includes both wages and employer social contributions. The Union Bank survey found that worker-hour costs in North America are almost double what they are in Great Britain, partly as a result of the sharp appreciation in the value of the U.S. dollar relative to the Swiss franc and the sharp decline in the value of the British pound against the Swiss currency.

LABOR PRODUCTIVITY

Should international managers scanning the Union Bank's results as reported in table 4.6 conclude that costs would be saved by shifting production from North America to Great Britain? Should North American producers conclude that their domestic markets will be flooded by low-cost British goods? In fact, such conclusions would be premature if based strictly on the data shown in table 4.6. For one thing, the data are based on averages across a wide range of industries. Therefore, they may be highly unrepresentative of specific industries. But more fundamentally, the data may be completely misleading if offsetting differences exist in labor productivity, defined as physical (or real) output per unit of physical labor input.

In practice, comparisons of labor productivity across countries are somewhat unreliable, since they reflect an averaging of heterogeneous goods and

TABLE 4.6   Cost per Worker-Hour in Swiss Francs

1.	Great Britain	=	14.08
2.	France	=	16.53
3.	Italy	=	17.29
4.	Switzerland	=	23.86
5.	Canada	=	25.31
6.	U.S.	=	25.57

Source: John Wicks, "U.K. Labor Costs among the Lowest," *Toronto Globe and Mail*, June 18, 1984, p. IB4. Reprinted by permission of the *Financial Times* of London.

services. That is, output produced differs across countries, and methods of aggregation to obtain total real output are imprecise. Nevertheless, the concept of labor productivity is still a useful and relevant one, since it qualifies the significance of cost per worker-hour differences in the manner shown by equation 4.6:

$$(4.6) \quad \frac{C_i}{Q_i} = \frac{C_i}{L_i} \times \frac{L_i}{Q_i}$$

Assuming (for simplicity) that all costs of production and distribution are directly or indirectly related to labor, cost per unit of output in the ith industry (C_i/Q_i) will equal the cost per worker-hour (C_i/L_i) multiplied by the number of worker-hours required to produce a unit of output (L_i/Q_i). It can, therefore, be seen from equation 4.6 that if the quantity of labor required to produce a unit of output, i.e., the inverse measure of labor productivity, is lower in country A than in country B, it might more than offset a higher cost per worker-hour in country A.

An important implication of the foregoing discussion is that projections of overall cost behavior in different countries require forecasts of productivity growth as well as forecasts of cost per worker-hour or per worker. Assessing the likely behavior of productivity growth in different markets implies the need to identify and evaluate the factors that influence productivity growth. The list of factors influencing labor productivity is lengthy. It includes (among other things) the behavior of the capital/labor ratio. Specifically, an increase in this ratio will contribute to an increase in labor productivity, all other things constant. Similarly, an increase in the natural-resources/labor ratio will promote an increase in labor productivity.

Technological Change

As an empirical matter, the most important factor influencing the post-war growth in labor productivity has been technological change. The latter may be loosely defined as the rate at which new production processes and new products are introduced into the economy. In the context of environmental scanning, both aspects of the technological-change process are relevant. Specifically, the introduction of new production processes abroad can facilitate lower costs of production and distribution in overseas markets. Moreover, as noted in the section on demand functions, the introduction of new substitute products represents a potential source of intensified competition for the international firm, while the introduction of new complementary products represents a source of increased demand for the firm's products.

Forecasting the rate of technological change is an extremely treacherous activity, particularly as the focus of one's interest narrows to the level of an individual industry. Nevertheless, technological-forecasting techniques of greater or lesser complexity have been applied in a wide variety of circumstances. One broad approach, called the Delphi technique, involves a structured approach to soliciting the opinions of experts in a field. Thus, if one were interested in the future pace and direction of technological change in the textile industry in a specific region, one might solicit the opinion of chemical engineers and equipment manufacturers with experience in the textile industry in that region. The aim of the Delphi approach is to elicit (through an iterative process described in more detail in the next chapter) a consensus view of the future from the chosen panel of experts.[10]

Statistical approaches to technological forecasting have also been undertaken. In these approaches, the researcher ordinarily focuses on the rate at which one or more new products or production processes spread through a given population of potential users. This focus is relevant in a variety of contexts. For example, if management is considering setting up retail food outlets in overseas markets, it may be interested in the rate at which local food suppliers computerize their distribution activities, since the costs of operating retail food outlets will depend, in part, upon the efficiency of their suppliers.

In one statistical approach to technological forecasting, the prospective rate of adoption of an innovation is extrapolated from the observed adoption patterns for earlier innovations. In effect, one assumes that the past is prologue, unless there are strong grounds for assuming otherwise. Historically, the adoption paths of many innovations have tended to follow the patterns shown in figure 4.1. The horizontal axis in this figure represents time, and the vertical axis measures the ratio of actual adopters to potential adopters of an innovation. More precisely, A is taken to represent the number of adopters at any point in time, while M represents the number of potential adopters. The adoption process is usually considered to be underway when 10 percent of the population of potential adopters are using the innovation. Clearly, the maximum value the ratio can attain is 1.

It is unnecessary to explain the rationale behind the S-shaped function that is widely employed to forecast the time path for the adoption of a new product or production process. The important point is that the S-shaped path establishes a basis for forecasting the future acceptance of an innovation once the adoption process begins.[11] It also tends to be generally true that the adoption process starts earlier and proceeds more quickly in the U.S. than elsewhere. This is illustrated in figure 4.1 by the $(A/M)^1$ function lying below the (A/M) function. The latter may be taken to be the diffusion path for an innovation introduced in the U.S., while the former represents the diffusion path for the same innovation outside the U.S. The figure shows that at any time, the adoption rate is higher in the U.S. than elsewhere.

---

[10]For some general background on the use of Delphi, see William Wedley, "New Uses of Delphi in Strategy Formulation," *Long Range Planning*, 10 (December 1977), 70-78.

[11]For a discussion of diffusion models in market research and analysis, see H. Jones and B. C. Twiss, *Forecasting Technology for Planning Decisions* (New York: Macmillan Co., 1978).

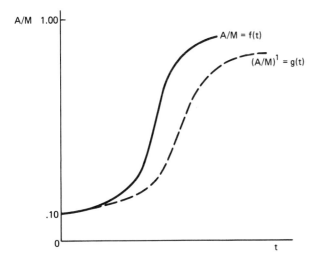

Figure 4.1 The Logistic Model of Technological Change

To put the general relationship between (A/M) and $(A/M)^1$ into some perspective, it has been found that the mean age of technologies transferred to overseas subsidiaries in developed countries by U.S.-based multinational firms was about six years, while the mean age of the technologies transferred to overseas subsidiaries in developing countries was about ten years. However, the average age of technology transferred abroad has declined over the postwar period. For example, the percentage of new products introduced in foreign markets within one year of U.S. introduction rose from 6 percent in 1945–1950 to 39 percent in 1971–1975.[12]

Education and Scale Economies

Another important factor that has been found to influence labor productivity is the educational level of a country's work force. As in the case of other economic characteristics that we have discussed in this chapter, there are considerable differences among countries in this variable as well, as illustrated in table 4.7. The data in table 4.7 report (for a sample of countries) the percentage of the population aged twenty-five years and older with postsecondary education. All other things the same, we would expect countries with more highly educated workers and managers to enjoy productivity advantages over other countries.

Formal education is only one aspect of a worker's overall education. On-the-job training also promotes improved labor productivity, while giving rise to so-called learning economies. Learning economies refer to declining unit costs of

[12]These data are discussed in Edwin Mansfield, "Technological Change: A Survey of Findings," pp. 11–12, University of Pennsylvania, mimeographed, 1984.

TABLE 4.7   **Percentage of Population Aged Twenty-Five Years or Older with Postsecondary Education**

COUNTRY	PERCENTAGE
1. Canada (1972)	17.8
2. United States (1971)	22.3
3. Brazil (1970)	2.0
4. Ecuador (1970)	2.8
5. India (1971)	1.1
6. Japan (1970)	5.5
7. Germany (1970)	4.3
8. Spain (1970)	3.7
9. Sweden (1970)	8.3
10. U.S.S.R. (1970)	4.2
11. Algeria (1971)	0.3

Source: United Nations, *Compendium of Social Statistics*, 1977, table III p. 33.

production and distribution owing to greater familiarity (on the part of both workers and managers) with their firm's production and distribution processes. Management-consulting companies have found that unit costs can decline quite dramatically with accumulated output in specific production activities. This suggests that the productivity of a work force will depend upon its experience as well as its attained education level.

ASSESSING PRODUCTIVITY PROSPECTS

Many of the factors influencing labor productivity change relatively slowly over time. For example, this is true for the education and skill levels of a country's work force, which are strongly influenced by demographic factors such as the age distribution of the population. It would therefore seem that a country's productivity performance should be reasonably stable and predictable over time, at least in comparison to the productivity performances of other countries.

In fact, there are several significant and consistent patterns in the productivity performances of different countries over the postwar period, as indicated by table 4.8. Specifically, the average annual growth in productivity over the postwar period was substantially higher in those economies that had been especially devastated by World War II, that is, Japan, West Germany, Italy, and France. Preliminary data for the early 1980s suggest a continuation of this basic pattern. As a result, absolute levels of labor productivity have converged quite dramatically in the past two decades to the point, for example, where Japanese productivity levels are higher than those in Canada and close to those in the U.S. In some industries, such as automobiles, Japanese productivity levels are substantially above those in North America.

TABLE 4.8 Average Annual Growth In Real Gross Domestic Product per Employed Civilian

COUNTRY	1950-73	1973-77	1973-80	1980-82
U.S.	2.1	0.3	0.6	-0.3
Canada	2.6	0.5	0.2	-1.1
Japan	7.8	2.7	3.4	2.2
France	4.6	2.9	n.a.	1.4
West Germany	5.0	3.3	n.a.	0.6
Italy	5.3	-0.2	2.2	1.2
United Kingdom	2.5	0.4	1.5	2.2

Source: Reprinted from an article appearing in *Cost and Management*, by Steven Globerman and Carolyne Smart, September-October 1983, by permission of the Society of Management Accountants of Canada, table 1, p. 5.

The factors underlying intercountry differences in productivity performance are imperfectly understood; however, the data in table 4.8 go a long way toward explaining why production costs in North America have increased relative to production costs abroad and why German and (especially) Japanese companies have become such formidable competitors in international markets. At the same time, rapid productivity growth in countries such as Japan and West Germany directly contributed to faster rates of growth of real income in those countries compared to North America. Hence, European and Japanese demand for goods and services has also increased at a relatively rapid pace in the postwar period.

To return to the questions we raised at the start of the section dealing with labor productivity, the relevant data suggest that North American producers may, indeed, find themselves under increased competitive pressure, although not so much from British producers as from their Japanese and German rivals. This assertion is further borne out by data presented in table 4.9. The table reports recent estimates of labor costs per unit of manufacturing output, where the U.S. ratio is taken to be the standard of reference. Clearly, Britain is still a high-cost producer relative to U.S. producers. But the other countries that have enjoyed rapid productivity growth over the postwar period, namely, Germany, France, and Japan, are lower-cost manufacturers than the Americans.

At the same time, a number of other Pacific-rim countries, such as South Korea, Singapore, and Taiwan, are experiencing rapid productivity growth rates while still maintaining relatively low wage rates. As a consequence, international production activity is beginning to move toward these newly industrialized countries (NICs), and salespeople from all over the world are becoming increasingly familiar with airline routes into Seoul, Singapore, and Taipei. The emergence of the Southeast Asian NICs as centers of economic growth reinforces the important point that early identification of rapidly growing, low-cost markets is a major goal of economic-scanning activities.

TABLE 4.9 Labor Costs per Unit, Manufacturing, 1983 (United States = 100)

Britain	136.0
Canada	129.3
Italy	107.2
Belgium	106.3
U.S.	100.0
W. Germany	92.3
France	86.5
Sweden	73.3
Japan	61.2

Source: Ronald Anderson, "Increasing Competitiveness Key to Lower Unemployment," *Toronto Globe and Mail*, August 16, 1984, p. B2.

OTHER FACTORS

To this point in the chapter we have discussed a variety of economic attributes influencing the potential international demand for a firm's products, as well as a number of variables affecting costs of production in different markets. The number and variety of factors discussed to this point suggest that the economic-scanning exercise is often a wide-ranging activity that imposes onerous information demands on management. While this can be true, it is sometimes the case that one specific economic attribute is especially important to management. For example, an international shipping company will be primarily interested in access to deep-water ports, while relative wage rates and productivity levels may be distinctly of secondary importance. As another example, service-oriented companies that rely heavily upon communications facilities to carry out their activities may be extremely mobile geographically. As a result, their primary motive may be to establish facilities in low-tax jurisdictions that possess up-to-date communications facilities. Hence the proliferation of banks and other financial-services companies in the Bahamas and other Caribbean countries.

The nature and extent of government regulation, along with taxation levels, often constitute the main concern of international managers considering the relocation of production facilities abroad. In identifying and evaluating differences in these economic attributes across countries, consulting companies and international accounting firms can be of assistance to management. But as with other dimensions of the economic environment, it is important for management to be forward looking, since the regulatory and tax environments of a country can change, in some cases quite rapidly. Indeed, the potential for sudden and unfavorable changes in a country's fiscal and regulatory environments contributes to more sleepless nights for international managers than perhaps any other feature of the international business landscape. It is therefore unsurprising that international companies often spend a good deal of time and money assessing the outlook for government actions in these two areas of the international economy. In many cases the outlook for discrete changes in government policy is addressed as part of the firm's analysis of political risk, a topic discussed extensively in the following chapter.

SOURCES OF INFORMATION

Obviously, even a fairly superficial screening of a region's economic environment imposes substantial information burdens on a firm's research function. Fortunately for many regions of the world, and especially for the developed countries, basic economic and demographic data are fairly readily available. International agencies, national governments, and private organizations are all reasonably good sources of background data and information.

The U.S. Government's Department of Commerce prepares a number of especially good statistical publications, including *Foreign Economic Trends and Their Implications for the U.S.* This publication consists of a series of brief reports on more than one hundred countries that are prepared by U.S. embassies and consulates. These reports provide current data on GNP, foreign trade, unemployment, wages and prices, and so forth, for the countries surveyed. Another publication, *International Economic Indicators and Competitive Trends*, contains economic data on the U.S. and seven principal industrial countries. Included are statistics on GNP, industrial production, trade, prices, finance, and labor. The International Trade Administration of the Department of Commerce also publishes updated business guides for different geographical regions, including government regulations and other relevant features of the commercial environment.[13]

Economic data for the European economies are especially good owing to the publications of the Organization for Economic Cooperation and Development (OECD) and the European Community Information Service. In particular, the former publishes annual surveys that offer discussions of current economic trends and statistics for each member country. A private organization, the Economic Intelligence Unit, also provides detailed studies of consumer markets in major European countries.

Basic economic data for both developed and developing countries can be found in the United Nations' *World Statistics in Brief*. This publication contains basic statistics on demographic, economic, agricultural, and educational characteristics of over 150 countries. A number of privately owned organizations, such as Gale Research Company, also publish detailed information on

---

[13]A comprehensive description of these and other data sources discussed in this section can be found in Cynthia C. Ryans, *International Business Reference Sources* (Lexington, Mass.: Lexington Books, 1983).

demographic, economic, and technological characteristics of countries located in Asia, Africa, and South America.

While this foregoing overview of information sources is far from comprehensive, it should suggest to the reader that the real issue facing international managers is typically not a lack of basic economic information but the need to be selective in acquiring and evaluating information.

SUMMARY AND CONCLUSIONS

Management's primary concern in scanning the economic environment is to assess opportunities to market its products in overseas areas and (or) to locate some or all of its production and distribution activities outside of the firm's domestic economy.

The two main components of the economic environment are demand and cost conditions in foreign markets. The key factors influencing current demand and future demand growth are captured in the demand function. The demand function expresses the statistical relationship between quantity demanded and the major variables that influence quantity demanded. The task for management is to identify the impact of these variables on demand in different geographic regions and to forecast future values of these variables.

In carrying out the environmental-scanning exercise, management should also be concerned with keeping both time and money costs under control. One way to do so is to segment potential markets by a small number of especially critical variables. For example, the demand for expensive household appliances, such as washing machines, is likely to be quite limited in countries with relatively low wage rates, since maids and other servants will be relatively cheap in those countries. Thus, one can eliminate low-wage countries from the screening exercise and focus strictly on high-wage areas.

The cost function identifies the statistical relationship between total cost and the quantity of output produced. Since the bulk of costs in most industries consists of labor costs, a focus on average wage rates and the productivity of labor is an appropriate aspect of the environmental-scanning exercise. Labor productivity is determined by a number of factors. Perhaps the most important are the rate of technological change and the education and skill levels of the work force. Whereas the latter are relatively easy to identify and change fairly slowly, the former is more elusive and is difficult to predict with precision, especially when the focus in on a specific new product or new production process. Nevertheless, historical evidence on adoption patterns for new technology combined with past productivity growth patterns can provide management with insights into future unit labor costs in different countries.

It should be emphasized that the economic-scanning exercise is not intended to quantify the profitability of specific overseas investment projects with any precision. Rather, individual project profitability must be estimated by more detailed cash-flow analyses undertaken as part of a firm's capital-budgeting activities. Environmental scanning is intended to separate more promising georgraphical regions from less promising regions for purposes of more detailed analysis at the stage when specific production and marketing strategies must be chosen.

DISCUSSION QUESTIONS

1. Are productivity trends in foreign countries relevant to managers of firms that produce and sell their output entirely in a single domestic market? What other aspects of the foreign economic environment might be relevant to the firm that has determined to specialize entirely within the domestic market?

2. Assume that you are responsible for marketing a new computerized telephone set for a major North American manufacturer of telecommunications equipment. What specific variables do you think would be important in the demand function for the telephone set?

3. How can the economic-scanning exercise be adapted so that it sheds some light on the potential risk-diversification benefits of international business expansion?

4. What relationship (if any) would you suggest exists between a country's productivity performance and the behavior of the country's exchange rate? What would be the relevance of the relationship identified above for managers of firms contemplating international expansion into that country?

5. In scanning global markets for economic trends, what procedures might you employ to reduce the amount of information and data analysis required? Is there some way that occurs to you to group countries for purposes of environmental scanning and assessment?

6. Develop a list of macroeconomic variables that you consider potentially relevant for use in scanning the international economic environment. For each variable, elaborate on the information it conveys about the economic outlook for a region or country.

REFERENCES

CLELAND, DAVID, AND WILLIAM KING, "Competitive Business Intelligence Systems," *Business Horizons*, 18 (December 1975), 19–28.

CRAVENS, D. W., G. E. HILLS, AND R. B. WOODRUFF, *Marketing Decision Making: Concepts and Strategy.* Homewood, Ill.: Richard D. Irwin, 1980.

GLUECK, WILLIAM F., *Strategic Management and Business Policy*, chap. 3. New York: McGraw-Hill, 1980.

O'CONNELL, J. J., AND J. W. ZIMMERMAN, "Scanning the International Environment." *California Management Review*, 22 (Winter 1979), 15–23.

RODRIGUEZ, JAMIE, AND WILLIAM KING, Competitive Information Systems," *Long Range Planning*, 10 (December 1977), 45–50.

THOMAS, PHILIP S., "Environmental Scanning—The State of the Art," *Long Range Planning*, 13 (February 1980), 20–28.

CHAPTER FIVE

Scanning
the Political
Environment

INTRODUCTION

In the preceding chapter we identified and discussed some important economic attributes that management should evaluate when scanning geographic regions for their international business prospects. But no matter how attractive the economic prospects of a given region or country, doing business in that area might prove to be financially disastrous for the international firm if host governments inflict onerous financial penalties upon it or if imperfectly anticipated events lead to the loss of income-producing assets. Perhaps the supreme contemporary illustration of the potential hazards associated with doing business internationally is provided by the 1979 revolution in Iran, which led to the overthrow of the Shah's government and the exposure of U.S. companies to potential losses totaling $1 billion.

Certainly, the management at General Telephone and Electric (GT&E), a large U.S. telecommunications company, became acutely aware of the importance of political events to international business activities through its experience in Iran. In December 1977 GT&E signed a contract for more than $500 million with the Iranian government, the largest communications-equipment deal at that time. As part of the agreement, the company had to advance Iran $94 million in open lines of credit. But GT&E's contract did not spell out the grounds on which the Iranian government could call the letter of credit, and the company did not have insurance to cover such risk. Negotiations between GT&E and the regime of

Ayatollah Khomeini came to an end on the day that the U.S. embassy was seized, leaving GT&E facing a $50 million loss in unpaid expenses and the liability posed by the letters of credit.[1] To be sure, GT&E was not alone in its experience. Starrett Housing Corporation left Iran leaving behind a group of uncompleted luxury condominiums and a sunken investment in the project ($38 million) greater than the company's net worth.

Political-risk assessment has become a glamorous and expanding business since the Iranian revolution. The large monetary losses resulting from the widespread and, ultimately, mistaken belief that the Shah's regime was secure have encouraged a wide variety of companies to incorporate political-risk analysis into their overseas investment and operating plans. By political-risk analysis (or assessment), we have in mind a set of integrated activities that include scanning political environments abroad and incorporating the information and perceptions gathered into the formulation of managerial strategies.

The purpose of this chapter is to describe and discuss fundamental issues related to scanning the political environment and utilizing the information collected to formulate and/or modify international business plans. We start by defining the underlying concept of political risk.

DEFINITION OF POLITICAL RISK

While there is no consensus on the precise meaning of the term *political risk*, one popular view considers political risk to exist when unanticipated discontinuities affecting corporate profitability and resulting from political changes can occur in the business environment.[2] The important dimensions of this definition of political risk are captured in the terms *unanticipated, discontinuities,* and *political.* Clearly, if changes in the environment could be fully anticipated, they would not represent a source of risk to management, since they would always be fully incorporated into the firm's business plans and profit expectations. In a related fashion, if changes were smooth and continuous over time, they would (seemingly) become easily predictable and therefore cease to be a significant source of risk; however, a number of observers have stressed that while environmental discontinuity significantly increases the difficulty of political assessment, discontinuous change is not necessary to create political risk.[3] That is, risk will exist as long as the actions of governments are incapable of being forecasted with certainty.

The qualification that changes in the environment must be politically ini-

---

[1] See Louis Kraar, "The Multinationals Get Smarter about Political Risks," *Fortune,* March 24, 1980, pp. 86–100, for a discussion of GT&E's experience in Iran.

[2] This view of political risk is proposed, for example, in Lars Thunell, *Political Risks in International Business* (New York: Praeger Publishers, 1977), and Stefan Robock and Kenneth Simmonds, *International Business and Multinational Enterprises* (Homewood, Ill.: Richard D. Irwin, 1983).

[3] See, for example, Stephen J. Kobrin, *Managing Political Risk Assessment* (Berkeley: University of California Press, 1982), p. 42.

tiated is anything but straightforward since virtually all environmental changes affecting corporate profits will ultimately take the form of changes in one or more economic variables, such as tax rates and output prices. While some macroeconomic and microeconomic variables will be under the direct and primary influence of government, others will be only indirectly affected by political actions. Yet the latter variables may in some cases have a more profound influence on overall corporate profitability than the former.

For example, the election of a government that is philosophically inclined toward the free-enterprise system might encourage optimism among investors leading to higher savings and investment rates, lower interest rates, and faster growth in real income. Conversely, the election of a Socialist regime might lead to sharp escalations in inflationary expectations and a deterioration in the value of the country's currency. This was apparently true, for example, in the case of France following the election of François Mitterand's Socialist government. The point we are making is that the boundary between risks created by political factors and those created by economic forces is often quite vague.

In finance theory, political risk is often equated with forces that are not systematically related to the business cycle, while economic (or business) risk is related to cycles of expansion and contraction in the economy.[4] In practice, this distinction is also difficult to make since both sources of risk may at times be interrelated. For example, adverse economic conditions may encourage host governments to adopt a more conciliatory attitude toward foreign businesses operating in the host economy, as the author has found to be true in the case of Canada's Foreign Investment Review Agency (now Investment Canada).[5] Conversely, severe economic hardship has periodically contributed to political upheaval and the suspension of the property rights of foreign investors.

In summary, there is no completely satisfactory way to isolate political risk for purposes of environmental scanning and assessment. Nevertheless, even when the primary potential cause of a change in the profitability of an international business venture or activity is economic in nature, political risks (or contingencies) may be said to exist whenever identifiable political events can significantly alter the economic environment.

IDENTIFYING POLITICAL RISK

The assessment of political risk involves identifying the nature as well as the potential effects of different political contingencies that might arise in the future. With regard to the nature of political risk, students of international business speak of two broad categories: macrorisk and microrisk. Political risk is of a macro nature

---

[4]This distinction is suggested in Joseph Micallef, "Political Risk Assessment," *Columbia Journal of World Business*, 16 (Summer 1981), 47.

[5]See Steven Globerman, "The Consistency of Canada's Foreign Investment Review Process—A Temporal Analysis," *Journal of International Business Studies*, 18 (Spring/Summer 1984), 119–29.

when politically inspired environmental changes affect all foreign enterprises. It is of a micro nature when the environmental changes are intended to affect only selected fields of business activity or foreign enterprises with specific characteristics.

To date, macrorisk has been the focus for almost all political-risk evaluations undertaken by corporations. This macro-orientation implicitly assumes that there is a direct correlation between the destiny of the host country's political environment and the destiny of all foreign-owned firms doing business in that country. However, recent research suggests that this assumption may be inappropriate given a shift by host governments from confiscation of assets to constraints and controls, accompanied by increasing corporate-specific discrimination.[6] Researchers and practitioners in the political-risk area are therefore recommending that international managers view political risk as being primarily micro in nature. This effectively means that the relevant variables to use as criteria for evaluating a new investment proposal or for reevaluating existing business activities should be industry and corporate specific rather than simply country specific.

Macrorisk and Microrisk

We can elaborate on the distinction between macro- and micro-based political risk by listing the sorts of considerations that appear in assessments of political risk. Table 5.1 reports the percentage of respondents to one study who indicated that the consideration identified was an important aspect of the overseas

TABLE 5.1   Most Important Aspects of Overseas Environment

CONSIDERATION	PERCENTAGE OF RESPONDENTS
1. Political stability	79.5
2. Foreign investment climate	79.5
3. Profit remittances/ exchange controls	69.4
4. Taxation	51.4
5. Expropriation	28.4
6. Political-party attitudes toward foreign investors	24.2
7. Labor strikes and unrest	21.1

Source: Stephen J. Kobrin, "The Assessment and Evaluation of Noneconomic Environments by American Firms: A Preliminary Report," *Journal of International Business Studies*, 11 (Spring/Sum-

---

[6]Among other contributions, see Warnock Davies, "Unsticking the State of the Art of Political Risk Management," *Sloan Management Review*, 16 (Summer 1981), 59–63.

environment. At the top of the list are political stability and the foreign investment climate. Third in importance is the imposition of controls on the remittance of profits and on the conversion of foreign exchange followed by taxation. While it may be somewhat surprising that expropriation is as far down the list as it is, given the severity of the action, its placement in the hierarchy of managerial concerns reflects the fact that expropriation is a relatively rare event.

In reviewing table 5.1, it is obvious that several of the environmental concerns are macro in nature, including political stability and political-party attitudes toward foreign investors. Others such as taxation and expropriation are more evidently "micro" in nature; however, the classification of a number of the concerns listed is not at all obvious. For example, labor strikes and unrest can be widespread, thereby affecting a wide range of firms and industries. As an illustration, there was a surge in strike activity in the Philippines in 1984, with many of the strikes being illegal. In many cases, a few workers forced factories to shut down. Some observers interpreted the strike activity as a concerted effort by left-wing groups to disrupt the economy in order to topple the country's government. On the other hand, labor relations problems may be specific to certain plants or industries. For example, two years after Aris Gloves established a plant in El Salvador, the facility was hit by political turmoil. Specifically, leftist dissidents held the subsidiary's president and about 120 local employees as hostages for nine days—until the company agreed to wage increases that it claimed it could not afford.[7] At the same time, production went on fairly smoothly elsewhere in the economy.

If political-risk assessment is to be useful to management, concerns about changes in the political environment will need to be translated into specific potential impacts on the firm. In this regard, concepts such as political stability and the foreign investment climate are vague and not readily linked to the outcome of specific international business ventures. Hence, the value to management of focusing on these dimensions of political risk is questionable.

A somewhat more specific set of environmental concerns is provided by the list of political-environmental events reported in table 5.2. In the survey underlying these data, corporate respondents were asked to select from a list of thirteen political-environmental events, the nine most important and to rank them according to their potential impact on overseas operations. Thus, all of the contingencies listed in table 5.2 are defined in terms of specific impacts on operations.

For business activities in less developed countries, the contingencies of greatest concern are civil disorder, war, and expropriation. For activities in industrialized countries, labor disruptions and price controls pose the greatest threats to profitability in the view of international managers. Evidently international managers are more concerned with conflict-related contingencies in less developed countries. The somewhat more macro-oriented concerns of managers in less developed countries in part reflect the fact that international businesses in

[7]Ibid., p. 87.

TABLE 5.2 Relative Importance of Specific Risks to Overseas Operations (median rankings by country groups)

RISK	LESS DEVELOPED COUNTRIES	INDUSTRIALIZED COUNTRIES
1. Civil disorder	1.8	5.5
2. War	3.6	8.4
3. Labor disruptions	5.5	3.7
4. Price controls	6.0	3.2
5. Expropriation	2.4	6.0
6. Contract cancellation	7.6	7.2
7. Fiscal changes	7.3	5.5
8. Remittance restrictions	5.3	4.4
9. Partial expropriation	5.7	6.9

Source: Stephen J. Kobrin, *Managing Political Risk Assessment* (Berkeley: University of California Press, 1982), p. 118.

these countries are often involved in natural-resource-extraction activities. Natural resource assets have been especially prone to broad expropriation.[8]

Since discrete political events such as the overthrow of a government or the suspension of the convertibility of a nation's currency can have serious impacts upon an international company's long-run profitability, management has a clear vested interest in identifying the relevant risks and taking steps to deal with those risks. However, future political events may represent opportunities and not just threats to the international firm, as when the procapitalist government of Edward Seaga was installed in Jamaica displacing the socialist, antiforeign-investment government of Michael Manley. Where management can identify potentially favorable future political events, it might want to factor those events into its assessment of the overall attractiveness of specific regions.

As a matter of policy, international firms tend to concentrate on identifying the "undesirable" consequences of political actions rather than evaluating the full range of potential political actions, including those that might improve business prospects in a region. While this asymmetric approach has been criticized by some experts, it represents a conservative approach toward environmental scanning that is quite appropriate for management concerned with minimizing the risks associated with international expansion. Specifically, once management has identified the "downside" risks associated with an international investment, it can proceed with confidence if the expected rate of return on that investment exceeds management's required rate of return after factoring the relevant downside risks into the analysis. On the other hand, conservative managers may choose to ignore potential, but uncertain, favorable political actions, especially when international

---

[8]The survey on which table 5.2 is based is discussed in Kobrin, *Political Risk Assessment*, along with a more detailed interpretation of the results.

expansion would not be warranted in the absence of such actions. In short, an asymmetric focus on political risk may be quite appropriate for many companies.

IDENTIFYING RISK-RELATED VARIABLES

Obviously, the goal of management is to anticipate the contingencies listed in table 5.2 and take appropriate action before the fact. This in turn implies a need to identify factors in the environment that reliably signal the risk of any specific contingency materializing. As an illustration, managers doing business in industrialized countries abroad will be interested in identifying a set of (quantifiable) variables that reliably foreshadow the imposition of price controls. Managers of international business activities centered in less developed countries would presumably be especially interested in identifying variables that signal an increasing risk of violence and/or expropriation of corporate assets.

In various approaches to quantifying political risk, both macro- and micro-oriented variables are linked to potential changes in the political environment. Macrovariables are related to broad socioeconomic conditions in a country, whereas microvariables are related to conditions specific to the sector in which the firm operates or to the firm itself. The relative importance of macrovariables versus microvariables will depend upon the nature of a firm's international business activities. For example, oil companies doing business in a narrow (albeit important) area of an overseas economy will presumably focus on microvariables, since they will be primarily affected by localized and specific political actions. On the other hand, international banks concerned about the risk of default on loans to foreign governments will be more concerned with monitoring the overall economic health of foreign countries, especially those variables related to the debt-servicing capacity of borrowing governments, such as foreign public debt as a ratio of gross domestic product or debt-service requirements as a ratio of export income.[9]

Macroeconomic indicators concerned with the financial integrity of a country should also be relevant in assessing the likelihood of foreign governments imposing various forms of trade restrictions and currency controls. Since the latter are frequently introduced to conserve foreign exchange, it is often the limited availability of foreign exchange relative to its demand that triggers political events curtailing the freedom of international businesses to buy and (especially) to sell local currencies. Foreign governments in both developed and less developed countries have occasionally imposed exchange controls on international corporations restricting the amount of host-country currency the latter can sell or otherwise take out of the country. Such exchange controls can impede the ability of sub-

[9]A variety of macrovariables used by banks in statistical models of loan-related risk analysis are discussed in Robert R. Davies, ''Alternative Techniques for Country Risk Analyses,'' *Business Economics*, 22 (May 1981), 34–41.

sidiaries to purchase goods and services from—and pay dividends to—their parent affiliates.

Most country-risk analysis studies contain extensive descriptions of the nation's financial health and stability. Relevant indicators typically included for study are the behavior of the domestic money supply, domestic credit expansion, and foreign borrowing. The presumption is that local financial conditions will be related to inflation and exchange-rate performance as well as to the rate of real economic growth in the country. These dimensions of overall economic performance are thought to be linked to the political stability of a country. Implicit in this view is the premise that real economic growth combined with stable prices enhances both the actual and perceived welfare of domestic residents, thereby encouraging them to support the status quo or (at a minimum) to forego efforts at making radical changes to existing legal and political institutions.

Macroeconomic variables are often used as proxies for political variables, since political characteristics of a market are sometimes extremely difficult to quantify. Conceptual examples of variables related to a country's political structure include the power base of the existing government, mechanisms for the orderly succession of leadership, consensus regarding priorities, and relationship to the United States. While some of these variables are susceptible to relatively objective quantification, others can be established only in a subjective way.

In contrast to the broad nature of the macroeconomic variables listed above, microvariables include such considerations as the economic sector in which a company operates, the age of the company, the extent to which domestic residents hold key managerial positions in the firm, and the degree to which ownership in the firm's underlying assets is shared with local residents.

The premise supporting a focus on these and other microvariables is that the way in which an international business is structured and the way it operates are of greater importance to how it is treated by overseas authorities than are the general socioeconomic conditions of host countries. For example, if a company brings skills and resources to a country that are perceived by the host government to be "irreplaceable," that company's presence might be encouraged, notwithstanding a hostile attitude toward foreign investment generally. Along the same lines, relinquishing some degree of ownership to foreign nationals might lead to a foreign subsidiary's enjoying a more favorable status than would be the case if the parent company insisted on 100 percent ownership of the subsidiary.

QUANTITATIVE MODELS OF POLITICAL RISK

Given one or more potential political contingencies or events that might significantly influence the outcome of an international business venture, a goal of management should be to assess the probability that such events will occur. Perhaps the most sophisticated, if not necessarily the most insightful or accurate, approach to estimating the probabilities of political contingencies involves the use of multivariate statistical models.

A common feature of these models is the use of a set of independent variables (of both a socioeconomic and a political nature) that are somehow combined to yield a numerical estimate of the likelihood of one or more political contingencies. In models of international lending risk, for example, the contingency of primary concern (default) is ordinarily quantified as a function of a number of macrovariables cited above, including the ratio of a country's external debt-service requirements to its export income and the national inflation rate.

The general structure of quantitative risk-assessment models found in the literature takes the general form shown in equation 5.1:

$$(5.1) \quad E_i = b_1 Z_{1i} + b_2 Z_{2i} + \ldots + b_n Z_{ni}$$

where E_i is the likelihood of a particular contingency or event, and the Zs are macro- and microvariables that the analyst believes influence E_i. Each b coefficient therefore represents an estimate of the impact that a change in some Z will have on E_i. For example, if E_i is the likelihood that Latin American countries will form a "debtors' cartel" and repudiate all foreign debt, while Z_{1i} is the average rate of unemployment in Latin American countries, b_1 shows how much the risk of repudiation goes up for each unit increase in the unemployment rate. By multiplying each Z variable by its corresponding b coefficient and then adding all the product terms, the analyst can (conceptually at least) obtain a numerical estimate for E_i.

Equation 5.1 illustrates the critical requirements of quantitative political-risk-assessment models. One is the need to specify the Z variables. That is, the analyst must have some idea of the variables that influence the contingency of interest. Second is the requirement to attach numerical values to the b coefficients. This latter requirement is often the undoing of quantitative risk-assessment models. In particular, historical data required to perform the statistical analyses that yield estimates of the b coefficients are often unavailable. In addition, there is often no firm basis for believing that the b coefficients will remain constant over time or from region to region. Indeed, there are often good reasons for believing that the converse is true. As an example, in Venezuela, models of expropriation are irrelevant to the oil industry because nationalization of the industry has already occurred. As a general caution, quantitative models are usually based upon the "average" experience of numerous foreign investors; however, the average experience may be a very unreliable guide to the likely experience of any individual international business.

OTHER APPROACHES TO POLITICAL-RISK ASSESSMENT

Given the complexities associated with using quantitative models to assess the political environment, it is not surprising that less than 20 percent of large international firms use quantitative-assessment methodologies on a regular basis.[10] The majority of firms use one or more of the other techniques listed in table 5.3.

Delphi Techniques

Delphi techniques are methods to solicit, collect, evaluate, and tabulate the opinions of experts. A typical Delphi application is initiated by a questionnaire, which requests participants to evaluate the importance of selective elements influencing a country's political destiny, such as the size of its armed forces or political-party attitudes toward foreign investors. The questionnaire might also require the experts to estimate the probabilities of occurrence of specific events, such as the imposition of price controls, given the selective elements evaluated in previous stages. The results of this initial round of questioning are summarized, and statistics summarizing the distribution of the responses are fed back to the respondents with a request that they revise their first estimates where appropriate. After the initial response, individuals are asked to request any information they need or to specify what information they have that can aid others in the decision process.

On succeeding rounds those individuals whose opinions deviate greatly from the majority are requested to give the reasons for their extreme opinions. A collection of these reasons is presented to each participant along with new distribution statistics, and participants are given another opportunity to reconsider and revise earlier opinions or estimates. The process is continued through an iterative number of rounds until there seems to be sufficient convergence of opinion on the evaluations or estimates. The last step is to aggregate the responses into an overall measure or index of political risk.

An interesting and sophisticated application of the Delphi approach was initially developed by Shell Oil in the U.S. and modified by Chase World Information Corporation, a subsidiary of Chase Manhattan Bank. The first step in this approach is to construct a series of political, social, and economic issues that would threaten the continued viability of a particular subsidiary in a specific country. Such issues might include the implementation of price controls or profit-remittance restrictions. Factors are listed that might cause each issue to come up, and arguments for and against the possibility of their developing are provided to define further both the factors and their causal link to the issue or issues of concern.

Next, a group of experts from various fields are given the list of issues and causal factors and asked to analyze the likelihood of each issue's developing as a result of each factor, in the short run and the long run, under both an optimistic and a pessimistic scenario. Each expert writes a paragraph for each scenario on the likelihood that each causal factor will arise and three paragraphs on the possibility

---

[10]See Stephen Kobrin, "The Assessment and Evaluation of Noneconomic Environments by American Firms: A Preliminary Report," *Journal of International Business Studies*, 11 (Spring/Summer 1980), 32–47.

TABLE 5.3   Techniques of Political-
Risk Assessment

1. Quantitative models
2. Delphi techniques
3. Qualitative approaches
   (a) "Old-hands"
   (b) Grand tours
   (c) Contextual analysis
4. Consultants' evaluations

that that factor will precipitate the issue. Then each expert quantifies this assessment by rating both the probability that each issue will develop from each factor for the various scenarios and the confidence the expert feels in these individual assessments. Mathematical techniques are used to aggregate the expert's factor probabilities. Next a composite of all the assessments is prepared with majority and minority opinions broken out. Finally, looking at the number and kinds of issues likely to develop, countries are ranged on a matrix showing relative risks versus rates of return on investment (separately derived).[11]

It might be noted explicitly that the Delphi approach described above is effectively an attempt to have experts identify the important Zs and assign values to the bs in equation 5.1. As such, Delphi techniques may circumvent some of the data availability and statistical problems that plague quantitative modeling techniques. However, Delphi approaches are likely to produce a "conventional" estimate of political risk, even if experts of different backgrounds are assembled and the identities of the experts are hidden from each other. Furthermore, lack of expertise about the company's activities may lead to mistaken Delphi estimates of political risk.

Qualitative Approaches

Difficulties associated with obtaining and interpreting quantitative estimates of political risk have encouraged international managers to rely heavily on interpersonal contact for their background information about the political environment. In what is probably the most commonly employed technique for assessing political risk, the so-called Old-Hands approach, management canvasses the opinions of individuals possessing area or country expertise, including individuals both inside and outside the corporation. However, as shown in table 5.4, corporate managers overwhelmingly turn to colleagues and associates inside affiliated companies for information about the political and administrative aspects of specific foreign environments.

[11]This description of Shell Oil's Delphi approach is taken from Robert D. Kramer, "Political Risk Assessment: A Brief Review of the State of the Art," *New International Realities*, 6 (August 1981), 21.

TABLE 5.4   Relative Importance of Information Sources (percentage of respondents rating source as relatively important)

INFORMATION SOURCE	PERCENTAGE
1. Subsidiary managers	74.6
2. Regional managers	68.9
3. Corporate headquarters personnel	64.8
4. Banking community	44.6
5. External consultants	28.0
6. Business periodicals	24.9
7. Other firms	22.8
8. Agents and outside counsel	22.3
9. U.S. embassies	17.6
10. U.S. government domestic agencies	16.6
11. Professional journals	14.5
12. Trade associations	13.0
13. International organizations	10.9
14. Newspapers, radio, television	10.4
15. Academics	9.3
16. American Chamber of Commerce	8.3
17. Journalists	8.3

Source: Stephen J. Kobrin, *Managing Political Risk Assessment* (Berkeley: University of California Press, 1982), p. 118.

While the use of line managers in foreign affiliates is a convenient source of information about political conditions in foreign countries, it is not necessarily an unbiased one. Subsidiary managers quite naturally have a desire to expand the amount of corporate resources under their direction. Therefore, they have a strong incentive to present headquarters management with an optimistic assessment of political and economic conditions in the region where the subsidiary is located. One way for headquarters management to combat this bias is to use outside experts as an additional source of information. The outside sources listed in table 5.4, including educators, diplomats, and journalists, can be given some of the responsibility for identifying political issues likely to affect the corporation's economic welfare and for grouping the issues by priority.

Gulf Oil's use of ''outside'' analysts has become somewhat legendary in the field. In the late 1960s the company hired a former foreign-service officer to recruit other analysts from government and universities to tap sources that few managers had the time or knowledge to pursue, such as specialized publications. The analysts were completely removed from Gulf's operations, to ensure their objectivity. Gulf's team of analysts encouraged headquarters management to make deals in nations that looked quite forbidding at first glance. Perhaps the most daring recommendation was for the company to work with the Marxist regime in Angola following that country's civil war in 1975. Gulf's African analyst correctly foresaw the emergence of a well-organized Marxist group as both the dominant force and a potentially stable business partner. As things turned out, Angola became one of Gulf's largest and most successful overseas production sources.[12]

Another approach toward obtaining subjective assessments of political risk involves the "grand tour." Just as the name implies, this technique involves dispatching an executive or a team of people on an inspection tour of the relevant market area, usually after some preliminary market research has been done. Conferences are held with government officials and business leaders "on the spot." The insight gathered from these conferences, along with the impressionistic evidence gained from the site-inspection exercise, is then integrated into headquarter's political-risk analysis.

As in the case of the Old-Hands approach, there is a great danger that information gathered on tours will be biased in a selective fashion. For example, government officials concerned about the employment impacts of foreign investment may paint a more favorable picture of the future political environment for foreign investors than is likely to materialize. Other local representatives of the particular region may also be motivated by pecuniary self-interest to encourage additional foreign investment in the area, and their self-interest can be expected to promote bias in their stated perceptions.

As long as headquarters management is aware of the bias inherent in the grand-tour approach, the technique can provide very useful insights into the political risk attached to new and ongoing overseas activities. For example, face-to-face encounters can inform management about the personalities of the political leaders they will be dealing with and tell them whether those leaders literally and figuratively speak the same language they do. Also, serendipitous (or unscheduled) events observed on the tour can be very informative to management.

An excellent (albeit fictional) example of serendipity is provided in the film *The Godfather II*. The protagonist, Michael Corleone, takes a grand tour of Havana during the Batista regime to examine the attractiveness of investing in the gambling-casino business in that city. He is wined and dined by Batista officials and by other American underworld figures with interests in that region. In all his conferences, he is strongly advised that the rebel forces led by Fidel Castro are a rabble that pose no serious threat to the existing government. However, Michael acquires a strong sense of the risk associated with investing in the area when he witnesses a rebel with explosives strapped to his body blow himself up along with a number of government soldiers. The dedication of the rebel persuades Michael that the political risks attached to casino investments in Havana are substantially higher than he has been led to believe.

A more broad-based (contextual) approach toward subjective political-risk assessment involves synthesizing diverse and extensive secondary research material with the first-hand impressions of old-hands and other experts. Secondary research inputs include historical and cultural analyses of a region as well as

[12]See Kraar, "Multinationals Get Smarter," pp. 87–88.

current information on external and internal sources of political pressure. Some order is brought to this potpourri of information by developing and evaluating patterns of causal and correlative relationships between historical socio/political conditions and political events in a region. That is, how have background conditions in a country influenced political events in the past? Then an effort is made to evaluate whether contemporary and prospective conditions are similar in important ways to conditions in some previous period.[13]

Consulting Evaluations

Some firms prefer to turn the political-risk-assessment exercise over to consultants, rather than conduct the analysis in-house. In part, this preference reflects a commitment on the part of management to keep overhead expenditures down by holding down the number of staff employees. But it also reflects a belief on the part of some managers that the specialization practiced by political-risk consulting companies gives the latter a cost and quality advantage over in-house analysts.

A number of well-known consulting companies offer regularly updated political-risk assessments in the form of indices. For example, Business International (BI), an advisory service for multinationals, calculates an index similar to that published by another consultant, Business Environment Risk Information (BERI). Both rank countries on a scale from 1 to 100, where higher numbers indicate a higher degree of political risk. The World Political Risk Forecasts (WPRF) service of Frost and Sullivan, a business research organization, estimates the probability of a major business loss in the future owing to political developments. For example, in January 1980 it saw a 31 percent chance that a company doing business in Indonesia would suffer a major business loss owing to political developments and a 45 percent chance of loss within five years. By contrast, the WPRF loss probability for Singapore was only 19 percent over the next five years.[14]

These rating services are attractive to many multinational companies since they are relatively cheap, and they boil down complex forecasts to simple numbers. However, the rankings are based on macroenvironmental variables and may, therefore, be misleading evaluations of the political risk facing any individual company involved in one or more specific international business ventures.

Other consulting firms undertake focused political-risk-assessment assignments for individual companies. A number of these firms draw upon the services of ex-CIA personnel. For example, William Colby, director of the Central Intelligence Agency from 1973 to 1976, is currently a senior adviser for International Business-Government Counsellors, Inc., a company whose clients include

---

[13]See Kramer, ''Political Risk Assessment,'' p. 23, for a description of an approach similar to the one described here.

[14]Grant Winthrop, ''Can a Computer Tell the Ratio of Risk?'' *Fortune*, March 24, 1980, p. 95.

Bank of America, General Motors, Nestlé, IBM, ITT, Ciba-Geigy, Unilever, and Xerox. Richard Helms, another former CIA director, now runs a company called Safeer that specializes in offering high-priced opinions to the major oil companies on issues such as the impact of the Iran-Iraq war on Middle East alliances and the potential for the OPEC cartel to fall apart. Henry Kissinger has also announced his entry into the private global intelligence business with the formation of his own new consulting company, Kissinger Associates.[15]

While offering a more micro-oriented focus to the risk-evaluation exercise, the services of the latter companies are substantially more expensive than those of the rating services. Moreover, it is still up to management to translate the consultant's appraisal of the environment into the implications for the company.

THE CONTEXT OF POLITICAL-RISK ASSESSMENT

One can quite rightly argue that purely domestic firms also face political risk. For example, many privately owned public utilities at the turn of the century were ultimately brought under government regulation or, in some cases, nationalized. The giant telephone company, AT&T, ran afoul of the U.S. Justice Department continuously during the 1960s and 1970s and ultimately agreed to divest its ownership of the local Bell Telephone Companies rather than face the prospect of even more severe penalties. What is unique about the political risk that confronts the international firm?

Part of the answer to this question is the recurrent one: A broader scope and greater variety of political environments complicate the international manager's scanning activities. Moreover, management's basic level of familiarity with political processes and individual personalities is bound to be higher as it pertains to domestic business activities. But perhaps of greater importance is the fact that a rising spirit of economic nationalism has promoted, if not outright hostility toward international businesses, at least distrust of them among many sovereign governments. A growing concern with threats to political sovereignty and increasing scepticism about the benefits conveyed by the activities of multinational companies make unfavorable intervention on the part of foreign governments more likely than intervention on the part of home governments.

Adding to the complexity facing international managers is the fact that remedies to any "unfair" treatment meted out by foreign governments are often quite limited. Disputes with host governments are inevitable, if only through misunderstandings. When they cannot be satisfactorily negotiated away, the international business can try to obtain resolution through either arbitration or litigation.

Arbitration involves the use of neutral third parties who listen to a dispute

[15]Daniel Burstein, "The Risk Analysts Survive a Shakeout," *International Management* (October 1983), p. 48.

and rule in favor of one or the other party to the dispute. An example is provided by an International Chamber of Commerce (ICC) arbitration between an Italian contractor and the government of Zambia. The dispute was over Zambia's non-payment for construction work. The ICC recommended an Iranian arbitrator, and the proceedings took place in Iran. The Zambian government did not make an appearance and the arbitrator found for the contractor. At first, there was no response from Zambia. But after about a year, the contractor received a check in the mail for the full amount.[16]

More than fifty countries are signatory to an agreement honoring foreign arbitration awards and will enforce any award made in another signatory country. Furthermore, there are a number of international agencies that administer commercial arbitration as well as agencies in nearly all trading countries of the world that administer arbitration in those countries. Notwithstanding this impressive arbitration apparatus, however, there are substantial hindrances to concluding arbitration agreements. In particular, disputes can arise over where arbitration is to be held as well as over the nature of the law to be applied. For example, new governments in Africa and Asia have sometimes claimed that agreements negotiated with preceding regimes were unfair and exploitative, even where those agreements had clear arbitration clauses.

In some cases home governments have intervened on behalf of international companies, as the French government did regarding the appropriation of shares and assets of French oil companies by the Algerian government. However, there is no guarantee that the intercession of a national government will be successful. Where the home-country government can bring substantial economic leverage to bear upon host-country governments, the former can be a powerful ally for international firms involved in disputes with foreign governments. On the other hand, broader political objectives may encourage the home-country government to play down any specific international trade (or investment) issue, thereby depriving international management of valuable political support.

Where the process of arbitration fails, for one reason or another, the option of litigation—or going to court—might be considered. At this level the requisite procedures become truly byzantine and have served to enrich generations of lawyers. International law, in fact, is neither a complete nor a unitized jurisprudence.[17] Since controversies are mainly litigated in municipal courts located around the world, there will, of necessity, be divergent formulations of international law since different courts may make different rulings on essentially the same issue. And given the sovereignty of host governments, the international firm can find itself (following a decision rendered in a host-country court) without an effective appeal ''short of heaven or war.''[18]

[16]This case is described in Robert Blanchard, ''Settling International Contract Disputes Through Arbitration,'' *International Management,* 36 (May 1981), 46.

[17]A comprehensive discussion of international litigation is found in Henry Harfield, ''Litigation,'' in H. R. Hahls, J. G. Smith, and R. W. Wright, eds., *Nationalism and the Multinational Enterprise* (Dobbs Ferry, N.Y.: Oceana Publications, 1975), 221–32.

[18]Ibid., p. 232.

International litigation is therefore more of a process than a solution. When disputes arise, satisfactory resolution (from the perspective of the international company) will often require the intervention of the home government, since the freedom of sovereign governments to determine their own destiny deprives international law of the forceful implementation mechanisms familiar in Western domestic legal disputes.[19] In some cases intervention by the home government will be successful. For example, in 1974 the U.S. government negotiated a settlement with Peru for compensation payments to a number of American resource companies involved in a series of expropriations. On the other hand, virtually no compensation has been realized for the approximately $1.6 billion in American business properties on the island of Cuba that was seized by the Castro government over the period 1959–1961.

There is a good deal more that might be said about the special difficulties that confront international firms in resolving commercial disputes with foreign governments. An implication is that careful attention should be paid to avoiding such disputes in the first place, partly through effective political-risk assessment. Another implication is that management should consider acquiring "political-risk insurance" where appropriate. For example, governments in most developed countries have established programs that insure credit risks for exports. In the U.S., export credit insurance is provided by the Foreign Credit Insurance Association (FCIA), an association of some fifty private commercial insurance companies operating in association with the Export-Import Banks of the U.S. government.

The FCIA insures exporters for an agreed percentage of loss from commercial and/or political risk. Losses due to commercial risk are those that result from insolvency or default of the buyer owing to events such as droughts, floods, fire, and so forth. Political risk involves losses arising from political actions of governments beyond the control of buyer or seller. Insurance covers various contingencies including the imposition of export restrictions prior to date of shipment; war, hostilities, civil war, and so forth; expropriation or confiscation of the business of the buyer; any action having the force of law which, under circumstances not due to the fault of the buyer, prevents the buyer from making a payment.[20]

The Overseas Private Investment Corporation (OPIC) offers insurance for U.S. private investments in less developed countries and an investment-guaranty program for overseas project financing. The latter provides protection against loss from political risks by arranging for repayment of principal and interest on loans made to eligible borrowers and a direct-investment fund, which offers dollar financing from OPIC's own resources. Around two-thirds of all U.S. nonpetroleum private investment in less developed countries are currently insured by OPIC. Insurance coverage exists for three types of political risk: inconvertibility;

[19]Bruce Welling and Richard McLaren, "The Use of Law and Lawyers in International Trade," *Business Quarterly*, 48 (Summer 1983), 85.

[20]This description of the FCIA is taken from David Eiteman and Arthur Stonehill, *Multinational Business Finance* (Reading, Mass.: Addison-Wesley Publishing Company, 1979), pp. 513–14.

expropriation; and war, revolution, and insurrection.[21] Other countries also offer insurance against expropriation, confiscation, and currency inconvertibility. The availability of insurance does not eliminate political risk as an issue for management, since assessments of relevant risks will need to be made to evaluate whether the purchase of insurance makes sense. Also, recurrent claims for insurance payments may threaten a firm's eligibility under the available insurance programs.

UTILIZING POLITICAL-RISK ASSESSMENTS

William Colby, the former director of the Central Intelligence Agency, has remarked that while the CIA gathered the world's best factual information, often the information might just as well have been floated down the Potomac River in a canoe.[22] The point he was making is that information is essentially useless unless it is integrated into an organization's planning activities. In this regard, the primary outlets for political-risk assessments are investment decision making and strategic planning. In both sets of activities, political-risk assessments are integrated as qualitative (and often verbal) inputs to decision making. For example, a written evaluation of the political environment may be included in the appraisal of an overseas investment prospect. When employed in this way, political analyses serve as qualitative screening devices to sort out high- and low-risk environments.

Decision Analysis

While subjective assessments can be useful in decision making, specific numerical estimates of political risk are especially beneficial in capital-budgeting appraisals, since numerical estimates facilitate comparisons across projects located in different countries. In theory, political risks should be incorporated directly into the capital-budgeting process by making appropriate adjustment to anticipated cash flows. Decision analysis represents a set of techniques that incorporate risk into the evaluation of alternative choices. The utility of decision analysis can be illustrated most simply with reference to a firm's decision to make a specific capital investment in a given country. We assume that a firm faces a simple dichotomous choice: either to make the investment or to forego the investment. The two alternatives are identified as I (invest) or NI (not invest). For additional ease of illustration we assume that there is a related political question of prime importance to the outcome of the investment decision: whether the existing government (which favors foreign investment) remains in power over the life of the investment or whether the opposition party (which favors confiscating foreign property) comes to power.

---

[21]See Ibid., pp. 206–8.

[22]See William Colby, "Awash in facts," *Princeton Papers* (September 1983), pp. 11–12.

For purposes of decision analysis, management must assign probabilities to the relevant political events. Assume that through its political-assessment analysis, management assesses the probability of the existing government (EG) remaining in power as equal to .6; it assesses the probability of the existing government confiscating its property to be only .01. On the other hand, if the opposition party (OP) comes to power (with probability of .4), the likelihood of confiscation is .9.

Four relevant political possibilities therefore confront the firm: (1) existing party remains in power and does not confiscate; (2) existing party remains in power and confiscates; (3) opposition party comes to power and does not confiscate; and (4) opposition party comes to power and confiscates. These joint probabilities are calculated as follows: The joint probability of the first event, denoted as (*EG, NC*), equals .6 × .99 or .594; the joint probability of the second event (*EG, C*) equals .6 × .01 or .006. In similar fashion, the joint probabilities of the third (*OP, NC*) and fourth (*OP, C*) events are .04 and .36. These joint probabilities are summarized in table 5.5.

The critical political risk for management in this investment decision is the potential for the firm's assets to be confiscated. The probability of confiscation is calculated by summing the probabilities in the first column of table 5.5. This probability equals .366. The probability of no confiscation equals .634, which is obtained as the sum of the probabilities in the second column.

While the probability of confiscation is substantially less than the probability of no confiscation, the decision to proceed (or not to proceed) with the investment requires estimates of the net returns to the investment, given alternative outcomes. For purposes of illustration, assume that if the firm's assets are confiscated after the election, the present value of the estimated negative net cash flow equals $10 million. On the other hand, if the assets are not confiscated for the length of their productive lives, the investment option is assumed to have a positive net cash flow (in present value terms) equal to $15 million. The expected value of the investment option is therefore:

$$(5.2) \quad E(I) = .366 \, (-\$10 \text{ million}) + .634 \, (\$15 \text{ million}) = \$5.85 \text{ million}$$

If management is not extremely risk averse, and if there is no need to ration financial capital, this hypothetical investment should be undertaken since it will

TABLE 5.5 Probabilities of Relevant Compound Events

	C	NC	TOTAL
EG	.006	.594	.600
OP	.360	.040	.400
Total	.366	.634	1.000

increase the firm's net worth. In working through this hypothetical example, we see that a useful political-risk-assessment effort should provide insight into both the likelihood and the consequences of specific political events, such as asset confiscation.

THE DECISION-TREE TOOL

The investment decision described above can be visualized as a set of branching contingencies, with a specific outcome attached to each branch. Indeed, this tree metaphor characterizes a tool used in decision analysis known as the decision tree. Figure 5.1 describes the decision tree for the preceding investment evaluation.

In the simple problem described, our hypothetical firm has two choices: invest or don't invest. If it chooses the latter course, we assume there are no explicit cash-flow consequences. That is, the expected value of the decision is zero. On the other hand, if the firm chooses to invest, the outcome will depend upon two related things: the government in power and that government's treatment of the firm's assets. The first contingency is modeled as two branches extending from the "invest" option. That is, there is a 60 percent chance of moving along the "existing government" branch and a 40 percent chance of moving along the "opposition party" branch. At the end of each of these branches is a node that describes the probabilities of continuing along the "confiscation" or "no confiscation" branches, respectively.

At the end of each branch, one finds the appropriate monetary outcome. The overall expected value of the decision to invest E(I) is found by multiplying the monetary value at the end of each branch by the probability of arriving at that point on the tree and then adding the respective values. The appropriate calculation is shown in figure 5.1.

The use of a decision tree makes it less likely that the analyst will ignore important attributes of the environment that potentially affect the outcome of a decision. Of course, the greater the number of such attributes, the more complex the decision tree is; however, even complex decision-analysis problems are easily solved using computers. While our hypothetical example is quite easy to solve, it illustrates why—to be useful—a political-risk-assessment exercise should provide insight into both the likelihood and the consequences of specific political events, such as the confiscation of assets.

INTERNATIONAL LENDING RISKS

Perhaps the most pressing international economic issue of the 1980s has been the debt crisis confronting many Third World countries. One recent estimate puts the total debt owed to Western banks and governments at around $650 billion in 1983

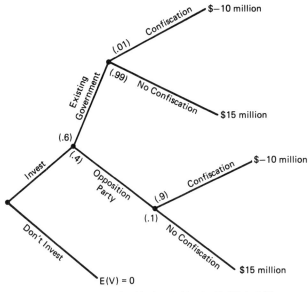

$E(I)=.6(.01)(-10)+.6(.99)(15)+.4(.9)(-10)+.4(.1)(15)=5.85$

Figure 5.1 A Sample Decision Tree

dollars.[23] Big debtors, such as Mexico and Brazil (see table 5.6), have been allowed to forego principal payments and have been bailed out by loans from the U.S. Treasury and the International Monetary Fund. The major threat facing Western bankers is that one or more debtor governments will repudiate their debt, thereby triggering a sequence of massive defaults. This international debt crisis has refocused attention on the nature of international lending risks.

As with many other attributes, the risks facing international lenders are substantively similar to those facing firms that restrict their lending to the domestic market. However, the scope and complexity of the relevant risks are generally greater for international lending. This point is underscored by considering the various categories of international lending risk: (1) credit risk, (2) legal risk, (3) documentation risk, and (4) funding risk.

Credit risk derives from the difficulties involved in analyzing the true degree of security provided by the collateral of international borrowers, as well as the financial condition of borrowing companies and the quality of their managers. Legal risk is related to complexities in the myriad of credit and debt laws enforceable in foreign countries and also the many unwritten legalities of international banking that exist without solid legal procedures to back them up.

TABLE 5.6   Bank Debts of Twelve Major Borrowers
($ billion U.S.)

	AMOUNT	
COUNTRY	OWED TO ALL COMMERCIAL BANKS (12/31/83)	OWED TO U.S. BANKS (12/31/83)
Mexico	71.3	25.4
Brazil	73.4	21.6
Venezuela	28.3	10.9
Argentina	26.7	8.8
Chile	12.1	5.9
South Korea	25.1	12.4
Philippines	15.8	5.5
Indonesia	13.3	3.2
Taiwan	7.4	3.9
Algeria	7.8	1.1
Nigeria	10.1	1.8
Egypt	5.9	1.4

Source: Morgan Guaranty Trust Co., New York, December 1984.

Documentation risk is associated with the possibility that merely extrapolating the required domestic contracting procedures for making loans may be inappropriate in the international context. Finally, funding risk is related to the exchange-rate risks described in chapter 3 as well as to risks of political actions by sovereign governments, including default and expropriation.[24]

It is apparent from this brief discussion of the sources of international lending risk that risk evaluation is a more complicated task for international lenders than for banks and other financial organizations that restrict their loans to borrowers in the home economy. Unsurprisingly, the massive scale of the debt-repayment problem has caused the major international banks to acknowledge shortcomings in their environmental-assessment practices and to reconsider ways of evaluating and managing international lending risks. Shareholders, among others, have been sharply critical of the apparent failure of bank managers to recognize the risks associated with making large loans to a relatively small number of borrowers.

In fact, empirical research has shown that the international banks are not unique in their seemingly casual approach toward risk assessment. Specifically, few companies appear to use sophisticated risk-assessment techniques. Rather, managers tend to rely heavily on interpersonal contact for their information.

A number of problems in effective risk assessment have been identified. One

---

[24]This categorization of international lending risk is found in Christopher M. Korth, ''Risk Minimization for International Lending in Regional Banks,'' *Columbia Journal of World Business*, 16 (Winter 1981), 21–28.

is the fact that the preparation of an in-depth political-risk study can be a time-consuming process, while management may be confronted with business opportunities that require an immediate commitment of resources. Another is that management is frequently overwhelmed with information to the point where it begins to ignore the information it receives. However, these problems are obviously not insurmountable. The first problem can be dealt with by trying to anticipate investment opportunities and initiate environmental-scanning activities in advance of the anticipated need. The second problem can be addressed by identifying the information needs of management and tailoring the intelligence gathered through the scanning activity to specific decision-making activities.[25]

SUMMARY AND CONCLUSIONS

No matter how attractive the underlying economic environment in a region is, the international firm might find it unprofitable to do business in that region if the host government inflicts onerous penalties upon the firm's activities. Potential penalties include the imposition of special taxes and barriers to trade as well as controls on the remittance of profits and foreign exchange from foreign subsidiaries to the parent affiliate. Perhaps the most severe action a sovereign government can take against the international firm is the confiscation of its property (expropriation) without adequate compensation.

Political-risk analysis is concerned with the identification and assessment of potentially significant changes in the overseas political environment that could have a significant impact on the profitability of doing business in that environment. While (conceptually) management should be concerned with the opportunities as well as the threats posed by such changes, conservative managers may be correct in focusing their primary attention on the threats posed by adverse government attitudes and actions.

Researchers have distinguished between macropolitical and micropolitical risk. The former encompasses risk that all firms confront in doing business in a given region. The latter refers to risk that is specific to certain firms or to particular economic activities. A variety of qualitative and quantitative techniques have been employed to assess and forecast political risk. The qualitative techniques are somewhat less demanding in terms of data requirements and statistical methodology; however, the quantitative approaches have the advantage of prompting managers to be explicit on how they see specific variables (or political conditions) affecting political risk. They also facilitate comparisons across different countries and regions.

In practice, the conflicting demands of political-risk assessment require a

---

[25]These and other problems associated with political-risk assessment, along with suggested solutions, are considered in B. Mascarenhas and C. Atherton, "Problems in Political Risk Assessment," *Management International Review*, 23 (1983), 22–32.

blend of both qualitative and quantitative analysis. For example, quantitative approaches that try to be overly precise may tend to be ignored by "practical" decision makers or may trigger extensive arguments over essentially irrelevant methodological issues. On the other hand, qualitative approaches may be difficult to incorporate into specific corporate decision-making activities, such as capital budgeting. In the final analysis, of course, there is no substitute for good judgment and a flexible attitude on the part of management.

DISCUSSION QUESTIONS

1. Define *political risk*. What are the various interrelated components of political-risk assessment?
2. Distinguish between macropolitical risk and micropolitical risk. Give examples of each type. What types of international businesses do you think would be most concerned with macrorisk factors? What types would be most concerned with microrisk factors?
3. Major international banks have for a long time engaged in environmental analysis of countries to which they extend loans. Yet at the present time they are extremely worried about major borrowers, including Argentina, Brazil, and Mexico, defaulting on their debts. What explanations can you offer for the apparent inability of major international banks to accurately anticipate default risk among Third World countries?
4. The country of Changedom is currently ruled by a military junta that is quite favorable toward foreign investment. However, the junta's stability is threatened on one side by an emerging coalition of political parties and on the other side by Communist guerrillas who are active in the countryside. The best guess is that the current junta will retain power and that foreign investments in Changedom will be left alone. However, there is a nontrivial probability that the junta will be displaced, either by an election or by a Communist takeover. As the manager of a company with capital investments in Changedom, how might you go about evaluating the net benefits of holding on to these investments versus selling them out to other investors?
5. What specific kinds of information would you look for to assist your decision making in question 4? What political-risk-assessment techniques would you find potentially useful?
6. Discuss the pros and cons of quantitative versus qualitative political-risk-assessment techniques.

REFERENCES

BLANK, STEPHEN, ET AL., *Assessing the Political Environment: An Emerging Function in International Companies.* New York: Conference Board, 1980.

BUNN, D. W., AND M. M. MUSTAFAOGLU, "Forecasting Political Risk," *Management Science,* 24 (1978), 1557–67.

FITZPATRICK, MARK, "The Definition and Assessment of Political Risk in International Business: A Review of the Literature," *Academy of Management Review*, 8 (1983), 249-54.

HANER, F. T., "Rating Investment Risks Abroad," *Business Horizons*, 22, no. 2 (1979), 18-23.

JONES, RANDALL, JR., "Empirical Models of Political Risks in U.S. Oil Production Operations in Venezuela," *Journal of International Business Studies*, 15 (Spring/Summer 1984), 81-95.

KNUDSEN, H., "Explaining the National Propensity to Expropriate: An Ecological Approach," *Journal of International Business Studies*, 5 (1974), 51-71.

NAGY, P., "Quantifying Country Risk: A System Developed by Economist at the Bank of Montreal," *Columbia Journal of World Business*, 13, no. 2 (1978), 135-47.

RUMMEL, R. J., AND D. A. HEENAN, "How Multinationals Analyze Political Risk," *Harvard Business Review*, 56, no. 1 (1978), 67-76.

WALTER, INGO, "Country Risk Assessment," in Ingo Walter and Tracy Murray, eds., *Handbook of International Business*. New York: John Wiley & Sons, 1982.

CHAPTER SIX

Scanning the Sociocultural Environment

The preceding two chapters discussed the importance of scanning the international economic and political environments and described a variety of approaches to the scanning exercise. This chapter considers a third major aspect of the firm's environment, namely, the social values and cultural institutions that influence the behavior of a firm's internal and external "stakeholders," including its employees, its customers, and host governments.

The well-known sociologist Geert Hofstede defines a value as "a broad tendency to prefer certain states of affairs over others."[1] He defines culture as " . . . the interactive aggregate of common characteristics that influence a human group's response to its environment."[2] Hence, personal value systems provide a framework that influences the general nature of an individual's behavior, while the aggregate of these personal values defines a society or a culture.

If we accept the importance of cultural influences on social behavior, it is apparent that yet another complexity confronts the international manager. Specifically, individuals in different countries may have different value systems and may not react in the same way to a given environment. Therefore, business practices

---

[1] Geert Hofstede, *Culture's Consequences: International Differences in Work-Related Values* (Beverly-Hills, Calif.: Sage Publications, 1980), p. 19.

[2] Ibid., p. 25.

that are successful in one set of countries may be entirely inappropriate in other sets of countries. While we will amplify on this theme extensively in this chapter, an example at the outset should help motivate the discussion.

The example refers to the use of the management technique known as management by objectives (MBO). The MBO approach involves employees and their immediate superiors jointly establishing employee objectives and performance milestones for an upcoming period. It was advanced as a way to motivate employees and remove arbitrariness and secrecy in the employee-evaluation process. While MBO was considered quite successful, by and large, in North America, it did not work well in France. Apparently, the main reason is that MBO presupposes self-imposed authority in the form of the individual's own objectives, whereas the French are accustomed to a highly personalized authority in the form of hierarchical superiors. Put more simply, French workers expect their managers to mandate performance standards and objectives rather than establish objectives in conjunction with the employee.

Cultural differences are not irrelevant to purely domestic managers since it is certainly true that different cultures often coexist within the same country. For example, American businesses are increasingly recognizing the unique tastes of Hispanic consumers in their approaches to domestic marketing and advertising. However, there is a prevailing view that individual countries are characterized by "core values" and that new arrivals to a country assimilate (over time) these core values to a substantial degree. Furthermore, in some countries, such as Japan, the society is alleged to be quite homogeneous, and relatively little adaptation to different tastes and preferences is required on the part of purely domestic companies.[3] In short, most researchers believe that cultural differences across countries are greater than those within countries.

HOW SIGNIFICANT ARE
INTERNATIONAL CULTURAL DIFFERENCES?

Even relatively modest efforts to scan and assess the sociocultural environments of different countries will involve a substantial commitment of the firm's resources. Clearly, many managers believe that this commitment is worthwhile as evidenced by the substantial percentage of firms that engage in social assessment and forecasting. In this regard, one study found that almost 43 percent of large U.S. firms responding to a survey were classified as having institutionalized the practice of social forecasting, and over 69 percent of the responding companies anticipated initiating or intensifying their efforts at social forecasting in the near future.[4] Nevertheless, a number of well-respected economists and marketing ex-

[3] For an exploration of this theme in the context of Japan, see Edwin O. Reischauer, "The Twain Shall Meet: Japanese and American Cultural Differences," *Speaking of Japan*, 3 (February 1983), 15–26.

[4] As reported in Kenneth E. Newgren and Archie B. Carroll, "Social Forecasting in U.S. Corporations—A Survey," *Long Range Planning*, 12 (August 1979), 60.

perts have argued recently that the importance of international cultural differences in formulating business strategies may be vastly overrated by international managers.

One such expert is Theodore Levitt, a professor of marketing at Harvard University. Levitt contends that technology has produced markets for standardized consumer products on a previously unimagined scale of magnitude. As a result, accustomed differences in national or regional preferences have largely disappeared. Indeed, he argues that many of today's differences among nations as to products and their features actually reflect the "respectful accommodation of multinational corporations to what they believe are fixed local preferences. They believe preferences are fixed, not because they are but because of rigid habits of thinking about what actually is." [5] According to Levitt, if a company keeps its costs and prices down and pushes quality and reliability up, while maintaining "reasonable" concern for suitability, customers will prefer its world-standardized products.

A key qualification in Levitt's argument is the requirement that international companies maintain concern for the suitability of their actions in overseas economies. In effect, Levitt is making a distinction between values and attitudes. The latter are susceptible to influence by a company's actions, say through advertising, whereas the former are more durable and stable motivations for behavior. Levitt can be seen as arguing that attitudes can change within a stable value system.

DeBeers is a company whose experience supports Levitt's globalization hypothesis. As some married readers may know, DeBeers is the largest miner and wholesale distributor of diamonds in the Western world. Indeed, a recent study estimates that the company controls more than 85 percent of the world's supply of uncut diamonds. In the late 1930s, the company embarked on a major campaign to promote the sale of diamonds in the U.S. Specifically, the company promoted diamonds as a symbol of the marital pledge and everlasting love. Needless to say, it was highly successful, as the diamond engagement ring became an institution in North America.

In the 1960s DeBeers turned its attention on Japan. While the diamond engagement ring was something of a tradition in the U.S. before DeBeers's entry into that market, the diamond engagement ring did not have a strong cultural precedent in Japan. For example, in the late 1960s, only 5 percent of Japanese women received diamond engagement rings. However, following DeBeers's intensive marketing campaign over the years, nearly 60 percent of all Japanese engagements are now sealed with a diamond ring.[6] DeBeers's campaign was obviously successful, perhaps because it did not conflict with a deeply held cultural value. After all, engagement rings were an accepted institution in Japan, although diamond rings were not widely purchased.

---

[5]Theodore Levitt, "The Globalization of Markets," *Harvard Business Review*, 61 (May/June 1983), 97.

[6]Susan M. Duffy, "DeBeers Is Forever," *Barrons*, October 31, 1983, pp. 6–7.

Not only have patterns of consumption apparently been altered through the efforts of multinational companies, but also seemingly unchangeable labor practices have been significantly modified. A striking example is provided in the case of the Japanese car maker Mitsubishi Corporation's takeover of Chrysler's manufacturing operations in Australia. Observers claim that industrial disruption in Chrysler's former plants, a notorious feature in earlier times, has fallen away with the introduction of Japanese-style labor relations. In particular, Mitsubishi has been able to offer something close to Japanese lifetime employment to its Australian work force on the basis of increasing volume through the plant and improving productivity.

Productivity increases have been accomplished by, among other things, training employees to perform more than one task at different locations on the assembly line, thereby providing more flexibility in the use of personnel and allowing management to cope with absenteeism. Plant management ensured that the work force was informed about its personnel plans and made efforts to instill a "company orientation" in the work place. Both of these practices are characteristically Japanese; however, more traditional Western-style incentives schemes were also introduced to encourage a positive attitude toward productivity and quality.[7]

Although tastes and preferences in different countries may not be immutable, they are often more difficult to modify than the DeBeers experience in Japan would indicate. For example, it has been suggested by some consultants that as a result of the adoption of Western styles of living, the number of small retail stores in Japan should have declined rapidly. But, in fact, about 60 percent of Japanese retailers have no more than two employees. Apparently, many Japanese homemakers have an abiding preference to buy fresh food on a daily basis within walking distance. Small shops also specialize in other items like clothing, pharmaceuticals, and furniture. The owners buy goods from each other, and personal ties between them and their customers are reinforced by shared community activities such as festivals and schools.[8] A number of international companies, including Pizza Hut and Dairy Queen, have been quite successful in Japan by operating neighborhood convenience and fast-food shops. In effect, these companies cater to the Japanese taste for shopping in small retail outlets.

THE BOUNDARIES OF SOCIOCULTURAL SCANNING

In most cases, international managers will find it in their firms' best interests to strike a balance between accepting local attitudes and preferences as given and fixed and trying to "engineer" changes in local tastes. But striking a proper

[7] See "Australia Takes to the Japanese Style," *International Management* (January 1983), p. 42.

[8] See "Frustrating Foreign Businessmen," *Far Eastern Economic Review* (December 3, 1982), p. 83.

balance requires a knowledge and appreciation of the nature and strength of established values. Any effort to modify local behavior patterns that does not respect deeply held values is doomed to failure. Many international business experts warn that the most important mistake management can make is to overlook relevant cultural differences. Simply put, the international company has to understand regional differences in behavior before it can develop strategies to minimize their impacts on the company's worldwide operations.

CASE STUDY: *CULTURAL IMPACTS ON JOINT VENTURES IN JAPAN*

An excellent illustration of the potential impact of cultural differences on international businesses is provided by the experience of Canadian firms undertaking joint ventures in Japan. Professor Richard Wright found that for smaller Canadian firms, cultural differences between Japanese and Canadian managers intruded into various aspects of negotiating and managing joint-venture agreements.

At the outset, problems were experienced with the speed of negotiation. Canadian executives, expecting to conclude joint-venture agreements quickly, perceived the Japanese as unwilling or unable to make firm decisions. Thus, joint-venture negotiations dragged on much longer than anticipated, causing anger and frustration. On the other side, the Japanese partners emphasized that they were not trying intentionally to delay. Rather, the consensus decision-making process in Japan requires much more discussion and study than in the West.

Another fundamental negotiating difference between the Japanese and Canadians was the role of written contracts. Several negotiations were frustrated by what the Canadians saw as an unwillingness of the Japanese to enter into precise contractual agreements. Compared to North Americans, the Japanese place relatively little emphasis on written contracts but (rather) rely on mutual understanding and personal agreement. Wright reports one Japanese negotiator as saying: "As long as the music plays and the heart is in the right place, you will make a deal. Just listen to the music, not the words."

Areas of conflict also arose in the course of managing joint ventures. The most fundamental problems arose from differing objectives between the Canadian and Japanese partners. For example, while the Canadian orientation was toward profit maximization, the Japanese orientation was toward growth of sales volume and market share. Because of the lifetime employment tradition in most large Japanese companies, continued growth in the size of the company is important to maintain morale among managers and employees.

Other common sources of conflict, apparently associated with cultural differences, related to selling methods and personnel policies. Specifically, whereas several Canadian managers reported that they considered their Japanese partners too humble and timid in selling, Japanese managers considered Canadian selling methods too aggressive for Japan. Furthermore, in periods of recession, Canadian managers expressed a preference to implement employee-layoff programs. The

This case discussion is taken from Richard W. Wright, "Canadian Joint Ventures in Japan," *The Business Quarterly*, Autumn 1977, Western University.

Japanese partners were reluctant to lay off workers, since it would go counter to the tradition of lifetime employment in their wholly owned affiliates.

Wright concludes that one obvious lesson of the experience of Canadian managers is to get acquainted with the foreign culture, since the effects of cultural differences permeate every management decision and every business relationship.

Since a society's values will ultimately shape its economic, political, and cultural institutions, it would seem that sociocultural scanning activities must embrace a firm's entire environment. In fact, distinctions between economic, political, and cultural variables are by no means easy to make, as indicated by table 6.1. This table reports the responses of a sample of industrial firms to an inquiry about the most significant social factors affecting their activities. The two most frequently cited factors, government behavior and employment trends, could well be considered contingencies associated with scanning the political and economic environments, as might pressure-group activity and population distribution/levels. On the other hand, life styles, aspirations, and attitudes

TABLE 6.1   The Most Significant Social Factors

SOCIAL FACTOR	NUMBER OF FIRMS CITING FACTOR
Government behavior	19
Employment trends	18
Population distribution/levels	15
Pressure-group activity	15
Life styles	15
Income distribution/levels	10
Child/youth behavior/education	7
Group aspirations	7
Attitudes to work	7
Union behavior	6
Local opinion/circumstances	6
Industrial developments	6
Attitudes—general	5
Political climate	5
Too numerous to list	5
Discrimination attitudes/legislation	4
Leisure patterns	4
Economic climate/process	3
Consumer tastes	1
Independent agency activity	1
Health	1

Source: Reprinted with permission from *Long Range Planning*, vol. 13. April 1980, p. 84, J. C. Higgins and D. Romano, "Social Forecasting: An Integral Part of Corporate Planning?" Copyright 1980, Pergamon Press, Ltd.

toward work are environmental attributes that are more readily characterized as "cultural" in nature.

Clearly, management should not become "hung up" on labels. The important point is that environmental factors motivating human behavior in a given region need to be identified, evaluated, and incorporated into the firm's business plans. In some firms, the corporate-planning department integrates social forecasting with economic and technological forecasting. This is especially true in smaller companies. On the other hand, many large firms have specialists or use specialized consultants to assess specific areas of the environment. For example, economists tend to examine the economic situations in countries, while political scientists assess the political situation.

A de facto separation of the various scanning activities also frequently takes place as a result of the fact that certain variables and manifestations of behavior are readily measurable, while others are not. The former are usually "economic" in nature, such as income levels and inflation. Hence, economic scanning and, to a lesser extent, political scanning are more amenable to quantitative analysis than are scanning activities associated with identifying, assessing, and forecasting underlying social attitudes.

The sociocultural scanning exercise can obviously be quite open-ended, given its focus on such characteristics as attitudes toward consumption and work. However, many specific social attitudes and preferences can be seen as manifestations of a relatively small number of broad societal characteristics. One suggested list of background cultural characteristics includes the following:[9]

1. Temperament

This concept covers a number of group-personality characteristics, including emotionalism, the need for formal rules, and a tolerance for uncertainty and ambiguity. Several broad generalizations have been drawn in the literature regarding differences across countries in national temperament. For example, it is suggested that in Latin countries and Japan, individuals prefer structured relationships, especially in the workplace, whereby individual roles and responsibilities are well defined. On the other hand, in Anglo and Nordic countries neither work processes nor relations among people are rigidly prescribed. As another example, while American managers are suggested to value achievement quite highly, Australian managers are alleged to place a low value on such concepts as achievement, success, and risk.[10]

2. Attitudes Toward Work by Employees

A variety of personality traits are subsumed under this category, and they have extremely important implications for the labor-relations function in interna-

---

[9]See F. T. Haner, *Global Business Strategy for the 1980's* (New York: Praeger Publishers, 1980).

[10]George England, *The Manager and His Values: An International Perspective from the United States, Japan, Korea, India and Australia* (Cambridge, Mass.: Ballinger Books, 1975), p. 10.

tional firms. Some perceptions, although widely held, may be unacceptable stereotypes, such as the view that Latin Americans have a "poor" attitude toward work while the Chinese will work hard, regardless of the country in which they live.

Other distinctions in national attitudes toward work are firmly grounded in empirical research. For example, Japanese workers are believed to place the interests of their companies and fellow workers ahead of their own individual interests, whereas the American ideal is one of rugged individualism and an ability to rely on one's own skills and resources. As a consequence, decision making that relies upon cooperation and consensus is the rule in Japan. Moreover, disciplinary measures are rarely taken against Japanese workers, since peer-group pressure is usually sufficient to bring "shirkers" back into line. And while Japanese employees will work for one company their entire careers, American employees (especially managers) will typically work for a number of companies over the course of their working lives.

3. Structure of the Culture

In many parts of the world, traditional guidelines related to religious practices, family relationships, and the like, dictate the ambitions and behavior of individuals. For example, it has been suggested that in Catholic countries there is a greater emphasis on avoiding uncertainty than in Protestant countries. This is in turn related to Catholicism's stress on absolute certainties, like the infallibility of the Pope and the uniqueness of the Church. On the other hand, Protestantism (and especially Calvinism) encourages worldly ways to cope with uncertainty (technology and law).[11] One alleged implication of this difference is a greater mobility of workers and managers in Protestant countries, both geographically and occupationally. The comparative mobility of the Protestant is, in turn, a manifestation of a higher propensity to accept risk in Protestant countries.

The demands of the Islamic religion significantly constrain behavior in Moslem countries with associated implications for international business. In some cases the implications are profound, including absolute prohibitions on activities such as the sale and consumption of alcoholic beverages or the use of sexual imagery in advertising. The rise of Islam has been identified by spirits companies as a major factor slowing their worldwide sales growth. But so have tougher impaired-driving laws in North America.

4. Fractionalization

Differences within societies in language, ethnic mix, and religion can significantly affect the climate for international business in specific regions, in both economic and political dimensions. For example, the diversity of religious sects in India has been a constant source of turmoil that has periodically flared into

---

[11]Hofstede, *Culture's Consequences*, p. 181.

violence, including violent confrontations between the Indian government and the Sikh religious minority. For international managers concerned with the risk of civil unrest, the religious fragmentation in India poses a distinct hazard.

The ethnic split in Canada between English- and French-speaking cultures obliges companies in that country to do business in two official languages. This in turn implies additional costs related to packaging and duplicative advertising. It also has posed a risk, from time to time, of political separation of the province of Quebec from the rest of the country.

5. Corruption

In some cases, what is considered to be a cultural value might actually be a manifestation of economic conditions. For example, in many countries unofficial payments to government administrators are considered to be an acceptable way of doing business, whereas in North America and Western Europe, they often constitute grounds for criminal prosecution. Hence, most Asians make a distinction between bribery and prebendalism. The latter is the right of an official, because of holding an office that provides little pay, to receive extra fees. This suggested difference in "values" might therefore actually reflect differences in economic circumstances. Specifically, a well-developed tax system provides the wherewithal to pay public officials in North America adequate wages to keep the jobs filled. On the other hand, less developed countries often have primitive tax systems. Hence, while government workers are poorly paid, it is expected that they will supplement their official salaries with unofficial gratuities.

As noted above, cultural differences do not as a rule prohibit doing business internationally, although they often oblige management to modify the way business is done from region to region. While modifications may be required, to a greater or lesser extent, in virtually all of the international firm's activities, the particular areas that seem to be most affected by cultural differences are the marketing and personnel-relations functions. Some relevant evidence on this point is provided in table 6.2. This table reports responses from the same survey providing the data for table 6.1. In the case of table 6.2, respondents were asked to name decision areas for which social information provides a useful decision input. As seen, the overwhelming majority of citations were for market assessment/customer relations and personnel/industrial relations.

TECHNIQUES OF SOCIAL ANALYSIS AND FORECASTING

While there is a recognized need to assess social attitudes and mores in overseas markets on an ongoing basis, there is no consensus on how broad the assessment should be nor on the assessment and forecasting techniques that should be employed. As a result, firms differ with respect to the geographic scope and the futurity of the scanning exercise. In the case of some firms, such as Citicorp and

TABLE 6.2 Decision Areas for Which Social Information Provides
a Useful Decision Input

DECISION AREA	NUMBER OF FIRMS CITING FACTOR
Market assessment/customer relations	23
Personnel/industrial relations	21
Premises/location	9
Investment	8
Product development/management	7
Corporate business policy	6
Environmental considerations	4
Policy toward government/government regulations	4
Decisions affected by demographic change	4
Public relations policy	4
Pricing	3
None	2
Advertising	2
Wage policy	2
Union relations	2
Too numerous to list	2
Acquisitions	1
Technical considerations	1
Policy toward pressure groups	1
Resource planning	1

Source: Higgins and Romano, "Social Forecasting," p. 85.

IBM, it appears that management trades off a global coverage of near-current conditions against a futurist leap based on a geographically narrower data set.[12]

Sociocultural Checklist

In one approach to the scanning exercise, a checklist of potentially important social forces is developed and monitored over time. The approach is illustrated by the business environment studies (BES) performed by General Electric, a pioneer in sociopolitical forecasting. The company's initial BES effort was a broad survey of the whole prospective business environment of the 1970s. General Electric's BES group viewed social change as the interaction of eight developing forces for change: (1) increasing affluence, (2) economic stabilization, (3) rising levels of education, (4) increasing pluralism and individualism, (5) changing attitudes toward work and leisure, (6) emergence of the postindustrial society, (7) growing interdependence of institutions, and (8) the urban/minority problem.[13]

---

[12]For a discussion of environmental scanning in major U.S. companies, see Philip S. Thomas, "Environmental Scanning—The State of the Art," *Long Range Planning*, 12 (February 1980), 20–28.

[13]See Ian H. Wilson, "Socio-Political Forecasting: A New Dimension to Strategic Planning," *Michigan Business Review* (1974), pp. 15–25.

The identification of these eight broad forces established the priorities of the BES group for more detailed studies and analyses. For example, it is felt by company officials that an early focus on minority problems gave General Electric a jump on predicting the emergence of the women's rights movement. The success of the BES group in identifying changing social attitudes that held potentially significant implications for the company led to the sociopolitical planning process being integrated into General Electric's overall strategic-planning system.

While General Electric's approach to sociopolitical analysis and forecasting is more ambitious than that of most companies, the focus of GE's analysis is quite representative. That is, many companies that evaluate sociocultural trends on a regular basis focus on issues such as the attitudes of people toward work and leisure, attitudes toward nonconformity and individualism, and popular concerns about the social responsibilities of business. The emphasis given to particular issues will naturally be influenced by a company's main business interests. For example, General Mills—a large, diversified consumer-goods company—is especially interested in understanding and forecasting overall movements in consumer attitudes.[14]

While the checklist is a structured way to monitor contemporary social values and attitudes, international managers must also guard against being surprised by value shifts in a society. An example of a significant value shift during the 1960s and 1970s was a growing disaffection among European employees working in large business units, as manifested by increased absenteeism and an increased incidence of strikes and industrial disputes. This growing worker discontent led to government action. In Sweden, for example, laws were passed in 1973 and 1977 enabling trade unions to participate in strategic decision making alongside top management. For companies unprepared to cope with this new labor-relations environment, worker participation in management proved to be a source of further conflict between employees and host governments on one side and management on the other side.[15]

Delphi

In chapter 5 we described the use of the Delphi technique to evaluate the extent and nature of political risk. A comparable procedure has been used on occasion to forecast major social changes. Potential participants in the Delphi exercise include sociologists, anthropologists, and other social scientists along with journalists and other so-called opinion leaders. As in applications of Delphi to political-risk assessment, expert opinion is solicited, collected, evaluated, and tabulated in an interactive process.

In a typical Delphi social-forecasting effort, participants would be asked to evaluate the importance of selective elements influencing a nation's social at-

[14]Thomas, ''Environmental Scanning,'' p. 26.

[15]For a discussion of cultural forces affecting European businesses, see Bernard Taylor and Luigi Ferro, ''Key Social Issues for European Business,'' *Long Range Planning*, 16 (1983), 42–69.

titudes and values. For example, they might be asked to evaluate the importance of the women's rights movement in less developed countries, or the likelihood of a widespread return to orthodoxy in religious practices. Obviously, the Delphi exercise will be valueless to management if irrelevant attributes of social change are chosen as elements for the experts to consider. For social forecasting to make a contribution to the strategic-planning process, management must have a preliminary notion of what social forces are particularly relevant to the corporation.

Extrapolation

This technique represents an attempt to forecast social change in a region by statistically projecting historical trends into the future. In effect, the approach embodies the notion that "the past is prologue."

There are several problems associated with the extrapolation method. One is that certain phenomena that the analyst would like to forecast, such as alienation of the work force, are not directly measurable; however, in order to statistically project a perceived trend, the phenomenon of interest must be quantifiable. In some cases the extrapolation method can be used by employing a "surrogative" measure or indicator for the (unquantifiable) variable of direct interest. For example, a commonly used proxy or "surrogative" measure of worker alienation is the number of days lost through strikes.

Another problem with the extrapolation approach is that trends often can be identified only after they are well established; by then it may be too late for the international firm to exploit the commercial opportunities created by the trend, or (alternatively) to avoid the unfavorable economic or political consequences. Since the extrapolation approach is not concerned with the factors that underlie cultural change, the technique cannot provide management with any advance warning about fundamental changes taking place in long-standing social attitudes and preferences. And fundamental changes in attitudes and even values do occasionally take place. For example, a number of observers suggest that the willingness of Japanese workers to sacrifice their personal lives for a job well done is beginning to diminish and that younger workers are less committed to teamwork, are more individualistic, and are more detached from their jobs than their elders are.[16] If such changes are taking place in Japan, they might have profound consequences both for Japanese companies and for international companies that compete against the Japanese in world markets.

Attitude Surveys

On the surface it would seem that the most direct way to gain insight into contemporary social forces as well as changes in those forces is to survey segments of the population. A substantial number of companies are in the survey business,

---

[16]See Lee Smith, "Cracks in the Japanese Work Ethic," *Fortune*, May 14, 1984.

and techniques for sampling segments of the population in order to identify attitudes toward specific issues have been well worked out. But while attitude surveys are useful for assessing popular opinion on specific issues, they are often poor indicators of future behavior.[17] This is likely to be especially true when respondents to surveys are unconcerned about the costs of their indicated preferences. For example, a majority of respondents to surveys express concern about environmental pollution, yet individuals will oppose government actions to prevent environmental damage when such actions pose a threat to their own employment.

Another shortcoming of attitude surveys is that social sentiment toward specific issues can change quite dramatically as a result of specific events. As an example, revelations of ITT's involvement in the overthrow of a socialist government in Chile contributed to a sharp increase in suspicion and hostility directed toward multinational companies by governments of many developing countries. A further problem is that small swings of opinion often produce large effects. This point is illustrated by the experience of multinational oil companies in Canada. The presence of large foreign-owned oil companies had been a long-standing source of concern to many Canadian nationalists, but substantial (and punitive) action was taken against them by the Canadian government only after a number of studies had been published arguing that these companies were making "excessive" profits.[18] While these shortcomings should be kept in mind, it is clear that developing value profiles through attitude surveys and the like can provide international managers with potentially useful insights into cross-cultural differences in tastes and preferences.

THE USE OF MULTIPLE SCENARIOS

Most candid observers of social forecasting conclude that attempts to quantify and project trends in public attitudes and values are likely to be unreliable, given the current state of the art, except perhaps in the very short term.[19] As a result, an increasing number of companies have turned to the use of multiple scenarios as part of the corporate-planning function. A scenario depicts some "plausible" or "possible" future state that identifies critical issues or variables.[20] Usually, more

[17]A critique of attitude surveys is provided in Tom Pint, "Measuring Change in Social Attitudes—Leading Indicators," in Brian C. Twiss, ed., *Social Forecasting for Company Planning* (London: Macmillan & Co., 1982).

[18]Among other things, the Canadian government retroactively assumed a 25 percent interest in the revenues earned by foreign-owned oil companies on acreage leased from the Crown. Of course, there is no way of proving that this action would not have been taken in the absence of such studies.

[19]See, for example, Peter M. S. Jones, "Discontinuities in Social Attitudes," in Twiss, *Social Forecasting*, p. 92.

[20]This definition is taken from Robert E. Linneman and Harold Klein, "The Use of Multiple Scenarios by U.S. Industrial Companies: A Comparison Study 1977-1981," *Long Range Planning*, 16, no. 6 (1983), 94-101. Much of the following discussion of scenarios draws on this article.

than one scenario is useful in providing a range of conditions likely to be encountered in the future area of interest. For example, international oil companies will ordinarily consider a range of scenarios for oil prices, including, say, a breakup of OPEC that would lead to a sharp decline in world oil prices. Since a scenario is a possible future, it need not be taken as a direct forecast. However, scenarios are often qualified in terms of their likelihood, such as "best case," "worst case," and "base case."

Typically, the use of multiple scenarios involves developing—and putting into writing—more than one relevant possible future external environment facing the firm. For example, a company contemplating the prospect of doing business in Saudi Arabia might be especially concerned about a strong upsurge of religious fervor in that country, which in the extreme might lead to an Iranian-style Islamic revolution. The scenarios developed might therefore consider a set of possibilities ranging from the preservation of the status quo to a strong popular uprising by a radical Muslim sect.

The value of the scenarios developed is not so much in forecasting the likelihood of an upsurge of religious fervor in Saudi Arabia as in laying out a set of contingencies for management to consider. Hence, well-written scenarios should describe important features of the environment that could be associated with a particular event. For example, an upsurge of fundamentalist religion in Saudi Arabia might conceivably be accommodated within the current political system, with only modest changes in business practices required to respect tighter codes of behavior pertaining, say, to dress, socializing, and so forth. At the other extreme, a strong religious upsurge could lead to the overthrow of the ruling government and an ensuing period of political and economic chaos.

The general nature of the multiple-scenario activity can be further illustrated with reference to figure 6.1. For purposes of discussion, three alternative

Figure 6.1   Multiple Scenarios Concerning Religious Attitudes in Saudi Arabia

SCENARIO 1	SCENARIO 2	SCENARIO 3
EVENT	EVENT	EVENT
No change in current attitudes	Modest intensification of fundamentalist pressures	Iranian-style revival of religious fundamentalism
IMPLICATIONS	IMPLICATIONS	IMPLICATIONS
Impact on government Impact on government policy Impact on business practices	Impact on government Impact on government policy Impact on business practices	Impact on government Impact on government policy Impact on business practices Impact on investments in the area

scenarios are put forth for consideration. Each is taken to imply certain consequences for the political and economic environments. A well-drawn scenario should describe explicit linkages from an event to its environmental consequences in order to assist management in evaluating the plausibility of each scenario. In some cases the implications of an event may be quite benign under all of the alternative scenarios, thereby suggesting that the event itself has no substantive managerial implications. In other cases the implications of an event may be so devastating for the economic and political stability of a region that even a relatively small probability of its occurring represents an unacceptable risk to management.

CASE STUDY: *THE MULLAS AND THE BANKERS*

A heightening of Islamic religious fervor in Middle Eastern and certain Southeast Asian countries, such as Malaysia, has had a significant impact on business practices in those countries and threatens to have more widespread and profound impact in the future. One area of business affected is banking. Pakistan was the first Muslim country to move toward converting the country's banking system into an Islamic one. In 1979, President Zia set up a panel of economists, bankers, and *ulema* (Muslim theologians) to do away with interest-oriented banking. Muslim fundamentalists argue that according to the Quran, the taking of interest is sinful for all Muslims.

As a result of this fundamentalist interpretation, customers are not paid interest on their deposits but are allowed to share in the bank's profits. Banks, in turn, charge a markup for investing in noninterest-bearing ventures, such as commodity buying and selling. Many Pakistanis debate whether profit is just another name for interest. However, the system has forced banks to change the way they finance companies. Specifically, banks provide working capital to companies in exchange for a partnership share, or *musharaka*, in the profits or losses of the "borrowing" company. If a company makes a loss on the *musharaka*, the bank can buy up company shares as compensation. Obviously, banks are being extremely cautious and are entering into *musharaka* deals only with well-established companies possessing healthy profit records.

At the time of writing, there were seventeen foreign banks with fifty-seven branches, and they were all excluded from the new Islamic banking system. However, the *mullas* (religious leaders) on the Council of Islamic Ideology were keen to force foreign banks to Islamicize.

Imagine that you are a senior manager of a foreign bank in Pakistan or in a neighboring Muslim country. How much emphasis would you give to this growing religious commitment in your business plans? What further studies, if any, would you recommend your company undertake to more accurately assess the likelihood that the *mullas* will have their way on Islamicizing foreign banks?

The information in this case was taken from Almid Rashed, "Pakistan Leaps into the Unknown," *Euromoney*, December 1983, pp. 110–12.

CROSS-IMPACT ANALYSIS

In most cases, the utility of multiple scenarios as a decision-making tool comes from linking the scenarios to potential impacts on the firm. Of course, this qualification can be made of all environmental-assessment and forecasting techniques. Unfortunately, it is not always easy to do. A procedure discussed in the literature that is useful in linking cultural events to their firm-level impacts is cross-impact analysis. This procedure is especially well suited for use with the multiple-scenario technique, since the latter is potentially capable of generating a rich and extensive list of influences on a firm's environment.

The nature of cross-impact analysis is illustrated in figure 6.2. In essence, it is a way of systematically evaluating the influence of a limited number of environmental factors on variables that are important to the firm's operations. Typically, the analysis is set up in the form of a matrix, where social as well as economic and political factors are arrayed along the side of the matrix, and variables relevant to managing the firm are arrayed along the top.

For example, in figure 6.2 the first row of entries in the matrix might represent the impact of increased individualism in Japanese society on various social, economic, and political variables relevant to firms doing business in Japan or with Japanese companies. Hence, SE_{1i} might be a measure of the impact of increased individualism on employee-turnover rates. Presumably, employee-turnover rates will increase as individualism increases, since workers will be more prone to switch jobs, substitute hobbies for work, and so forth.

As another example, the mth row of entries in the matrix might represent the impact of an aging Japanese population on relevant business-related variables. Thus, SS_{mi} might be a measure of the impact of an aging population on required

Figure 6.2   Cross-Impact Analysis

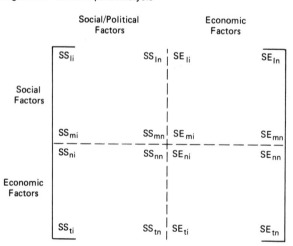

corporate pensions and health benefits. Presumably, a rapidly aging population will lead to increased social and political pressure on corporations to fund retirement programs. Indeed, increased individualism in Japanese society might also have a similar influence, since working people may be less disposed to help out their retired parents and other elderly family members on a voluntary basis. Hence, SS_{I_i} will also take a positive value, as it is the cell that corresponds to the interconnection between increased individualism (row 1) and sociopolitical pressures to increase corporate pension and other retirement benefits (column 1).

In the case of certain social forces there may be no obvious relationship to a variable of direct interest to the firm. For example, the aging of the Japanese population has no evident implications for the price of energy in Japan. In this case the appropriate cell in the cross-impact matrix would be empty. And more often than not, it will be impossible to quantify the impact of any particular social force on variables of interest to the firm. In these cases the appropriate cells in the cross-impact matrix might merely indicate the direction of the impact.

In effect, the cross-impact matrix is a structured way to incorporate perceptions about current and future social forces into the firm's planning process. As such, it represents one of several stages in the overall sociocultural-scanning exercise.

SOCIOCULTURAL SCANNING
AND FORECASTING AS A PROCESS

The social-assessment and forecasting activity is, on balance, best thought of as a process. To this end, Morris describes a number of steps to be taken in designing and installing a system for social forecasting.[21] The stages of this process are discussed below and are summarized in table 6.3:

1. Apprise the entire organization of the exercise (organizational involvement).
2. Identify those who are the most likely users of the analysis.
3. Identify the issues, that is, the problems and factors in the external environment that affect, or potentially could affect, the organization.
4. Find out the information needs of specific user groups and incorporate the findings into the design of the social-assessment system.
5. Evaluate the current corporate intelligence system; e.g., what type of information is available on a routine basis? Where does the information come from?
6. Evaluate the likelihood of the development of major trends in a given time frame and the impact of each trend on the organization.
7. Based upon steps 3 and 6, determine the relative priorities of the social-assessment information system.

[21]Geoffrey K. Morris, "Designing and Installing a System for Social Forecasting," in Twiss, *Social Forecasting*.

TABLE 6.3   Key Stages of the Social-Forecasting Exercise

1. Organizational involvement
2. Identify users
3. Checklist of issues
4. Identify specific information needs
5. Evaluate corporate intelligence system
6. Evaluate major trends
7. Determine issue priorities
8. Communicate information
9. Act on information if appropriate
10. Install a monitoring system
11. Ensure sufficient funding to perpetuate system
12. Provide adequate training

Source: Geoffrey K. Morris, "Designing and Installing a System for Social Forecasting," in Brian Twiss, ed., *Social Forecasting for Company Planning* (London: Macmillan & Co., 1982). By permission of Macmillan, London and Basingstoke.

8.   Communicate relevant information, as identified by step 7, on a continuing basis to those who need to know.
9.   Translate the information into action.

From table 6.3 it can be seen that the process of assessing and forecasting cultural trends is an activity within a broader management-information framework, just as in the case of economic and political scanning. Its utility to management will therefore depend upon whether the relevant issues are addressed, and whether the information that is gathered and analyzed is communicated to the appropriate people in the organization. Finally, it will also depend upon whether the information is used by management in making decisions about investments, marketing strategies, and labor relations.

SOURCES OF INFORMATION

Obviously, for effective scanning and forecasting of the sociocultural environment, management must have access to information that is in many cases difficult to gather and interpret. These difficulties relate to the fact that social values are to a significant extent open to interpretation. Furthermore, they are usually not codified in a convenient published form as are national economic data.

Fortunately for international management, there are sources that provide interpretive analyses of sociocultural forces and trends in both developed and developing countries. For example, the European Community Information Service issues a number of publications covering social conditions in several Western European countries. Major management-consulting companies, such as Price Waterhouse, publish manuals on how to do business in different countries. These manuals tend to emphasize the cultural influences on overseas business ventures. A number of universities housing international business centers publish reviews of cultural trends in foreign countries on both a regular and irregular basis.

In addition to published sources of information, an increasing number of consulting companies are offering training courses on how to do business in overseas markets. Many of these courses tend to emphasize cultural dos and don'ts for specific regions of the world. Often videocassettes and computer software are used in the training courses, allowing managers to practice cultural protocol before actually embarking on overseas business trips.

AVOIDING THE PROBLEM OF SELF-REFERENCE CRITERIA

It is not sufficient to gather information about foreign cultures. The interpretation of the information should be relatively free of what has been called a self-reference bias. This is a bias associated with studying foreign cultures from one's own frame of reference. While one cannot escape completely from one's own cultural heritage, international managers should try to be aware of how their own backgrounds may be shaping their interpretation of behavior in other cultures. In some cases such an awareness may help prevent management from wrongful stereotyping. For example, a North American or Western European manager might deplore the Latin American's seeming disregard for promptness and consider it an undesirable but essential feature of the Latin temperament. In fact, the North American's standard for promptness is developed against the background of relatively efficient transportation systems. The Latin American must typically cope with a much less reliable transportation infrastructure. In the latter context it makes less sense to set "tight" time schedules. But this is more a rational response to economic conditions than an imbedded cultural value. The Latin manager when transferred to North America might be every bit as time conscious as his or her colleagues.

The readjustment of focus away from self-reference criteria could, for example, help the North American manager to use his or her time more efficiently when doing business in Latin America. As one illustration, the manager might take work along to meetings in order to use time productively in the event of unforeseen delays. It should also help reduce misunderstandings and hostilities that impede successful business transactions.

INTEGRATING THE ENVIRONMENTAL ANALYSES

Ultimately, the various environmental screening exercises carried out to identify the economic, political, and sociocultural characteristics of different geographic regions must be brought together in an overall assessment as to which regions are promising for international business activities and which are not.

There is no single method that is used to integrate the disparate information into a single overall evaluation of a region's attractiveness. The economic, political, and social variables evaluated under the various assessment exercises will likely be quantitatively incomparable. For example, some may be cardinal measurements, e.g., GNP per capita, while others may be ordinal measurements, e.g., high or low entrepreneurship. In order to combine these cardinal and ordinal variables into an overall measure, some common basis of measurement must be chosen.

Typically, these various ordinal and cardinal measures are combined as index numbers. Specifically, on each of the dimensions used to evaluate the attractiveness of a region, various countries might be rated relative to some base-case number. For example, the rating might be taken on the basis of 100. Thus, for GNP per capita the country with the highest GNP per capita would be assigned a value of 100 for this particular attribute. A country with a GNP per capita half that of the first country would be assigned a value of 50, and so forth.

For the qualitative variables, such as stability of political institutions, an index-ranking approach can also be used. For example, if this variable is ranked on a basis of 100, the country perceived to have the most stable political institutions would be assigned the highest possible value. Countries deemed to be only half as stable would be assigned a value of 50. And so on for other countries. Clearly, differences in the index values assigned to countries or regions are more arbitrary when they are based upon ordinal measurements to start with—e.g., subjective evaluations of greater or lesser political stability—than when they are based upon cardinal measures. Therefore, the overall index obtained by combining all the individual environmental attributes (expressed as index numbers) must be viewed as a ranking device and not necessarily as a precise measure of how much more desirable one region is than another. Nor is the index a measure of the potential profitability of any one region.

Since the overall index is primarily relevant as a ranking device, the precise scale chosen is somewhat arbitrary; that is, scaling on the basis of 1 to 10 can be as meaningful as scaling on the basis of 1 to 100. What is crucial, however, is determining how a specific variable is related to the overall attractiveness of a foreign region. For example, how does an ''individualistic ethic'' affect prospects in the overall index?

Attempts have been made to develop overall indices of the business environment in foreign markets. To illustrate, an attractiveness ranking developed by Haner, which is based upon index values for a set of human and physical variables, is reported in table 6.4.[22] Haner's index suggests that the developed countries are far more attractive sites overall for international investment than most of the developing countries. In fact, the developed countries tend to score better with respect to most environmental attributes. But within the group of developed countries, the rankings are quite sensitive to weightings given to in-

[22]See Haner, *Global Business Strategy*, p. 26.

TABLE 6.4 Attractiveness Ranking for International Investment, 1985–1989, Based upon a Set of Human and Physical Variables

1. United States	14. Denmark
2. Switzerland	15. New Zealand
3. Germany	16. Argentina
4. Singapore	17. Spain
5. Sweden	18. Israel
6. Australia	19. Brazil
7. Japan	20. Taiwan
8. Netherlands	21. Greece
9. Canada	22. Ireland
10. Norway	23. South Korea
11. U.K.	24. Malaysia
12. Belgium	25. Chile
13. France	

Source: F. T. Haner, *Global Business Strategy for the 1980's.* Copyright © 1980 Praeger Publishers. Reprinted by permission of Praeger Publishers, p. 26.

dividual attributes. For example, Canada would score significantly higher on the scale were less emphasis given to its poor record for strikes and lockouts. This observation emphasizes the importance of designing an index that suits the individual firm. For example, for a highly automated business, labor conditions in overseas markets may be a relatively small concern compared to tax policies for depreciation.

SUMMARY AND CONCLUSIONS

The international manager is fundamentally concerned with human behavior as it affects the demand for his or her firm's output and the costs of producing and distributing that output. To a significant extent, current human behavior and differences in human behavior over time and across markets will reflect the influence of economic stimuli. When properly done, economic analysis should alert management to the potential impacts of economic stimuli on the firm's business activities.

Similarly, human behavior in its impact on the firm will be influenced by the formal and informal political environments in which the firm operates. Legislation and regulations resulting from the political process can directly affect the organization's profitability, or they can motivate behavior that is either helpful or harmful to the firm's prospects in specific market areas. Hence the importance of effective scanning of the political environment.

While not detracting from the importance of scanning economic and political features of the environment, most researchers would agree that human attitudes and behavior will also reflect social values that are not directly linked to economic or political factors. Thus, there is a need to assess cultural values in foreign markets of potential interest and to forecast potential changes in those values as they affect societal preferences. There are various techniques to accomplish the sociocultural assessment and forecasting exercise, including checklists, extrapolation, Delphi, attitude surveys, and multiple scenarios. Cross-impact analysis is a procedure that ties forecasts of emerging social forces to an evaluation of their impacts for the firm. Notwithstanding the availability of various techniques, however, most observers agree that scanning the sociocultural environment remains much more an art than a science.

Some researchers argue that there are too few significant differences in social attitudes and mores—either across cultures or over time—to make the evaluation and forecasting of social forces a worthwhile exercise for the firm. The anecdote of the major breakfast food company that failed in its strategy to sell cereals in Brazil because Brazilians generally do not eat breakfast is one of many examples that might be cited to reject this notion.[23] Another is the major mistake made by the Marlboro Company when it took its famous "lone cowboy" advertisement to Hong Kong in the early 1960s. The image of the cowboy off in the distance by himself led the Chinese to wonder what he had done wrong. The Chinese have no romantic myth of the individual, the self-made person, the cowboy on the lone prairie.[24] Even a modest assessment of cultural attitudes presumably would have prevented such mistakes or at least would have alerted management to the need for "modifying" the ad to meet the tastes of foreign consumers.

DISCUSSION QUESTIONS

1. Discuss and evaluate some techniques for forecasting social change.
2. Imagine that you are the manager of a pharmaceutical company that distributes birth-control pills on a worldwide basis. What specific cultural values and attitudes might you be especially concerned with monitoring as an aspect of formulating corporate strategy?
3. In what ways is the job of social assessment and forecasting more complex for the international firm than for the purely domestic firm?
4. Give some examples of changes in social attitudes in your own country. How quickly did they take place? Were they related to any underlying economic or political developments?
5. Following your answer to question 4, how might international companies doing business in your country be affected by the changes in social at-

[23]These and similar examples are discussed in Steven Globerman and Carolyn Smart, "Strategic Planning in International Business," Simon Fraser University, mimeographed, 1983.

[24]This anecdote is taken from George Renwick, "The Multicultural Company," *Princeton Papers* (October 1983), p. 220.

titudes that you identified? Would you expect the impact on international companies to be different from the impact on purely domestic firms located in your country?

6. What constraints and pressures upon management might limit the firm's commitment to, and effectiveness of, sociocultural assessment and forecasting?

REFERENCES

AGUILAR, FRANCIS J., *Scanning the Business Environment*. New York: Macmillan, 1967.

HOFSTEDE, GEERT, "Culture and Organizations." *International Studies of Management and Organization*, 10, no. 4 (1981), 15–41.

LAMMAS, C. J., AND D. J. HICKSON, EDS., *Organizations: Alike and Unlike*. London: Routledge & Kegan Paul, 1979.

LEE, JAMES A., "Cultural Analysis in Overseas Operations." In Douglas N. Dickson, ed., *Managing Effectively in The World Marketplace*. New York: John Wiley & Sons, 1983.

MAURICE, MARC, ARNDT SORGE, AND MALCOLM WARNER, "Societal Differences in Organizing Manufacturing Units: A Comparison of France, West Germany and Great Britain." *International Studies of Management and Organization* 10 (1981), 74–100.

ROMANO, D. J., AND J. C. HIGGINS, "The Role of Social Forecasting in Business Planning: A Survey of Current Practice." Bradford Management Centre, October 1978.

SETHI, PRAKASH, "A Conceptual Framework for Environmental Analysis of Social Issues and Evaluation of Business Response Patterns." *Academy of Managment Review* 4 (1979), 63–74.

CHAPTER SEVEN

The International Firm and Capital Financing

In chapter 1, we noted that profitable business strategies are generally character-ized by a matching of opportunities in the business environment to the particular competitive strengths of the firm. Conversely, business strategies that require capabilities lying outside a firm's core set of skills are usually recipes for financial disaster. To this point in the book we have outlined a set of approaches to evaluating opportunities and threats in the international business environment. In this chapter and the next we discuss the identification of competitive strengths and weaknesses in the international firm.

Clearly, there are a large number of factors underlying the competitive strengths and weaknesses of different firms. A partial list of factors would include access to low-cost labor or low-cost natural resources; ownership of proprietary technology in the form, say, of patents; superior management; well-known brand-name products; exceptionally cordial relationships with sovereign governments, and so forth. Management should be competent to identify its firm's unique com-petitive advantages in the marketplace and exploit those advantages to the shareholders' benefit. In this respect there is no real difference between managing in the international firm or in the purely domestic firm. However, assessing the firm's competitive strengths and weaknesses is ordinarily a more complex task in the case of the international business. In particular, engaging in international business activities might itself enhance certain competitive strengths enjoyed by a firm in the domestic market while mitigating others.

While this assertion might be illustrated with regard to a number of required business inputs, we will restrict our analysis to the financing and labor-relations activities, since studies indicate that regardless of whatever else a firm has going for it, adequate financing and motivated and efficient employees are generally prerequisites for business success. In this chapter we consider how "going international" affects a firm's ability to acquire the financial capital needed to purchase and deploy productive assets. While purely domestic firms often have access to the same sources of capital as international firms of comparable credit worthiness, the latter confront a somewhat different set of financing opportunities as well as different incentives to exploit international sources of financing.

CAPITALIZING THE FIRM

Traditionally, the issue of how to capitalize a firm amounted to a concern about how to finance the firm's activities at the lowest possible cost. By contrast, contemporary theories of corporate finance recognize that the volume and composition of financing are tied to the volume and structure of assets the firm wishes to hold. Modern theories therefore suggest that financial managers must address three basic questions:

1. What is the volume of assets to be held by the firm?
2. What is the structure of these asset holdings?
3. What is the composition of financing to be used?[1]

While these three questions are closely interrelated and, in principle, should be addressed simultaneously, we will follow the practice of most textbook writers in treating the sourcing and using of capital as separable activities.

It is widely accepted that the primary goal of management should be to maximize the firm's net present value or net worth, defined as the expected flow of all future net cash flows attributable to the firm's assets divided by the required rate of return needed to justify the use of capital and minus the amount of equity capital required to acquire the assets involved. This definition of net worth obliges us to discuss in some detail both the concept of a firm's cost of capital and the components of a firm's capital structure.

COMPONENTS OF CAPITAL STRUCTURE

Financial managers typically face an array of financing alternatives. In broad terms, however, the alternatives fall into two broad categories: debt and equity.

---

[1] An early statement of these interrelated financial management issues is found in Ezra Solomon, *The Theory of Financial Management* (New York: Columbia University Press, 1967).

Debt capital represents financing provided the firm in exchange for a contractual obligation to repay the amount of capital borrowed plus interest, according to a specific time schedule. The lender's claim on the borrower's long-run profits is limited to the amount of the principal and the interest accumulated over the period of the loan. Equity capital represents financing provided the firm in exchange for a share of the company. The equity investor in a firm is essentially a residual claimant, in that his or her payment comes out of the net profits of the firm in the form of dividends that are paid at the discretion of the board of directors.[2]

The potential payback to an equity investor is therefore theoretically unlimited on the upside; however, the equity investor may fail to realize any payback if the firm fails to earn revenues in excess of all operating, administrative, and debt-financing costs. On the other hand, the debt holder's payback is limited on the upside by the contractual interest rate on the issued debt.[3] But the debt holder can institute proceedings against management for failing to adhere to the repayment schedule, and he or she is entitled to first claim on the liquidated value of the borrower's net assets, up to the amount of the outstanding principal plus interest.

THE COSTS OF THE COMPONENTS

The firm's cost of capital is the required rate of return needed to justify the use of capital.[4] Effectively, it represents a cutoff rate for the allocation of capital to investment projects. It can be shown that if management undertakes projects that promise to yield less than the firm's cost of capital, the action will lower the shareholders' net worth. Since capital funds can be sourced in different ways, it is relevant to consider the costs of the two broad categories described above: debt and equity capital.

Cost of Debt

The explicit cost of debt is the discount rate, r, which equates the net proceeds of the debt issue with the present value of interest plus principal payments.[5] For students who have not yet studied finance, I will define present value. It is a monetary measure that effectively expresses future cash flows in terms of an equivalent number of "today's dollars." The use of present value is required to

---

[2] Preferred shares represent a special form of equity capital, in that dividend payments are made so as to provide the investor a specified yield on the share price. Preferred dividends must be paid before any dividends can be disbursed to common shareholders.

[3] We are ignoring here the possibility that the original debt holder will sell the debt instrument for more than he or she paid for it, thereby earning a capital gain and realizing a yield that exceeds the contracted interest rate.

[4] As defined in James C. Van Horne, *Financial Management and Policy*, (Englewood Cliffs, N.J.: Prentice-Hall, 1974), p. 101.

[5] This is the definition provided in ibid., p. 103.

acknowledge the reality that a dollar to be received in the future is worth less than a dollar received today.

As a simple illustration of the cost of debt, assume a company was able to sell a new issue of twenty-year bonds with a 10 percent coupon rate to realize net proceeds (after underwriting expenses) of $1,000 for each $1,000 face-value bond. In this case the before-tax cost of debt (r) is 10 percent. Since interest expenses are deductible from income for tax purposes, a better measure is the after-tax cost of debt (r) defined in equation 7.1:

$$(7.1) \quad r_i = r(1 - t)$$

where t is the firm's marginal tax rate. Thus, the after-tax cost of debt for our hypothetical firm issuing 10 percent bonds and in a 50 percent marginal tax bracket would be 5 percent.

Cost of Equity

For a variety of reasons, the costing of equity capital is a more complicated procedure than the costing of debt capital. While much of the relevant discussion is beyond the limited scope of this chapter, an essential point is that modern capital theory recognizes a firm's cost of equity as being determined in the context of the overall market for equities. That is, the required return on a company's shares is determined by how those shares "fit" into stock portfolios that can be created in the capital markets.

The cornerstone of equity-costing procedures is the well-known capital-asset pricing model. According to this model, the rate of return required by investors on the equity-financed portion of investment projects consists of a so-called risk-free rate and a premium for risk.[6] For practical purposes, the risk-free rate of interest can be thought of as the yield on government Treasury bills. The risk premium is primarily related to the covariance of returns for a given equity issue with those of the entire stock market. The latter relationship is, in principle, a measure of how closely the expected earnings from a given set of assets correspond to the earnings pattern expected from the set of assets held in the general economy.

The lower the expected covariance, the lower the perceived business risk associated with holding a given set of assets and, consequently, the lower the required return on equity capital. The reason is that "low-covariance" assets offer the investor some relief from the vagaries of the business cycle. That is, the anticipated earnings on the investor's portfolio of assets will be more stable, over time, with the inclusion of low-covariance stocks. Since it is presumed that greater stability of earnings is a characteristic valued by investors, low-covariance assets will have a lower cost of equity capital (k_e), all other things the same.

---

[6] A basic overview of the capital asset pricing model is provided in the appendix to this chapter. A more extensive treatment of the model can be found in any finance textbook. For example, see Jack Francis and Stephen Archer, *Portfolio Analysis,* 2nd ed. (Englewood Cliffs, N.J.: Prentice-Hall, 1979), chap. 8.

THE WEIGHTED AVERAGE COST OF CAPITAL

The overall cost of capital for evaluating investment opportunities (or the required return on investment) is (under conditions to be specified) a weighted average of the required returns on debt and equity capital. More formally, it is defined as:

$$(7.2) \quad k = r(1 - t) \frac{D}{D + E} + k_e \frac{E}{D + E}$$

where

r = interest rate paid on borrowings
k_e = required return on equity
D = total market value of debt financing
E = total market value of equity financing
t = the firm's marginal tax rate

Several assumptions underlying the use of this weighted average cost of capital should be made explicit. One is that the proportion of debt $[D/(D + E)]$ and the proportion of equity $[E/(D + E)]$ in the firm's overall capital structure will remain constant as the amount of financing done by the firm increases. A second is that individual investment proposals have identical risk characteristics. This latter assumption is especially treacherous and is more likely (in practice) to be violated than obeyed; however, when deviations from "average" risk characteristics are relatively small, the average cost of capital is probably quite acceptable for use in evaluating individual investment projects.

The "Optimal" Debt-Equity Ratio

Equation 7.2 is a traditional calculation framework for a firm's overall cost of capital. The task for the financial manager is to estimate r and k_e for any mix of debt and equity. This brings the manager squarely up against the issue of whether or not there is an optimal debt-to-equity ratio for the firm; that is, is there some distribution of capitalization that minimizes k, the overall cost of capital? This issue has been the subject of a long and venerable debate in the corporate finance literature.[7]

The traditional position in the debate is that the cost of capital can be influenced by varying the proportions of debt and equity financing employed in the capital structure. This view is summarized in figure 7.1. The key notion embodied in this diagram is that the after-tax interest rate paid on debt is typically below the required return on equity capital. Therefore, as long as the cost of equity is relatively insensitive to the degree of leverage the firm employs, that is,

---

[7] For a thorough overview of this debate, see Nahum Biger, *Finance: A Conceptual Approach* (Toronto: Butterworths, 1981), chap. 8.

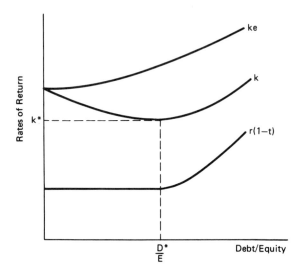

Figure 7.1   Traditionalists' View of Capital Structure and Cost of Capital

the relative amount of debt in the firm's capital structure, the aggregate cost of capital (k) will decline by substituting debt for equity financing.

Since debt represents a contractual burden on the firm, increasing the ratio of debt to equity imposes on shareholders an increasing (financial) risk, so that in the event of unforeseen downturns in corporate revenues, the firm may have to liquidate assets in order to pay contractual claims. Shareholders will expect to receive a higher rate of return on their equity to compensate them for assuming increased financial risk. It might therefore be expected that beyond some point, increases in the cost of equity capital (associated with greater leverage) will outweigh the benefits of employing lower-cost debt capital, thereby leading to an overall increase in the aggregate cost of capital.

The traditional view therefore suggests that the cost of capital will follow a U-shaped pattern when plotted as a function of the debt-to-equity ratio, as shown in figure 7.1. The location of the optimum leverage point—or range—for any given firm will vary with the amount of business risk associated with its operations and with the attitude of investors toward this uncertainty.

A simple example can illustrate the concept of the optimum leverage point. Assume that the after-tax cost of debt is 6 percent, while the cost of equity is 14 percent. For simplicity, assume that the initial debt/equity ratio is 1.0. The overall cost of capital is therefore 10 percent.[8] Now assume the debt/equity ratio increases to 2.0. If the cost of equity remains constant, the overall cost of capital will decline to 8.64.[9] However, if (as a result of the debt/equity ratio rising to 2.0) the cost of

---

[8] The relevant calculation is .5(6) + .5(14) = 10 percent.

[9] Calculated as: .67(6) + .33(14) = 8.64 percent.

equity increases to, say, 20 percent, the overall cost of capital will equal 10.62 percent. The cost of capital might be even higher if the after-tax cost of debt also started increasing with increased leverage. This might happen if potential lenders became concerned about the possibility that the highly leveraged firm would go bankrupt.

The debt-to-equity ratio associated with the lowest average cost of capital for the firm described in figure 7.1 is D/E^*. This means that this firm would find it cheapest to increase its financing in the debt-to-equity ratio given by D/E^*.

The nontraditional view in the debate is taken by economists who maintain that two companies characterized by identical assets, that is, assets offering the same expected net cash flows over time, must have the same total market value (and therefore the same cost of capital) regardless of differences in leverage. According to this view, a firm's cost of capital is independent of its capital structure, abstracting from the fact that interest payments are deductible in computing corporate income taxes while dividend payments are not.

Unfortunately (for practitioners) the issue of the optimal capital structure is unsettled. The empirical evidence suggests that the cost of capital is constant over a wide debt-to-equity ratio and then rises; however, the evidence is by no means conclusive. While the issue is central to determining a firm's capital structure, it is not very important for the practical task of measuring a company's cost of capital. And it is the latter task that occupies most of the attention of financial managers.

The chapter, to this point, reads like a *Reader's Digest* condensed version of a financial management textbook. While not the most enthralling subject matter, the concepts discussed are essential to an understanding of the main issues in international finance. Given the complexity of modern finance theory, we have undoubtedly misrepresented the state of knowledge in the field. However, our limited goal was to provide sufficient background to enable the reader to appreciate how financing decisions differ between the international firm and the purely domestic firm. The patient reader may now realize his or her reward.

INTERNATIONALIZATION AND DEBT FINANCING

We begin our main agenda by considering the impact of internationalization on the cost and availability of debt financing. Credit-worthy firms can often borrow funds abroad, even if their business activities are confined to a single domestic economy. However, holding the issue of credit worthiness constant, it is frequently less risky and less costly for the international firm to obtain debt financing outside of its home-country capital markets.

To expand upon this point, we must recognize that a firm borrowing funds abroad will ordinarily incur liabilities denominated in one or more foreign currencies. As far as the shareholders of the borrowing firm are concerned, the true carrying cost of the accumulated foreign debt is the after-tax interest rate on that debt in equivalent home-currency units. Therefore, the domestic shareholder will be concerned that foreign currencies in which the firm has issued debt may appreciate in value against the home-country currency.

Consider the following hypothetical example. Imagine that a U.S.-based firm borrows £10 million to finance a capital investment in Great Britain. It borrows the funds by floating a bond issue in the London market, which bears an interest rate of 10 percent per annum with a maturity of five years. The firm must therefore make pretax interest payments of £1 million per year for five years and must then retire the debt principal of £10 million. Assume that while the exchange rate at the time of the bond issue was $1.50 U.S. = £1.00, the British pound increases in value to $1.60 U.S. by the time the first interest payment has to be made and that it remains at that level for the next five years. In this case, the firm will have realized the equivalent of $15 million from the bond issue, but the annual pretax interest burden will be $1.6 million and not the $1.5 million anticipated. In addition, the principal repayment will be in the amount of $16 million. Hence, the U.S. dollar-equivalent pretax cost of the £10 million bond issue would be 10.67 percent per annum ($1.6 million divided by $15 million), plus the present value of the $1 million exchange-rate loss associated with the repayment of principal (from $1.5 million to $1.6 million).[10]

This example illustrates the concept of exchange-rate risk associated with borrowing in foreign currencies. At this point, the perceptive reader might interject that interest-rate differentials across domestic capital markets will ordinarily be sufficient to offset any risks associated with adverse exchange-rate movements. For example, if the hypothetical firm in our preceding example faced a domestic interest rate of 19 percent per annum, it would consider the debt issued in British pounds to be a bargain, notwithstanding the appreciation of the pound against the U.S. dollar.

In theory, interest-rate differentials across national credit markets should reflect anticipated changes in currency values as discussed in chapter 3. However, the "market" is frequently wrong in its implied forecasts of future exchange-rate relationships. Management should not assume that interest-rate differentials necessarily compensate for exchange-rate risk associated with foreign borrowings. Many North American managers learned to their sorrow that the "cheap" interest rates in Switzerland and Germany in the mid-1970s were not so cheap after all when interest and principal had to be repaid in Swiss francs and German marks that had appreciated, in some cases, by 30 percent or more against the U.S. dollar.

Exchange-rate risk associated with foreign-denominated debt is therefore a legitimate additional cost of the firm's debt. The potential advantage of the international firm is that it may have future cash flows denominated in the same currency as its foreign debt and, as a result, will not be faced with the same amount of risk as will a purely domestic firm undertaking an equivalent amount of foreign

---

[10] Exchange-rate losses on current and capital expenditures can ordinarily be treated as capital losses.

borrowing. To illustrate this point, imagine that our hypothetical U.S. firm expects to meet its £1 million-per-year interest obligation from earnings in Great Britain, while the repayment of principal will be made by selling the assets acquired with the proceeds of the bond issue. In this case, the firm's pound-denominated debt obligations are hedged, and no additional home-country currency will be required to meet higher payments denominated in British pounds. This will not necessarily be true for firms whose cash flows are entirely denominated in U.S. dollars.[11]

Trizec Corporation is a Canadian-owned company whose borrowing activities further illustrate the points being made in this section. Founded in 1960, the company currently has about 60 percent of its $3 billion in assets in the United States. Borrowing in U.S. dollars for its U.S. operations is part of a corporate policy of matching the terms and nationalities of its money: long-term investments are financed with long-term debt, and Canadian and U.S. projects and operations are financed with Canadian and U.S. funds. The president of Trizec recently stated his belief that all of his company's competitors in the real estate development business have the matching principle as the most critical component of their business plan.[12]

To the extent that international firms find it less risky to borrow abroad, it would be especially advantageous if well-developed capital markets existed outside their home country. In fact, major international capital markets do exist which offer large firms a variety of borrowing options. The most prominent international capital markets are the so-called Euromarket banking centers.

EUROMARKET BANKING CENTERS

Perhaps the most significant institutional development in international finance in the past twenty years is the substantial growth of the so-called Euromarkets. These international capital markets consist of markets for short-term bank deposits and loans (the Eurocurrency market) and for the placement of commercial paper (Eurocredit market) or bonds (Eurobond market).

A Eurocurrency deposit (loan) is a bank deposit (loan) denominated in currencies other than those of the countries in which the issuing banks are located, and the Eurocurrency market is the market for these deposits and loans. Eurocurrency deposits usually take the form of large short-term time deposits, typically in units of $1 million. The bulk of Eurocurrency deposits (around 68 percent) are denominated in U.S. dollars. These U.S. dollar-denominated deposits held outside the U.S. are referred to as *Eurodollars*. In a similar manner, the term

---

[11] To be sure, there are other ways to hedge foreign debt exposure. The point remains, however, that the international firm may be "naturally" hedged as a result of its business activities.

[12] See Patricia Lush, "Trizec Finds Name-Building Speeds Financing in Europe," *Toronto Globe and Mail*, December 2, 1983, p. B1.

Euroguilder refers to deposits of guilders in banks not resident in the Netherlands; the term *Euroyen* refers to deposits of Japanese yen in banks not resident in Japan. And so forth.

The emergence of the Euromarkets can be traced to the growth of U.S. dollar-denominated deposits in banks located outside the United States beginning in the mid-1960s. This dramatic growth is illustrated by the data in table 7.1. Initially, the bulk of the deposits whose growth is described in table 7.1 were made in British banks located in London. Over time, however, subsidiaries of large U.S. banks as well as other European and Japanese banks began to compete aggressively for Eurodollar deposits. At present, major Eurocurrency markets exist in other European capitals besides London as well as in Singapore, Hong Kong, Japan, and several Caribbean countries. Nevertheless, London remains the focus of the Eurocurrency market. It has been estimated that the size of the Eurodollar market in 1985 amounted to around $2 trillion.

Several hypotheses have been put forward to explain the rapid growth of Eurodollar deposits over the 1960s and 1970s. One theory credits the growth to large U.S. balance-of-payments deficits in the late 1960s and early 1970s. These large annual deficits ostensibly led to a considerable buildup of dollar balances held by foreigners, and these dollar balances may well have been invested in European banks rather than sold in the foreign-exchange market. While superficially plausible, researchers have shown that there is no stable statistical relationship linking the growth of the Eurodollar market to the U.S. deficit.[13] Furthermore, persuasive arguments have been made that no theoretical link need exist. For example, a French corporation might convert its franc-denominated cash balances into dollar-denominated deposits without necessarily bringing about a balance-of-payments surplus in favor of France vis-à-vis the United States.

A second and probably more relevant explanation for the growth of the Eurodollar market is restrictions imposed by the U.S. government on the workings of domestic credit markets. For example, until recently, interest-rate ceilings existed on time and savings deposits in the U.S. Furthermore, banks in the U.S. that are members of the Federal Reserve System must keep a certain percentage of their deposits on reserve at their federal reserve bank. These required reserves also restrict the ability of U.S.-based banks to compete by offering higher deposit rates since not all of the deposits taken in can be used to make loans and, thereby, earn income. On the other hand, Eurobanks are largely exempt from reserve requirements and interest ceilings on the Eurodeposits. As a result, the latter can afford to pay higher interest rates on deposits.[14]

---

[13] See Gunter Dufey and Ian Giddy, *The International Money Market* (Englewood Cliffs, N.J.: Prentice-Hall, 1978).

[14] For a historical overview of the development of the Eurocurrency markets, see Ronald McKinnon, *The Eurocurrency Market*, Essays in International Finance, no. 125, Princeton University, December 1977. In the past few years, the major federal restrictions on the interest rates that banks can pay depositors have been eliminated.

TABLE 7.1   Growth of the Eurocurrency Market

YEAR	NET SIZE ($ BILLIONS U.S.)	RATE OF GROWTH OF NET SIZE (PERCENT)
1966	21	23
1967	25	19
1968	34	36
1969	50	47
1970	65	30
1971	85	31
1972	110	29
1973	160	45
1974	215	34
1975	250	16
1976	305	22
1977	355	15

Source: Gunter Dufey and Ian Giddy, *The International Money Market* (Englewood Cliffs, N.J.: Prentice-Hall, 1978), p. 108.

Borrowing in the Euromarkets

The Eurocurrency bank-loan market is now the most important source of international bank financing, providing more than half of the medium- and long-term borrowing in the international capital markets. Most transactions are between banks acting for their clients. However, large international companies also borrow funds in the Eurocurrency market. The size of individual loans varies from several million to several billion dollars, with maturities extending from one to fifteen years. Most loans are made by syndicates of banks in order to spread the risk of default among a number of lenders.

The growth in Eurobank lending, illustrated by the data in column 4 of table 7.2, also largely reflects restrictions imposed on the U.S. banking system in the 1960s. For example, guidelines were imposed in 1965 on American commercial banks that limited the amount of foreign loans they could book. And in 1968 a requirement was imposed that American multinational corporations raise funds for direct investment outside the U.S. Both of these measures were introduced to prevent further flow of U.S. dollars abroad, which would aggravate the hemorrhage of dollars that was already taking place as a result of expenditures on the Vietnam War. But perhaps the greatest stimulus to the development of the international capital markets was the interest equalization tax introduced by President Kennedy in 1963, which imposed a substantial levy (in the form of a withholding tax) on sales of foreign bonds and equities in the U.S. As seen in the third column of table 7.2, the international bond market has grown substantially since the early 1960s.

The commercial-paper market consists of short-term debt obligations issued

TABLE 7.2   Funds Raised on International Markets ($ millions U.S.)

YEAR	TOTAL FUNDS	INTERNATIONAL ISSUES OF BONDS	INTERNATIONAL MEDIUM- AND LONG-TERM BANK LOANS
1972	19858.3	6933.6	8672.6
1973	30865.0	4208.8	20826.3
1974	40828.4	3396.1	28521.9
1975	42648.5	8742.6	20607.2
1976	63021.9	14705.2	28442.4
1977	70255.9	18724.3	34197.9
1978	111158.2	14960.7	73804.6
1979	119926.2	18690.7	79327.6
1980	120762.9	20394.2	80953.7
1981	200552.5	31294.1	91263.3
1982	178927.5	50328.6	90750.5
1983	157613.2	50094.5	60216.6

Source: OECD, *Financial Market Trends*, 28 (June 1984), 53–68. The difference between column 1 and the sum of columns 2 and 3 represents short-term international bank loans.

by large commercial banks and corporations. Typically, the promissory notes issued mature in three or six months from issue date and are priced to offer yields slightly above the London Inter-Bank Offer Rate (LIBOR). Most commercial paper issued in Euromarkets is denominated in U.S. dollars. And owing to a tax loophole discovered by lawyers for the Security Pacific Corporation, commercial paper is exempt from the U.S. government's 30 percent withholding tax on interest paid to foreigners.

The overseas bond market has two components: the Eurobond (or international) market and the foreign bond market. Foreign bonds are those issued by a borrower in a foreign country but denominated in the currency of the lending country and underwritten and sold by a national underwriting and selling group of the lending country. For example, a Canadian company might float a bond issue in Switzerland, underwritten by a Swiss syndicate and denominated in Swiss francs. The bond issue will therefore be traded in the Swiss domestic capital market.

In contrast, Eurobonds are deliberately offered for sale in more than one country simultaneously, through international syndicates of underwriting and selling banks. The critical distinction between the two markets, therefore, is that Eurobonds are marketed in countries other than the country of the currency in which they are denominated. As a result, Eurobonds are not subject to national restrictions, such as financial disclosure laws. Another advantage to investors is the fact that Eurobonds are almost always in bearer form, which means that the holder's identity can be kept confidential from the tax authorities, among others.

As shown in table 7.3, Eurobonds (indicated in the table as international issues) are typically denominated in U.S. dollars, while the bulk of foreign bonds

TABLE 7.3   International and Foreign Bond Offering ($ billions U.S.)

	1982	1983
International issues	50.33	50.10
Foreign issues	25.20	27.05
Total	75.33	77.15
International issues by currency		
U.S. dollar	42.23	39.23
Deutsche mark	3.25	4.04
ECUs	0.82	2.19
Sterling	0.84	2.15
Canadian dollar	1.20	1.07
Dutch guilder	0.62	0.75
Yen	0.60	0.23
Other	0.77	0.44
Total	50.33	50.10
Foreign issues by market		
Switzerland	11.32	13.50
United States	6.02	4.73
Japan	3.32	3.85
Germany	2.11	2.62
Netherlands	0.85	0.93
United Kingdom	1.13	0.85
Other	0.45	0.57
Total	25.20	27.05

Source: OECD, *Financial Market Trends*, 28 (June 1984), 54.

are underwritten in Switzerland. Most international bond issues are denominated in a single currency. However, a small (but growing) number of issues are denominated in a composite of national currencies, such as the European Currency of Account (ECUs). The main feature of multiple-currency bonds is the diversification advantage to the lender, who can request payment in a contract currency that has appreciated most (or depreciated least) against his or her home currency. With this advantage, multiple-currency bonds often carry lower interest rates than single-currency bonds.[15]

Implications for the Cost and Availability of Debt

It is time to bring together the various strands we have been weaving in regard to the cost and availability of debt capital to the international firm. To this

[15] For a thorough discussion of the international bond market, the reader should consult Yoon S. Park, *The Euro-Bond Market: Function and Structure* (New York: Praeger Publishers, 1974). A more up-to-date description is provided in Harvey Poniacheck, "International Financial Markets," in Ingo Walter and Tracy Murray, eds., *Handbook of International Business* (New York: John Wiley & Sons, 1982), chap. 18.

point, we have argued that the international firm might enjoy a lower effective cost of debt owing to lower exchange-rate risk associated with foreign-currency-denominated debt. Given the opportunity to issue dollar-denominated debt in the Euromarkets, this may not be a major consideration for U.S. firms. However, it may well be an important concern for many non-U.S. firms, especially when interest rates in the international capital markets are lower than those in domestic capital markets.

For non-U.S. based firms, borrowing rates in Eurobanking centers are quite likely to be lower than in domestic capital markets. In part, this is due to the fact that international capital markets are more competitive than the cartellike arrangements of many domestic banking systems.[16] There is also evidence that lenders in the Eurobond market are more innovative than lenders in European domestic capital markets. For example, the former seem more receptive to new types of debt instruments, such as convertible bonds, that enable corporate borrowers to shave debt costs.[17]

Technically minded economists would identify debt markets in various countries as being "segmented." This simply means that the risk-adjusted costs of debt are not equal in all national debt markets. Non-U.S. firms, in particular, may be in a position to benefit from lower costs of borrowing if they can tap into the Eurocredit markets. In addition, access to international markets provides firms with a source of funds in times of domestic credit rationing. While terms for equally credit-worthy borrowers should be comparable in the Euromarkets, international firms may have an advantage over purely domestic firms in Euromarket borrowing. Besides a lower exchange-rate risk, which is relevant when Euromarket borrowing is done in foreign-denominated debt, international firms ordinarily enjoy a higher "visibility" among foreign lenders. This is a potentially important advantage in the Euromarket, where debt ratings have not permeated the investment community as they have in the U.S.

While most observers acknowledge that the U.S. domestic capital market is highly competitive, there are still advantages to American firms that can borrow in the international (or Euro-) capital markets. Until recently, foreigners had to pay a 30 percent tax on the interest they earned from owning U.S. securities, if those securities were issued in the U.S. However, large U.S. companies—such as Coca-Cola and Texaco—were able to set up offshore subsidiaries to issue bonds for sale on European capital markets. As a result, their bond issues escaped the 30 percent withholding tax. This enabled companies such as Coca-Cola and Texaco to borrow at lower rates than their small, purely domestic rivals. Indeed, Coca-Cola estimated that the 12.81 percent yield on a recent Eurobond issue was a full percentage point less than the company would have had to pay in the United States.[18]

---

[16]For a discussion of this point, see McKinnon, *The Eurocurrency Market*, p. 20.

[17]Some evidence on this point is provided in "Hybrids That Buy Eurobonds," *Business Week*, August 3, 1981, p. 78.

[18]See Fred Bleakley, "U.S. Dropping Investment Barrier," *Toronto Globe and Mail*, July 16, 1984, p. B5.

The Tax Reform Act of 1984 effectively repealed the 30 percent withholding tax, thereby eliminating this specific advantage enjoyed by large international companies. As a result, many observers expect a substantial increase to occur in domestic borrowing by U.S. companies relative to overseas borrowing. Whether this tax change can offset other remaining advantages of overseas and offshore capital markets, including anonymity, absence of red tape, and—in some cases—no domestic income taxes on lending institutions remains to be seen.[19] As long as U.S. and overseas debt markets are segmented, at least to some extent, international firms headquartered in the U.S. should enjoy certain advantages in raising debt capital compared to small, domestically oriented businesses.

GOVERNMENT FINANCING ASSISTANCE

In the preceding section, we suggested that large international companies enjoy easier access to international debt markets than their smaller, purely domestic counterparts do. In a very deliberate sense, we were vague about whether the easier access is due primarily to the international activities of a firm or to its large size. To some extent, the distinction is immaterial, since most large firms also engage in international business. However, there are large firms, such as public utilities, that do business in a single country yet also borrow funds in the Euromarkets.

On balance, it seems fair to conclude that both large size and an international presence ease a firm's access to international capital markets, although the impact of either attribute has not been persuasively quantified. However, the impact of engaging in international business on a firm's access to debt capital is quite a bit clearer when it comes to government financial assistance. Specifically, there are sources of low-interest government loans and loan guarantees accessible to firms doing business abroad (especially through foreign affiliates) that are not accessible to purely domestic firms.

For example, the Export-Import Bank of the U.S. is an independent government agency that plays a key role in the financing of U.S. exports. Short-run financing programs are based on the export credit insurance program, which enables exporters to obtain or offer prospective buyers better financing. More specifically, the Export-Import Bank offers insurance against commercial and political risks on debt obligations acquired by banks from U.S. exporters. This protection allows banks to charge lower rates to borrowers who require temporary financing of their export sales.

The Export-Import Bank also has long-term programs designed to promote the export of specific U.S. products, most notably capital equipment. These programs include direct credits to overseas buyers and financial guarantees to elicit

---

[19]With no income taxes, lending institutions might be willing to accept lower yields than U.S. banking institutions, whose income is taxed; however, strict microeconomic theory would refute this assertion.

long-term private-sector lending. In many cases these two types of assistance are blended together, thereby allowing foreign public- and private-sector importers, as well as U.S. exporters, access to funds at lower interest rates and for longer maturities than are generally available in the commercial sector.[20]

In recent years the Export-Import Bank has lent money in support of a range of business activities including cotton sales to Japan, communications-equipment sales to Peru, and the sale of nuclear power plants to South Korea. But the single largest beneficiary of the bank's funding activities has been the Boeing Corporation, which received almost $3 billion in credits and loan guarantees in 1981 alone.

Another important U.S. government agency offering financial assistance to international businesses is the Overseas Private Investment Corporation (OPIC). Operating as a component of the International Development Cooperation Agency, OPIC makes direct loans to help finance start-up projects or expansions of existing projects that involve significant U.S. equity participation. These loans usually range from $200,000 to $3 million, but OPIC will guarantee loans made by private U.S. financial institutions up to a maximum of $50 million for any one project. It also offers financial assistance for preinvestment activities such as feasibility studies and investment missions to developing countries. In addition, the insurance that OPIC offers against such political risks as expropriation and inconvertibility of currency serves as an indirect subsidy to firms with overseas assets.

The United States is certainly not the only country that subsidizes the international business activities of domestically owned firms, as indicated by table 7.4. For example, the Export-Import Bank of Japan provided some form of official support for $56 billion worth of exports in 1980. The British, French, German, and Canadian governments—the latter through the Export Development Corporation—are also quite generous in their support of international business.

The increasing competition among sovereign governments to promote the overseas sales of their national companies has become a major issue in intergovernmental economic relations. But as the president of Canada's Export Development Corporation pointed out, much of the potential new export business for international companies is concentrated in a few major areas, in particular the Pacific-rim and Middle Eastern countries.[21] With a relatively large number of companies vying for the business of a fairly small number of customers, it is not surprising that the latter are able to demand and extract financial concessions. Nor is it surprising that the former seek (and often rely upon) financial assistance from their respective government to remain competitive in those areas.

---

[20] A comprehensive description of the Export-Import Bank and other government agencies providing financial assistance to international business is found in Jonathan Menes, "Government Aids and Services," in Walter and Murray, eds., *Handbook of International Business,* chap. 10.

[21] See Hyman Solomon, "Export Financing Deals Are Made Easier," *Financial Post* (Toronto), 12 (November 19, 1983), 1-2.

TABLE 7.4   Value of Exports Supported by Government Credit and Insurance Programs, 1980 ($ billions U.S.)

COUNTRY	AMOUNT
Japan	$56
United Kingdom	43
France	35
U.S.	19
West Germany	14

Source: Marilyn Much, "How the U.S. Has Stumbled in Export Finance," *Industry Week*, January 10, 1983, p. 38.

For large U.S. companies, the availability of government financial support for overseas business activities is welcome but perhaps not essential, given the extensive availability of long-term debt capital in U.S. domestic capital markets. However, many European companies face great difficulty in borrowing at fixed interest rates for longer than five to ten years into the future. Hence, government subsidies of one sort or another are seen by managers of European-based international companies as essential to compete against North American-based companies.

INTERNATIONALIZATION AND EQUITY FINANCING

The relationship between "going international" and a firm's access to equity capital can perhaps best be evaluated by recalling the three main characteristics that influence a firm's cost of equity capital: the risk-free rate, business risk, and financial risk. All three characteristics were discussed earlier in the chapter. The issue that confronts us in this section is whether any or all of these characteristics vary depending upon the geographical distribution of a firm's business activities.

While this issue is not easily or obviously resolved with respect to any one of the characteristics mentioned, it is probably safe to say that the risk-free rate of interest confronting shareholders of a purely domestic firm equals the risk-free rate confronting shareholders of an international firm, where (for practical purposes) the uniform risk-free rate is the yield on short-term government debt. Unfortunately, matters become less simple when considering business risk.

As noted in chapter 2, business cycles are not perfectly synchronized across different countries. As a result, a firm doing business in a number of countries can be expected to have an earnings profile that varies less systematically with home-country business-cycle conditions than would a company doing all of its business in the home country. However, if home-country investors can—cheaply and efficiently—assume minority shareholding positions in a wide range of foreign-based companies, any geographic diversification provided by a single company's international business activities may be redundant. That is, investors can presumably realize any desired geographical diversification of their wealth simply by calling their stockbrokers. In this case investors will not reward the international firm with a lower cost of equity. On the other hand, if equity capital markets are segmented, for example, by high information costs or by restrictions on portfolio investments outside the home country, the opportunities for geographic diversification provided by international companies may be highly valued by investors, and this should be reflected in a lower cost of capital for the international firm.

Whether or not business risk is lower for the international firm therefore boils down to an empirical question of whether or not there are significant barriers to efficient international investing. One often hears anecdotes about how undiscovered "bargains" were found lurking on foreign stock exchanges, which if true to any great extent, would signal the existence of barriers to efficient international equity investing. An example sometimes cited to support the argument that information about foreign equities is highly imperfect is Novo Industries, a Danish producer of enzymes. One U.S. portfolio manager claims to have made his reputation by discovering Novo in 1980 before a single research report had been written in the U.S. on the company. The price of the company's shares went up six-fold following the portfolio manager's purchase.

There is an obvious danger in placing too much emphasis on such "war stories," since portfolio managers are especially prone to publicizing their successes while burying their failures. More reliance should be placed on statistical studies that draw upon large samples of companies. In this regard, there is some evidence that multinational companies are rewarded with a lower cost of equity capital than purely domestic companies.[22] However, the available studies are plagued by theoretical and empirical difficulties, which makes it difficult to generalize about the impact of internationalization on a firm's cost of equity capital.

In some cases there are clear legal restrictions that prevent institutional investors from making extensive investments in foreign securities. For example, Canadian pension funds are prevented from holding more than 10 percent of their assets in the form of foreign securities.[23] Thus, they are quite restricted in their ability to invest in, say, Exxon or Gulf Oil in the United States. However, they can—if they wish—hold more than 10 percent of their assets in the bonds or common stock of Imperial Oil and Gulf Canada, the Canadian subsidiaries of these two U.S. companies. Such legal restrictions offer one plausible rationale for why investors may not be able to achieve a desired degree of geographic diversification through portfolio investment.

The third characteristic—financial risk—refers to the potential for fixed

[22] For a review and discussion of some relatively recent studies, see Marjorie Thines Stanley, "Capital Structure and Cost-of-Capital for the Multinational Firm," *Journal of International Business Studies* (Spring/Summer 1981), pp. 103–20.

[23] More specifically, tò qualify as a registered retirement savings plan, and thereby gain tax-exempt status for the funds deposited in the plan as well as for the income on the funds deposited, pension fund investors must obey the so-called 10 percent basket clause.

financial obligations to claim all of the net cash flow of an organization, thereby depriving equity shareholders of the opportunity to receive dividends or to build further equity in the corporation. In the extreme, debt obligations that are not serviced can result in a company's bankruptcy.

While financial risk is traditionally associated with leverage, as discussed earlier, shareholders in the international firm may be exposed to unique sources of financial risk, including direct or indirect government restrictions on dividend payments to parent-company shareholders. Indirect restrictions often take the form of local currency inconvertibility, as in the reputed case of several U.S. multinational oil companies, which in the 1960s held on to pound balances instead of converting those balances to dollars, in order to "help" the Bank of England in

CASE STUDY: *IT'S NOT NECESSARILY WHAT YOU KNOW,*
IT'S WHO KNOWS YOU—THE CASE OF NOVO INDUSTRI A/S

On July 8, 1981, Novo Industri A/S, a Danish multinational firm in the industrial enzyme and pharmaceutical field, became the first Scandinavian firm to sell equity through a public issue in the U.S., as well as the first to list on the New York Stock Exchange. This culminated an intense four-year program on the part of Novo's management to internationalize the company's sources of capital.

Novo's management believed that the Danish capital market was "segmented." Specifically, management believed that the cost of equity capital was lower in other capital markets than in the Danish market. Furthermore, management was concerned that the relatively small Danish stock market could not absorb the large amount of equity the company would need to sell in order to finance its long-range growth strategies.

There were several reasons underlying the belief that lower-cost equity capital could be raised outside the Danish capital market. One was a perception that more favorable tax treatment for bond investments in Denmark made it necessary to offer relatively high (by international standards) required returns on equities. Another was the belief that international investors would perceive Novo's shares as a vehicle to increase their portfolio diversification, and, as a result, would require lower rates of return on those shares than would Danish investors, other things being equal. A relevant concern, of course, was whether Danish stocks would be seen by foreigners to carry more "financial" risk than their own domestic securities, thereby offsetting any diversification benefits realized by including Novo's shares in their portfolios.

Novo took a number of steps to make its equity offering attractive to North American investors. For example, the company sponsored an American Depositary Receipts (ADR) system in the U.S. Under this system, a U.S. bank or trust company holds a given number of underlying foreign securities. Then they issue American Depositary Shares (ADS) against these securities. The ADS may be issued at a different price than the underlying shares to bring the price into a range more usual for

Source: Arthur I. Stonehill and Kare B. Dullum, *Internationalizing the Cost of Capital* (Chichester, England: John Wiley & Sons, 1982). Reproduced by kind permission of John Wiley & Sons Ltd.

U.S. companies in the same or similar industries. This was the çase with Novo's shares, which were split five for one in the U.S. market by issuing five times as many ADS as the underlying Danish kroner shares held in the bank.

The ADR system offered two important advantages to U.S. shareholders: (1) they received dividends paid in dollars rather than kroner, and they could trade the securities in dollars rather than kroner. As a result, exchange-rate risk was reduced, and (2) shareholders could transfer securities physically in the U.S. rather than abroad. Transactions costs to U.S. shareholders were further reduced by Novo's adoption of English as its official corporate language and by amending the company's accounting principles to meet U.S. general accounting principles.

Stonehill and Dullum provide persuasive evidence that Novo's cost of equity capital did, indeed, decline after it made its shares available for trading in the U.S. stock market. The liquidity of the company's shares also increased, as witnessed by a sharp increase in the average trading volume in Novo's shares. The two researchers caution, however, that merely listing on foreign exchanges will not necessarily guarantee a lower cost of equity capital. The secret is to offer an unusual investment opportunity and tailor equity shares to suit the unique characteristics of foreign equity markets.

its fight to maintain the value of the pound.[24] While relatively infrequent, the most serious international financial risk is the potential for shareholders' assets to be seized by hostile foreign governments.

Shareholders in international companies therefore face certain financial risks that shareholders in purely domestic companies do not face. The magnitude of these additional risks depends upon the nature of a firm's international activities. Specifically, international financial risk will reflect the macropolitical and micropolitical risks associated with a firm's foreign business ventures. As we noted in an earlier chapter, these risks are very difficult to quantify.

OTHER CONSIDERATIONS

The extent and nature of a firm's international business activities may also affect the firm's ability to retain earnings for reinvestment. This would be true, for example, if international firms enjoyed lower effective tax rates than their purely domestic counterparts did. In fact, the emphasis of many national governments to boost export sales in an effort to promote job creation has resulted in tax legislation that in many cases treats foreign-earned income more favorably than income earned domestically.

In the U.S., for example, the Foreign Sales Corporation (FSC), enacted as part of the Deficit Reduction Act of 1984, grants tax incentives to exporters. The

[24] David Eiteman and Arthur I. Stonehill, *Multinational Business Finance*, 2nd ed. (Reading, Mass.: Addison-Wesley Publishing Co., 1979), p. 170.

FSC was developed by the U.S. government as a replacement for the Domestic International Sales Corporation (DISC), which a number of other countries claimed violated GATT rules against export subsidies. Under the new regulations, export sales must be made through a foreign sales corporation incorporated outside U.S. territory. Generally, 15 percent of the FSC's export income will be exempt from federal taxation. To qualify for the FSC benefit, certain management activities of the corporation, such as shareholder meetings, must take place outside the U.S. The principal bank accounts of the FSC must also be abroad, and all dividends must be paid from that account. Additionally, 50 percent of the direct costs of a specified set of activities, including advertising, the processing of customer orders, and transportation, must be incurred outside the U.S.[25]

Other features of government tax codes as they apply to multinational companies are too complex for us to treat in any detail in this introductory book. Suffice it to say, certain features of the U.S. tax code have been criticized as favoring the multinational company. In particular, the Internal Revenue Code specifies that foreign earnings can be taxed only when they are repatriated. The U.S. parent pays no U.S. tax on the earnings of its foreign subsidiaries if they are retained abroad. Of course, increased retained earnings in foreign affiliates constitute a source of equity capital for the multinational firm's international business activities. Clever management and pricing of interaffiliate payments can also transfer funds back to the parent company without triggering a tax obligation in the U.S. For example, an affiliate can make funds available to the parent by delaying the collection of accounts owed by the parent for goods and services received from the affiliate. Other techniques for moving funds within the multinational firm will be discussed in later chapters. The main point to note is that these techniques provide financing flexibility to the international firm as well as gargantuan incomes for the international finance and tax experts who develop and refine them.

INTERNATIONALIZATION AND ACCESS TO CAPITAL
—IMPLICATIONS FOR MANAGEMENT

The preceding discussion suggests that the impact of a firm's international business activities on its overall cost of capital is highly uncertain and depends upon the precise nature of those activities. Nevertheless, it seems fair to conclude, on balance, that the international firm has greater access to debt capital (and possibly to equity capital) than the purely domestic firm. A potentially important implication is that the international firm may find it easier than the purely domestic firm to maintain its optimal debt-to-equity ratio as it expands its capital budget. If so, the net impact of this improved access to international capital

---

[25] This description of FSC is taken from "Policy and Legislation," *International Business Review*, vol. 3 no. 6(May 1984).

markets is a possible reduction in the marginal cost of capital (*MCC*) for the international firm.

This argument can be further developed with reference to figure 7.2. The *MCC* function represents the incremental (or marginal) cost of each additional dollar of capital financing done by the firm. Looking back at figure 7.1, we see that if the firm increases its capitalization with a ratio of debt to equity given by D^*/E, its cost of capital should remain constant at approximately k^*, other things constant. This is illustrated in figure 7.2: the *MCC* curve for the international firm (*MCC$_I$*) remains flat over a wide range of budget commitments. On the other hand, if a purely domestic firm must borrow more than would be dictated by its optimal debt/equity ratio, say because it does not have access to low-cost sources of debt capital available to the international firm, the *MCC* curve for the domestic firm (*MCC$_D$*) will increase (beyond some point) with additional budget commitments and corresponding needs for additional financing. Hence, beyond some point, financing the expansion of a purely domestic firm may become more expensive than financing the expansion of an international firm in essentially the same line of business.

The *MRR* curve in figure 7.2 represents the expected rate of return to an additional dollar of capital invested by the firm. It is presumed to be downward sloping, since firms will invest in higher yielding projects initially before moving on to more and more marginally profitable investments. The capital budget (or commitment of capital) that maximizes the net worth of a company is determined at the point where *MRR* = *MCC*. For the international firm, this implies a capital budget of K_I, while the optimal capital budget for the purely domestic firm is K_d. The implication is that, all other things constant, the international firm can profit-

Figure 7.2   Cost of Capital and Financial Structure
David K. Eiteman and Arthur I. Stonehill, *Multinational Business Finance*, 2nd edition (Reading, Massachusetts: Addison-Wesley Publishing Co., 1979), p. 364.

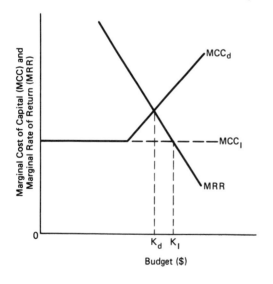

ably undertake a greater number of capital investments than the purely domestic firm.[26] We hasten to add, of course, that the international firm must carefully evaluate any specific project's expected profitability relative to its cost of financing, since any one project may be dissimilar to other investment projects undertaken by the firm.

SUMMARY AND CONCLUSIONS

An important competive attribute of any firm is its access to financial capital. One summary measure of a firm's relative financial strength is its cost of capital. The main theme of this chapter is that a firm's international business activities may affect its cost of capital as well as its access to financial capital. Therefore, in evaluating their firm's competitive strengths and weaknesses along the dimension of financing capacity, international managers face a more complicated task than do managers of purely domestic firms.

While it is not possible to be precise about how "going international" affects a firm's financing capabilities, it would seem that international businesses, on average, enjoy easier access to both debt and equity markets than their purely domestic counterparts. In particular, the international firm that invests abroad is often eligible for a variety of low-interest funds from host-government and multilateral agencies that are not available to the purely domestic firm. Also, institutional investors abroad may be legally able to invest in debt and equity securities of foreign subsidiaries, although they cannot invest in the securities of the parent companies. The impact of a firm's international business activities on its financing capabilities is therefore related both to government policy and to the segmentation of national capital markets.

Perhaps the most significant institutional development in the international financial markets over the post-World War II period has been the development and growth of Euromarket banking centers. This development can be seen as a partial response to restrictions on the free flow of capital between national capital markets. As a result, a number of international financial centers have emerged in which financial intermediaries (most notably, affiliates of large multinational banks) can operate largely free of restrictions on deposit-taking and lending activities imposed by government authorities and central banks.

In principle, the Eurocurrency and Eurobond markets are accessible to both international and purely domestic companies of a minimum size and credit worthiness. In practice, however, international firms may be more familiar to Eurobank lenders and therefore deemed to be more credit worthy. Furthermore, most Euromarket lending is done in U.S. dollars. Companies based outside the U.S. but earning income denominated in U.S. dollars are therefore less exposed to exchange-rate risk than their purely domestic rivals. This feature lowers the former group's effective cost of debt.

---

[26] This analysis is taken from Eiteman and Stonehill, *Multinational Business Finance*, pp. 362–66.

DISCUSSION QUESTIONS

1. Define the components of a firm's cost of capital. Give some reasons for why you agree or disagree with the traditional assumption that the cost of capital will have a U-shaped relationship when plotted against the firm's debt-to-equity ratio.
2. Explain how a firm's cost of capital might be influenced by the extent and nature of its international business activities.
3. In recent years, major brokerage companies such as Merrill Lynch have created mutual funds for investing in foreign securities, notably in European and Japanese companies. Do you think the creation of these funds has (or has not) affected the cost of equity capital for U.S. multinationals? If it has, in what way?
4. What are the main factors influencing the cost of equity capital? Discuss how a specific investment by firm X in a less developed country might affect each of the factors identified?
5. Discuss the significance of the development and growth of the Eurobanking centers to international businesses.
6. Distinguish among: Eurocurrency markets, Eurobond market, foreign bond market.

REFERENCES

AGMON, TAMIR, and DONALD R. LESSARD, "Investor Recognition of Corporate International Diversification," *Journal of Finance*, 22 (September 1977), 1049–55.

ARDITTI, FRED, and HAIM LEVY, "The Weighted Average Cost of Capital as a Cutoff Rate: A Critical Analysis of the Classical Textbook Weighted Average," *Financial Management*, 6 (Fall 1977), 24–34.

COLLINS, J. MARKHAM, and WILLIAM S. SEKELY, "The Relationship of Headquarters Country and Industry Classification to Financial Structure," *Financial Management*, 12 (Autumn 1983), 45–51.

MEHRA, RAJNISH, "On the Financing and Investment Decisions of Multinational Firms in the Presence of Exchange Risks," *Journal of Financial and Quantitative Analysis* (June 1978), pp. 227–44.

ROBBINS, S. M., and R. B. STOBAUGH, *Money in the Multinational Firms.* New York: Basic Books, 1973. A classic study.

RODRIGUEZ, R. M., and E. E. CARTER, *International Financial Management*, 2nd ed. Englewood Cliffs, N.J.: Prentice-Hall, 1979.

APPENDIX 7A: AN OVERVIEW
OF THE CAPITAL-ASSET PRICING MODEL (CAPM)

For more than two decades, the CAPM has been the focal point for financial theorists concerned with how corporate securities are priced in the capital markets. The conclusions of the CAPM are dependent upon several assumptions: (1) capital markets are efficient, in the sense that the price of each security closely approximates its correct equilibrium value; (2) well-informed investors keep the prices of securities from diverging away from their equilibrium values; (3) investor valuation of securities prices is positively related to the expected return on the security and negatively related to the riskiness of the security. The investor is assumed to measure return per period as the appreciation in share price plus dividends received over the period. Risk is assumed to be measured as the statistical variance of the price of a security.

Under these assumptions, it is demonstrated that:

(A1) $k_e = \beta(R_m - R_f) + R_f$

where

k_e is the cost of equity to the firm
R_m is the return on the total market for equity securities
R_f is the risk-free rate of return

Beta (β) is a measure of the volatility of the equity security with respect to the return on the total market for equity securities. Specifically, it is equal to the covariance of the return of the security with respect to the return on the market (σ_{em}) divided by the variance of the return on the market (σ^2_m) as in equation A2:

(A2) $\beta = \sigma_{em}/\sigma^2_m$

Substituting A2 into A1, we get:

(A3) $k_e = R_f(1 - \sigma_{em}/\sigma^2_m) + R_m(\sigma_{em}/\sigma^2_m)$

Traditional financial analysis also assumes that changes in the debt-to-equity ratio of a firm's capital structure affect the perceived riskiness of the firm's securities. That is, a higher debt-to-equity ratio will be associated with a higher beta, other things the same.

Source: Equations A1 through A3 and the associated discussion are taken from a more extensive description of the cost of capital found in Edward M. Graham, ''Multinational Firms and the Cost of Capital,'' in John S. Oh, ed., *International Financial Management: Problems, Issues and Experiences* (Greenwich, Conn.: JAI Press, 1983), pp. 114-15.

CHAPTER EIGHT

Human Resources and the International Company

In most businesses, personnel costs amount to between 60 and 80 percent of the total costs of doing business. Obviously, if human resources are not managed effectively and efficiently, the typical company has little hope of successfully meeting its corporate objectives. In this regard, several international business experts have argued that the primary causes of failure in multinational ventures stem from a lack of understanding of the essential differences in managing human resources.[1]

All organizations face a difficult and sensitive task in carrying out key personnel decisions, including personnel planning, administration, and control; however, this task is substantially more complex for the international firm, primarily because of the more diverse environment in which international businesses operate. For example, language differences can distort communications between corporate headquarters and overseas affiliates, thereby impeding the ability of headquarters management to motivate, direct, and monitor the performance of overseas personnel. Moreover, in some societies remuneration may not be a strong motivating force, while in other societies it will be. Hence, cultural differences can result in specific employee-motivation programs succeeding in certain countries while failing dismally in others.

[1] See R. L. Desatnick, and M. L. Bennett, *Human Resource Management in the Multinational Company* (Westmead, England: Grover Press 1977), p. x.

Differences in the international political environment also complicate the task of managing human resources. For example, labor practices that are legal in some countries may be illegal in others. Furthermore, in some countries government bureaucrats may intervene actively in the day-to-day operations of affiliates, whereas in other countries affiliate managers may be given comparatively free rein to make decisions in the interests of the company's shareholders. The labor-relations function in the international company must therefore be sufficiently flexible to accommodate different sociopolitical environments. At the same time, headquarters management must ensure that minimal standards of performance are being met by all foreign and domestic affiliates.

In this chapter we focus our attention on how ''going international'' can affect personnel administration, including the selection, development, and compensation of employees. We leave to chapter 15 a discussion of how the international company might deal with the issue of personnel control, that is, ensuring that the pursuit of individual self-interest in the organization does not subvert the achievement of broad corporate goals. In the first part of the chapter, we consider issues particularly relevant to selecting, developing, and compensating managerial personnel. We then consider issues surrounding the management of nonsupervisory personnel in international business.

MANAGERIAL PERSONNEL

Many observers believe that a shortage of trained managers is the most serious economic problem confronting the less developed countries. At the same time, the magnificent salaries earned by many upper-level managers in North America suggest that talented managers are a scarce resource everywhere. Given the skills allegedly required of effective international managers, they are likely to be an especially rare breed. For example, consider one observer's description of the characteristics possessed by the ideal international executive:

> . . . a flexible personality, with broad intellectual horizons, attitudinal values of cultural empathy, general friendliness, patience and prudence, impeccable educational and professional (or technical) credentials—all topped off with immaculate health, creative resourcefulness, and respect of his peers. If his family is equally well endowed, all the better.[2]

It is difficult to imagine anyone who could satisfy all of the criteria listed in this idealized portrait. Certainly most companies would settle for less. Nevertheless, most observers agree that staffing executive positions in international companies is a substantially more demanding task than in purely domestic companies. In particular, international managers must have a greater breadth of

---

[2] See Jean E. Heller, ''Criteria for Selecting an International Manager,'' *Personnel*, 57 (May-June 1980), 46.

knowledge than their purely domestic counterparts, including an understanding of the economic, social, and political life in countries other than their own. This requirement ordinarily obliges the international organization to hire managers from both inside and outside its own country, which imposes the unique need to coordinate a multinational mix of managers. Coordinating a multinational mix of managers, in turn, often forces the human-resources manager to make difficult trade-offs between different sets of management skills.

EXECUTIVE-STAFFING ALTERNATIVES

In the international firm, managerial personnel can be classified as belonging to one of three possible groups: parent-company nationals (PCNs), host-country nationals (HCNs), and third-country nationals (TCNs). The first group are drawn from the home country of the international organization. The second group (in any country) are recruited from that country, with their most typical assignments being to manage in a subsidiary located in that country. The third group of managers are typically recruited from affiliates located in other countries or from areas where the firm has no presence.

As Heenan and Perlmutter note, there is an important element of arbitrariness in determining who is a ''foreign'' manager and who is a ''domestic'' manager in a worldwide company, since as a company expands internationally, the ''home country'' is not home for an increasing number of executives.[3] Furthermore, a constant reference to the nationality of executives could lead to a perception among some groups of managers that they are second-class citizens in the international organization. This perception, if not dealt with, poses a grave liability to the global enterprise.

In fact, while distinctions among managers based solely on geographic location can be extremely dysfunctional, there tend to be unique benefits and costs associated with selecting managers from the headquarters country. Similarly, there are unique benefits and costs associated with selecting managers from outside the headquarters country. Specifically, PCNs are typically best acquainted with the objectives and operating procedures of the global organization. Furthermore, they are often most knowledgeable about the management and engineering techniques being put in place in the various international affiliates and divisions of the company. On the other hand, in any country, managers drawn from the local labor force are typically best able to build satisfactory relationships with the local affiliate's stakeholders, including governments, labor unions, and suppliers. Indeed, more and more governments are pressuring multinational companies to hire local managers for responsible executive positions in the international

---

[3] David A. Heenan and Howard V. Perlmutter, *Multinational Organization Development* (Reading, Mass.: Addison-Wesley Publishing Co., 1979), p. 61.

organization. Another consideration is that it is typically more costly to staff affiliates with PCNs than with HCNs and TCNs.[4]

Ethnocentric Staffing Problems

Ethnocentrism has been defined as the expression of parent-company attitudes and the application of parent-country standards at overseas affiliates.[5] An ethnocentric staffing policy, then, is characterized by a general preference for using PCNs to fill senior management positions in overseas affiliates, and to reward PCNs more generously for their work. In some cases, ethnocentrism might reflect simple prejudice on the part of headquarters management. In other cases, it might reflect a lack of knowledge about the availability of capable managers in other countries. Whatever the cause, it can be expected that an ethnocentric human-resources program will create problems in the organization. For example, HCNs are likely to feel frustrated about limited promotion opportunities and about their perceived need to conform to headquarters-style management procedures and mores. But even stronger grievances will likely center on the superior salaries and fringe benefits earned by PCNs.

Besides the grievances created among non-PCN managers, an ethnocentric policy can inflict undue hardships on PCN managers, to the extent that the latter are involved in frequent and extended overseas tours of duty. PCN (and even TCN) managers frequently express anxiety about transfers, especially regarding their unfamiliarity with the local environment.

Executive Expatriation

Once transferred abroad, managers frequently exhibit inappropriate leadership style, especially nonparticipatory decision making, in trying to reconcile their behavior to both headquarters requirements and the needs of their subordinates. It has also been found that new expatriate managers in well-established overseas subsidiaries have a tendency to promote short-range, low-risk, quick-result-type projects in an effort to demonstrate their competence in unfamiliar surroundings. Indeed, their concern with demonstrating competence to headquarters management frequently results in their covering up mistakes and censoring downward flows of information.

Ironically, a successful adjustment to an overseas posting is often associated with anxiety and trauma experienced by PCNs when they return to their home country. Upon their return, PCNs frequently have to accept a cut in their salaries and a loss in fringe benefits. They may have to buy a new house, often at a much higher price than they sold at because of inflation. Readjustment to life styles at

---

[4] These dimensions are discussed in Yosup Lee and Laurie Larwood, ''The Socialization of Expatriate Managers in Multinational Firms,'' *Academy of Management Journal,* 26 (1983), 657–65.

[5] See Howard Perlmutter, ''The Tortuous Evolution of the Multi-National Corporation,'' *Columbia Journal of World Business,* 5 (January–February 1969), 9–18.

home is traumatic, not only for the returning employee but also for the entire family. The family often experiences a loss of status after being used to "club-life" living and affordable live-in domestic help.

The returning expatriate will perhaps experience the greatest difficulty in readjusting to the head-office corporate structure. He or she may find that while away, new and unfamiliar people have reached the top positions in headquarters. Often, returning expatriates experience a feeling of loss of independence, since while abroad they enjoyed much greater decision-making authority. Managers living abroad also frequently hobnob with people in an elite social stratum not usually accessible in the home country. These elite often include senior managers from the home country who occasionally tour their overseas affiliates.

All of the above problems can cause the repatriated executive to exhibit dysfunctional behavior or even to leave the organization to join a competitor. Also, other suitable candidates for overseas assignments will be disinclined to accept those assignments after they see such negative effects on their colleagues.

One way for companies to minimize the costs and inefficiencies of poorly executed relocation decisions is to incorporate "adaptability screening" into their selection and orientation programs for overseas transfers. Companies using adaptability screening generally take into account two factors in measuring a family's suitability for life abroad: its success in handling similar transfers within the home country and its reaction to discussion of the stresses that life in a foreign country will entail. Trained psychologists are often employed to carry out the screening interviews.[6] Such interviews typically last one or two hours and cost about $100. Since it can cost between $20,000 and $30,000 to move a family overseas, adaptability screening can be an extremely cost-effective program, even if it only saves a company one or two bad transfers a year. Furthermore, evidence suggests that adaptability screening combined with culture-orientation programs can reduce expatriate attrition rates by up to 75 percent.

Problems associated with repatriating managers can also be reduced by planning for repatriation before an executive departs the home country. One expert recommends a four-phase program for dealing with repatriation:

1. Planning expatriation—overseas position is classified, and possible repatriation problems are assessed.

2. Pre-expatriation—purpose of the foreign assignment, career plans, and the traumas of repatriation are discussed with the candidates.

3. Expatriation—expatriate's performance is evaluated from time to time, thereby allowing two-way communication with corporate headquarters and serving as a motivational factor.

4. Readjustment—expatriate is assisted in readjusting to domestic life through reorientation programs, financial counseling, and so forth.[7]

[6] See "Gauging a Family's Suitability for a Stint Overseas," *Business Week*, April 16, 1979, 127.

[7] This approach is discussed in Michael Harvey, "The Other Side of Foreign Assignments: Dealing with the Repatriation Dilemma," *Columbia Journal of World Business* (Spring 1982), pp. 53–59.

It is also recommended that international companies employ individuals to look after expatriates' affairs (predeparture training, communication with expatriates, and repatriation). As an example, Exxon assigns each expatriate a "contact person" in the home country, someone he or she can talk to apart from the people the expatriate reports to in the normal course of business. The creation of a position in the personnel department of the firm to deal with international executives should result in more effective personnel planning and alleviation of morale problems experienced by those executives.

Promoting Executive Mobility

The problems associated with expatriating and repatriating PCNs and (to a lesser extent) TCNs can be substantially reduced through appropriate staff and training policies and creative compensation programs. Researchers have found that international companies employing more rigorous and well-defined training and selection methods for overseas assignments have a lower failure rate of expatriates than companies displaying less concern in this area.[8] In particular, studies stress the importance of "relational abilities" of expatriates, as well as their family situations. Relational abilities refer to an expatriate's capacity to understand and operate in another culture, which includes some degree of fluency in the local language.

Several researchers have distinguished between factors necessary to ensure success and those necessary to avoid failure. For example, Hays identifies technical competence in the job as a prerequisite for success, relational abilities as important for achieving success, and an adaptive and supportive family as a prerequisite for avoiding failure.[9] A number of other factors have also been suggested to improve an expatriate's on-the-job performance. One is the expatriate's ability to find good substitutes for the recreational and cultural activities he or she pursued at home. Another is an ability to develop friendships with host-country nationals. The expatriate's confidence and willingness to use the host culture's language also have an influence on successful adjustment. Finally, an important piece of emotional luggage, experienced dispatchers of expatriates say, is a sense of humor.

While it is unclear whether expatriate managers can be socialized in foreign values and concepts prior to their assignments outside the parent affiliate, many experts suggest that predeparture training be given the expatriate manager, including an area-studies program (history, geography, politics, and so forth, of the country in question), language training, sensitivity training (developing attitudinal flexibility of the candidate), and field experience (sending the candidate

---

[8] See, for example, Rosalie Tung, "Selection and Training of Personnel for Overseas Assignments," *Columbia Journal of World Business*, 16 (Spring 1981), 68–78.

[9] Richard Hays, "Expatriate Selection: Insuring Success and Avoiding Failure," *Journal of International Business Studies*, 2 (1971), 40–46.

to the country in question or to a microcosm of the foreign culture in the home country).

Another suggested way to develop an individual's relational abilities vis-à-vis foreign cultures is to enroll the executive in a management-development program in an overseas institution, for example, INSEAD in France or IMEDE in Switzerland. This allows executives to interact with managers of other cultural backgrounds and to develop contacts among important opinion leaders in foreign countries.

Volvo Car Corporation, part of Sweden's giant AB Volvo group, recently implemented an interesting management-training program. A select group of high-ranking managers were given an eight-month leave from their jobs to take up temporary positions in other companies around the world. These included Volvo Car subsidiaries and sales companies, as well as outside companies such as Renault in France, Hughes Aircraft and American Motors in West Germany, and a major Belgian bank. The objective of the program was to broaden the managers' experience and expose them to new cultures, different companies, and alternative production and management methods. The initial program was considered sufficiently successful so that similar programs were scheduled for the future.[10]

OTHER STAFFING APPROACHES

The problems associated with an ethnocentric approach to executive staffing suggest that alternative approaches should be carefully evaluated. These include polycentric, regiocentric, and geocentric approaches to managing international business activities. In a polycentric organization, local nationals occupy virtually all the key positions in their respective local affiliates. Headquarters management essentially allows local managers almost full autonomy over their local operations.

The regiocentric approach emphasizes the recruitment and assignment of managers on a regional basis. This approach is sometimes accompanied by establishing multiple headquarters, such as IBM's decision to dissolve its world trade headquarters in New York and replace it with two international headquarters—IBM Europe (in Paris) and IBM Americas/Far East (in New York). In the geocentric organization, the company takes a global view of the selection and utilization of managers. Executive expertise is recruited on a worldwide basis without regard to nationality.

Each of these alternative staffing approaches has its own strengths and weaknesses. For example, a polycentric approach allows for an intensive exploitation of local knowledge about the immediate economic, political, and sociocultural environments. HCNs presumably best understand the ways of their own countries,

---

[10] The program is described in George Bickerstaffe, "A $1 million Training Investment to Meet the Challenge of the 1990s," *International Management,* 36 (July 1981), 33.

and they should be able to function most effectively in the host-country environment. Furthermore, staffing with HCN executives might encourage a more favorable attitude toward the international firm among host-government authorities. On the other hand, an intensive use of local managerial talent may insulate the affiliate from an awareness of global trends. This was the concern that encouraged Volvo to implement the management-training program described above.

The regiocentric and the geocentric approaches, especially the latter, tend to bring an increasingly ''global'' outlook to the management of the company's various affiliates. Thus, they enhance the likelihood that the best available managerial talent will be employed and that policies consistent with global corporate objectives will be implemented. However, these benefits come at the potential expense of greater unfamiliarity with specific environments in which the company operates. The regiocentric and geocentric approaches also carry a greater risk that affiliate managers will not interact well with host-government officials, and therefore that unfavorable political actions may be taken against the international firm's activities in specific countries.

All three alternative staffing approaches suffer from a common shortcoming that is especially acute in the case of rapidly growing, technology-based companies. Namely, specific corporate skills and managerial philosophies may be extremely difficult to transfer from head office to local affiliates without also transferring head-office managers. This may be the case, at least in part, because these skills and philosophies are ingrained in the corporation's ''culture.'' That is, they must be acquired in the process of managing at the head office. It is also often the case that few managers outside the home country have the technical background to assume specific managerial responsibilities without training under the tutelage of head-office managers.

Training employees drawn from developing areas to use modern technology (including management techniques) efficiently is obviously a more difficult proposition than training employees drawn from developed countries. Some experts argue that the most difficult task is to induce local managers to accept the efficient organization of effort as a focus of their managerial responsibilities. The international firm must therefore be prepared to provide managers not only with an in-depth understanding of the global organization's policies and practices but often with an intensive training in professional management.

STAFFING BY STAGES

While a geocentric approach toward executive selection and placement is in some sense a theoretical ideal, very few international businesses actually employ such an approach. In many cases, the conditions appropriate for implementing a geocentric approach do not yet exist, especially given the ethnocentric and polycentric pressures that often exist in the home and foreign environments of multinational companies. The preceding discussion suggests that for most companies an evolutionary approach to overseas staffing may be preferable, where the specific approach chosen is sensitive to the age and stage of development of the international business. A specific elaboration of this theme is provided by Lawrence Franko's survey of twenty-five European and U.S. multinationals, the main results of which are summarized in table 8.1.[11] Franko identified four stages that a multinational company goes through: export, initial foreign manufacturing, poststartup/growth stage, and area-headquarters stage.

In the export stage, international businesses rely on sales forces made up of foreign personnel (HCNs) to carry out the marketing function. In the initial foreign manufacturing stage, these firms (now technically multinational companies) send PCN expatriates to the subsidiaries for the start-up period. In the poststart-up/growth stage, U.S. multinational companies begin to replace expatriates with HCNs, while in European multinationals the very top positions are retained by PCNs. In the fourth stage, area headquarters (regiocentric approach) are put in place by companies that adopt a strategy of extending a limited product line around the globe. In this last stage, a realignment of subsidiaries occurs. Subsidiary heads (HCNs) are replaced by PCNs in order to ensure global standardization of the multinational's goals and products. After this realignment occurs, HCNs and PCNs are again used to fill top subsidiary positions.

OTHER STAFFING CONSIDERATIONS

The approach to staffing outlined in table 8.1 suggests a general approach based upon the stage of development of the international company. Of course, there may be specific circumstances that dictate a departure from this general pattern.

TABLE 8.1   Staffing-Policy Stages

STAGE	STAFFING CHARACTERISTICS
1. Exporting	1. Sales forces are made up of HCNs.
2. Foreign manufacturing	2. PCN expatriates are employed for start-up.
3. Poststart-up: growth	3. U.S. companies begin to replace PCNs with HCNs; European companies retain PCNs.
4. Area headquarters	4.
(a) Realignment	(a) HCNs replaced by PCNs.
(b) Postalignment	(b) HCNs used to fill top affiliate positions; TCNs are also used.

Source: Lawrence Franko, "Who Manages Multinational Enterprises?" *Columbia Journal of World Business*, 8 (Summer 1973), 30–42.

[11] See Lawrence Franko, "Who Manages Multinational Enterprises?" *Columbia Journal of World Business*, 8 (Summer 1973), 30–42.

For example, specialized management positions may continue to be filled by TCNs simply because qualified local managers are not available. This was the situation faced by the large Italian company Montedison in the early 1980s.

In 1982, in a last-ditch effort to avert financial disaster, Italy's hard-pressed chemical giant, Montedison, began importing foreign—notably American—managers. Montedison chairman, Mario Schimberni, went overseas to fill key jobs, from strategic planning to managing the company's pharmaceuticals, dyestuffs, and oil operations—the battle horses that Schimberni hoped to ride to profitability in the future.

The basis for the staffing strategy was explained by Schimberni: "I had to change the mentality here to a profit mentality from one of waiting for the Italian state to bail out the company. This is a provincial welfare mentality that has built up over the past ten years. I needed proven outside leadership in specific sectors such as fine chemicals. I couldn't find what I needed in Italy, so I went abroad."[12]

In a related fashion, HCNs are used to a much greater extent at all levels of management in developed regions of the world, as compared to the less developed regions, since the developed nations have a larger pool of individuals possessing the necessary managerial and technical skills to staff executive positions. As a case in point, the Chinese government recently approved plans to import foreign managers to take control of some of China's ailing industries. Skilled foreigners will be invited to serve as advisers or to take over directorships of various industrial enterprises.

PCNs may be kept in management positions abroad to gain international experience and to facilitate coordination and control within the multinational organization. Furthermore, transfers of PCNs from headquarters to subsidiaries and of TCNs between subsidiaries (and to headquarters) help to reinforce a shared international ideology, which in turn assists in maintaining coordination among subsidiaries. In many large international companies—such as Ford, Coca-Cola, and Dow Chemical—putting in time abroad is increasingly a required and critical step in a manager's progress up the corporate executive ladder. A major reason is that these companies believe the personal qualities that enable an executive to negotiate his or her way through a job overseas—an ability to understand the position of others and a capacity to make decisions even in the face of extreme uncertainty—are precisely those qualities needed for senior positions at corporate headquarters. An expatriate tour has therefore become in many companies a screening process for determining whether an executive has the capacity to perform as an upper-level manager.[13]

Some insight into the relative importance of these and other determinants of staffing the international firm is provided in a comprehensive survey of the ex-

[12] See "Recruiting Foreigners to Rescue Montedison," *Business Week*, November 7, 1982, p. 45. It might be noted parenthetically that the strategy was seemingly successful, since by 1984 Montedison was a profitable company.

[13] For a further discussion of this point, see Walter Kiechel, III, "Our Person in Pomparippu," *Fortune*, October 17, 1983, p. 213.

ecutive selection and training procedures in U.S., European, and Japanese multinational companies. The findings of the survey are summarized in table 8.2. For U.S. companies, the most important reasons mentioned for staffing with PCNs were (1) the foreign enterprise was in a start-up phase; and (2) technical expertise was lacking in the host country. These were also among the most important reasons cited by European multinationals for staffing with PCNs. In addition, the European firms cited the goal of developing an internationally oriented management for headquarters. For the Japanese sample, the most important reason given for staffing with PCNs was that the parent-country national was the best person for the job.

Familiarity with the host-country culture and knowledge of the local language were the two most important reasons cited by U.S. and European multinationals for staffing with HCNs. In addition, U.S. multinationals mentioned lower costs and good public relations. The Japanese multinationals again reported that they staffed with HCNs when the latter were the best people for the job.

Both U.S. and European multinationals emphasized that TCNs were selected because they were the best people for the job. A need to import technical

TABLE 8.2   Motives for Staffing—Results of a Survey

REASONS CITED AS MOST IMPORTANT FOR STAFFING WITH:	
PCNs	
U.S. multinationals	1. Foreign enterprise in start-up phase
	2. Technical expertise
European multinationals	1. Management development
	2. Technical expertise
	3. Foreign enterprise in start-up phase
Japanese multinationals	1. PCN best person for job
HCNs	
U.S. multinationals	1. Familiarity with culture
	2. Knowledge of language
	3. Reduced costs
	4. Good public relations
European multinationals	1. Familiarity with culture
	2. Knowledge of language
Japanese multinationals	1. HCN best person for job
TCNs	
U.S. multinationals	1. TCN best person for job
European multinationals	1. TCN best person for job

Source: Rosalie L. Tung, "Selection and Training Procedures of U.S., European, and Japanese Multinationals," © 1982 by the Regents of the University of California. Reprinted from *California Management Review*, Vol. XXV, No. 1, pp. 57–71, by permission of the Regents.

expertise was also cited by American companies as an important motive for staffing with TCNs. On the other hand, Japanese multinationals rarely used TCNs.[14]

The use of PCNs, HCNs, and TCNs in senior management positions varies among different firms. For example, Japanese multinational companies employ considerably more PCNs in their overseas operations than do U.S. and European multinationals. Until recently, however, top managerial positions in overseas affiliates of most firms have been occupied by PCNs.

MANAGEMENT COMPENSATION

One of the touchiest issues in international human-resource management is the establishment of reward systems that are widely seen to be fair and that fulfill the function of motivating employees. In principle, performance-appraisal and compensation mechanisms should be free of ethnocentric bias. That is, evaluative techniques should blend the best available approaches from around the world, and compensation should be based upon performance, irrespective of nationality. In practice, there are substantial difficulties associated with implementing a geocentric approach toward performance appraisal and compensation.

One such difficulty is that, historically, companies headquartered in the United States felt a necessity to pay PCN managers relocated abroad more than comparable HCN managers, since management incomes in the U.S. were substantially above those elsewhere. Hence, even given the lower cost of living in many foreign countries, the ''opportunity costs'' of American managers necessitated payment of substantial salaries and ''hardship'' bonuses for tours of duty in foreign affiliates.

The cost of using parent-country managers in affiliates of U.S. multinational companies escalated sharply with the passage of the Tax Reform Act of 1976. Hailed in the U.S. as a step in halting the privileged treatment of ''pampered'' executives ''living it up'' overseas, the bill sharply increased the income tax burden on American managers working overseas.

The impact of the Tax Reform Act is suggested by the following statistic. In the 1960s and early 1970s, the rule of thumb was that to assure an executive assigned overseas the same standard of living he or she enjoyed in the U.S., foreign compensation had to be 50 percent greater than the executive's compensation in the U.S. By the late 1970s, the required compensation differential had increased to 100 percent or more. Predictably, U.S. multinationals began to substitute HCNs for PCNs in their overseas affiliates. In Belgium, for example, the U.S. business population shrank from about six thousand executives to less than three thousand over the period from 1977 to 1979.[15]

---

[14] Full details of this survey are reported in Rosalie Tung, ''Selection and Training Procedures of U.S., European and Japanese Multinationals,'' *California Management Review*, 25 (Fall 1982), 57–71.

[15] As discussed in Thomas A. Byrnes, ''U.S. Executives Abroad: A Vanishing Breed,'' *Dun's Review* (August 1980), pp. 89–91.

While American managers are still very well paid by worldwide standards, foreign salaries have recently been rising faster than salaries in the U.S. By some measures, Swiss and German managers are better paid than their American counterparts. As background, table 8.3 reports recent data on compensation levels for middle- and upper-middle managers.

While the data in table 8.3 give the impression that international salary differences can be precisely estimated, the cash-compensation figures reported are, at best, a rough assessment of how well managers in different countries are rewarded. For example, while the Japanese executive's salary is modest by American standards, Japanese companies pay up to 50 percent of interest charges on mortgages for all employees, including managers. As an executive moves up the Japanese corporate ladder, his company provides him with a car and a chauffeur, a larger expense account, and membership in exclusive golf clubs and country clubs known as "castles."[16]

Outside the U.S. and especially in high-tax jurisdictions such as Holland, Belgium, and Australia, companies typically emphasize payment in noncash prerequisites. For example, a Mexican executive earning the equivalent of $25,000 a year will have a company-supplied car and chauffeur, along with a specified amount of groceries and liquor delivered to his home twice monthly. In some countries, as much as 50 percent of executive-compensation packages are in noncash forms.

CASE STUDY: *VOLKSWAGENWERK'S COMPENSATION POLICIES
FOR HCN MANAGERS*

Volkswagenwerk is a well-known German auto company with subsidiaries in various countries including Belgium, France, Brazil, Mexico, the U.S., Canada, and South Africa. It incorporates a number of factors into the determination of an optimum salary range for overseas managers. These factors are taken into account in its so-called balance-sheet approach illustrated in the table.

The basis for the company's overseas compensation is the German base salary that would be paid for a comparable position in the country of transfer (number 1). Then a general overseas allowance is added on, regardless of the place of assignment. In this hypothetical illustration, it is assumed to be 15 percent of the base salary. At the place of assignment B, where working and living conditions are less attractive, a "conditions-of-living" allowance of 10 percent of the base salary is granted. This allowance can vary from country to country, but it will be zero in areas with condi-

Adapted from P. Frerk, "International Compensation: A European Multinational's Experience." Reprinted from the May 1979 (vol. 24) issue of *Personnel Administrator*, copyright 1979, The American Society for Personnel Administration, 606 North Washington Street, Alexandria, Va. 22314.

[16] This discussion of the components of executives' salaries in different countries is taken from Lisa Miller Mesdag, "Are You Underpaid?" *Fortune*, March 19, 1984, pp. 22–23.

Volkswagen's Balance-Sheet Approach

SALARY COMPONENTS	SUMS IN DM PER MONTH	
	PLACE OF TRANSFER A	PLACE OF TRANSFER B
1. Basic Salary, DM	4,500.00	4,500.00
2. Overseas Allowance (15% of Base Salary)	+ 675.00	+ 675.00
3. Conditions of Living Allowance (In % of Base Salary Depending on Country)	—	+ 450.00
4. Cost-of-Living Allowance	+ 600.00	− 150.00
5. Residence Allowance	+ 400.00	− 100.00
6. Overseas Gross Salary (Before Taxes)	6,175.00	5,375.00
7. Assumed Taxes in Germany (On Base Salary)	−1,200.00	−1,200.00
8. Contribution to Company Pension Plan	− 333.00	− 333.00
9. Statutory Payments in Country of Assignment	—	+ 200.00
10. Net Sum Paid Out to Individuals During Overseas Assignment (After Taxes)	4,642.00	4,042.00

Source: Peter Frerk, "International Compensation: A European Multinational's Experience," *The Personnel Administrator*, 24 (May 1979), 33.

tions similar to those in Germany. Adjustments for cost of living (number 4) and residence (number 5) reflect the assumption that they are higher/lower in A/B than in Germany.

The total of the components from numbers 1–5 is the overseas gross salary (before taxes) in number 6. The basic rule that personnel should not obtain any tax advantge or disadvantage from an overseas assignment may be complied with by deducting the assumed German taxes on the base salary (number 7)—which would have been payable if working in Germany—from the overseas salary. At the same time, the company pays all taxes due overseas. A further deduction is made for the German company's pension plan (number 8). Finally, the statutory payments in the country of assignment must be taken into account (number 9). For example, Social Security payments must be made in location B. These contributions are reimbursed by the company on the presumption that the expatriate is unlikely to collect the Social Security benefits. The net amount paid overseas is shown in number 10. The individual receives the full amount, since Volkswagen pays the associated income tax.

While the procedure outlined in the table appears to be quite mechanical, it actually requires a good deal of judgment, especially regarding the values of adjustments for cost-of-living differences. Volkswagen also attempts to ensure that the salaries of its expatriates fit into the social structure of the host country. This often obliges the company to offer promotions to expatriates (along with higher corresponding salary classifications) to balance off generally lower local salary levels.

TABLE 8.3 Total Cash Compensation for Executives (in thousands)

COUNTRY	YEAR	MIDDLE MANAGERS		UPPER MIDDLE MANAGERS	
		BEFORE TAX	AFTER	BEFORE TAX	AFTER
United States	1983	$65.0	$54.1	$112.0	$85.1
($12.5)	1981	58.0	49.1	112.0	88.5
	1979	44.0	38.5	96.0	74.8
Switzerland	1983	73.7	55.2	130.9*	91.6
($17.2)	1981	68.1*	51.4	125.6*	88.4
	1979	N.A.	N.A.	N.A.	N.A.
West Germany	1983	58.0	41.0	117.4	70.9
($13.5)	1981	56.5	40.6	120.5	72.9
	1979	62.4	43.2	124.2	74.3
France	1983	49.0	43.9	89.3	74.9
($12.1)	1981	53.4	47.9	N.A.	N.A.
	1979	55.5	49.3	93.4	77.8
Canada	1983	48.6	36.9**	80.2	55.7**
($11.2)	1981	46.5	35.5**	82.2	56.8**
	1979	33.5	27.1**	57.6	42.5**
Brazil	1983	40.9	27.1	79.2	42.7
($2.2)	1981	33.7	23.2	67.7	41.5
	1979	N.A.	N.A.	N.A.	N.A.
Italy	1983	40.1	30.1	58.6	42.6
($6.8)	1981	37.4	28.4	63.0	43.6
	1979	30.5	23.9	55.5	41.4
Australia	1983	38.6	24.9	63.9	34.9
($11.2)	1981	25.3	18.4	43.7	26.9
	1979	N.A.	N.A.	N.A.	N.A.
Spain	1983	33.9	27.4	51.6	38.1
($5.8)	1981	38.6	30.5	60.1	42.3
	1979	40.1	31.4	71.6	47.5
United Kingdom	1983	33.2	26.0	58.8	41.0
($9.0)	1981	33.5	26.0	57.6	40.4
	1979	33.7	26.5	58.9	41.0
Japan	1983	29.6*	25.6	39.0*	31.8
($10.3)	1981	29.8*	26.0	39.3	32.5
	1979	27.1*	24.3	36.0	30.3
Mexico	1983	28.6*	15.9	65.2*	33.7
($2.3)	1981	61.4*	31.0	149.4*	72.0
	1979	N.A.	N.A.	N.A.	N.A.

Source: *Fortune*, March 19, 1984, p. 22. The number shown in the parenthesis under the name of the country is the per capita GNP in thousands for 1981. The Hay Group for compensation figures; TPFC for after-tax calculations; Population Reference Bureau for latest 1981 per capita GNP figures.

Fortune estimate.

**Includes Ontario Provincial.

The foregoing observations underscore another difficulty in implementing a geocentric compensation program. Namely, nationality, economic, and cultural differences across countries often necessitate regional modifications to compensation approaches. For example, it is argued that Americans seem to care more about cash, while executives elsewhere seem to focus more on how they live or are seen to live. Since they do not face such cultural complexities, purely domestic firms have a much less difficult job in designing and implementing "equal pay for equal work" reward systems.

Another relevant complication in implementing a geocentric compensation program is that the amount of time worked by executives differs across countries. Whereas American executives tend to take three or four days' vacation at a time, European and Latin American executives enjoy their four-to-six-week holidays. Other "quality-of-life" differences may also be inadequately captured in converting pecuniary compensation to a U.S. dollar equivalent, as is done in table 8.3. This point is made succinctly in the following comment of Ove Sundberg, president of KemaNobel, Sweden's largest chemical company, whose salary in 1983 was $130,000: "We love living in Sweden. Taxes are a nuisance, but we live a decent life. You can only eat one steak a day anyway."[17]

MANAGING NONMANAGERIAL PERSONNEL

Up to this point we have focused on issues concerned with staffing and managing executive positions in the international firm; however, the majority of employees in any company are typically not middle- or upper-level managers. Therefore, the particular complexities associated with managing line employees in overseas companies are also of vital concern to international management.

A growing number of management-consulting experts are stressing that effective personnel management is a critical ingredient to the success of any organization. The authors of the best-selling book *In Search of Excellence,* in assessing the success of Japanese companies over the past three decades, concluded: "Treating people—not money, machines, or minds—as the natural resource may be the key to it all." This view tends to be supported by Japanese executives themselves, one of whom notes: "We are very different from the rest of the world. Our only natural resource is the hard work of our people."[18]

A number of the special complexities associated with managing managers in the international context are also relevant to managing other personnel. For example, determining levels of compensation and working conditions is typically more difficult in the international firm than in the purely domestic firm, for reasons described earlier in the chapter. However, the labor-relations function in

---

[17] Ibid., p. 25.
[18] See Thomas J. Peters and Robert H. Waterman, Jr., *In Search of Excellence* (New York: Warner Books, 1982), p. 39.

the international firm is rendered especially complicated by the fact that firms operating in different countries must deal with a number of different unions and observe collective-bargaining practices and labor legislation unique to individual countries. In other cases, multinational firms confront International Codes of Conduct, which influence their behavior toward employees across a range of labor practices.

The Codetermination Process

One very important feature of the international labor environment is the emphasis that governments and labor unions have increasingly placed on involving employees more directly in the corporate decision-making process. This so-called codetermination movement has arguably had its greatest impact in Europe. Indeed, most European countries have (to a varying degree) rules and regulations on codetermination. The specific legislation varies from country to country, but the general thrust of the process can be illustrated with reference to the German experience.

The German mining and steel industries were the first to come under codetermination in the Works Constitution Act of 1952. The act, as amended in 1972, governs codetermination by the employees in the companies in which they are employed by works councils elected by them. These works councils, consisting of employees of the company, have extensive rights in many areas related to personnel administration, including establishing criteria for hiring, firing, promoting, and laying off workers.

Another key element of the codetermination system is the supervisory board, which has responsibilities for general policy decisions within the firm. It is composed of five stockholder representatives, five employee representatives, and one neutral person elected by a majority vote of the other ten members. This board has the task of electing the members of the management board, which in turn is responsible for day-to-day business operations. The management board usually consists of three executives, at least one of whom must receive the vote of the majority of the employee members of the supervisory board.[19] The practical implication of this codetermination structure is that management is required to share information with workers on a larger number of issues than is the case for North American companies, as well as to consult and share decision making on a broad range of specific operational issues.

Partly as a result of codetermination legislation, the ease with which management can hire and (especially) fire or lay off workers is much more constrained in European countries than in North America. This condition is also the result of a seemingly greater preference for stability and continuity in employment

[19] For a full description of the German codetermination process, see Trevor Bain, "German Codetermination and Employment Adjustments in the Steel and Auto Industries," *Columbia Journal of World Business*, 48 (Summer 1983), 40–47. Also, see Johannes C. Welbergen, "Codetermination In Europe," in *International Management Newsletter*, 8 (February 1985), 2–3.

relations on the part of both European managers and workers. For example, in the German steel and auto industries, the employment relationship is much less the "employment at will" system followed in the U.S. and much more the lifetime-employment approach characteristic of major Japanese companies. But unlike the procedure in Japan, where agreements are implicit, in Germany all levels of employees, including managers, sign a contract with the company that can be terminated only by mutual agreement.

The relative success of the West German economy and, to a greater extent, the Japanese, over the postwar period has led some observers to argue that labor-relation practices in these two countries should be transplanted to other affiliates of the international company, including plants in North America. Whether such transplantation can or should take place is a question that may only be answerable over time as multinationals from Japan and other countries increase their business activities in North America. However, there are certain employment practices, especially in Japan, that are not widely admired. Specifically, large Japanese firms employ many smaller firms in subcontracting roles. During business downturns, the burden of making employment layoffs is transferred to these smaller subcontractors. Another feature of the Japanese labor market that is inconsistent with North American principles is the apparently widespread exploitation of female workers. To a much greater extent than North American women, Japanese women are constrained to take menial jobs. In many cases, they make less than a third of what males doing similar jobs get paid.

One labor-relations practice where substantial differences apparently exist between the North American affiliates of Japanese-owned companies and their domestically owned counterparts relates to management's attitudes toward other employees. For example, in comparing his experience as general manager of Mitsubishi Electric Company's Canadian subsidiary with his twenty-four-year stint as plant executive with Canadian General Electric, M. D. Colliver notes: "The Japanese treat all employees virtually the same and listen to them, rather than just call them a clock number. They are treated like people instead of an adjunct to a machine tool."[20]

It also appears that more fundamental changes in labor-relations practices within North American plants are taking place under Japanese management. For example, in Mitsubishi's Canadian plant, there are no job designations of foreman, plant foreman, or superintendent on the organizational chart. Technicians and engineers do not sit in offices. They work on the plant floor. And quality control is part of the marketing manager's job, with each worker responsible for his or her own work quality.[21]

While changes introduced by Japanese managers in the way North

---

[20] See Edward Clifford, "Japanese Adjust Work Style For Canada," *Toronto Globe and Mail*, February 4, 1984, p. B1.

[21] Ibid. Other distinguishing characteristics of Japanese-managed plants will be discussed in the chapter dealing with production in the international firm.

American factories are organized have been substantive, the human-relations component of Japanese personnel practices should not be underestimated. For example, in Matsushita Industrial Canada Ltd. of Toronto, worker input is invited from a plant committee consisting of fifteen employees elected by their fellows. It meets monthly with management to discuss company affairs and get involved in the decision-making process. During a recessionary period in which Matsushita laid off workers, the company did all the paperwork for employees in securing unemployment benefits, providing interest-free loans to get them over difficult financial periods and generally tried to insulate them from the effects of being jobless.[22]

A point worth emphasizing here is that international managers must be cognizant of host-country cultures and local attitudes before transplanting human-resource-management practices from the home country to overseas affiliates. For example, the Japanese practice of "management by whiskey"—described in the following brief case study—might be fairly well received in the North American business environment, but it would invite severe legal penalties in Muslim countries.

CASE STUDY: *JAPANESE "MANAGEMENT BY WHISKEY"*

An important point that emerges from any consideration of Japanese labor-relations practices is the emphasis placed on cooperation and employee morale. Sometimes the techniques employed in pursuit of this emphasis can be quite unorthodox indeed. Nowhere is this statement more dramatically illustrated than by Japan's $300 million, four-year research program known as the Very Large Scale Integrated (VLSI) Semiconductor Project. Launched in 1976, the project resulted from a government initiative that brought together five large Japanese electronics manufacturers in a research and development association.

The amount of money invested in the project was ample but by no means extravagant. For example, it was about the same amount of money as Texas Instruments Inc. of Dallas, the largest U.S. component supplier, was already spending on its own. But the project was unique in that it was staffed by researchers seconded by the five companies, and those researchers did the basic R&D work. Previously, companies had always divided up the research.

Initially the companies involved resented the arrangement, and as fierce commercial competitors, they were prone to mutual suspicion and squabbling. As a result, it took them six months just to agree on a site for the cooperative laboratory. Similar friction beset the laboratory's one hundred researchers—at least for the first few months. Credit for turning the squabbling units into an effective and integrated team has been given to Masato Nebashi, the VLSI association's managing director.

This story is reported in Guy de Jonquières, "Japanese Microchip Feat Partly Achieved by Drinking," *Toronto Globe and Mail*, May 18, 1985, p. B15. Reprinted by permission of the *Financial Times*.

[22] Ibid.

A retired civil servant with considerable experience in project management, Mr. Nebashi concentrated on what he called "the human problem." From the outset, he urged participants to air their grievances and inhibitions openly, deliberately encouraging confrontation as a way to break down social and professional barriers. He also impressed on them that they were an elite, charged with a special mission, and that their performance was of keen interest worldwide.

"I wanted them to become good friends, communicate to each other, and open their hearts," Mr. Nebashi recalled later. The method he chose was, by his account, typically Japanese: "All I did for these four years was to drink with them as frequently as I could." One researcher described Mr. Nebashi's style as "management by whiskey." Gradually, an esprit de corps developed as members of the team met night after night to fill their glasses and empty their souls. By the end of the project, many had become firm friends, and an alumni association was formed with its own newspaper.

INTERNATIONAL CODES OF CONDUCT[23]

Codes of conduct intended to regulate activities of multinational firms have emerged since the mid-1970s under the auspices of intergovernmental agencies such as the Organization for Economic Cooperation and Development (OECD), International Labour Organization (ILO), the United Nations Commission on Transnational Corporations (UN/CTC), and the European Community (EC). By mid-1983, the OECD and the ILO had developed and issued codes of conduct, and the UN bodies and the EC were continuing discussions in regard to various codes.

OECD Employment
and Industrial-Relations Guidelines

The relevant sections of the OECD guidelines, that is, those dealing with employment and industrial relations in the multinational corporation, are reported in table 8.4. The guidelines are voluntary and do not supplant national law and practice in the field of industrial relations. Nevertheless, they do prescribe a code of conduct for multinationals that has been agreed upon by member governments. Furthermore, unions have seen the code as a move toward binding regulations of the multinational firm. Indeed, several challenges under the OECD guidelines, dealing with such matters as access to decision makers at headquarters level and approval privileges with respect to investments and plant closings, have been brought forward by labor unions.

In one such challenge known as the Badger case, a subsidiary of the

---

[23] The bulk of the discussion in this section is drawn from Richard L. Rowan and Duncan C. Campbell, "The Attempt to Regulate Industrial Relations Through International Codes of Conduct," *Columbia Journal of World Business*, 18 (Summer 1983), 64–72.

TABLE 8.4 Employment and Industrial Relations Guidelines—OECD

Enterprises should, within the framework of law, regulations and prevailing labour relations and employment practices, in each of the countries in which they operate,

1. respect the right of their employees to be represented by trade unions and other bona fide organisations of employees, and engage in constructive negotiations, either individually or through employers' associations, with such employee organisations with a view to reaching agreements on employment conditions, which should include provisions for dealing with disputes arising over the interpretation of such agreements, and for ensuring mutually respected rights and responsibilities;

2. a) provide such facilities to representatives of the employees as may be necessary to assist in the development of effective collective agreements,
   b) provide to representatives of employees information which is needed for meaningful negotiations on conditions of employment;

3. provide to representatives of employees where this accords with local law and practice, information which enables them to obtain a true and fair view of the performance of the entity or, where appropriate, the enterprise as a whole;

4. observe standards of employment and industrial relations not less favourable than those observed by comparable employers in the host country;

5. In their operations, to the greatest extent practicable, utilise, train and prepare for upgrading members of the local labour force in co-operation with representatives of their employees and, where appropriate, the relevant governmental authorities;

6. in considering changes in their operations which would have major effects upon the livelihood of their employees, in particular in the case of the closure of an entity evolving collective lay-offs or dismissals, provide reasonable notice of such changes to representatives of their employees, and where appropriate to the relevant governmental authorities, and co-operate with the employee representatives and appropriate governmental authorities so as to mitigate to the maximum extent practicable adverse effects;

7. implement their employment policies including hiring, discharge, pay, promotion and training without discrimination unless selectivity in respect of employee characteristics is in furtherance of established governmental policies which specifically promote greater equality of employment opportunity;

8. in the context of bona fide negotiations* with representatives of employees on conditions of employment, or while employees are exercising a right to organise, not threaten to utilise a capacity to transfer the whole or part of an operating unit from the country concerned nor transfer employees from the enterprises' component entities in other countries in order to influence unfairly those negotiations or to hinder the exercise of a right to organise**;

9. enable authorised representatives of their employees to conduct negotiations on collective bargaining or labour management relations issues with representatives of management who are authorised to take decisions on the matters under negotiation.

Source: OECD, Declaration on International Investment and Multinational Enterprises (June 21, 1976).
*Bona fide negotiations may include labour disputes as part of the process of negotiation. Whether or not labour disputes are so included will be determined by the law and prevailing employment practices of particular countries.
**NOTE: This paragraph includes the additional provision by OECD Governments at the meeting of the OECD Council at Ministerial level on 13th and 14th June, 1979.

American company Raytheon (the Badger Company) decided to close its office in Antwerp, Belgium, in January 1977, affecting some 250 employees. The company claimed bankruptcy, and Raytheon refused to supplement Badger's assets on grounds that the Belgian company enjoyed limited liability. The Belgian government and the affected unions argued, on the other hand, that Raytheon had failed to observe relevant provisions of the OECD guidelines.

The specific issues raised in the Badger case were, first, whether a parent company must assume the financial obligations of a subsidiary operating as a limited liability company in a particular country, and, second, what constitutes "reasonable notice" and appropriate attempts to "mitigate the adverse effects" of plant or company closings. The challenge before the OECD led to negotiations between Badger and the Belgian government, which in turn led to Raytheon supplementing the assets of Badger.

In another case, the American auto-rental company Hertz brought in employees from other parts of Europe when its Danish affiliate was hit by a strike. Following a settlement of the strike, Hertz reorganized its Danish operation, transferring some functions to its German affiliate and reducing employment in Denmark. The unions involved presented the Hertz case to the OECD as an example of the ineffectiveness of voluntary corporate guidelines for multinationals. The essential question raised by the case is whether a multinational company can legitimately transfer employees across national boundaries in order to maintain operations at a struck facility. Although the OECD declined to act on this individual case, the Hertz case did lead to an amendment of the guidelines, as indicated in paragraph 8 of table 8.4.

In another recent challenge, Viggo—a Swedish subsidiary of the London-based British Oxygen Company International (BOCI)—announced a decision to expand its operations outside of Sweden. Viggo's management discussed its investment plans with the Swedish labor federation, in compliance with the Swedish Codetermination at Work Act, and the unions attempted to convince the company to expand its plant in Sweden rather than to invest overseas. When the management of Viggo refused, the union tried to draw corporate headquarters into the dispute by bringing their case before the OECD. As a result of this challenge, a clarification of paragraph 9 of the OECD guidelines was issued, which established that management of the decision-making center could either delegate authority to the subsidiary's management, send representatives to sit with the subsidiary's management negotiating team, or enter directly into negotiations with the employee representatives.

Other Relevant Complexities

Perhaps the most significant long-term concern of multinational companies relates to the efforts of international trade unions to implement global collective bargaining. The main focus for international unionism is the international trade secretariats, such as the International Metalworkers Federation. The international secretariats are industry-based confederations covering fifteen industries, including mining, metal working, chemicals, agriculture, and transportation. Their activities range from providing information to transferring funds in support of strikes. While the secretariats have been successful in coordinating activities against specific companies in isolated instances, by and large the geographic diversity of membership has, to date, limited their effectiveness in coordinating employee actions against individual companies.

Supporters of international unionism have been strong supporters of the Vredeling Proposal, which at the time of writing is awaiting approval by the Economic Community's Council of Ministers. If passed by the council, the proposal would become law in the Economic Community's ten member states within a specified time period.

The Vredeling Proposal has two major aspects. First, it would obligate the employer to disclose information to employee representatives on specific items at stipulated intervals without waiting for a union request for the information. Second, the directive would require companies to consult employees on certain decisions, with the company to carry out the planned action only after this consultation. Responsibility for consulting with employees ultimately rests with the parent company.

Although the proposed directive does not mention bargaining explicitly, it does state that the required consultation shall be held ''with a view to attempting to reach agreement on the measures planned.''[24] The directive has aroused intense opposition from business on the grounds that it does not adequately safeguard the confidentiality of business secrets, since companies would be required to give projected data related to the future plans of the corporation as a whole and not just historical data on specific subsidiaries. The intention is to build a picture of the overall strategic plans of the multinational company as well as to provide more limited operational data. A major fear of the multinationals is that unions will begin to share and use information across national borders, thereby substantially altering the framework of labor relations.

HOMOGENEOUS OR HETEROGENEOUS APPROACHES TO LABOR RELATIONS?

The various codes of conduct described above, as well as emerging legislation such as the Vredeling Proposal, may be seen as attempts to promote a minimal uniformity in the way that international companies conduct labor relations in different geographic jurisdictions. These initiatives highlight the broad issue for management that exists in virtually all functional areas of the international com-

[24] This description of the Vredeling Proposal is taken from Geoffrey W. Latta and Janice R. Bellace, ''Making the Corporation Transparent: Prelude to Multinational Bargaining,'' *Columbia Journal of World Business,* 18 (Summer 1983), 75–76.

pany; namely, Should the company seek to define a set of uniform procedures to apply in all of its affiliates, or should it try to tailor labor-relations practices to best suit the individual environments in which its affiliates operate?

There are advantages in terms of administrative convenience in adopting standardized labor-relations practices on a worldwide basis. However, legislative and cultural differences across countries make complete standardization either illegal or ill-advised. Perhaps the best prescription for international managers is to work toward implementing a geocentric approach toward human-resource management that is sufficiently flexible to recognize strong cultural, economic, and political differences across national labor markets.

SUMMARY AND CONCLUSIONS

All companies, whether international or purely domestic, must ensure that their employees are working efficiently in pursuit of the objectives of the global organization; however, this task is a particularly difficult one for the international company, given the diversity of environments in which it operates. In particular, since headquarters management will ordinarily be less familiar with the overseas environment than with its own immediate domestic environment, the international organization is under an especially pressing obligation to ensure that the behavior of its employees (including its managers) is compatible with the goals and objectives of the global organization. This observation implies that the management of human resources is an especially critical task in international business and that effective staffing and incentive systems are a required strength of successful international companies.

An important aspect of staffing the international business is determining an ''optimal'' nationality mix of executives. Three broad executive categories encompass parent-country nationals, home-country nationals, and third-country nationals. There are advantages and disadvantages associated with each category. For example, while parent-country nationals are presumably most familiar with the overall objectives and operating procedures of the parent company, they are typically least knowledgeable about the host-country environment. A task of human-resource managers in the international company is to strike a proper balance between the use of different nationals in the management function.

Expatriating and repatriating management personnel also create unique challenges for the international firm. On balance, the approach to staffing will depend upon the firm's stage of development. Directionally, the use of parent-country nationals will decrease, while the use of home-country and third-country nationals will increase as the firm matures.

Environmental diversity also complicates labor relations with respect to nonmanagerial employees in the international firm. Labor legislation and union practices vary from country to country. In some cases, these differences in accepted practice are codified, as in legislation governing codetermination in West Germany. In other cases, they are implicit in the culture of the country, as in the case of lifetime employment practices within large Japanese companies. Further complicating the international-labor relations function is the emergence of various codes of conduct administered by international and supernational agencies. While these codes do not yet have the status of law, they have been appealed to by unions and governments dissatisfied with specific decisions taken by multinational companies. Strengthened codes of conduct threaten to seriously constrain the decision-making autonomy of multinational managers with respect to labor-relations practices.

Human-resource managers in the international firm face a difficult task in ensuring that workers in different regions are treated equitably while also taking care that strong cultural preferences are not ignored. For example, Japanese labor-management practices, which emphasize intensive socializing and dialogue between workers and their managers, would not fit well in the current French industrial structure. The French worker demands a separation between his or her work life and social life and does not expect to have to share decision-making responsibilities with higher-level managers. In simply transplanting practices that are well received in one country, management runs a risk of seriously alienating other parts of its international work force.

DISCUSSION QUESTIONS

1. Discuss the advantages and disadvantages of using host-country nationals (HCN's) to manage overseas affiliates.

2. Imagine the case of two international companies. One is a designer and manufacturer of state-of-the-art scientific instruments. The other is a financial institution. What differences would you expect to find between the management staffing policies of the two companies?

3. Describe the problems associated with the repatriation of parent-country nationals (PCNs). How can they be reduced?

4. As a manager in an international company, what concerns might you have about the imposition of international codes of conduct respecting labor relations? Would you see any benefits to your company from the imposition of such codes?

5. As a human resource manager in an international company, what factors would you consider in establishing the salaries of workers transferred from one affiliate to another?

6. Give some examples of how cultural differences may affect labor-relations practices in different countries.

REFERENCES

BANKS, R. F., and J. STIEBER, EDS., *Multinationals, Unions and Labor Relations in Industrialized Countries.* Ithaca, New York: Cornell University, New York State School of Industrial and Labor Relations, Publications Division, 1977.

ENDERWICK, PETER, "Labour and the Theory of the Multinational Corporation," *Industrial Relations Journal,* 13 (Summer 1982), 32-43.

FELDMAN, D. C., "The Multiple Socialization of Organization Members," *Academy of Management Review,* 6 (1981), 309-18.

HARRIS, P. R., and R. T. MORAN, *Managing Cultural Differences.* Houston, Texas: Gulf Publishing, 1981.

JAIN, H. C., "Disinvestment and the Multinational Employer—A Case History From Belgium," *Personnel Journal* (March 1980), pp. 201-5.

CHAPTER NINE

Measuring and Evaluating Foreign-Exchange Risk

As noted in chapter 3, fluctuating currencies are a ubiquitous feature of the international business landscape that impose certain unique risks on international managers. These risks, in turn, oblige international managers to evaluate and implement strategies that are not particularly relevant for their purely domestic counterparts. Specifically, international managers generally must develop approaches to deal with three broad categories of risk related to fluctuating currency values: transaction risk, translation risk, and economic risk.

Transaction risk (or exposure) refers to the potential increase (gain) or decrease (loss) in cash flows denominated in a foreign currency. A gain or loss could be realized if the exchange rate between that foreign currency and the home currency of the relevant affiliate or division changed over time.

Translation risk (or exposure) refers to the potential gain or loss associated with the conversion (for financial consolidation of the balance sheets) of the foreign-exchange-denominated assets and liabilities of overseas affiliates into home-currency values.

Economic risk is the broadest concept of exchange-rate exposure in that it encompasses all potential changes in the net worth (or discounted net cash flow) of a company that are related to exchange-rate changes. Thus, it incorporates the effects not only of accounting-related changes in the net worth of the company but also of changes in future revenues and costs that follow from fluctuating currency values.

The objective of this chapter is to define these various sources of foreign-exchange risk in more detail, elaborate on how overall measures of foreign-exchange exposure can be developed, and discuss when and how management can hedge its corporate exposure to foreign-exchange risk. We begin by considering the nature of transaction risk.

TRANSACTION EXPOSURE

Consider the following hypothetical example. The Acme Computer Company, headquartered in San Francisco, has booked an order to sell a large quantity of its computer disk drives to the Canadian government through its distribution subsidiary based in Toronto. The Canadian government has agreed to pay Acme $2 million Canadian on the basis of a 10 percent discount for payment up to thirty days after receipt of delivery, or the full amount after that. The current (or spot) rate of exchange between the Canadian and U.S. currencies is $1.00 Cdn. = $.8020 U.S. Thus, if Acme were to receive payment in full that same day from the Canadian government and converted the Canadian dollars received into U.S. dollars, it would realize $1,443,600 U.S. This is calculated as:[1]

(9.1) $2,000,000 \times (1 - .10) \times .8020 = \$1,443,600$ U.S.

Since it will take at least two weeks to ship the disk drives from the company's warehouse in California to the distribution depot in Toronto and then another week to distribute the drives to the Canadian government's offices in Ottawa and Hull, payment for the drives might not be received until at least three weeks after the order is booked. And typically the Canadian government takes a full thirty days to pay after taking delivery. Hence, the rate of exchange that seems relevant to Acme in calculating the U.S. dollar value of the Canadian government's order is the spot rate expected to prevail between fifty and sixty days from the order date.

Suppose for the sake of argument that the spot rate at the time Acme actually receives payment turns out to be $1.00 Cdn. = $.7920 U.S. Acme's revenues from the disk sales would then amount to:

(9.2) $2,000,000 Cdn. $\times (1 - .10) \times .792 = \$1,425,600$ U.S.

This is $18,000 U.S. or approximately 1.25 percent less than the amount ($1,443,600) Acme would have realized (in U.S. dollar terms) had the value of the Canadian dollar remained stable from the date at which the order for the disk

---

[1]The calculation assumes that the Canadian government receives the 10 percent discount for early payment.

drives was booked. The difference between the "booked" value of the transaction and the realized value (i.e., $18,000 U.S.) represents a foreign-exchange loss.

If Acme had no short-term liabilities or payables denominated in Canadian dollars at the time the Canadian government order was booked, the company would have been exposed to transaction risk in an amount equal to $2 million Canadian between the time of booking and the date that payment was received. However, if Acme also had payables denominated in Canadian dollars, its transaction exposure would have been less than $2 million. More specifically, its net Canadian dollar transaction exposure would equal the difference between receivables and payables denominated in Canadian dollars.

To elaborate on this concept of net exposure, imagine that at the time Acme receives the disk-drive order from the Canadian government, Acme issues $1 million Canadian in commercial paper in Toronto's money market. The debt issued must be redeemed in sixty days. Assume that the spot rate at the time of issuance is $1.00 Cdn. = $.8020 U.S. and that by the time the commercial paper is redeemed, the rate is $1.00 Cdn. = $.7920 U.S. Acme would therefore enjoy an effective reduction in the U.S. dollar value of its commercial paper liability. Specifically, the booked value of the debt would be $802,000 U.S.; however, the realized value of the debt payment is $792,000 U.S. This $10,000 gain partially offsets the $18,000 exchange-rate loss on the disk-drive sale. Thus, for the period over which the $2 million receivable and the $1 million payable is carried by

CASE STUDY: *THE FOREIGN-EXCHANGE "SQUEEZE PLAY"*

A good illustration of the transaction-risk concept in the real world is provided by the recent experience of the Toronto Blue Jays baseball team. In 1983, the ball club paid out U.S. $6 million in salaries to its players, most of whom are Americans who negotiate their contracts in U.S. dollars. In addition, the club has other U.S.-dollar-denominated expenditures related to spring-training facilities, scouting, travel, accommodations, and minor league operations. At any point in time, salary obligations and other costs incurred in U.S. dollars represent a source of transaction risk (or exposure) for the Blue Jays management. Since around three-fourths of the club's revenues are denominated in Canadian dollars, its gross U.S. dollar transaction exposure is almost equivalent to its net exposure.

Canada's other professional baseball team—the Montreal Expos—face a similar source of foreign-exchange risk. A declining Canadian dollar in the first half of the 1980s cost the Montreal ball club dearly. For example, Expo group vice-president, Pierre Gauvreau, estimated that a one-half-cent decline in the value of the Canadian dollar in the first week of June 1984 cost the Montreal team about $400,000 (Canadian)—almost enough to buy the services of a good outfielder, since the average National League salary was $343,000 U.S. in 1984.

Source: Jennifer Hunter, "Sagging Canadian Dollar Hits Blue Jays, Expos Hard," *Toronto Globe and Mail,* June 7, 1984, pp. 1-2.

Acme, the company's net Canadian dollar transaction exposure is $1 million Canadian.

Over the course of an accounting period, many receivable and payable positions will be booked and subsequently liquidated. It would be extremely cumbersome for each booked transaction to be accounted for at the spot rate of exchange at the time the receivable or payable position is liquidated. Therefore, in practice an average exchange rate for the period is used to convert transactions in foreign currencies into the home currency of the parent. The net foreign-exchange gain (or loss), as summed over all foreign-currency-denominated transactions, is typically accounted for as an addition to (or subtraction from) the operating income of the international company for that period, since it represents either a real addition to (or deduction from) the company's overall cash flow.

TRANSLATION EXPOSURE

Typically a company will carry more than short-term receivables and payables on its balance sheet. For example, it will ordinarily have working-capital assets in the form of cash and liquid instruments such as Treasury notes. It is also likely to be carrying finished and semifinished inventory and long-term assets such as plant, machinery, and equipment. On the liabilities side of its balance sheet, the firm will probably be carrying long-term debt (in addition to short-term payables), as well as various reserve accounts and shareholders' capital.

A company's balance-sheet (or translation) exposure in any foreign currency will be measured as the difference between the value of assets and the value of liabilities that are "translated" at the current rate of exchange. The term *translation* in this context is essentially equivalent to the term *conversion*.

The precise way in which the assets and liabilities of foreign affiliates and divisions are translated (or converted) into home-currency units for purposes of financial reporting is a matter of accounting convention. From January 1, 1976, to January 1, 1983, U.S. accounting standards for consolidating the financial statements of foreign affiliates were established in accordance with Financial Accounting Standards Board statement number 8: "Accounting for the Translation of Foreign Currency Transactions and Foreign Currency Financial Statements."

The FASB-8 rules for translating balance-sheet items of foreign affiliates and divisions into the parent's consolidated balance sheet are summarized in table 9.1. The recently revised translation rules (FASB-52) are reported in the column alongside the FASB-8 summary. Under FASB-8, the exposure of a foreign affiliate was determined as the difference between its monetary assets (cash plus accounts receivable) and monetary liabilities (accounts payable plus long-term debt) denominated in currencies other than the parent's. Inventories and plant and equipment were considered real assets and were translated at the exchange rates in effect when the assets were booked. Net worth was calculated as the residual between translated assets and translated liabilities.

TABLE 9.1   FASB-8 and FASB-52 Rules for Balance-Sheet Translation: Foreign-Currency Items from the Viewpoint of the Parent

ASSETS	FASB-8 EXCHANGE RATE	FASB-52 EXCHANGE RATE
Cash	Current	Current
Accounts receivable (A/R)	Current	Current
Inventories	Historic	Current
Plant and equipment	Historic	Current
LIABILITIES		
Accounts payable (A/P)	Current	Current
Long-term debt	Current	Current
Net worth	Residual	Residual

Source: Reprinted by permission of the publisher from *Exchange Risk and Exposure: Current Developments in International Financial Management,* edited by Richard M. Levich and Clas G. Wihlborg, (Lexington, Mass.: Lexington Books. D. C. Heath & Co., copyright 1980, D. C. Heath & Co.), and Financial Accounting Standards Board. *Foreign Currency Translation,* exposure draft, June 30, 1981.

Under FASB-8 a decline in the value of an affiliate's local currency (against the U.S. dollar) would result in a decrease in the translated net monetary assets of that affiliate, all other things constant. The net decrease of all affiliates' net monetary assets was ultimately accounted for as a deduction from earned income in the parent's income statement and as a corresponding debit to net worth on the parent company's balance sheet. Conversely, a revaluation in the local currency of an affiliate resulted in an increase in the translated net monetary assets of the affiliate, which in turn was accounted for as a contribution to income on the income statement and an increase in net worth on the parent's balance sheet.

The accounting procedures mandated by FASB-8 created a great deal of controversy among corporate treasurers, who argued that the accounting conventions imposed were arbitrary and were imposing erratic—and sometimes dramatic—windfall deductions from operating profits. Some financial economists argued that the required translation procedures did not provide reliable information to managers and shareholders about the outlook for the international company's long-term profits, basically because translation gains or losses are not directly related to changes in long-run corporate cash flow.[2] These economists further argued that management's time would be better spent worrying about how to improve long-run operating efficiency rather than about how to minimize translation exposure.

The reliability and practical relevance of the information provided under FASB-8 accounting procedures were further called into question by empirical

[2]We shall elaborate on this point below.

studies demonstrating that, by and large, the issuance and implementation of FASB-8 did not significantly affect the security returns of U.S. multinational corporations. Many observers interpreted this finding as evidence that investors ignored or completely discounted the reported income gains and losses resulting from exchange-rate changes, since investors apparently did not demand a higher rate of return on equity shares of multinational companies as compensation for the apparent increase in risk, that is, the greater variance in reported income presumably associated with translation gains and losses.[3]

FASB-8 was superseded by FASB statement number 52: "Foreign Currency Translation." Under FASB-52 all of a foreign entity's assets and liabilities are to be translated from that entity's functional currency into the parent company's reporting currency using the current exchange rate, that is, the rate in effect on the balance-sheet date. Thus, referring again to table 9.1, FASB-52 would have cash, accounts receivable, inventories, plant and equipment, accounts payable, and long-term debt all translated at the current exchange rate.

Under FASB-52 the exchange-rate exposure imposed by foreign affiliates on the parent is therefore measured as the net foreign-asset position(s) of the affiliates at the last (balance sheet) reporting date. Changes in the translated values of net foreign assets (or liabilities) are not included in the determination of net income, as was the case under FASB-8. Rather, the translation gains or losses are accumulated in a separate reserve account until the net-asset (or liability) position is substantially or completely liquidated, or until it is determined that a permanent impairment of the net-asset position of the foreign entity has taken place.

FASB-52 addresses one frequently raised concern about FASB-8; namely, that the exchange-risk exposure on long-term debt is effectively hedged in many cases by the foreign currency revenue potential of long-term assets. Under FASB-8, the appreciation of a foreign currency would result in an increase in the translated value of long-term debt, while leaving the translated value of plant and equipment unchanged. All other things constant, this would lead to a translation loss and a corresponding deduction from operating income. But presumably the revenues earned from operating plant, equipment, and other long-term assets of the affiliate will be worth more in home-currency units. The FASB-8 translation procedure did not recognize this "hedging" feature of long-term assets. In particular, during the 1960s and early 1970s, when the value of the U.S. dollar declined (on average) against the European currencies, the translated value of foreign-denominated debt increased for U.S. multinationals, but no corresponding increase was recorded for foreign-denominated inventories and other physical assets financed by that debt.

---

[3]Many criticisms have been levied against statistical studies of the impact of FASB-8. One major criticism is that most firms had accounting conventions similar to FASB-8 in place prior to its formal implementation. In this case, one would not necessarily expect the market to acknowledge that there was any major impact from codifying what was already a common practice.

THE CONCEPT OF ECONOMIC EXPOSURE

For a variety of reasons, most economists agree that accounting translation procedures described in the preceding section do not give a reliable insight into the relationship between exchange-rate changes and changes in the future net cash flows of affiliates of international companies. Perhaps of greatest fundamental importance, accounting-based measures of exchange-rate exposure do not consider the impact of exchange-rate changes on the prices that affiliates can charge for their products and services as well as on the prices they must pay for the goods and services they buy.

The most encompassing measure of exchange-rate risk (or exposure) is economic risk. Economic exposure is concerned with the impacts of exchange-rate changes on the net present value of the international firm's cash flows. In effect, economic risk relates potential changes in a firm's net worth to changes in foreign-exchange rates.

Unfortunately, there is no straightforward measure of economic risk that can be derived from the firm's books of account. This is because changes in the translated values of the international firm's foreign assets and liabilities may not perfectly correspond to changes in the long-run cash flows of the firm's various affiliates. Therefore, one cannot simply infer long-run profitability impacts of exchange-rate changes from their balance-sheet implications.

To develop this point in a bit more detail, consider the following hypothetical (and simplified) example. The U.S. affiliate of a large Canadian real estate developer owns a number of office towers in several northeastern cities. The towers were entirely financed by issuing mortgages denominated in U.S. dollars.[4] Assume that all short-term assets and liabilities of the affiliate are also denominated in U.S. dollars. Currently, the rent from the office towers equals U.S. $10 million per year, while operating and interest expenses are U.S. $7 million per year. This leaves the affiliate with net earnings of U.S. $3 million either to pay the parent as a dividend or to reinvest itself. At an exchange rate of $1 Cdn. = U.S. $.80, the Canadian parent can expect to receive a dividend of $3.75 million Canadian from its U.S. affiliate.

Of course, the exchange rate between the Canadian and U.S. currencies will vary over time. Assume that over the following five years, faster inflation in the U.S. will push the Canadian dollar to parity against the U.S. dollar. What would be the impact of this exchange-rate change on the Canadian developer? Since we've assumed that the affiliate has offsetting assets and liabilities denominated in U.S. dollars, there is no translation effect under FASB-52.[5] If the developer's

---

[4]This assumption in unrealistic, but it is expedient. The points that follow are not affected in any essential way by the assumption.

[5]We are ignoring the likelihood that some portion of the mortgage principal will be paid down over the five-year period, thereby increasing the affiliate's net asset position.

rental income and expenses remained constant, the parent's anticipated dividend would decline to $3 million Canadian. However, it is unlikely that rental income and expenses would remain unchanged, especially in the face of significant inflation. If, for example, both the affiliate's rental income and its rental expenses increased by 50 percent over the five-year period—to $15 million and $10.5 million respectively—U.S. dollar profits at the end of the period would be $4.5 million. Given our assumption of exchange-rate parity, the Canadian parent, at the end of the five-year period, would enjoy increased net cash flows denominated in Canadian dollars.[6]

On the other hand, if we assume that both rental income and rental expenses increase by only 10 percent over the ensuing five-year period, U.S. (and Canadian) dollar profits at the end of the period would equal $11.0 − $7.7 = $3.3. In this case, the depreciation of the host currency would result in a lower Canadian-dollar-denominated dividend available to be paid to the parent: compare $3.3 million to $3.75 million. Obviously, there is some assumed increase in U.S. rental incomes and rental expenses that would give the affiliate a Canadian-dollar equivalent profit of $3.75 million. In this case, the depreciation in the U.S. dollar would be exactly offset by an increase in U.S.-dollar-denominated profits. As an exercise, calculate this "breakeven" increase in rental income and rental expenses. You should not be surprised to find that it equals the assumed appreciation in the value of the Canadian dollar.

The previous example is meant to illustrate the following point: If changes in foreign-denominated revenues and costs do not exactly offset changes in foreign-currency values, exchange-rate changes will impose cash-flow gains or losses on the international firm. At this point in the discussion, the reader might be wondering about the potential relevance of the purchasing-power-parity theory described in chapter 3. In our explanation of that theory, as applied to the preceding example, the depreciation in the U.S. dollar should precisely equal the difference between the U.S. and Canadian inflation rates.

In appendix 9A we demonstrate that if the revenues and costs of a firm's foreign divisions always change in the same proportion as—but in the opposite direction to—the change in the value of relevant foreign currencies, international companies would not face economic risk. Equivalently, this requires the revenues and costs of the foreign divisions to change at a rate dictated by purchasing-power parity. However, this is unlikely to be true for most individual international companies. Specifically, differences across domestic markets in such factors as technological change, seller concentration, union bargaining power, and government regulations make it likely that there will be a wide divergence in the rates at which individual domestic prices change over time. That is, inflation will not have an equivalent impact on individual companies. This point is underscored by data presented in table 9.2. The data are Canadian selling-price indices for a variety of products. Quite clearly, individual prices do not all rise or fall at the same rate.

[6]Compare $3.25 million to $4.5 million.

TABLE 9.2   Industry Selling Price Indexes—Selected Goods (1981 = 100)

	BREAD	COTTON YARN	MOTOR GASOLINE
1980	85.5	91.4	70.3
1981	100.0	100.0	100.0
1982	107.5	95.5	118.0
1983	113.8	94.8	123.4

	PASSENGER CARS	MARGARINE	FABRIC SOFTENERS
1980	90.0	99.0	89.8
1981	100.0	100.0	100.0
1982	109.1	100.8	106.0
1983	108.0	102.6	109.2

	COPPER	ASPHALT	STEEL CASTINGS
1980	117.2	73.7	91.4
1981	100.0	100.0	100.0
1982	88.7	102.4	107.8
1983	92.8	109.1	114.2

Source: Statistics Canada, *Industry Price Indexes*, June 1984.

Therefore, the purchasing-power-parity theory has limited relevance for any individual international company contemplating the economic effects of exchange-rate changes.

COMPONENTS OF ECONOMIC RISK

The basic components of economic risk can be described more clearly with reference to equation 9.3. The variable on the left-hand side (II_h) represents profit expressed in the home-country currency. $Q_A{}^q$ is the physical quantity of output sold in country A; P_A is the average price of the output sold in country A; $Q_A{}^i$ is the physical quantity of inputs purchased in country A; while C_A is the average cost of the inputs purchased in A. Similar interpretations would be given to $Q_B{}^q$, P_B, $Q_B{}^i$, and C_B, e_A is the number of home-currency units required to purchase a unit of currency A, and e_B is the number of home-currency units required to purchase one unit of currency B.

$$(9.3) \quad II_h = e_a P_A Q_A{}^q + e_b P_B Q_B{}^q - e_a C_A Q_A{}^i - e_b C_b Q_B{}^i$$

Looking at equation 9.3, we can envision two main ways in which II_h can be affected by exchange-rate changes:

1. One or more of the *P*s and *C*s fail to change in exact inverse proportion to changes in the corresponding *e*.
2. The quantities of outputs and inputs demanded are influenced by changes in the *e*s.

In evaluating the economic exposure of an international firm, management should evaluate these two broad influences on the profitability of its international activities expressed in home-currency units. In the context of equation 9.3, transaction risk can be seen as an aspect of a broader set of cash-flow risks associated with exchange-rate changes. More specifically, economic risk encompasses both short-term and long-term cash-flow risks. This abstract discussion of equation 9.3 can be made more concrete by discussing some real-world examples.

Laker Airways

The dramatic appreciation in the value of the U.S. dollar over the first half of the 1980s offers numerous illustrations of real-world exchange-rate risk. One especially noteworthy example is the British company Laker Airways, which went out of business in part because of its failure to adequately anticipate and deal with the substantial decline in the British pound in the early 1980s.[7]

Laker was a highly leveraged firm with an outstanding debt of more than U.S. $400 million. Hence, as the pound began its depreciation against the dollar in 1981, Laker's pound-equivalent cost of debt increased substantially. The company also had operating expenses denominated in both pounds and dollars. Specifically, the salaries of most of its employees and office and administrative expenses in the U.K. were incurred in sterling, while administrative expenditures made in the U.S. as well as the salaries of its U.S.-based employees were denominated in dollars. However, the bulk of Laker's expenses were fuel and debt servicing, and both of these expenditures were denominated in U.S. dollars.

In the airline industry, ticket prices denominated in different currencies are set on the basis of some assumed relationship between those currencies. Ticket prices remain in force until changed; they are not changed every day. Laker's ticket sales in Britain, therefore, resulted in a sterling cash inflow, while its ticket sales in the U.S. resulted in a dollar cash inflow. In Laker's case, fares were set on an assumed currency relationship of $2.25 U.S. to the pound. Indeed, Laker's entire financial budget was prepared on the basis of this assumed relationship.

In terms of equation 9.3, if the b subscripts indicate dollar-denominated variables and the a subscripts denote pound-denominated variables, the bulk of Laker's costs would be represented in the product term $C_B Q_B{}^i$, and the bulk of the company's revenues would be represented in the product term $P_A Q_A{}^q$. That is, the position of Laker in the early 1980s was that its dollar expenses were far in excess of its dollar revenues, while its sterling revenues were higher than its sterling expenses. As a result, if the pound declined in value against the dollar, Laker's expenses could be expected to increase relative to its revenues.

To see this result directly in terms of equation 9.3, note that e_B (the number of pounds equivalent to one U.S. dollar) would rise with a depreciation of the

---

[7]This example and the related discussion is taken from S. L. Srinirasulu, "Currency Denomination of Debt: Lessons From Rolls-Royce and Laker Airways," *Business Horizons* Vol. 26, September–October 1983, 19–21.

pound; e_A of course would equal one at all values of the pound, since the A subscript represents the pound denomination. Since $C_B Q_B{}^i$ exceeds $P_B Q_B{}^q$, the home-currency profits of Laker would decline.

In actual fact, the British pound plunged from a price of around \$2.40 in 1979 to \$1.60 during 1981–1982. Since the dollar price of jet fuel and Laker's dollar-denominated interest payments did not decline, Laker's pound-equivalent costs skyrocketed; however, Laker's pound-denominated ticket prices failed to keep pace with the depreciation in the pound owing to lags in scaling up ticket prices as well as fierce competition on North Atlantic routes, which kept a lid on prices that Laker could charge its British customers.

Canadian Forest-Products Companies

A somewhat more complex illustration of the impact of exchange-rate changes on corporate profits is provided by the recent experience of Canada's major forest-products companies. About 75 percent of Canadian forest products are sold in U.S. dollars. As a result, a declining Canadian dollar translates directly into increases in the Canadian dollar value of forest-products sales. In terms of equation 9.3, if e_B represents the number of Canadian dollars required to purchase a U.S. dollar, and the b subscript denotes U.S.-dollar-denominated quantities, $Q_B{}^q$ constitutes the bulk of total forest-products sales. Since a decline in the Canadian dollar is equivalent to an increase in e_B, the home-currency revenues of forest-products companies can be expected to increase, other things constant.

The direct impact of exchange-rate changes on corporate profits can be quite substantial. For example, Abitibi-Price, Inc., of Toronto estimates that for every one-cent change in the value of the Canadian dollar relative to the U.S. dollar, the impact is \$3 million to \$3.5 million on its after-tax corporate profit, or fourteen to fifteen cents a share. At MacMillan Bloedel Ltd. of Vancouver, the one-cent currency move affects pretax profits by \$5 million.[8] These estimates represent the direct effects of an exchange-rate change primarily associated with a change in the value of e_B. But there are potentially important indirect effects to consider as well. For example, when the U.S. dollar is strong in relation to the Canadian dollar, it will generally be strong against other currencies. Since Canadian forest products sold outside of North America are ordinarily priced in U.S. dollars, Canada's wood products will become relatively more expensive in offshore markets.

Higher-priced Canadian products in offshore markets will lead to lower sales in those markets for Canadian companies. The indirect impact of a decline in the value of the Canadian dollar is therefore to reduce sales made by Canadian companies. But since only about 25 percent of Canada's forest-product exports are offshore, the direct effect of a declining Canadian dollar (that is, the increase in e_B) will outweigh the indirect effect (the decline in $Q_B{}^q$ sold in other markets).

---

[8] These estimates and the accompanying discussion are taken from Harvey Enchin, "U.S. Canadian Dollar Spread Crucial to Forest Firms' Profits," *Toronto Globe and Mail,* May 30, 1984, B1.

To recapitulate, international businesses confront a variety of risks related to the instability of exchange rates. Translation exposure, an accounting measure of risk, is approximated by the net foreign-currency asset or liability position of a company. Economic exposure is a cash-flow concept that relates exchange-rate changes to changes in an international company's long-run profitability valued in its home currency. In principle, economic exposure is the appropriate concept of risk for the wealth-maximizing firm to focus on; however, in practice it is often difficult for firms to identify the cash-flow impacts of exchange-rate changes, especially given the varied (and often conflicting) influences of market forces on corporate profitability. As a result, many corporate treasures believe that translation gains and losses are useful approximations to the long-run cash-flow effects of exchange-rate changes. To the extent that investors take translation gains and losses into account when valuing a company's equity, financial managers should not ignore the net-asset exposure of their firm's foreign affiliates and should consider ways to reduce translation exposure.

CALCULATING THE BENEFITS AND COSTS OF HEDGING

Before considering the benefits and costs of hedging, we should offer a formal definition of the hedging process. A hedge represents a transaction that is entered into in order to protect the home-currency value of foreign-currency-denominated assets or liabilities. It represents an attempt to balance the firm's exposure in foreign currencies.

Whether or not a firm should actively hedge its foreign-exchange risk depends upon both the benefits (associated with risk reduction) and costs of hedging. It also depends upon management's tolerance of risk. A hypothetical example will illustrate the foregoing points. For simplicity, we will assume that our hypothetical American company (U.S. International, Inc.) has a single subsidiary (Canus Ltd.), which is located in Canada. As of a given balance-sheet date, Canus's assets and liabilities (in Canadian dollars) are reported in table 9.3.

Following the procedure for calculating translation exposure under

TABLE 9.3   Canus Ltd. Balance Sheet ($ millions Cdn.)

ASSETS		LIABILITIES	
Cash	$ 10	Accounts payable	$ 30
Accounts receivable	40	Long-term debt	70
Inventory	20		
Plant and equipment	100	Net worth	70
	$170		$170

FASB-52, U.S. International's net asset exposure through its Canus subsidiary is $70 Canadian. Assume that the Canada-U.S. exchange rate is $1 Cdn. = $.80 U.S. at the time Canus's balance sheet is prepared. Further, the management of U.S. International expects that one year from the current balance-sheet date, the exchange rate will be $1 Cdn. = $.76 U.S. As a result, if nothing is done to hedge the company's net asset exposure in Canadian dollars, U.S. International faces a potential translation loss equal to $2.8 million U.S. on its net asset position.[9]

Under FASB-52, translation losses can be placed in a separate reserve account until the net asset (or liability) position is substantially or completely liquidated, or until it is determined that the net asset or liability position is permanently impaired. In Canus's case, it would probably be prudent accounting to acknowledge a permanent impairment of receivables and payables, since these items will likely be liquidated in the near future at (or near) the current exchange rate. Taking accounts receivable minus accounts payable as Canus's short-term net asset position, an exchange-rate decrease from $1 Cdn. = $.80 U.S. to $1 Cdn. = $.76 U.S. would result in a deduction from U.S. International's operating income of $400,000 U.S.[10]

In fact, if any component of Canus's balance sheet is actually liquidated over the year, the liquidated net asset (or net liability) position is translated at the average exchange rate over the period and is directly deducted from (or added to) operating income. For example, if Canus liquidates its receivables and payables over the course of the year, and if the average exchange rate over the year is $1 Cdn. = $.78 U.S., U.S. International would suffer a deduction from operating income of $200,000 U.S., associated with the transaction loss from liquidating a $10 million Canadian net asset position at $.78 U.S., when the net assets were carried on the books at $.80 U.S.

In the foregoing example, if U.S. International's management could lock in a price for the Canadian dollar, or otherwise hedge its net asset exposure in Canadian dollars, at a cost less than the expected transaction loss of $200,000, it would seem an appropriate expenditure on management's part. For example, management might consider selling forward $10 million Canadian dollars at the prevailing one-year forward rate. Let us assume that as of the date at which the spot rate of exchange is $1 Cdn. = $.80 U.S., the one-year forward rate is $1 Cdn. = $.79 U.S. In this case, when $10 million Canadian in net short-term assets are liquidated over the course of the year, the funds raised can be used by the parent (if it so desires) to purchase $7.9 million U.S. dollars. The one-year forward sale of Canadian dollars locks in a price for the excess of Canus's receivables over its payables that exceeds the expected average price over the period (i.e., $.78 U.S.). In effect, by selling forward the relevant net-asset position, U.S. International ac-

---

[9]This is calculated as $70 million Cdn. X (.76 − .80) = −$2.8 million U.S.
[10] This is calculated as ($40 million − $30 million) X .04; an additional $50 million X .04 = $2.4 million is assigned to a reserve account as a future deduction against earned income.

cepts a certain (before tax) loss of $100,000 U.S. to save an estimated $200,000 U.S.[11]

Numerous examples can be cited of international firms selling forward foreign-currency-denominated receivables—or buying forward foreign currency required to cover liabilities. For example, Great Lakes Forest Products of Thunder Bay, Ontario, sells U.S. dollars forward to lock in a certain Canadian dollar value for its lumber sales in the U.S. Thus, while hedging is widely practiced, it is unclear in our hypothetical example whether (1) the entire $70 million net asset position should be hedged, and (2) whether management should hedge Canus's net-asset exposure whenever the expected value of the hedged position exceeds the expected value of the unhedged position.

The benefits from hedging the full translation exposure of a firm are less obvious than the benefits of hedging anticipated near-term transactions. This is because in hedging long-run assets or liabilities the manager is essentially trading the uncertainty of an accounting loss that may never materialize for the certain cost of eliminating translation risk.[12] Recall that FASB-52 allows the firm to carry translation losses (from period to period) in a reserve account until the net-asset (or liability) position is substantially or completely liquidated, or until it is determined that the net-asset position is permanently impaired. Hence, it is quite possible that, in the case of long-term assets and liabilities, future exchange-rate changes may reverse the translation effects of previous exchange-rate changes, and the translation losses incurred in any period may never materialize as a deduction against income.[13] Furthermore, as suggested by our discussion of economic exposure, the long-run impact of currency fluctuations on the net present value of any individual firm may be inadequately captured by the firm's translation exposure. In this case, knowledgeable investors will ignore changes in the firm's reserve account for translation gains and losses.

While theoreticians continue to express reservations about the appropriateness of hedging translation exposure, many practitioners and management consultants argue that the international firm's liabilities should be structured in such a way that any unanticipated change in the return on assets is offset, as far as possible, by a change in the effective cost of liabilities.[14] In the case of U.S.

[11] In effect, the expected benefits from hedging are defined as the foreign-exchange losses expected from an unhedged position. The (before-tax) costs of hedging in the above case are the losses associated with selling forward the Canadian currency at a discount. We shall discuss hedging techniques more fully in the next chapter.

[12] There are cases when a foreign-exchange gain (net of transactions costs) can be earned when selling foreign currency forward; that is, when the foreign currency is at a premium to the home currency.

[13] Several authors have noted a reservation to this point. Namely, unanticipated capital gains and losses that a firm experiences owing to random-currency fluctuations may influence valuation through the effect on debt capacity; e.g., accrued losses may reduce a firm's capacity to raise debt. See Dennis Logue and George Oldfield, "Managing Foreign Assets Where Foreign Exchange Markets are Efficient," *Financial Management* Vol. 2 (Summer 1977), 16–22.

[14] See, for example, Gunter Dufey and Ian Giddy, "International Financial Planning: The Use of Market Based Forecasts," *California Management Review* Vol. 21 (Fall 1978), 69–81. Various posi-

International, for example, this would imply offsetting the $70 million net asset position in Canadian dollars with additional liabilities of $70 million Canadian. If additional financing is being considered for the Canus subsidiary, the net asset exposure in Canadian dollars provides one reason for raising the required capital in Canada. Specifically, a $70 million Canadian issuance of debt would leave U.S. International with zero net translation exposure in Canadian dollars.

The benefits of issuing debt in a currency that is expected to depreciate, such as the Canadian dollar in our hypothetical example, is that the value of the debt in U.S. dollars will decrease to the same extent as the devaluation. This is why borrowing to offset a net asset position acts as a hedge. But recall the interest-arbitrage model discussed in chapter 3. An implication of the model is that interest rates will be higher on assets and liabilities that are denominated in currencies expected to decrease in value against other currencies. In our example, given that the Canadian dollar is at a discount in the one-year forward market,[15] interest rates in Canada should be higher than in the United States. To the extent that they are higher by the amount of the expected depreciation over the life of the loan, there is no anticipated benefit to borrowing in a depreciating currency.

In summary, when the anticipated benefits of hedging exceed the anticipated costs, management should hedge the firm's exposed foreign-currency positions. The benefits of hedging are more obvious in the case of cash-flow exposure (of which transaction exposure is a component) than in the case of translation exposure. But even in the former case, efficient money markets and foreign-exchange markets would ensure that the costs of hedging short-term expected cash flows equal the anticipated benefits of hedging in most situations. While the relevant markets in which hedging takes place are not always efficient, international managers should guard against the tendency to "overhedge"; that is, they should not spend more on risk reduction than that risk reduction is worth to the shareholders of the firm.

EXCHANGE EXPOSURE IN MULTIPLE CURRENCIES

Our preceding discussion of the various forms of exchange-rate risk was implicitly cast in terms of exposure in a single foreign currency. When short-term and long-term assets and liabilities are denominated in a number of foreign currencies,

---

tions on hedging translation risk are reviewed in Laurent Jacque, "Management of Foreign Exchange Risk: A Review Article," *Journal of International Business Studies* Vol. 12 (Spring/Summer 1981), 81-101.

[15]The forward premium (or discount) is calculated as: $\dfrac{F_s - E_s}{E_s} \times \dfrac{12}{\text{number of months forward}} \times 100$

where F_s is the forward rate and E_s is the spot rate.

estimates of foreign-exchange exposure must be modified to take into account interrelationships in exchange-rate movements.

A simple example will illustrate this point. Recall our discussion of the Acme Computer Company, which has an account receivable outstanding in the amount of $2 million Canadian. Now let us assume that while Acme has no short-term liabilities or payables denominated in Canadian dollars, it does have accounts payable equal to £1.11 million. The Canadian dollar value of these accounts payable would equal approximately $2 million at an exchange rate of £1.00 = $1.8025 Cdn. In this case, what is Acme's foreign-exchange exposure?

On the surface, it would appear that Acme has an asset exposure of $2 million Canadian and a liability exposure of £1.11 million and, therefore, should contemplate hedging both its "open" Canadian-dollar and British-pound positions. But this would lead to excessive hedging behavior if movements in the Canadian and British currency units are positively correlated. For example, in the extreme case where the two currencies moved by identical relative amounts against the U.S. dollar, a change in the U.S. dollar value of Acme's Canadian receivables would be exactly matched by the change in the U.S. dollar value of Acme's sterling payables.

To verify this claim, we need to explicitly introduce the notion of cross-exchange rates. Recall that exchange rates are conventionally quoted in terms of the U.S. dollar. Obviously, exchange ratios for non-U.S. currencies are implicit in the exchange rates quoted in terms of the U.S. dollar. These implicit rates are called cross-rates. For example, if the relevant spot rates are $1.00 Cdn. = $.81 U.S. and £1.00 = $1.46 U.S., the implicit exchange rate between the Canadian dollar and the British pound is

$$(9.4) \quad £/\$Cdn. = £/U.S. / \$Cdn./\$U.S. = {}^{1/}1.46/{}^{1/}.81 = .5548$$

That is, $1.00 Canadian will exchange for £.5548; or equivalently, £1.00 = $1.8025 Cdn.

If over the maturity period for Acme's receivables and payables, both the Canadian dollar and the British pound decrease by 10 percent against the U.S. dollar, the new spot rates will be $1.00 Cdn. = $.7290 U.S. and £1.00 = $1.3140 U.S. The new cross-rate will therefore be:

$$(9.5) \quad £/\$Cdn. = {}^{1/}1.3140 / {}^{1/}.7290 = .5547$$

This example shows that when currencies are perfectly correlated in their movements against the U.S. dollar, the respective cross-rates will be constant.[16] In Acme's case, therefore, the depreciation in the value of its Canadian-dollar-denominated receivables will be exactly matched by the depreciation in the value of its British-pound-denominated liabilities. In this case, Acme's outstanding

---

[16]The slight difference between the cross-rates calculated in equations 9.4 and 9.5 is entirely the result of rounding.

British pound liabilities should be fully netted from its outstanding Canadian dollar receivables to obtain the company's net transaction exposure. In this highly stylized example, Acme's net transaction exposure would be extremely limited.[17]

(9.6) $2 million Cdn. − £1.11 million = $2 million Cdn.
− (£1.1 million × $1.8025) = $17,250

Hence, Acme should hedge neither its exposed receivable nor its exposed payable position.

The Acme example was highly simplified by our assumptions that given the initial spot rates, Acme's receivables and payables were equal in U.S.-dollar-denominated value and that relative price changes in the Canadian dollar and the British pound were perfectly correlated. It is worth briefly considering how the evaluation of multicurrency-transaction risk might proceed under more realistic circumstances.

To keep the analysis relatively simple, we continue to assume that Acme has a $2 million Canadian receivable and a £1.11 million payable. But now we assume that the initial spot rates are $1.00 Cdn. = $.80 U.S. and £1.00 = $1.50 U.S.[18] Furthermore, we assume that the Canadian dollar and the British pound tend to move in the same direction against the U.S. dollar but not necessarily in perfect unison. As shown in table 9.4, this assumption is more realistic than the preceding

TABLE 9.4   Cross-Rates For Major Currencies*

	DM/CANADIAN $	£/CANADIAN $	DM/£
1981	1.8874	.4120	4.5811
1982	1.9581	.4634	4.2255
1983	2.0721	.5353	3.8709
	SWEDISH KRONA/ DM	SWEDISH KRONA/ CANADIAN $	SWEDISH KRONA/ £
1981	2.2385	4.2251	10.25
1982	2.5881	5.0906	10.98
1983	3.0039	6.2245	11.63
	JAPANESE YEN/ DM	JAPANESE YEN/ CANADIAN $	JAPANESE YEN/ SWEDISH KRONA
1981	97.49	184.01	43.55
1982	102.58	201.77	39.64
1983	93.01	192.74	30.96

Source: *Federal Reserve Bulletin*, May 1984, p. A64.
*Annual averages of daily closing rates.

[17]Recall our assumption that at the start of the period £1 = $1.8025 Cdn.
[18]The implied cross-rate is therefore £1.00 = $1.8750 Cdn.

assumption that cross-rates are constant. More specifically, the data in table 9.4 report cross-rates for major foreign currencies at selected dates. Clearly, cross-rates vary over time, including the Canadian dollar–British pound cross-rate. While not obvious from the data in table 9.4, it is also true that historical relationships between foreign currencies are often inaccurate guides to future relationships. Consequently, management needs to make explicit forecasts of future cross-rates in order to evaluate multicurrency-exchange-rate risk.

A convenient way in which to carry out this exercise is through the construction of a tableau such as the one presented as table 9.5. The tableau shows the change in multicurrency receivables and payables (in home-currency values) under various assumed future spot rates. Specifically, the first column of table 9.5 shows the values of receivables and payables and the net exposure position of the firm at current spot rates. The next three columns show what these values would be under three assumed future spot rates for the relevant foreign currencies. The second column is based on a "most pessimistic" scenario for the Canadian dollar and the British pound. That is, it incorporates the lowest values for each currency (against the U.S. dollar) that management foresees over the period. The third column is based on a "most optimistic" scenario, while the last column represents a "most likely" or base-case scenario.[19]

The bottom row in the table shows the change in the firm's net receivables or net payables associated with the various implied exchange-rate changes. For example, we see that under the pessimistic scenario, the firm can expect to realize a before-tax transaction gain of $11,000 U.S. This gain arises because the decline in the British pound payable (in U.S. dollar terms) exceeds the decline in the Canadian dollar receivables. Similarly, under the optimistic scenario, there is an expected transaction gain of $44,500 U.S. Conversely, the firm will experience a $17,800 U.S. pretax transaction loss under the base-case scenario.

The tableau presented in table 9.5 is therefore a convenient way to identify the potential for transactions gains or losses when receivables and payables are denominated in imperfectly correlated currencies. Conceptually, the same approach can be employed to assess translation risk when long-term, as well as short-term, assets and liabilities are denominated in multiple foreign currencies.

The tableau results can provide important insights to managers on how to minimize the costs of hedging. For example, in the case described by table 9.5, hedging would only be a relevant strategy in the base-case scenario, since the other relevant scenarios promise a likelihood of exchange-rate gains. Therefore, if management did not see a high probability that the base-case scenario would materialize, it might choose to forego any hedging activity. On the other hand, if management held strongly to the base-case scenario, it might choose to hedge. But it would need to hedge only a portion of its foreign-exchange exposure.

---

[19] It is not essential to elaborate on how the various future spot rates are developed. Presumably the base-case forecast would bear a close relationship to the relevant forward rates, where such forward rates are available or can be inferred from interest-rate differentials.

TABLE 9.5 Multicurrency Transaction-Exposure Tableau

	SPOT RATE	ASSUMED FUTURE SPOT RATES		
	£1.00 = $1.50 U.S. $1.00 CDN. = $.80 U.S.	£1.00 = $1.40 U.S. $1.00 CDN. = $.75 U.S.	£1.00 = $1.55 U.S. $1.00 CDN. = $.85 U.S.	£1.00 = $1.48 U.S. $1.00 CDN. = $.78 U.S.
Value of receivables in home currency	$1,600,000	$1,500,000	$1,700,000	$1,560,000
Value of payables in home currency	1,665,000	1,554,000	1,720,500	1,642,800
Net receivables (payables) in home currency	(65,000)	(54,000)	(20,500)	(82,800)
Change in receivables—change in payables		(100,000) – (111,000) =	100,000 – 55,500 =	(40,000) – (22,200) =
		+ 11,000	+ 44,500	– 17,800

235

TABLE 9.6   The Effect of Liquidating a Portion of Acme's Canadian Dollar Receivables

CASE ONE

Acme liquidates $1 million Cdn. at the start of the period at the assumed rate: $1 Cdn. = $.79 U.S. It therefore realizes $790,000 U.S. on this portion of its receivables.
It is assumed that the remaining $1 million Cdn. is liquidated at the base-case rate: $1 Cdn. = $.78 U.S. Acme realizes $780,000 U.S. on this portion of its receivables.
It is assumed that the entire British pound liability position is "closed out" at the base-case exchange rate.
The realized U.S. dollar value of Acme's receivables will therefore be $790,000 + $780,000 = $1,570,000 U.S.
**The change in receivables — change in payables = (30,000) — (22,000) = — 8,000

CASE TWO

Acme liquidates $1.5 million Cdn. at the start of the period at the assumed rate: $1 Cdn. = $.79 U.S., thereby realizing $1,185,000 U.S. on this portion of its receivables.
Acme would then realize $390,000 U.S. on the remainder of its receivable position.
The realized U.S. dollar value of Acme's receivables will therefore be $1,185,000 + $390,000 = $1,575,000.
**The change in receivables — change in payables = (25,000) — (22,000) = — 3,000

Consider, for example, a case where management has an opportunity to liquidate some or all of its Canadian dollar receivables at the rate of $1 Cdn. = $.79 U.S.[20] Table 9.6 shows that the potential transactions losses under the base-case scenario can be cut in half by liquidating half the Canadian-dollar-receivable position. The potential loss can be reduced by over 80 percent by liquidating three-fourths of the exposed Canadian dollar position.

SUMMARY AND CONCLUSION

Fluctuating currency values impose a variety of risks upon firms that engage in international business. Three broad types of risks are described in the international business literature: transaction risk, translation risk, and economic risk.

Transaction risk (or exposure) refers to the potential change in realized cash flow associated with forseeable transactions denominated in foreign currencies. Typically, these transactions involve liquidating near-term receivables and payables. The risk involved is that assets denominated in foreign currencies will decrease in home-currency value, while liabilities denominated in foreign currencies will increase in home-currency value. Transactions gains or losses are usually accounted for as an addition to or subtraction from current income, although in some cases transactions gains are treated as capital gains. Thus, they constitute real cash-flows gains or losses for the international firm.

---

[20]We leave to the next chapter, a discussion of different ways to hedge foreign-exchange exposure without using the forward market.

Translation risk (or exposure) is related to the difference between the value of foreign assets and foreign liabilities that are consolidated into the parent company's balance sheet at the current exchange rate. It is therefore a function of the distribution of a broad maturity range of assets and liabilities denominated in foreign currencies. Under new accounting procedures for U.S. companies, translation gains or losses are treated as reserve items and are not directly added to or subtracted from current income. Thus, they do not have an immediate effect on a firm's cash flow.

The broadest concept of exchange-rate risk (economic risk) refers to potential changes in the long-run profitability of the international firm associated with exchange-rate changes. Economic risk is therefore concerned with direct changes in the home-country value of liquidated assets and liabilities as well as with the impact of exchange-rate changes on the competitive position of the international firm. In the long run, the indirect (or competitive) impacts of exchange-rate changes are likely to have the greatest relevance for management. Unfortunately, these competitive impacts are often difficult to quantify; however, they will typically be manifested in either changing costs of production or changes in the firm's unit sales volume.

There tends to be disagreement between theoreticians and practitioners about how much attention should be paid to translation exposure. A substantial number of academics argue that translation gains or losses are merely bookkeeping entries that have little relationship to the firm's long-run net worth and should therefore be ignored. On the other hand, many managers continue to believe that investors are concerned about recorded translation gains and losses and, therefore, that managerial efforts to reduce translation exposure are in the shareholders' interest. This remains an area where ''best practice'' is uncertain.

Unlike translation exposure, transaction exposure has direct cash-flow implications for the firm. Yet there is still contention, especially among academicians, about the wisdom of hedging transaction risk. The primary caution is that if money markets and currency markets are efficient, the costs of hedging will approximately equal the anticipated benefits. However, since there is reason to question whether relevant markets are efficient at all times, many management experts continue to support the hedging of transaction risk as a legitimate practice. Furthermore, reduced uncertainty itself may have value to decision makers, even if (on average) the costs of reducing uncertainty are at least as great as the costs avoided through hedging. Nevertheless, international managers are advised to weigh the costs of hedging against the anticipated benefits in order to minimize uneconomic expenditures on risk reduction.

DISCUSSION QUESTIONS

1. Explain the distinctions among transaction exposure, translation exposure, and economic exposure.
2. Where forward markets exist for foreign exchange, managers can

evaluate the risks of transaction and translation losses against the market forecasts of experienced currency traders. But forward rates are not normally quoted beyond one year into the future. Is there any other source of information that can provide managers with market forecasts of more distant exchange-rate relationships? (Hint: recall the interest-arbitrage model.)

3. What is the relevance of purchasing-power parity to the concept of economic risk? Discuss why you do or do not believe that purchasing-power parity is a useful theory for international managers to incorporate in their decision making?

4. A simplified balance sheet as of December 1984 for Internatcan, the Canadian subsidiary of New York-based Internat, Inc., is reported below. For simplicity, assume that the spot rate of exchange as of this balance-sheet date was $1 U.S. = $1 Cdn. Show how Internatcan's balance sheet would be consolidated into the parent company's balance sheet, assuming that the exchange rate on the next balance-sheet date is $1.00 Cdn. = $.80 U.S. Use both the old translation procedure (FASB-8) and the new procedure (FASB-52). Assume also that the balance-sheet items remain unchanged between reporting dates.

Internatcan Ltd. Balance Sheet ($ millions Cdn.)

ASSETS		LIABILITIES	
Cash	$ 50	Accounts payable	$ 70
Accounts receivable	80	Long-term debt	95
Inventory	25		
Plant and equipment	110	Net worth	100
	$265		$265

5. Evaluate arguments for and against hedging translation risk.

6. Which specific U.S. industries do you think enjoyed the greatest economic benefits from the sharp appreciation in the U.S. during the early 1980s? Which do you think suffered economic hardship as a result of the dollar's appreciation? Explain your answer.

REFERENCES

Choi, F. D. S., and G. G. Mueller, *An Introduction to Multinational Accounting.* Englewood Cliffs, N.J.: Prentice-Hall, 1978.

Eiteman, David K., and Arthur I. Stonehill, *Multinational Business Finance,* 2nd ed., chap. 3. Reading, Mass.: Addison-Wesley Publishing Co., 1979.

Frank, W. G., "An Empirical Analysis of International Accounting Principles." *Journal of Accounting Research* (Autumn 1979), 593–605.

Kubin, Konrad, "Financial Accounting and Reporting for International Business Operations." In H. Peter Halzer, ed., *International Accounting.* New York: Harper and Row, Publishers, 1984, 47–104.

OFFICER, LAWRENCE, "Effective Exchange Rates and Price Ratios Over the Long-Run: A Test of the Purchasing-Power-Parity Theory." *Canadian Journal of Economics* Vol. 13 (May 1980), 206-31.
POWELL, WILLIAM J., JR., "The Superdollar's Latest Victim." *Business Week,* March 4, 1985, 28-29.

APPENDIX 9A: TRANSLATION PROCEDURES IN OTHER COUNTRIES

There are various methods used to consolidate foreign-denominated assets and liabilities for purposes of headquarters financial reporting. The main methods include:

1. Current/noncurrent: All current assets and current liabilities of foreign affiliates are translated into the home currency at the current exchange rate; i.e., at the exchange rate in effect on the date of the statement. Noncurrent assets and liabilities are translated at historic rates; i.e., at the rates in existence on the date the assets were acquired or the liabilities incurred (used in Argentina, Brazil, Mexico, and other Latin American countries).

2. Monetary/nonmonetary: Acquisition-date exchange rates are used for nonmonetary items; monetary assets (cash, marketable securities, accounts receivable, and long-term receivables) and monetary liabilities (long-term and current) are translated at current exchange rates (used in Canada and South Africa).

3. Temporal: Assuming historical cost accounting, the temporal method follows the monetary/nonmonetary approach. Differences would be apparent if, for example, generally accepted accounting principles supported the use of inflation adjustments to assets and liabilities, e.g., replacement-cost valuation techniques.

4. Closing or current rate: All assets and liabilities are translated at the current exchange rate. Equity is translated at the historic rate but is adjusted up or down by the net foreign-exchange gain or loss (used in Great Britain and Continental Europe).

When the transaction and settlement dates for foreign-currency transactions are within the same accounting period, exchange gains and losses are treated as realized and, as such, generally are recognized in the income statement.

Current practice around the world varies significantly with respect to the treatment of unrealized gains with a somewhat greater degree of harmonization as to unrealized losses. The recognition of exchange losses on unsettled transactions (except on certain hedging and intercompany transactions) in the income statement is either required or predominant practice in most countries. The practice of recognizing gains on monetary items in the income statement is widespread; however, in some countries all gains are deferred on the grounds of prudence.

The material in this appendix draws heavily on Hanns-Martin W. Schoenfeld, "International Accounting: Development, Issues and Future Directions," *Journal of International Business Studies* 12 (Fall 1981), 83-100.
The definition of economic exposure presented in this appendix is taken from Clas G. Wihlborgk, "Currency Exposure: Taxonomy and Theory," in Richard Levich and Clas Wihlborgk, eds., *Exchange Risk and Exposure: Current Developments in International Financial Management.* Lexington, Mass.: Lexington Books, D. C. Heath and Co., Copyright 1980, D. C. Heath and Company, reprinted by permission of the publisher, 1980, pp. 23-44.

In some countries, e.g., West Germany and Austria, translation gains and losses are generally recorded directly in shareholders' equity. In Canada, translation gains and losses are recorded directly in income except for those on long-term monetary items that are deferred and amortized to income over the period of the item.*

APPENDIX 9B: DEFINING ECONOMIC EXPOSURE

The concept of economic exposure can be brought into clearer focus by defining the value of a foreign affiliate as the present value of the stream of dividends paid by the affiliate to the parent, where the dividends are adjusted for exchange-rate changes and for price changes. This value is given as the solution to equation 9B.1, where we assume for purposes of the example that the parent-company shareholders are U.S. residents:

$$(9B.1) \quad V_0 = \frac{D_{i,U.S.}}{(1+r).P_{i,U.S.}} + \ldots + \frac{D_{n,U.S.}}{(1+r)^n.P_{n,U.S.}} + \frac{F_{n,U.S.}}{(1+r)^n.P_{n,U.S.}}$$

where

$F_{n,U.S.}$ = face value or realization of the affiliate in period n in U.S. dollars
D_i = expected dividend payments to shareholders in period i
$P_{i,U.S.}$ = expected price levels in the U.S.
r = discount rate in real terms (assumed to be constant over the period)

The dividend stream, in turn, is given as equation 9B.2:

$$(9B.2) \quad D_{i,U.S.} = (Y_i P_i^o - Y_i P_i^I - Y_i.P_i^L - \delta.P_i^K.K_i - g_i)(1-t)_i e$$

where

Y_i = quantity of goods sold by the affiliate in period i
P_i^o = price of output in country of sales in period i
P_i^I = price of inputs in country of purchase in period i
P^L_i = unit labor costs in the country of production in period i
P^K_i = price level of plant and equipment in country of production in period i
K_i = capital stock (plant and equipment) in period i in real terms
δ = depreciation rate
g_i = realized gains and losses on assets and liabilities other than plant and equipment in period i

*A discussion of the accounting treatment of exchange gains and losses is contained in Ernst and Whinney, "Foreign Currency Translation: A Comparison of International Translation," mimeographed, 1983.

t = tax rate

e_i = exchange rate in period i between U.S. dollar and the currency of denomination of the different components of profit

A company is exposed to economic risk if a change in the exchange rate (e_i) can be expected to affect V_0. How might changes in e_i be related to changes in V_0? Looking at equation 13.4, a change in e_i might affect V_0 if output and input prices do not change equiproportionately to the change in e_i. Consider the following case: All prices in the host economy increase by 10 percent, while prices in the U.S. remain constant. Further, the value of the affiliate's functional currency, that is, the currency in which the affiliate's revenues and costs are denominated, decreases by 5 percent against the U.S. dollar. Assuming that all asset and liability values rise by the rate of inflation (so that $g_i = 0$) and that the tax rate is constant, $D_{i,\text{U.S.}}$ will increase by 5 percent. This follows from the fact that local currency profit (that is, the difference between total revenue and total cost) will increase by 10 percent. However, local-currency profit will be worth 5 percent less in terms of the U.S. dollar. As a result, $D_{i,\text{U.S.}}$ will increase by 5 percent, and V_0 will increase.

CHAPTER TEN

Managing Foreign-Exchange Risk

There are numerous ways to hedge foreign-exchange risk, and all share a common characteristic: the hedger typically accepts a certain cost for the prospect of an uncertain benefit. In many cases, the anticipated benefit relates to lower transaction or translation losses associated with adverse foreign-exchange movements. In other cases, the anticipated benefit is associated with forestalling or reversing a deterioration in the firm's long-run competitive position in international markets. The costs associated with hedging also take various possible forms. Most typically, costs take the form of losses on selling forward foreign exchange at a discount or buying forward foreign exchange at a premium. In other cases, hedging costs take the form of foregone interest on assets or higher interest payments on liabilities. In all cases, brokerage fees and other transactions costs will be incurred in forward market-hedging operations and in hedging through readjustment of the firm's net asset position.

Before considering the various ways in which foreign-exchange risk can be hedged, we might restate our definition of hedging from the preceding chapter. Namely, a hedge represents a transaction that is entered into in order to protect the home-currency value of foreign-currency-denominated assets or liabilities, or foreign-currency-denominated prospective cash flows. As such, hedging represents an attempt to balance the international firm's exposure in foreign currencies. On the other hand, when management enters into forward market transactions in order to profit from imperfectly anticipated (by the market) movements in foreign-exchange rates, the firm is said to be engaging in speculation. While there have been cases of successful currency speculation by firms whose primary business does not involve currency brokerage services, in most cases, such speculative ventures have proven costly for the firm's shareholders. At the risk of sounding dogmatic, we would assert that the techniques discussed in this chapter are appropriate for "covering" exposed positions in foreign currencies and that it is irresponsible for managers to gamble on changes in the prices of currencies in which the firm has no existing or anticipated exposure.

DESIGNING A HEDGING STRATEGY

As one international finance expert has noted, the usefulness of a hedging strategy depends on both acceptability and quality. To be acceptable, a hedging strategy must be consistent with the values of top management and with the corporation's overall objectives. The latter, in turn, should reflect management's perceptions about how the capital markets will evaluate the firm's performance. The quality of a particular hedging strategy is related to whether or not the strategy will promote a higher valuation of the firm's performance by the capital markets.[1]

The most frequently encountered objectives, explicit and implicit, in management behavior toward foreign-exchange risk include the following:

1. Minimize translation exposure: focus on protecting longer-term foreign-currency-denominated assets and liabilities from changes in value that are due to exchange-rate fluctuations.

2. Minimize transaction exposure: protect foreign-currency-denominated assets and liabilities whose near-term liquidation or payment dates are known or are reasonably certain.

3. Minimize economic exposure: to achieve this goal, a firm must ignore the accounting impacts of exchange-rate changes and concentrate on reducing fluctuations over time in cash flow that are due to currency fluctuations.

4. Minimize quarter-to-quarter (or year-to-year) earnings fluctuations due to exchange-rate changes: this short-run focus primarily overlaps the objective to minimize transaction exposure.

5. Avoid surprises: prevent large foreign-exchange losses, whether or not these losses will ever be realized in the firm's income statement.[2]

Studies show that most companies attempt to balance off the costs and benefits of hedging. For example, most companies evaluate their exposure after netting out offsetting foreign-exchange positions, as described in the preceding

---

[1]See Alan C. Shapiro, *Multinational Financial Management* (Boston: Allyn & Bacon, 1982), p. 155.

[2]Ibid., p. 156.

chapter. As well, exposed positions are rarely fully hedged, especially in cases where assets are denominated in "strong" currencies and liabilities are denominated in weak currencies. However, hedging procedures are not always well thought out by management.

One study, for example, found that for a sample of international firms in Canada, a large majority lacked well-defined hedging policies and operating procedures.[3] With the exception of about 10 percent of the surveyed firms, statements of objectives were typically put in fairly simplistic and broad terms, such as "protecting the company against losses," "minimizing exchange losses and avoiding unnecessary and expensive coverage," or "avoiding speculation and pursuing a policy of full coverage whenever possible." A few firms specified a "threshold level" of exposure beyond which a certain action would be taken, but these constituted a minority. In some cases, there was difficulty in arriving at an estimate of the firm's foreign-exchange exposure because records were not kept in a manner that could easily provide such information. But the majority of sample firms lay between the few extreme cases of highly developed systems on the one hand and almost nonexistent systems on the other hand.

Similar studies for U.S. companies find that the two most common cases of exchange transactions, both of which management worries about, are remittances to the parent company from subsidiaries (dividends in particular) and specific large transactions denominated in foreign currencies—for example, payments for a plant purchased or built abroad. However, in the majority of companies no formal records of future exchange transactions are maintained. Furthermore, balance-sheet (or translation) exposure is often analyzed from reports that were as much as three months behind the period under review.[4] Of course, as firms gain experience with foreign-exchange-risk management, future surveys may find that international managers are increasingly formalizing and standardizing procedures toward hedging exchange-rate risk.

Perhaps the most important observation to note is that managers do not base their hedging decisions strictly on the basis of comparisons between the expected values of hedging and nonhedging alternatives. If they did, and if they believed that markets were efficient so that current forward market rates were the best available forecasts of future spot rates, there would be no net gains from hedging. On average, unexpected exchange-rate gains would equal unexpected losses. But managers are risk averse; that is, they are more concerned with avoiding losses than with realizing gains. Therefore, hedging strategies may be considered appropriate even when management assumes that foreign-exchange markets are efficient. The incentive to hedge an exposed position would increase to the extent

[3]Talaat Abdel-Malek, "Managing Exchange Risks Under Floating Exchange Rates: The Canadian Experience," *Columbia Journal of World Business* Vol. 11 (Fall 1976).

[4]See, for example, Rita M. Rodriguez, "An Analysis of the Exchange Management Decision in U.S. Multinationals," in John S. Oh, ed., *International Financial Management: Problems, Issues and Experiences* (Greenwich, Conn.: JAI Press, 1983), pp. 85–102.

that the maximum possible exchange loss exceeded the maximum possible exchange gain.

The extent to which any firm hedges foreign-exchange risk will therefore depend partly upon the degree of management's risk aversion, where management is presumably acting in the interests of the firm's owners. While one cannot talk about a universal ''best-practice'' approach to hedging foreign-exchange risk, one can conclude that given specific objectives, management should be efficient in its approaches toward hedging. That is, it should utilize the least expensive hedging alternatives available and should consider the implications of its hedging strategies on other activities in the firm, including marketing and working-capital management.

CASE STUDY: *PHILLIPS PETROLEUM'S FOREIGN-CURRENCY-EXPOSURE MANAGEMENT PROGRAM*

The foreign-exchange-risk-management program at Phillips Petroleum, while not typical of all large companies, illustrates the types of issues that any such programs must address. Phillips's foreign-currency-management program has historically been cash oriented, that is, hedging is undertaken for immediate cash-flow requirements. The management program is centralized with respect to policy guidelines, while hedging strategies are normally executed at headquarters and the company's field offices.

Phillips's management had traditionally been willing to accept translation fluctuations provided they were not excessive. However, with exposures at the $800 million level, coupled with significant currency movements in the late 1970s, substantial translation losses were experienced. Management subsequently amended its exposure-management guidelines, which are premised on the following:

1. Phillips is in the energy business and does not want to be exposed to large foreign-currency movements.

2. Phillips does not want translation results to exceed a stipulated amount each year. Thus, they have set tolerance levels of translation results assuming currency movements do not move by more than ± 10 percent against corporate exposures.

In summary, Phillips has embarked on an aggressive program to reduce corporate exposures so as to reduce expected translation results to levels which meet corporate objectives. The company is willing to forego opportunities for translation gains in order to protect earnings per share provided the cash costs are not considered prohibitive. The primary hedging technique used by Phillips involves forward foreign-currency purchases.

Source: J. J. Mulva, ''Phillips Petroleum Company Approach to Foreign Currency Exposure Management,'' in John S. Oh, ed., *International Financial Management: Problems, Issues and Experiences* (Greenwich, Conn.: JAI Press, Inc., 1983), pp. 103–8.

HEDGING IN THE FORWARD MARKET

The most popular technique for hedging the exposure of short-term assets and liabilities with known maturity dates (usually of less than one year) involves buying or selling forward foreign exchange. Specifically, to fully hedge a net short-term asset position denominated in a foreign currency, a firm would sell forward the foreign currency in an amount equal to the exposed net-asset position. A net-liability position would be covered by buying the foreign currency forward.

The traditional way of measuring the relative cost of a forward contract is to calculate the spread between the spot and forward rates at the time the contract is initiated. On an after-tax basis, expressed at an annual rate, this cost (excluding transactions costs) is given as equation 10.1:

$$(10.1) \quad CH = \frac{360}{n} \frac{(e_o - f_n)}{e_0} (1 - t)$$

where

CH	=	cost of hedging
e_o	=	the current spot rate
f_n	=	the forward rate on a contract of length n
t	=	the effective tax rate on forward contract gains or losses in the country in which the contract is sourced[5]

To illustrate the implications of equation 10.1, assume that the current spot rate of the Canadian dollar is \$.80 U.S., while the ninety-day forward rate is \$.79 U.S. If the company's marginal tax rate equals .5, the after-tax cost of selling Canadian dollars forward on a ninety-day basis (ignoring transactions costs) is:

$$(10.2) \quad CH = \frac{360}{90} \times \left(\frac{.80 - .79}{.80} \right) \times .5 = .025 \text{ or } 2.5\%$$

On the other hand, if the Canadian dollar is at a premium in the forward market (e.g., \$1 Cdn. = \$.81 U.S.), the cost of selling Canadian dollars forward would actually be negative (i.e., -2.5 percent). That is, the hedger would gain income by selling forward. Symmetrically, the cost of buying Canadian dollars forward would be positive if the Canadian unit was at a premium in the forward market, while the cost would be negative if the Canadian dollar was at a discount.

Some economists argue that the traditional method of measuring the cost of a forward contract is wrong because the relevant comparison is between the dollar value of foreign exchange received with hedging and the value that the firm expects to receive in the absence of hedging. That is, they argue that the real cost of

---

[5]Losses are commonly treated as a cost of doing business, whereas gains may be taxable as capital gains depending on the maturity of the contract and the country involved.

hedging is an opportunity cost. Following this viewpoint, the (after-tax) relative cost of hedging would be calculated as:

$$(10.3) \quad CH^1 = \frac{360}{n} \quad \frac{(e_n - f_n)}{e_0} \, (1 - t)$$

where

e_n = the future (expected) spot rate on the date of settlement
CH^1 = opportunity cost of hedging

Thus, if the firm's estimate of the future spot rate of a foreign currency exceeds the forward rate, the firm incurs an expected (positive) cost in selling the currency forward. In our preceding example, if management's best guess as to the future spot rate of the Canadian dollar ninety days hence is $.81 U.S., CH^1 would be calculated similarly to CH in equation 10.2, except that .81 would be used instead of .80 in the numerator. Note that if the firm's estimate of the future spot rate exceeds the forward rate, the cost of buying foreign exchange forward is negative, by this opportunity cost measure. And where management accepts the existing forward rate as its best forecast of the future spot rate, the opportunity costs of hedging are nil, since $e_n = f_n$.

In fact, equation 10.3 is most properly viewed as a decision rule rather than an accounting measure of the "out-of-pocket," or cash-flow, gain or loss associated with forward cover. There is certainly a compelling argument for buying (or selling) foreign-currency forward whenever $e_n > f_n$ or $(e_n < f_n)$. But for purposes of recording additions to, or deductions from operating income associated with foreign-exchange transactions, equation 10.1 is the appropriate measure of the cost of hedging.

Numerous examples can be cited of firms that use the forward market to hedge exchange-rate risk. One involves the Toronto Blue Jays baseball team. As we noted in the previous chapter, the bulk of the team's expenses consists of salaries denominated in U.S. dollars while most of its revenues are denominated in Canadian dollars. The Blue Jays management purchases U.S. dollars forward to hedge some of its contractual commitments. However, the rapid and continued slide in the Canadian dollar over the first half of the 1980s had the club's management likening its forward hedging to "applying a bandage when a tourniquet is needed."[6]

In the case of the Blue Jays, management did not hedge its entire exposed liability position in U.S. dollars, which (in retrospect) might be considered a mistake. In other cases, however, shareholders have regretted the hedging activities of management. For example, in 1982 Great Lakes Forest Products of Thunder Bay, Ontario, sold forward U.S. dollars it expected to receive from

---

[6]See Jamie Wayne, "Exchange Rate Catches Teams in Squeeze Play," *Financial Post* (Toronto), May 14, 1983, 40.

wood-products exports to the U.S. The forward exchange contracts for delivery of $690 million U.S. to the end of 1984 seemed a good way to lock in profit at $1.18 Canadian for $1 U.S. However, it turned out to be a cause for regret as the U.S. dollar continued to rise over the period to around $1.30 Canadian.

The point illustrated in these two examples is that hedging transactions exposure involves judgment calls that can often be criticized after the fact. In the case of the Blue Jays, management believed that the Canadian dollar was more likely to rise than to fall further. As a result, they limited their short-term hedging activity. Since most currency experts were surprised by the strength of the U.S. dollar's rise against other major currencies, including the Canadian dollar, the Blue Jays management was not alone in its poor forecast. Nevertheless, the club's shareholders might legitimately argue that the potential costs of inaccurate forecasting were sufficiently great to warrant more extensive hedging in the forward market.

Economists have developed fairly elaborate mathematical models to determine the "optimal" amount of hedging that international firms should do in the forward market. While consideration of these models is beyond the scope of this basic text, their fundamental deduction is that a greater proportion of a firm's exposed position should be hedged as the movement between spot and forward foreign-exchange rates becomes more closely correlated. As an empirical matter, it is generally inefficient for firms to hedge their entire net transactions exposure, especially when transactions costs of hedging are incorporated in the analysis.

The forward market is a popular instrument for short-term hedging, especially when the positions to be hedged are denominated in major currencies, since the associated transactions costs are relatively low.[7] Furthermore, forward hedging does not disturb the firm's asset/liability position, as is the case with some other hedging techniques that we shall discuss below.

Futures markets in foreign currencies can also be used to hedge short-run foreign-exchange risk. The majority of futures trading in currencies takes place on the International Monetary Market (IMM) of the Chicago Mercantile Exchange. In general, a futures contract differs from a forward contract in that the former is negotiable and the terms are standardized with respect to the size of the contract and the delivery date, whereas the latter is not standardized. The currency futures and forward-exchange markets accomplish pretty much the same hedging purposes, although they differ substantially in operation. While one or the other market may be better suited for any given firm, the currency-futures market possesses certain general advantages, including the availability of more buyers and sellers and high market liquidity. Very large firms may find the relatively small, fixed contract sizes traded on futures markets inconvenient for their hedg-

[7]Boothe estimates that the direct transactions costs of forward exchange commitments are on the order of ½ of 1 percent. The cost of maintaining a credit line to buy or sell forward contracts is also around ½ of 1 percent. So total transactions costs are around 1 percent. See Paul Boothe, "Speculative Profit Opportunities in the Canadian Foreign Exchange Market, 1974–78," *Canadian Journal of Economics* 16, November 1983, 607–8.

ing needs. On the other hand, smaller firms may find they have easier access to futures markets, since IMM contraçts can be bought (or sold) by anyone who puts up a security deposit, in contrast to forward contracts, which are arranged by banks with customers they deem credit worthy.

In many cases, employing forward (or futures) market cover is impractical, even for relatively short-term hedging needs because the precise timing of a foreign-currency-denominated transaction is uncertain. In this case currency options may be useful hedging tools.

HEDGING UNCERTAIN
FOREIGN-EXCHANGE-DENOMINATED TRANSACTIONS

Consider the following hypothetical example. General Electric bids against a number of Japanese companies to sell electrical generators to a large German utility company. If its bid is accepted, General Electric will receive an initial payment of DM4 million. The result of the bidding process will be known some time during the next two months. General Electric could sell the anticipated DM4 million forward, but if its bid is not selected, it will have an open position in DMs and could lose money. A similar conflict would confront a firm facing a potential liability denominated in a foreign currency. For example, a U.S. electrical utility might be contemplating the purchase of generating equipment from one of a number of European or Japanese firms. It may be unsure whether it will actually purchase the equipment as well as from whom the purchase would be made. As a result, if it buys a foreign-currency forward, it runs a risk that the foreign currency will not actually be needed for offshore purchases. The purchased currency might in turn have to be sold at a loss.

One possible way of hedging uncertain foreign-currency-denominated transactions is to arrange a forward exchange contract with a bank, where the date of execution of the contract is at the customer's choice within a specified period of time. The problem is that the customer must ultimately honor the forward commitment, even if the anticipated transaction does not materialize. An alternative way to hedge uncertain transactions is through the use of so-called foreign-exchange options.

PUTS AND CALLS

Options are financial instruments that convey the right, but not the obligation, to buy or sell a designated quantity of a foreign currency at a specific price (exchange rate). For example, the purchaser of a put option buys the right to sell a certain quantity of a foreign currency at a stipulated price. The purchaser of a call option acquires the right to buy a certain quantity of a foreign currency at a stipulated price. Currency options were sold in an unorganized fashion in the United States, but their illiquidity made them a relatively unused hedging tool. More recently, foreign-exchange options began to be traded on organized stock exchanges. As a result, they are becoming an increasingly important hedging instrument.[8] There are currently three major North American exchanges in which currency options are bought and sold: the Philadelphia Stock Exchange, the Chicago Mercantile Exchange, and the Montreal Exchange. But, in fact, most of the writing of currency options is being done by banks. Major banks offer options tailored to the individual specifications of very large customers. We can perhaps better appreciate the nature of these financial instruments by considering the contract specifications for puts and calls on the Philadelphia Stock Exchange as reported in table 10.1.

The first row in table 10.1 shows the standard contract size for a put or a call in the foreign-currency unit. For example, the standard contract for a put or a call on the Swiss currency is 62,500 Swiss francs. It might be noted that the standard contract sizes on the Montreal Exchange are substantially smaller than on the Philadelphia Stock Exchange. For example, puts and calls on the Deutsche mark and Swiss franc are for 25,000 units, while the contract sizes for the British pound and Japanese yen are 5,000 and 2,500,000 units, respectively. The contract size for Canadian dollars is 50,000 units on both the Philadelphia and Montreal exchanges.

The second row in table 10.1 shows the intervals at which the so-called strike prices for the various options will be set. The strike price is the contracted price (or exchange rate) at which the option can be exercised by the holder. On the Philadelphia exchange, the intervals are set at two cents for most currencies, with the exception of the British pound and Japanese yen. The strike-price intervals on the Montreal Exchange are set at one cent for the Deutsche mark, Swiss franc, Canadian dollar, and Japanese yen. The strike price interval for the British pound is five cents on both exchanges.

The strike-price concept can be illustrated by reproducing several contracts for Canadian dollar options as they were listed on the Montreal Exchange on January 16, 1984. Table 10.2 shows strike-price intervals for $.79 U.S.–$.82 U.S. The first entry in the table shows the bid and ask prices for a March .79 call. The bid price of .0131 shows the willingness of some currency traders to pay $.0131 U.S., per Canadian currency unit, for the option to buy $50,000 Canadian at an exchange rate of $1.00 Cdn. = $.7900 U.S. The expiration date for this option was the Saturday following the third Friday in March 1984. The total cost of this call option, presuming it was purchased at the bid price, equals ($.0131 × 50,000) = $655 U.S. In fact, the market clearing price for this contract probably lay somewhere between the bid price and the ask price ($.0140). Note that the March call series increases by one-cent intervals through $.82. Note also that options are ordinarily listed for up to nine months forward. In table 10.2, options contracts are listed through September 1984.

[8]An excellent description of currency options is provided in Ian H. Giddy, "Foreign Exchange Options," *Journal of Futures Markets* 3, (1983), 143–66.

TABLE 10.1 Contract Specifications for Puts and Calls Traded on the Philadelphia Stock Exchange

	DEUTSCHE MARKS	SWISS FRANCS	CANADIAN DOLLARS	BRITISH POUNDS	JAPANESE YEN
Underlying currency units	62,500	62,500	50,000	12,500	6,250,000
Exercise price intervals	2¢	2¢	2¢	5¢	.02¢
Exercise price and Premium quotations	Cents/ Unit	Cents/ Unit	Cents/ Unit	Cents/ Unit	Hundredths Cents/ Unit
Minimum premium charge	.01	.01	.01	.05	.01
Minimum contract price charge	$6.25	$6.25	$5.00	$6.25	$6.25

Source: Philadelphia Stock Exchange, Contract Specifications.

**TABLE 10.2   Options on the Canadian Dollar, 50,000 CAN.
Series Traded January 16, 1984—Montreal***

SERIES	BID	ASK	CLOSING PRICE FOR CURRENCY
March 79	.0131	.0140	.8030
March 79P	.0006	.0007	,,
June 79	.0137	.0146	,,
June 79P	.0009	.0010	,,
Sept. 79	.0141	.0150	,,
Sept. 79P	.0010	.0012	,,
March 80	.0035	.0043	,,
March 80P	.0008	.0012	,,
June 80	.0060	.8030	,,
June 80P	.0020	.0023	,,
Sept. 80	.0067	.0075	,,
Sept. 80P	.0029	.0034	,,
March 81	.0003	.0006	,,
March 81P	.0066	.0075	,,
June 81	.0012	.0016	,,
June 81P	.0071	.0080	,,
Sept. 81	.0024	.0028	,,
Sept. 81P	.0076	.0085	,,
March 82	.0001	.0003	,,
March 82P	.0166	.0174	,,
June 82	.0001	.0030	,,
June 82P	.0171	.0180	,,
Sept. 82			
Sept. 82P			

Source: *The Globe and Mail,* January 17, 1984, B14. By permission of The Canadian Press.
*Note: No prices were quoted for the September 82 series.

How would the March 79p (put) contract be interpreted? The bid price of $.0006 shows the willingness of currency traders to pay $.0006 U.S. per Canadian currency unit for the option to sell $50,000 Canadian at an exchange rate of $1.00 Cdn. = $.7900 U.S. The total cost of this put option, assuming a transaction at the bid price, would be $30 U.S. = ($.0006 U.S. × 50,000). Once again, the transaction price was likely between the bid and the ask price ($.0007). Table 10.2 shows prices quoted to the fourth significant digit. Hence, the minimum contract price change is $5.00 U.S. = (50,000 × .0001).

The following hypothetical example illustrates how option contracts on the Canadian dollar might be used by international businesses. Imagine that a U.S. steel company is contemplating buying $500,000 Canadian worth of coal from Nova Scotia Coal Ltd. The purchase depends upon auto-production activity, which varies quite markedly from quarter to quarter. As of January 16, 1985, the steel company sees the possibility of sharply expanded production of autos in the summer of 1985, in which case it will need to step up its production of steel and its purchases of coal. On the other hand, if a surge in auto production does not take place, increased future purchases of coal will not be needed. The U.S. steel company might therefore be reluctant to buy Canadian dollars forward in anticipation of buying coal, since it will then be obligated to take delivery of $500,000 Canadian or sell the $500,000 Canadian (possibly at a loss), if it later decided against the coal purchases.

In this situation, the U.S. steel company might contemplate buying options on the Canadian dollar. If it bought ten call options, it could lock in a price on $500,000 Canadian (that is, ten contracts worth $50,000 Canadian each) and would be under no obligation to take delivery of the Canadian currency. For example, the U.S. company might buy ten March 79 call options at, say, $.0136. This purchase would cost $6,800, plus brokerage commissions. If sometime before the expiration date, the company decided against buying additional coal, it could sell the ten call options. It is possible that the price received will be higher or lower than the original price paid. However, the most the company could lose is the initial $6,800, since it would simply allow the call options to expire if the price of the Canadian dollar dropped below $.79 U.S. before expiration.

FINANCIAL HEDGES

Borrowing or lending to hedge transaction exposure might be advisable where no forward market exists for a currency, where a currency is susceptible to the imposition of government exchange controls, or where other restrictions or imperfections in the forward market lead to systematic departures from covered interest parity.

Consider the case of a U.S. company holding net short-term receivables denominated in Indian rupees. This exposure could be hedged by borrowing the equivalent amount of rupees and converting them to U.S. dollars in the spot market. The borrowing would be paid off when the company liquidates the rupee receivables. In the meanwhile, it is fully hedged against any depreciation in the price of the rupee. Excluding transactions costs, the (annualized) cost of this financial hedge will be the difference in the annual rate of interest paid on the rupee borrowings and the annual rate of interest received on the U.S. dollars obtained through conversion in the spot market, where the latter would presumably be invested in some short-term interest-bearing asset. This type of financial hedge could conceptually be used to cover a long-term net-asset position denominated in rupees or some other foreign currency; however, in many areas of the world, long-term capital markets are simply insufficiently developed to accommodate the large-scale borrowing that might be required.

If the company had a net short-term payable position denominated in rupees, it would presumably reverse the transactions described above. Specifically, it would borrow U.S. dollars in the spot market, convert to rupees in the spot market, and invest the proceeds in rupee-denominated short-term assets. As a practical matter, however, most international companies would probably not hedge a net-liability position denominated in rupees, since the rupee is a weak currency prone to depreciation. In that case, rupee debts would decline in home-currency value, over time. Furthermore, opportunities to invest in liquid and safe, short-term rupee-denominated assets are quite limited. Therefore, the financial hedge described in this paragraph is of primary interest where short-term payables are denominated in currencies prone to revaluation.

It is easy to show that if covered interest arbitrage holds, the nominal cost of hedging through the forward market will approximate the nominal cost of financial hedging.[9] Consider, for example, a U.S. company with ninety-day net receivables equal to $1 million Canadian. Assume that the firm can borrow ninety-day money in Canada at an annual interest rate of 10 percent and that it can invest in a risk-free ninety-day U.S. dollar asset and receive a 9 percent annual yield. If it undertakes this financial hedge, it will receive (on a before-tax basis):

(10.4) $1,000,000 Cdn. × e + $1,000,000 Cdn. × e × (.09 − .10) × 1/4

where e is the spot rate of exchange. If e = $.80 U.S., the hedged value of the receivables will therefore equal $798,000. Since the firm will pay its Canadian dollar borrowings with its receivables when realized, the financial hedge described is an effective way of locking in the spot rate for the company's receivables at a cost of 1 percent interest.

Now consider what the firm's before-tax receipts would be if it sold $1 million Canadian forward. Given that ninety-day assets have a 1 percent per annum premium in Canada, covered interest arbitrage would put the price of the Canadian dollar in the ninety-day forward market at a 1 percent annual discount to spot. The ninety-day rate would therefore be $1 Cdn. = $.7980 U.S.[10] The U.S. firm would therefore receive $798,000 by selling forward its $1 million Canadian receivables position. Obviously, the greater the degree to which covered interest arbitrage holds, the more indifferent the firm will be about hedging in the forward market versus financial hedging.

Invoicing in Home Currency

The exchange-rate risk associated with international transactions can be eliminated by contracting for the transactions to be denominated in the company's home currency. Since this solution transfers the exchange risk to the other party, the latter will presumably insist on more favorable prices for

---

[9]There is an extensive discussion of this point in Laurent L. Jacque, Management of *Foreign Exchange Risk* (Lexington, Mass.: Lexington Books, 1978).

[10]Recall that the forward premium or discount is calculated as $\frac{360}{n}$ × $(\frac{e_0 - f_i}{e_0})$ × 100; setting this term equal to 1, when n = 90 and e = .80 yields f_i = .7980.

the underlying transactions. Where bargaining power is fairly evenly divided, the price discount (on foreign sales) or premium (on foreign purchases) should approximately equal the expected depreciation in the price of the foreign currency. Invoicing in the international firm's home currency would therefore prove to be a cheaper form of hedging than the forward market only when the international firm enjoys some special bargaining power vis-à-vis its trading partners.

LEADS AND LAGS

Firms can reduce foreign-exchange exposure by accelerating or decelerating the timing of payments that must be made in a different currency: that is, by "leading" or "lagging" the movement of funds. Leading and lagging may be done between affiliates or with independent firms. The technique has the effect of changing the asset or liability position in one affiliate with the mirror-image impact on the balance-sheet position of another affiliate. For example, if an international firm has liabilities denominated in currency A and receivables denominated in currency B, it might negotiate for early payment in currency B and use the proceeds of this transaction to eliminate its liability position in currency A.

It is substantially easier for the multinational firm to undertake leading and lagging operations than for the international firm that must deal at arms length with independently owned companies. This is because the headquarter's affiliate in the multinational can effectively dictate interaffiliate transfers of funds, whereas dealing with independent companies calls for negotiation in situations where the other party to the negotiation does not share the same profit objectives as the international company. Periodic payments are often made between units of a multinational firm, providing the opportunity for many types of leads or lags. For example, payments will typically be made for intracompany receivables and payables associated with intracompany shipments of raw materials, goods, and components. Payments may also be associated with royalties and license fees, management fees, and interest and dividend payments.[11]

The basic objective in this risk-management procedure is to lead payments from weak-currency affiliates and to lag payments from strong-currency affiliates. In this way, working capital is not tied up for any length of time in currencies that are depreciating in value but, rather, tends to be concentrated in currencies that are holding up or even increasing in value against the home currency. It is important to note that leading and lagging intracompany cash flows may have substantial impacts on the liquidity positions of various affiliates in the multinational corporate network. That is, the ability of the firm's affiliates to pay their bills in a

---

[11]A short description of how funds flows within the multinational corporate network may be subjected to leads and lags is provided in David K. Eiteman and Arthur I. Stonehill, *Multinational Business Finance,* 2nd ed. (Reading, Mass.: Addison-Wesley Publishing Co., 1979), chap. 4.

timely fashion may be affected by the transfer of working capital among affiliates and divisions. Therefore, the use of leads and lags to reduce exchange-rate risk is subsidiary to leading and lagging intracorporate cash flows in order to manage the international firm's overall working-capital position.

Where the parent affiliate uses leads and lags for exchange-risk management it must be careful to adjust its techniques for measuring profit and controlling the capital budgets of its various affiliates, so that the performance rating of affiliate managers is not affected when one unit "assists" another for the good of the overall enterprise.[12] For example, managers in weak-currency affiliates may have minimal working-capital balances on which to earn interest and other nonoperating income, whereas managers in strong-currency affiliates may be able to show handsome returns on invested capital, thereby boosting their affiliates' overall profit performance. Management should also be cognizant of restrictions that most governments impose on lead and lag periods. For example, the New Zealand government does not permit payment for exports due New Zealand-based companies to be delayed by more than 180 days, and it does not permit prepayment of imports into New Zealand, except on capital equipment where called for by usual trade practice.

Of the various short-term hedging techniques available, leading and lagging intracompany payments tend to be the most frequently used, followed by financial hedges and forward market transactions. Altering the currencies of denomination for arms-length contracts is infrequently undertaken, since interfering with marketing activities is seen to be outside the scope of exchange-risk management.

METHODS OF COVERING LONG-DATE EXPOSURE

Where the firm's foreign-exchange exposure is associated with foreign-currency-denominated long-term assets and liabilities of indefinite maturity, management is implicitly more concerned with translation exposure than with transaction exposure. In other cases, management may be concerned with hedging long-term foreign-currency-denominated assets or liabilities that have a known maturity date. Hedging either type of exposure will often draw upon the same "balance-sheet" techniques. For example, the creation of liabilities denominated in a weak currency in order to offset a net-asset position in that currency is potentially appropriate for hedging exposed assets of either definite or indefinite maturity. In other cases, however, techniques appropriate for hedging exposed positions of definite maturity are inappropriate for hedging long-term exposed positions of indefinite maturity.

---

[12]Working-capital management and capital-budgeting techniques are discussed in detail in chapter 15.

PARALLEL, OR BACK-TO-BACK, LOANS

These are paired loan agreements whereby one party, with excess liquidity in a particular currency, makes these funds available to a second party.[13] In exchange, the second party makes an equivalent amount of a second currency (in which it has excess liquidity) available to the first party. The parallel loans are transacted through separate loan agreements, one for each currency, with an interest rate applicable to each. The individual interest rates would presumably be appropriate for the term and risk of each loan in its respective currency. A typical agreement might provide for the cross-lending of dollars by a U.S. multinational company to the U.S. subsidiary of a British multinational company, matched by the cross-lending of British pounds by the U.K. parent to the British subsidiary of the U.S. multinational.

Parallel, or back-to-back, loans act as a hedging technique, since the foreign currency borrowed will be repaid at an exchange rate fixed at the time the deal is struck. However, their implementation relies on a mirror-image match by two parties of excess liquidity in one currency and capital requirements in another currency for like amounts and term to maturity. To bridge this difficult matching problem, banks often serve to bring parties together. With their wide range of contracts and their understanding of the foreign-exchange needs of commercial customers, international banks are in a position to be effective intermediaries between parallel lenders.

CURRENCY SWAP

Commercial currency swaps were introduced in the mid-1970s. They provide for the transfer of currencies between parties as of a given date and the reversal of the transfer at the maturity of the swap, normally at the same rate of exchange. Unlike a loan agreement there is no interest payment by either side. Instead a fee is normally paid by the provider of a stronger currency to the provider of the weaker currency, where the fee is set to compensate for the expected change in exchange rates over the life of the swap. The main advantage of swaps over back-to-back loans is that the former employs one agreement rather than two.

Commercial bank swaps have existed much longer than commercial currency swaps. In cases where the availability of a foreign currency is strictly controlled by the central bank, swap arrangements would ordinarily be negotiated between international companies and central banks. Typically, the international company will deposit a certain amount of its home currency with the central bank to obtain a given amount of local currency. The amount of home currency re-

---

[13]For a more detailed description of these and other long-date hedging techniques, see Carl Beidleman, John Hilley, and James Greenleaf, "Alternatives in Hedging Long-Date Contractual Foreign Exchange Exposure," *Sloan Management Review* Vol. 24 (Summer 1983), 46–51.

quired to be put on deposit will depend upon the so-called swap rate of exchange, i.e., the spot rate of exchange established by the central bank. Typically the swap rate will overvalue the local currency. As well, the international company ordinarily earns no interest on the home currency deposited but pays the negotiated rate of interest on the equivalent amount of local currency borrowed. The proceeds of the loan will presumably be invested in a capital project paying returns denominated in the local currency. From these returns the international company will pay back the loan and, ideally, earn its required rate of return.

Upon termination of the loan, the company will receive back its home-currency deposit. The cost of the swap will therefore consist of the foregone yield on the home-currency deposit plus the explicit interest cost of the local currency borrowed from the central bank. The expected yield on the local project (evaluated in home-currency terms) must exceed this swap cost for the project (and the swap arrangement) to be undertaken.

FORWARD SWAPS

Forward swaps (not to be confused with forward market hedges) are similar to currency swaps except that they do not provide for any currency transfers between parties on the day the agreement is formulated. An exchange of currencies is arranged for some future date at an agreed-upon forward rate. An example of such an arrangement would involve a U.S. company anticipating payment in British pounds at some distant date arranging to exchange those pounds for dollars with a British company expecting U.S. dollar receipts at about the same time.

In practice, the starting point for negotiating on agreed-upon forward rate begins with the interest-rate differential on government securities in the two currencies. For example, the five-year forward rate $(F) = \$/\pounds$ on a dollar-sterling forward contract would be based on the spot rate on day 1 (S_o) and the respective five-year interest rate on government securities denominated in each currency $(i_{5,\text{U.S.}})$ and $(i_{5,\text{U.K.}})$:[14]

$$(10.5) \quad F_s = S_o \left(\frac{1 + i_{5,\text{U.S.}}}{1 + i_{5,\text{U.K.}}} \right)^5$$

Since the forward-swap arrangement requires a coincidence of liquidity positions between international companies, much as in the case of back-to-back loans, long-date forward swaps are often arranged by a financial intermediary, such as a commercial bank, with extensive contacts among international firms. The forward contract is by far the most popular of all instruments available for covering long-date foreign-exchange exposure.[15]

[14]See ibid. for the development of this formula.
[15]Beidleman, Hilley, and Greenleaf, p. 52, estimate that 75 percent of long-date foreign-exchange hedging employs forward swaps.

The various ways of hedging transaction and translation exposure that we have discussed to this point are summarized in table 10.3. In fact, most of the methods discussed are especially appropriate for hedging transaction exposure, since the approach to hedging translation exposure most typically involves some variant of borrowing to offset an unwanted net-asset position or acquiring assets to offset an unwanted net-liability position; however, since a number of methods discussed are conceptually applicable to both financial-hedging concerns, economists tend to emphasize a distinction between short-term and long-term hedging instruments.

The various hedging techniques employed by Parker Pen Company illustrate the point that hedging operations ordinarily involve a number of the

TABLE 10.3   Hedging Approaches

TECHNIQUES FOR HEDGING SHORT-TERM FOREIGN-EXCHANGE EXPOSURE

1. Forward market sales or purchases:
   Especially appropriate for hedging net asset or liability positions of short-term and known maturity.
2. Foreign-exchange puts and calls:
   Appropriate for hedging uncertain near-term cash flows denominated in foreign currencies.
3. Financial hedges:
   Appropriate for hedging either where forward markets do not exist and (or) where capital markets are imperfect. When used for short-term hedging, typically involves buying or issuing short-term financial (or money market) instruments.
4. Invoicing in home currency:
   Appropriate particularly when international firm possesses bargaining power.
5. Leads and lags:
   Most appropriate for the international firm with foreign affiliates but subject to government regulation.

TECHNIQUES FOR HEDGING LONG-DATE FOREIGN-EXCHANGE EXPOSURE

6. Financial (or balance-sheet) hedges:
   Similar to short-term financial hedges only maturities of assumed liabilities (or assets) are longer term. In other cases, exposed assets (liabilities) may be liquidated rather than offset by assumed liabilities (or acquired assets).
7. Parallel or back-to-back loans:
   Appropriate where partners are available with excess liquidity in home currency and in need of unwanted foreign exchange.
8. Currency swap:
   Similar to #7, with convenience of requiring one agreement rather than two agreements.
9. Forward swap:
   Most frequently used long-date hedging procedure. Involves a currency exchange between transacting parties at some future date at an agreed-upon exchange rate.

CASE STUDY: *THE APPLICATION OF HEDGING TECHNIQUES—*
PARKER PEN COMPANY

Sharp fluctuations in exchange rates in the 1970s led many multinational companies to strengthen their foreign-currency-management activities. While some companies have large complements of staff and hundreds of specialists to handle their hedging activities, others rely largely upon the corporate treasurer and his or her assistants to handle the hedging function.

An example of the latter sort of company is Parker Pen. Parker's treasurer and his staff are responsible for the company's investment, borrowings, taxes, financial statements, insurance, capital spending, and currency management in the U.S. and the twenty-two foreign countries in which Parker does substantial business. Fifty-five percent of Parker's sales are overseas. One strategy used by the company to deal with the U.S. dollar's gyrations is "leading and lagging"—speeding up or delaying payments according to the changing values of various currencies. An example is provided by the purchase by Parker's German subsidiary of pen parts made by Parker's Spanish unit. Since the Spanish subsidiary bills in pesetas, when the peseta is weakening and the mark is strengthening, the German company will delay payment. On the other hand, if the mark were weakening, the German subsidiary would pay quickly.

Another strategy used by Parker's treasurer is to move as much excess cash as possible into stronger currencies. Still another is to borrow money in the local currency of a foreign subsidiary so that the company's assets there are at least partly offset by debt denominated in that money. And in 1976, Parker came up with a new way to set up liabilities in foreign currencies to offset exposed assets: a loan agreement which gives Parker the option to "redenominate" the balance of its debt (around $11 million in 1978) in Swiss francs, German marks, or other European currencies on thirty days' notice. The option gives Parker the flexibility to move in and out of currencies to balance off exposed assets in its foreign units.

Source: This example is taken from "Corporate Treasurers Face New Uncertainty over Currency Values," *Wall Street Journal*, November 3, 1978, 21. Reprinted by permission of *Wall Street Journal*, © Dow Jones & Co. Inc., (1978). All rights reserved.

techniques described in table 10.3. This theme is further illustrated by surveys of hedging techniques employed by international firms. For example, Abdel-Malek studied a national sample of Canadian firms involved in international business. Responses were obtained from sixty firms, most of which had foreign manufacturing subsidiaries in addition to their export-import operations. The responses are summarized in table 10.4.

The survey shows that forward market hedging is the most frequently used means of hedging foreign-exchange risk. The next most frequently used technique is to bill international transactions in Canadian dollars. Although the bulk of Canada's foreign trade is still financed in U.S. dollars and British pounds, the majority of Canadian firms denominate some of their foreign transactions in Cana-

TABLE 10.4 Means of Covering Foreign-Exchange Risk by Canadian Firms

MEANS OF COVERAGE	PERCENTAGE OF FIRMS
1. Hedging in forward market	
(a) As the only means	25
(b) As one of the means	54
Subtotal	79
2. Use of C$	62
3. Leads and lags	21
4. Local borrowing	19
5. Currency clauses	13
6. Intercompany transfers	19

Source: Talaat Abdel-Malek, "Managing Exchange Risks Under Floating Exchange Rates: The Canadian Experience," *Columbia Journal of World Business* Vol. 11 (Fall 1976).

dian dollars. This was made possible largely by the emergence of a sellers' market in raw-materials-based products in the 1970s, which enabled many Canadian exporters to establish the new practice despite resistance from their foreign customers.

MANAGING LONGER-TERM OPERATING (ECONOMIC) EXPOSURE

Exchange-rate changes can affect the long-run competitive position of an international firm. For example, output sales may decline if the currency in which the output is denominated increases in value against other currencies. As well, a firm's costs of producing and distributing output may be affected by exchange-rate changes. This type of exposure, which we identified in chapter 9 as a potentially important component of economic risk, can be managed through a number of marketing and production strategies.[16]

Potential marketing strategies to confront the competitive effects of exchange-rate changes include price adjustments and advertising and public relations programs. With regard to pricing, where the home currency depreciates (in real terms) against foreign currencies, a company presumably has the option of increasing unit profitability in the home market (by increasing its home-country prices) or expanding its market share (by keeping home-country prices constant and, therefore, allowing the relative prices of imports to rise). The lower value of the home currency effectively raises the home-currency cost of imported goods. By the same token, where the home currency appreciates in value against foreign cur-

[16]An extended discussion of these strategies is found in Shapiro, *Multinational Financial Management*, pp. 196–203.

rencies, companies with affiliates in the home country ostensibly have the option of lowering domestic prices to preserve market share or maintaining home-country prices by accepting the possible erosion of home-country market shares. The greater the price elasticity of demand in the home market and (or) the more significant the economies of scale in production, the greater the incentive of home-country firms to hold down their domestic prices.

In the case of a depreciation in a foreign currency, international firms exporting into that market might consider increasing the base prices of their products, thereby maintaining the home-currency values of their export sales; however, the existence of local competitors will impose something of a tradeoff between preserving the home-currency-denominated per unit markup on export sales and the total unit sales realized, since local producers may become stronger competitors with a decline in the value of the local currency. Again, the more price sensitive the demand in the foreign market and the greater the economies of scale, the stronger the motivation of international firms to maintain equivalency between their host-country prices and those of their competitors. As a practical matter, high-tech companies and others that sell mainly on the basis of product quality rather than price have more flexibility in dealing with the exchange-rate disadvantage of an appreciating home currency than companies competing on price alone. Thus, Hewlett-Packard (a U.S. firm) raised prices abroad on many computer and instrument products in 1983 and 1984 in order to maintain (home-currency) profit margins in the face of a soaring U.S. dollar. Hewlett-Packard believed that its customers would be willing to bear the added costs to get the sophisticated equipment they wanted.

Exchange-rate fluctuations may influence not only the prices but also the broader marketing strategy of the international firm. For instance, a foreign-currency devaluation or home-currency revaluation might require the international firm to reorient its product line completely and target it to a higher-income, less price-sensitive market. The example is sometimes cited of Volkswagen, which achieved its export prominence on the basis of a low-priced, standardized, low-maintenance car: the Beetle. The sharp appreciation in the value of the Deutsche mark relative to the U.S. dollar during the first half of the 1970s seriously eroded the ability of German auto makers to compete in the North American market primarily on the basis of price. As a result, Volkswagen's management determined that it would compete more intensively on the basis of quality and styling rather than on cost alone. A similar progression has taken place in Japanese automobiles, encouraged by the appreciation of the Yen in the 1970s as well as by "voluntary" quotas on exports of Japanese cars to North America. Over time, Japanese car makers have increased their exports of relatively more expensive models that enjoy higher profit margins and to which car buyers are less price sensitive than economy models.

The approximately 33 percent increase in the value of the U.S. dollar vis-à-vis other world currencies over the first half of the 1980s stimulated a major restructuring in the marketing strategies of various U.S. companies. Several large

U.S. manufacturers ceded production of key products entirely to foreign companies and now essentially act as marketing agents. The most dramatic example is in the auto industry, where General Motors is implementing its so-called Asian strategy: the company is selling small cars made by Japan's Suzuki Motor Company and Isuzu Motors Ltd., and by 1987 it will begin marketing subcompacts produced in South Korea by Daewoo Corporation. Caterpillar Tractor Company, another old-line U.S. manufacturer, has also decided to forego manufacturing certain products in favor of buying and distributing products made by other manufacturers. In Caterpillar's case, the company buys lift trucks from Daewoo.[17]

Exchange-rate fluctuations may also affect the timing of new-product introductions. For example, the period after a home-currency devaluation or a foreign-currency revaluation may be the ideal time to introduce a new brand product because of the competitive price advantage provided by a lower relative value of the home currency. Similarly, companies may continue to sell marginally profitable products domestically pending a home-currency devaluation, but they may have to discontinue such product lines entirely if instead of a devaluation, the home currency appreciated in value or remained stable relative to foreign currencies.

Companies also respond to economic risk by altering the way in which they produce output. Production management of long-term operating exposure primarily involves increased flexibility in sourcing parts and components, thereby enabling the international firm to take advantage of changes in relative (exchange-rate-adjusted) prices of critical parts and components. In particular, a firm drawing input supplies from plants located in different countries has some leeway to increase production in plants located in countries undergoing currency devaluations while cutting back somewhat on production in countries experiencing appreciations in their national currencies.

The sharp escalation in the value of the U.S. dollar has encouraged a number of U.S. companies to increase the extent to which they source components overseas. For example, Beckman Instruments, Inc., a medical- and laboratory-equipment subsidiary of Smith Kline Beckman Corporation, recently moved production of several product lines sold overseas from the U.S. to plants in Europe. It is also looking to expand operations in Ireland and Scotland. Further shifts of production are being actively considered by Beckman's management because they believe that exchange-rate-adjusted costs will be lower in Europe than in the U.S. for the indefinite future. Hewlett-Packard is another American company moving some manufacturing capacity abroad partly because of exchange-rate changes.

The auto companies have long used foreign sourcing of production as a way of coping with the impacts of exchange-rate changes. For example, Mercedes

---

[17]See "Drastic New Strategies to Keep U.S. Multinationals Competitive," *Business Week*, October 8, 1984, 171.

Benz switched the sourcing of its diesel trucks destined for the U.S. market from West Germany to Brazil in the 1970s to counter the effects of an appreciation in the Deutsche mark relative to the U.S. dollar. More recently Ford and General Motors have stepped up their purchases of components produced in such countries as Brazil, Mexico, and Portugal. The move by U.S. companies to increase outsourcing and foreign manufacturing has become a major source of concern to labor unions. Indeed, in recent negotiations with the auto companies, a key concern of the United Auto Workers was what it would get in return for the job losses associated with the companies' plans to buy more components abroad.

Since the costs of changing a company's sources of production can be quite considerable,[18] management needs to be reasonably sure that the cost advantages associated with increased overseas sourcing will persist for a substantial length of time. In the various approaches to managing longer-term operating exposure, the international firm should plan in advance for potential currency changes that could have a significant impact on the firm. Japanese companies are highly successful practitioners of this forward-looking approach to managing economic risk. Specifically, many Japanese exporters use a stronger yen exchange rate for planning purposes. By adopting a planning rate that is higher than the current market exchange rate, cost-reduction pressures are generated within the companies. As an illustration, while the spot exchange rate in January 1984 was 234 Japanese yen to the U.S. dollar, the Sony Corporation was using several yen-dollar exchange rates between 200 and 220 for planning purposes. Sony chairman, Akio Morita, stated: "Long range, we know the yen is going to get stronger, so we are already working to decrease production costs."[19]

Many observers believe that the powerful U.S. dollar forced many American companies to increase and accelerate plans aimed at boosting domestic productivity in the early 1980s. The key point is that planning allows the international firm to design and implement efficient marketing and production strategies. A danger is that while hastily put together responses to exchange-rate changes may mitigate some of the competitive disadvantages imposed by currency changes in the short run, they may impose even greater offsetting efficiency decreases or market-share losses in the future.

SUMMARY AND CONCLUSIONS

A variety of approaches might be taken by international managers toward hedging the major sources of exchange-rate risk described in the preceding chapter.

---

[18]In the case of General Motors, for example, the company agreed to spend $1 billion over six years to support workers displaced by imported parts and components while they are retrained or until they can be transferred to new jobs. And this is only one element of the costs of redistributing production. See ibid.

[19]See Don Currie, "Exporters Brace for the Shock of a Strengthening Yen," *Business Week,* January 9, 1984, 42.

Hedging is ordinarily undertaken to deal with two broad categories of foreign-exchange exposure: cash-flow risk and balance-sheet risk. The former encompasses what we have labeled economic risk, which includes transaction risk as a subset. Balance-sheet risk corresponds to what we have called translation risk. Certain techniques are appropriate for hedging both transaction risk and translation risk. In particular, borrowing to offset net-asset positions is potentially appropriate for hedging both types of risk, with borrowing concentrated in short-term liabilities to hedge transactions risk and longer-term borrowing used to hedge translation risk. Other types of financial hedges involve investing in foreign-currency-denominated assets to hedge net-liability positions in a foreign currency.

While financial hedges and/or direct adjustments of balance sheets are standard approaches to dealing with translation risk, there is a fairly wide range of approaches to hedging transaction risk. The latter are divided into approaches for hedging short-term and longer-term transaction exposure. Short-term hedging techniques for transaction risk include forward market sales or purchases, foreign-exchange puts and calls, invoicing in home currency, and leads and lags. Longer-term hedging techniques include back-to-back loans, currency swaps, and forward swaps.

Since economic risk refers to the long-run, comprehensive impact of exchange-rate changes on the international firm's profitability, hedging economic risk requires management to take a broad, long-run perspective on the outlook for exchange-rate changes and their likely impact on the firm. In many cases, implementing changes in marketing and production strategies can offset adverse competitive impacts of exchange-rate changes or enable the international firm to take advantage of competitive opportunities created by exchange-rate changes. Strategies include changing the home-currency-denominated prices of the company's products, adding or dropping products from the firm's overall product portfolio, increasing overseas sourcing of components and improving domestic productivity.

DISCUSSION QUESTIONS

1. On January 26, 1984, the spot rate of exchange between the U.S. dollar and the Canadian dollar was $1 U.S. = $1.2477 Cdn.; the three-month forward rate was $1 U.S. = $1.2478 Cdn. What was the "traditionally" measured (pretax) cost to a Canadian firm buying U.S. dollars three months forward?

2. If management of the Canadian firm described in question 1 expected the future spot rate (three months hence) to be $1 U.S. = $1.2475, what was the (pretax) "opportunity" cost of buying U.S. dollars three months forward.

3. Explain how the Canadian company in question 1 might have hedged its

purchase of U.S. dollars three months hence if the need for those dollars was not certain but was contingent on the firm's decision to expand capacity to meet new orders.

4. Under what conditions might a firm choose to use a financial hedge to cover an exposed foreign-exchange position rather than use the forward markets, assuming both options were available?

5. If a British company and a U.S. company are considering a forward swap, what would be a "reasonable" forward swap rate presuming that the spot rate is £1 = $1.4190 U.S. and that the yields on newly issued five-year British government and U.S. government notes are 10.25 and 11.75 percent respectively?

6. Are purely domestic firms based in the United States likely to be immune from the economic effects of a stronger U.S. dollar? Which types of firms are likely to have their profitability prospects enhanced by an appreciating dollar? Which will come under greater competitive pressure? What differences, if any, exist between purely domestic and international firms in terms of their potential behavior toward economic risk?

REFERENCES

ANKROM, ROBERT, "Top-Level Approach to Foreign Exchange Rate Problem." *Harvard Business Review* Vol. 52 (July–August 1974), 79–90.

BABBEL, DAVID F., "Determining the Optimum Strategy for Hedging Currency Exposure." *Journal of International Business Studies* Vol. 14 (Spring/Summer 1983), 133–39.

BIGER, NAHUM, *Finance—A Conceptual Approach.* Toronto: Butterworths, 1981, chap. 12.

LIETAER, BERNARD A., "Managing Risks in Foreign Exchange." *Harvard Business Review* Vol. 48 (March–April 1970), 127–38.

SOENEN, L. A., "Foreign Exchange Exposure Management." *Management International Review* Vol. 19 (1979), 31–38.

——, and E. G. F. VAN WINKEL, "The Real Costs of Hedging in the Forward Exchange Market." *Management International Review* 22 (1982), 53–59.

TRAN, VINH QUANG, *Foreign Exchange Management in Multinational Firms.* Ann Arbor, Mich.: University Microfilms International, 1980.

CHAPTER ELEVEN

Corporate-Government Relations in International Business

A unique feature of international business is the need for international firms to interact with foreign governments on a wide range of complex issues. As a result, international firms must possess expertise, in both line and staff positions, on how to structure and negotiate relations with sovereign governments. This expertise is extremely important since cordial and mutually trustworthy relations with both foreign and domestic governments can eliminate a good deal of risk in a firm's political environment. Moreover, continual interaction with governments will ordinarily be required in carrying out operational plans. For example, access to transportation facilities and hydroelectric power will often have to be negotiated with host governments. The importance of enjoying amicable relations with foreign governments is emphasized by the fact that in many cases, there is no realistic opportunity for appealing or overturning adverse decisions by those governments.

International managers must also be prepared to deal with initiatives taken by their home governments that would not necessarily be relevant to them if they were managing purely domestic companies. In some cases, these actions are taken because of a perception that the firm's international business activities are harming the home economy. In other cases, home-government initiatives may have nothing to do with the international activities of the international firm, per se. Rather, the international firm may find itself caught in a political cross fire between its home government and foreign governments. Indeed, dealing with conflicting pressures exerted by home and host governments is one of the most vexing strategic issues that can confront international managers.

The premise underlying this chapter is that a firm must have in place requisite skills and resources to deal with complex and often conflicting encounters with foreign and home-country governments before embarking upon substantive international business undertakings. The primary objective of the chapter is to identify and discuss the main issues that typically constitute the focus of business-government relations in the international context and to suggest some general strategies and procedural approaches that have been found to assist in the successful conduct of government relations. In this regard, while formal and informal negotiations with government officials must—to some extent—be structured to meet the unique needs of specific circumstances, general guidelines for successful government relations have emerged from the experiences of more or less successful companies. The point to stress is that implementation of these guidelines will require skilled personnel and a commitment of management to monitoring relations with host and home governments.

AN OVERVIEW OF CORPORATE-GOVERNMENT RELATIONS IN INTERNATIONAL BUSINESS

In outlining the nature of the government-relations activity, it is necessary to repeat an oft-stated disclaimer; namely, government relations is an important concern in many purely domestic firms as well. Thus, differences between international and purely domestic firms in their conduct of government relations is typically a matter of degree rather than of kind. Nevertheless, these differences are sufficiently important to warrant consideration.

Kapoor and Boddewyn summarize the main differences between domestic and international business-government relations as follows:[1]

1. Things are different: Political, legal, and economic systems differ widely across countries. In addition, the practices of foreign governments often differ from the stated rules.

2. People are different: Cultural and nationality gaps stemming from differences in social values and personal attitudes make business-government communication across national boundaries especially problematic.

3. Coordination is more complex: While both purely domestic and international companies may need to deal with three levels of government, that is, local, regional and federal, in carrying out their activities, the latter ordinarily need to coordinate actions on the international level as well. This may necessitate dealing simultaneously with government representatives from a number of different countries.

---

[1]See Ashok Kapoor and J. Boddewyn, *International Business-Government Relations: U.S. Corporate Experience in Asia and Western Europe* (New York: American Management Association, 1973), pp. 4–5.

4. Legitimacy is harder to acquire and keep: Foreign firms will ordinarily find it more difficult than local firms to win popular acceptance. For example, foreign businesses will be suspected of not understanding or rejecting what is in the national interest of the host country, owing either to ignorance of local aspirations or to a conflict of interest with activities in other parts of the world. As a result, international firms are often faced with political challenges that are not encountered by purely domestic firms.

These important differences between the international and purely domestic environments make business-government relations more complex and in some ways more important in the case of the international firm than in the case of the purely domestic firm. Nevertheless, the broad objectives of government-relations activities are similar in both types of firms. Namely, they are directed at making heard the firm's position on relevant policy issues and at exerting influence to obtain and maintain scarce property rights.

It should be stressed that there is nothing necessarily immoral or even inappropriate in a company's intervening in the public-policy process. Indeed, where impending government actions threaten to affect adversely the welfare not only of a specific firm but also of broad segments of society, management may be said to have an obligation to seek to prevent those actions. The legitimacy of management's intervention into the public-policy process will depend upon the extent to which the firm's profitability is consistent with broad social welfare and the extent to which management's actions lie within acceptable codes of political and social behavior in the relevant region. We will explore these considerations a bit more in a later section of this chapter.

BROAD SOURCES
OF BUSINESS-GOVERNMENT INTERACTION

It is difficult to be comprehensive about the issues that constitute the focus of international business-government relations since, as a rule, countries do not have a specific law or code that embodies all or most of their objectives with regard to international business. Instead, public policies toward international business emerge from a variety of sources, including laws and regulations affecting international trade and investment, bilateral agreements dealing with taxation, and various supranational treaties and conventions.

Table 11.1 suggests several major sources of business-government interaction in the international context. Most of the sources listed are related to actions initiated by host governments, although home-government initiatives are also relevant in a number of important dimensions of the international firm's activities. An indirect source of issues for international managers arises from actions taken by sovereign governments that are directed at third parties. In many such cases, international firms are incidental victims of disputes between national governments.

TABLE 11.1   Broad Sources of Business-Government Interaction

1. *Host-government actions*
   a. Regulation of international movements of capital
   b. Tariff and nontariff barriers to trade
   c. Incentives for international business (subsidies and grants)
   d. Rules regarding transfer prices
   e. Codes of conduct
2. *Home-government actions*
   a. Regulation of international movements of capital
   b. Export restrictions
   c. Taxation of foreign income
3. *Extraterritorial issues*
   a. Application of antitrust laws
   b. Trade sanctions
   c. Financial disclosure

Host-Government Trade Restrictions

In cases where the host government initiates policies affecting international businesses, it will ordinarily have a number of reasonably explicit objectives in mind. For example, tariff and nontariff barriers to trade have traditionally been implemented to stimulate or preserve domestic production activity in specific lines of business. These barriers to trade are alleged by many economists to be an important stimulus to the growth of multinational corporations. That is, companies have been encouraged by trade barriers to set up subsidiaries in the host country, thereby escaping tariff and nontariff barriers that restrict the amount of exporting that can be done from the home country. In some cases, governments have used trade barriers as a direct form of leverage to get foreign companies to undertake production activity in the host market. For example, the Canadian and U.S. governments have used the threat of formal quotas on exports of Japanese automobiles as an instrument to encourage Japanese companies to establish production facilities in North America.

Increasingly, many developing countries are turning to barter as a way to save foreign currency and to promote exports of goods. For example, Colombia passed barter legislation listing about thirty products, including construction equipment, whose purchase is being tied to the exporting of Colombian goods.

Over the past twenty-five years, a series of rounds of multilateral government negotiations has led to substantial reductions in tariff levels among developed countries under the auspices of the General Agreement on Tariffs and Trade (Gatt). Unfortunately, much less progress has been realized in dealing with nontariff barriers to trade. Some prominent examples of nontariff barriers include the practice of governments in a number of developed countries to purchase high-technology goods, such as computers and telecommunications equipment, only from local companies. Quotas such as those implicitly imposed by the U.S. and

Canadian governments on Japanese cars and textile products from China are other prominent examples of nontariff barriers to trade.[2]

Host-Government Restrictions on Capital Imports

The dramatic growth and geographical spread of multinational companies in the past three decades have led to a proliferation of formal and informal government regulations and policies restricting the freedom of international capital movements and in particular the establishment of foreign affiliates by international companies. A summary of the restrictions imposed on the inward movement of direct investment capital by OECD countries is provided in table 11.2.

As indicated by the information in table 11.2, host-government restrictions on the establishment of foreign affiliates within their political jurisdictions are the rule rather than the exception. Of the countries included in the table, only Germany, the Netherlands, and Switzerland have adopted an essentially laissez-faire attitude toward inward direct investment.

There are seemingly two broad reasons for the imposition of restrictions on inward movements of direct investment capital by host governments. One is a desire to preserve domestic ownership in specific industrial sectors for reasons of national defense or to maintain sovereignty over critical economic resources, such as energy. Another is to ensure that the initial inflow of foreign capital and the subsequent outflows related to dividend payments will not lead to sharp fluctuations in the price of the host currency.

Countries primarily concerned with the first set of reasons for regulating inward investment tend to have explicit restrictions on foreign ownership in specific sectors of the economy. In addition, a growing number of countries, including Australia, Canada, Finland, New Zealand, and Portugal, have agencies of government dedicated to examining specific types of incoming direct investment on a case-by-case basis, with an eye toward establishing whether permitting the investment would be in the national interest. Unfortunately for multinational managers the criteria applied are often vague and inconsistently administered over time.[3] In other countries, where currency stability is the main concern of authorities, inward investment is evaluated by the central bank.

[2]In the case of Japanese cars, the quotas are (technically) voluntarily adopted by the Japanese producers; however, they were adopted as a result of representations made by the U.S. and Canadian governments, with an underlying threat that formal quotas would be introduced if export restrictions were not implemented by the Japanese themselves. In March 1985, the U.S. government decided not to ask the Japanese to extend their "voluntary" car-export curbs. However, the Canadian government did not immediately follow suit. Interestingly, Japanese auto officials indicated that they would continue to show restraint in exporting cars to the U.S. market for fear that a flood of Japanese exports would lead to formal trade sanctions.

[3]For an evaluation of the consistency of the screening criteria employed by Canada's Foreign Investment Review Agency, see Steven Globerman, "The Consistency of Canada's Foreign Investment Review Agency—A Temporal Analysis," *Journal of International Business Studies* 15 (Spring/Summer 1984), 119–30. The name of Canada's review agency was recently changed to Investment Canada.

TABLE 11.2   Policies Toward Inward Investment—OECD Countries

COUNTRY	AGENCY OR DEPARTMENT THAT DOES SCREENING	CRITERIA
1. Australia	Foreign Investment Review Board	National economic benefits and costs
2. Austria	Austrian National Bank	Currency stabilization
3. Belgium	Ministry of Economic Affairs	Not explicit
4. Canada	Foreign Investment Review Agency	Significant benefit to Canada
5. Denmark	Ministry of Commerce	Not explicit
6. Finland	Commission for Foreign Investments	Not explicit
7. France	Ministry of Economics	Currency stability: exceptionally detrimental effects
8. Germany	No authorization required	
9. Greece	Bank of Greece	Currency stability
10. Ireland	Central Bank	Currency stability
11. Italy	Exchange Control Office	Currency stability
12. Japan	Bank of Japan	Not explicit
13. Netherlands	No authorization required	
14. New Zealand	Overseas Investment Commission	Benefits to New Zealand from development of natural and human resources
15. Norway	Norges Bank	General economic effects
16. Portugal	Foreign Investment Institute	Not explicit
17. Sweden	Sveriges Riksbank	Currency stability
18. Switzerland	No authorization required	
19. U.K.	Bank of England	Currency stability
20. U.S.	No authorization required	

Source: Organization for Economic Cooperation and Development, *International Direct Investment: Policies, Procedures, and Practices in OECD Member Countries* (Paris; OECD, 1979) pp. 4–32.

It is somewhat ironic that while many countries have barriers to the free flow of goods and capital, they also actively solicit specific types of foreign investment. For example, the Canadian government continues to compete strenuously for Japanese auto parts and assembly investments, notwithstanding the fact that foreign investment proposals in other sectors of the economy are occasionally rejected. Other countries, such as Ecuador and Colombia, encourage multinational investment in oil and mineral exploration through generous concessions of land and favorable taxes. At the same time, Colombia and Ecuador, along with Bolivia, Peru, Venezuela, and Panama, belong to the Andean Common Market. The Andean Pact has strict regulations on foreign investments, including a rule stipulating that foreign companies must agree to convert to ''mixed'' or ''national'' status by taking on government partners before they are allowed to participate in the enlarged Andean market. Foreign companies are further prohibited from repatriating more than 20 percent of their capital invested in these countries. Those multinationals refusing to abide by this rule must restrict their business activities exclusively within the national markets in which their affiliates are located. In this way, they are deprived of the benefits of tariff-free access to neighboring national markets.

The ambivalent attitudes of host governments toward inward direct investment reflect a host of internal political and economic influences, some of which are difficult for international managers to forecast. In many cases, the ambivalence reflects a tradeoff between preserving national economic and political sovereignty and creating jobs through foreign investment. The emphasis placed by host governments on one or the other objective will depend, among other things, on the overall health of the host economy and the political sensitivity of the sectors involved. For example, other things constant, a higher domestic rate of unemployment will encourage host governments to adopt a more favorable attitude toward inward direct investment.

BEHAVIORAL RESTRICTIONS
IMPOSED BY HOST GOVERNMENTS

In the initial stages of an international business venture, negotiations with host governments are concerned with conditions of entry, tax rates, degree of local ownership, and so forth. Once the venture is underway, interactions with host governments tend to focus on specific aspects of the international firm's behavior. For example, the labor-relations practices of foreign affiliates are an important focus of concern for host governments. In chapter 8 we discussed European legislation that would give unions a much greater voice in the European operations of multinational companies. Specifically, it would require the companies to share confidential, strategic information with their work force. It would also require companies to consult their unions on all major decisions and give unions the right to bypass local management and carry complaints and questions directly to corporate headquarters.

The enactment of legislation and codes of conduct prescribing acceptable behavior on the part of international firms constitutes one periodic source of friction between host governments and international management. Another source of friction is the transfer prices established for transactions between affiliates of the multinational firm. Specifically, the ability of the multinational parent to allocate expenses among affiliates and to charge one affiliate for services or capital at rates not charged to another allows the multinational enterprise to alter the tax base of the host country by altering the income of the affiliate.

Transfer pricing has been an especially contentious issue between multinational companies and host governments in less developed countries. The relatively underdeveloped customs valuation procedures in less developed countries are suggested by some observers to encourage tariff-pricing abuses. For example, some studies have found that multinational subsidiaries in Latin America underpriced their exports, on average, by some 40 to 50 percent relative to the prices being received by local firms. Overpricing of imports, in some cases ranging up to 700 percent, was also identified.[4] This is not to suggest that multinational companies regularly rip off host governments through improper interaffiliate transfer pricing. Rather, it is to suggest that the potential for abuse combined with an inherent difficulty in establishing ''fair'' transfer prices makes the issue a potentially contentious one. Host-government suspicion of international transfer pricing has been further aroused by occasional revelations of transfer-pricing abuses, as in the case of the Amway Corporation described in chapter 14.

Home-Country Concerns about Tax Revenue

Home-country authorities are also greatly concerned about the potential for multinational companies to avoid paying income taxes through the use of tax havens abroad and other incentives offered by host governments. The accompanying discussion of the use of tax havens by Canadian multinationals elaborates on the source of this home-country concern.

The existence of tax havens is encouraged by the fact that many national governments do not tax the earnings of the foreign affiliates of domestic companies until the earnings are repatriated in the form of dividends or other forms of profit remittances. On the other hand, foreign affiliates are ordinarily not eligible for accelerated depreciation allowances, investment tax credits, and other tax benefits available to domestic companies.

There are no definitive estimates of the extent to which multinational companies pay their fair share of taxes to home governments.[5] A number of estimates

---

[4] These studies are discussed in Ronald Müller, ''Poverty Is the Product,'' in Reed Moyer, ed., *International Business: Issues and Concepts* (New York: John Wiley & Sons, 1984), pp. 156–71.

[5] A more detailed consideration of this issue is provided in Robert G. Hawkins and Bertram Finn, ''Regulation of Multinational Firms' Foreign Activities: Home Country Policies and Concerns,'' in Moyer, *International Business*, pp. 233–45.

CASE STUDY: *HOW COMPANIES CAN EXPLOIT TAX HAVENS*

Canadian tax authorities have outlined a number of practices involving tax havens in the Caribbean countries that they claim are abuses of the tax system. In one approach, a company that buys a product abroad and then sells it—either in its original form or in a processed form—on the Canadian market could set up an affiliate in a tax haven and have that affiliate operate as an intermediary in the purchasing function. Thus, instead of the company in Canada buying the original product directly from its foreign source, that company has the intermediary do the purchasing. The intermediary affiliate then sells the product at a much higher price to the company in Canada.

A company operating in Canada, for example, could buy a product abroad for $1 and then sell it on the Canadian market for, say, $1.50, creating a 50¢ profit for itself in Canada. This profit would be subject to Canadian tax. But that same company could set up an affiliate in a Caribbean country with an effective corporate tax rate of close to zero. Then the affiliate could purchase the product for $1 and sell it to the Canadian company for, say, $1.40. The Canadian company could still sell the product on the Canadian market for $1.50, which would give it a 10 cent profit in Canada. But it manages to take a 40¢ profit in the tax-haven affiliate on which it pays no taxes.

For some industries, such as pharmaceuticals and electronics, tax-haven subsidiaries have been established that assemble or manufacture a small part of the product, often a fairly minimal part. In other industries, however, the product never goes near the tax haven, except on paper.

The Canadian government is, of course, aware of the use of tax havens by large Canadian firms. Indeed, it recently charged the Redpath Sugar Company with tax evasion for using a sales corporation to avoid more than $3 million in taxes over a six-year period. A confidential company memo described how the company could save taxes by establishing an affiliate in Bermuda to buy discount sugar cargoes, which it in turn could sell to the Canadian affiliate at market prices, taking the discount as its profits. While the court accepted that establishing the Bermuda affiliate procured a substantial tax saving for the company, it held that the company had not violated Canada's tax laws.

Source: Linda McQuaig, "How Big Corporations Beat the Tax Man for Billions," *The Globe and Mail,* March 10, 1984, 2.

that have been made for the U.S. suggest that the tax advantages enjoyed by multinational firms may be approximately offset by tax disadvantages, such as their inability to utilize home-country tax concessions. However, the Canadian government estimates that offshore transfers of income by Canadian and foreign-owned companies with overseas affiliates may have cost the government about $3.5 billion in 1982. Since the total income tax paid by corporations to the Canadian government in 1982 was $7.5 billion, the estimated loss is quite significant on both an annual and a cumulative basis.[6] But it is not just national governments

[6] These estimates are provided in Linda McQuaig, "How Big Corporations Beat the Tax Man for Billions," *Toronto Globe and Mail,* March 10, 1984, 2.

that are worrying about getting their fair share of tax revenues from multinational companies. Indeed, one of the most controversial tax provisions to be applied against multinational firms in recent years is the so-called unitary tax. In fact, the unitary tax is really a franchise fee levied by over a dozen American states on multinational companies operating within their borders.

The premise underlying this approach is that where a corporate group operates an integrated business—characterized by common interlinks of management, finance, products, and so on—the financial results of any one company in that group may not reflect its "fair" share of total profits. Accordingly, where a business is considered unitary, these states tax a portion of the corporate group's worldwide profits by applying an "apportionment factor" to the consolidated profits of the multinational. This apportionment factor may be based on the average ratio of the group's sales, wages, and investments in the state to the group's worldwide totals.[7]

The unitary tax has generated a firestorm of protest from multinational companies, especially from those companies with headquarters outside the U.S. A presidential working group chaired by former Treasury Secretary, Donald Regan and including the governors of California, Utah, and Illinois and the chief executives of several major American multinational companies failed to achieve a compromise on the issue, although agreement was reached that the states would not tax income that arises from business done outside the U.S.—unless that income was remitted as dividends to the parent from overseas subsidiaries.

The monetary issues at stake are substantial. It is estimated that states using the worldwide unitary method collect $750 million more a year than they would get by switching to a less global form of accounting, such as a straightforward levy on in-state operations. California alone gets some $500 million a year extra from its unitary tax.[8] Several companies have begun to apply economic pressure against the taxing states. For example, IBM announced it would terminate its investment plans in Florida because of the unitary tax and put up for sale two thousand acres it had purchased in northern Florida. This pressure has begun to bring results. In 1984, Florida and Oregon abandoned the unitary tax method.

HOME-GOVERNMENT TRADE RESTRICTIONS

Given the emphasis of sovereign governments on promoting economic activity to create jobs, restrictions on exports are relatively unusual. However, political considerations occasionally dominate economic objectives. This has been particularly true in the case of the U.S. government's intervention into international trade. Indeed, there is specific legislation that authorizes government intervention into the

---

[7]A discussion of the unitary tax is contained in Peter Bernstein, "A Taxing War on Sticky-Fingered States," *Fortune,* June 25, 1984, 113.

[8]Ibid., p. 113.

exporting activities of U.S. firms. The Export Control Act of 1949 and its successor, the Export Administration Act of 1969, give the president the authority to prohibit or curtail all commercial exports, including technical know-how to Communist countries from U.S. companies or their foreign subsidiaries. The Trading with the Enemies Act of 1917 empowers the President to regulate all commercial and financial transactions by Americans with foreign countries or nationals in time of war or national emergency.

In recent years U.S. computer manufacturers have been heavily hit by applications of the Export Administration Act. To keep computers with possible military applications from falling into Soviet hands, the U.S. government monitors computer sales, even those of personal computers, to all other countries, including allies. The Commerce Department tracks most business computers by requiring exporters to apply for special licenses. Furthermore, regulations require overseas customers to notify the U.S. government if they plan to resell an American-made computer to another country. Any case that seems less than routine is passed on to the Department of Defense or other agencies for further review.

Exporters of fewer than twenty-five machines a year and those who sell highly advanced systems need a separate license for every order. On the other hand, large companies such as IBM and Honeywell can apply for a distribution license, which allows them to make unlimited shipments of conventional computers to subsidiaries and approved agents. However, government approval is required for sales of advanced computers.[9]

On occasion the U.S. government has blocked the overseas sale of computer equipment. For example, in 1978 the Carter administration blocked the sale of a Sperry Univac 100 series computer to Tass, the Soviet news agency. Observers believe that the embargo was intended to express President Carter's displeasure with Soviet human-rights violations. More recently the U.S. government ruled against IBM's application for a license to sell its personal computer in Budapest. American companies have argued that export restrictions cost them millions of dollars in lost business while failing to prevent Eastern-bloc countries from acquiring the goods they want. As an illustration, one computer-company executive argues that Budapest is the personal-computer capital of the Eastern bloc. European, Japanese, and Taiwanese desk-top computers are readily available. Other computers can be obtained by simply buying them in Vienna and driving back across the border.[10]

Home-Government Policies toward Capital Exports

Home governments of major capital-exporting countries have been intensely interested in the potential effects of overseas investment on domestic

[9]This discussion of the U.S. government's policy toward computer export is taken from Monci Jo Williams, "How Not to Capture the Export Trade," *Fortune,* August 6, 1984, 69.

[10]Ibid., p. 69.

employment opportunities. The "jobs export" issue provides a major political rationale for restricting efforts of home-country multinationals to establish overseas subsidiaries. In the U.S. this concern is exacerbated by arguments that overseas direct investment is eroding the technological lead of U.S. companies by making new technology readily and cheaply available to other countries. In Britain, Sweden, and several other countries, a concern exists about the potential impact of large outflows of capital on the stability of the domestic currencies.

While less extensive than restrictions on inward capital flows, there are authorization requirements for outward foreign direct investments, as indicated in table 11.3. In almost all cases approval for large capital exports is required from the central bank. While the adoption of formal procedures for approving overseas investment has been discussed in the U.S., to date outflows of direct investment capital are unrestricted.

EXTRATERRITORIALITY ISSUES

It is sometimes the case that government policies that affect specific international businesses are initiated as a result of intergovernmental disputes. For example, of the sixteen conflicts cited by Behrman as arising from corporate activities among the Atlantic nations in the mid-1960s, twelve involved the American Trading with the Enemy Act. Under this act, U.S. firms, whether located at home or abroad, were legally forbidden to trade with a number of Communist countries. One dispute involved computer technology related to nuclear weapons, and three involved enforcement of United Nations sanctions.[11] In all of these cases the firms involved were confronted with extraterritorial applications of national laws. That is, their behavior was constrained by laws applied outside of the jurisdiction in which the laws were passed.

In the majority of cases where extraterritoriality has been an issue, applications of U.S. laws have been involved. The issue of extraterritoriality was especially pronounced in two relatively recent episodes. One involved restrictions on the sale of equipment and technology for use in building a natural gas pipeline from Siberia to Western Europe. The second involved the application of U.S. antitrust laws in the world uranium industry.

It should be noted explicitly that while the U.S. government has received the greatest criticism for extraterritorial applications of its laws, it is not the only government to extend its laws to affect foreign companies. For example, the Vredeling Proposal (discussed in chapter 8) will require foreign companies with subsidiaries operating within the European Economic Community to publish information about their overall operations, including activities outside the EEC. Thus, notwithstanding recent indications that national governments recognize

[11]As cited in Joseph S. Nye, Jr., "Multinational Corporations in World Politics," in Moyer, *International Business*, pp. 142–56.

CASE STUDY: *THE SOVIET PIPELINE CASE*

Contracts for equipment to build the pipeline were signed in October 1981 after six years of talks between the Europeans and the Russians. In December 1981, following the imposition of martial law in Poland, President Reagan tried to hinder construction of the pipeline by barring General Electric, Caterpillar, Dresser, Cooper Industries, and other American companies from supplying equipment for the pipeline because of Russia's presumed responsibility for the imposition of martial law in Poland. The issue of extraterritoriality arose from the fact that the 125 turbines the Europeans wanted to deliver for the pipeline depended on rotors and nozzles designed or supplied by G.E. The compressor stations relied on technology from Dresser and Cooper Industries.

On June 18, 1982, the sanctions were extended when President Reagan forbade the supply to Russia of oil and gas equipment by the foreign subsidiaries of American companies and equipment produced abroad under licenses issued by American companies. Violators were liable under American law to criminal penalties, including fines up to a maximum of $100,000 per item. It was estimated at the time that the restrictions affected about twenty companies, thirteen of them European-based licensees, and seven of them subsidiaries of American companies. The twenty companies affected were located in France, West Germany, Britain, and Italy.

As might be expected the companies affected by the sanctions protested vigorously, especially the European-based companies. The latter were joined by their national governments, who argued that the U.S. government was blocking the export of goods that were subject to neither export nor re-export provisions when they were purchased by European companies. U.S. government officials disputed this, citing a catch-all application-of-American-law clause in contracts, which they said legitimized the President's actions. At the time, it appeared to be a matter for the courts to decide, although substantial haggling might have been anticipated over whether it was to be an American, European, or international court.

In fact, the Reagan administration lifted export controls on some oil and gas equipment in November 1982, although manufacturers of this equipment were still required to apply to the Commerce Department for export licenses. And in June 1983, further steps were taken to ease trade curbs by removing all licensing requirements for exports of heavy pipe-laying machinery to Russia. It is unclear how much of the subsequent easing of trade curbs was due to pressure exerted by European governments and how much was due to a recognition that American companies were losing business to foreign competitors, including Komatsu Company, a large Japanese manufacturer of pipe-laying equipment. In this regard, the pipeline case may offer a valuable lesson to both the U.S. government and non-U.S. companies. Namely, that the power of national governments is often tempered by the realities of a competitive international marketplace.

Source: Much of the material in this case was taken from ''When Political Masters Fall Out, Whom Does Business Obey?'' *The Economist,* Vol. 284 (July 10, 1982), 59–60.

TABLE 11.3   Policies Toward Outward Investment—OECD Countries

COUNTRY	AGENCY OR DEPARTMENT THAT DOES SCREENING	CRITERIA
1. Australia	Reserve Bank	Promote Australian exports; involve a significant degree of Australian management participation
2. Austria	Austrian National Bank	Unspecified
3. Belgium	No authorization necessary	
4. Canada	No regulation of outward direct investment	
5. Denmark	Danish National Bank	Not used to circumvent restrictions on outward portfolio investments
6. Finland	Bank of Finland	Balance-of-payments impact: employment and tax impacts
7. France	Ministry of Economics	Unspecified
8. Germany	No regulation of outward direct investment	
9. Greece	Currency Committee	Potential benefit to Greek economy, including exchange-rate impact
10. Ireland	Central Bank	Balance-of-payments effects; strengthened trade links; securing essential raw materials

11.	Italy	Italian Exchange Office	Impact on exports and domestic employment
12.	Japan	Bank of Japan	Authorization is required in specific sectors
13.	Netherlands	Outward direct investments are free from any authorization requirements	
14.	New Zealand	Reserve Bank	Impact on exports and current account balance
15.	Norway	Norgesbank	Impact on balance payments
16.	Portugal	Bank of Portugal	Impact on domestic employment
17.	Spain	Council of Ministers	Unspecified
18.	Sweden	Sveriges Riksbank	Impact on exports and current account balance; impact on overall balance of payments and on employment
19.	Switzerland	No restrictions on outward direct investment	
20.	U.K.	No restrictions applicable	
21.	U.S.	No regulation of outward direct investment	

Source: Organization for Economic Cooperation and Development, *International Direct Investment: Policies, Procedures and Practices in OECD Member Countries* (Paris: OECD, 1979), pp. 34–57.

CASE STUDY: *THE URANIUM CASE*

In the late 1960s and early 1970s, the Westinghouse Electric Corporation contracted to build a number of nuclear power stations and to supply them with uranium. In 1975, faced with a skyrocketing price of uranium, Westinghouse declared itself unable to fulfill the terms of its contracts and brought a civil antitrust action against twenty-nine uranium-producing companies, including companies from South Africa, Australia, Canada, and the U.K.

When American prosecutors attempted to bring foreign executives into U.S. court proceedings, most resisted. For example, senior executives at Britain's Rio Tinto-Zinc Company pleaded the fifth amendment to the U.S. Constitution, protecting them against self-incrimination, when they appeared before an American judge at the American Embassy in London. Subsequently, the British House of Lords ruled that British executives were under no obligation to appear before American courts.

When four of its uranium companies were sued under the U.S. antitrust laws, the Australian government passed emergency legislation, first to bar the production of evidence from Australia and then to block the enforcement in Australia of foreign antitrust judgments. In May 1984 the Canadian parliament passed legislation prohibiting Canadian subsidiaries of foreign-owned companies from complying with extraterritorial measures taken by a foreign country, including the application of antitrust legislation. Indeed, subsequent to the uranium case Britain, Australia, France, and New Zealand enacted legislation similar to this Canadian statute.[12] Fortunately for the companies involved, the potential political vise they might have found themselves in was avoided by out-of-court settlements of Westinghouse's claims. Nevertheless, the potential exists in the future for international managers to find themselves in a position where obeying one country's laws means violating the laws of another country.

Source: "Kangaroo Leap by America," *The Economist* Vol. 284 (July 3, 1982), 56–57.

---

the need to coordinate their application of legislation, the problem of extraterritoriality is likely to be with international managers for some time to come.

It might also be emphasized that while international firms confront a variety of government initiatives, they tend to derive from a relatively small number of economic and political "pressure points." While our discussion (to this point) paints a somewhat negative picture of business-government relations, it is not the case that all interactions between international managers and government authorities focus on issues of conflict. In some cases, businesses and governments work harmoniously toward common objectives. For example, home-country governments frequently cooperate with domestically owned businesses to promote

---

[12]The relevant legislation was stimulated not only by the uranium case but also by the sanctions associated with the Russian gas pipeline. See Ann Silversides, "Foreign Measures Bill Surprise to Business," *Toronto Globe and Mail*, May 30, 1984, B21.

exports, while host-country governments and international agencies, such as the World Bank, often actively assist multinational companies to establish subsidiaries abroad. However, it is ordinarily in areas where business and government have conflicting objectives that procedures and strategies must be implemented with special finesse. Hence, our focus on managing areas of conflict in international business-government relations.

MAJOR TASKS IN MANAGING CORPORATE-GOVERNMENT RELATIONS

There are several major tasks for employees charged with managing their corporation's relations with governmental and extragovernmental agencies. One is to identify emerging problems in the organization's relations with different governments. A second is to gather specific information about the environment in order to better understand and forecast emerging government positions, thereby enabling management to position itself to take advantage of opportunities or to mitigate threats. A third is to generate support for the firm's actions from key public sector decision makers. This involves more than just effective public relations campaigns. It means demonstrating that the firm is promoting the broad public interest as well as its own self-interest. Frequently this involves dispelling false impressions about how the firm is conducting its international business activities. Finally, assistance should be provided to senior executives involved in negotiating with key government decision makers.

The emphasis given to each of these tasks, as well as the precise way in which the tasks are carried out will vary with the nature of the business activity in question (for example, gaining access to a foreign market through exporting versus establishing foreign subsidiaries), and it will also vary among constituent parts of the international business. Nevertheless, there are several recognized attributes of an effective corporate approach to managing government-relations activities, regardless of the specific issues involved. These attributes are summarized in table 11.4.

One attribute is the judicious use of intermediaries to assist in a company's interactions with foreign governments. Various intermediaries include interna-

TABLE 11.4   Elements of an Effective Government-Relations Strategy

1. Judicious use of intermediaries to assist in interacting with governments
2. Understanding of governments' priorities and of how the decision-making process is structured in different countries
3. A framework for structuring incoming information about emerging business-government issues
4. Use of former government employees in key negotiating roles
5. Continuing involvement of senior management

tional and host-country law firms, international and local banks, public relations firms, trade and industry associations, and home-country government institutions, particularly embassy officials. Each of these intermediaries may be of particular assistance with a specific problem or in carrying out a given activity. For example, banks can be of particular assistance in dealing with host governments on matters related to raising capital and repatriating foreign exchange. Obviously, to be effective an intermediary should be knowledgeable about conditions in the home or host country in his areas of expertise. It is also important for the intermediary to have good relations with appropriate government officials. In this regard, it is frequently advantageous for the intermediary to be a national of the country concerned.

The effectiveness of a firm's government relations will also depend upon management's understanding of government priorities as well as on how the political decision-making process is structured in different countries. One expert in this area argues that the problem is not that managers lack information about the political environment. Rather, the underlying reason for inadequate awareness and understanding of government priorities is that managers, for the most part, don't know what to do with all the incoming signals.[13] A number of frameworks have been suggested to structure incoming information about emerging business-government issues. Underlying these frameworks are several key questions: Who is affected by the issue? How are they affected? What can be done about the issue?[14] The answers to these questions help define the nature and magnitude of an issue and the way in which a corporate response to the issue can be structured.

Experts in the field of international government relations also argue that companies can improve their effectiveness in dealing with governments by employing former government employees in sensitive negotiating positions.[15] A leading proponent of the use of former government employees in negotiating roles with host governments is the large Canadian development company, Olympia and York. This company recently undertook one of the largest commercial development projects in the history of New York City. The complex plans associated with the project had to be approved by various municipal government agencies. All government officials involved in approving the project agreed that Olympia and York's management was remarkably attuned to the desires and concerns of city officials and frequently recommended modifications to the project that were highly innovative in the urban development context. The president of Olympia and York, Paul Reichman, credited the company's success in this regard to the fact that several senior managers in the Toronto City Planning Department

[13]See Peter F. Bartha, "Managing Corporate External Issues: An Analytical Framework," *Business Quarterly* Vol. 47 (Autumn 1982), 78–90.

[14]Ibid., pp. 82–83.

[15]See I. A. Litvak, "The Ottawa Syndrome: Improving Business/Government Relations," *Business Quarterly* 44 (Summer 1979), 22–29.

had been hired by Olympia and York for the express purpose of negotiating with municipal officials about the plans for large development projects.[16]

As noted earlier in this chapter, governments everywhere tend to be concerned about many of the same issues, including domestic employment, exports, technological development, balance of payments, local participation in management, and tax revenues. Nevertheless, priorities change, and different criteria become more or less important over time. By signaling changes in priorities, a structured approach to issues identification can give international managers an important advantage in negotiating with government officials. Specifically, management can concentrate on tailoring concessions to suit the circumstances of individual business proposals.

One other important characteristic of an effective government-relations program is the involvement of senior management in the process. Senior foreign government officials prefer to deal with their counterparts in private organizations. Moreover, senior management's involvement should be constant, not episodic. The striking success enjoyed by the Occidental Petroleum Company in establishing trade ties with Russia and China is in large measure due to the long-standing personal relations between Occidental's chairman, Armand Hammer, and leading Soviet and Chinese politicians. These relations were developed over decades and were solidified through Armand Hammer's continuing efforts to promote peaceful coexistence between East and West.

NEGOTIATING WITH FOREIGN GOVERNMENTS

It is more often the rule rather than the exception for major international business ventures to be contingent upon the formal or informal approval of foreign governments and/or upon the agreement of the company to specific conditions. This in turn obliges management to carry out both formal and informal negotiations with host governments.

Several of the characteristics we discussed in the context of effective government relations are prerequisite to the specific task of negotiating agreements with host governments, including the use of company personnel and intermediaries who are familiar with the objectives and decision-making processes in host governments. But in addition, successful negotiating requires the selection of appropriate strategies and tactics.

Kapoor defines negotiation as the use of common sense under pressure to achieve objectives.[17] He stresses that effective negotiation requires an understanding of underlying social, cultural, political, and economic systems as well as exper-

---

[16]See Judy Steed, "Battery of Talent Takes on N.Y.," *Toronto Globe and Mail*, January 14, 1984, 10.

[17]Ashok Kapoor, *Planning for International Business Negotiation*, (Cambridge, Mass.: Ballinger Books, 1975), p. 3.

tise in technical, financial, accounting, and legal analysis. The outcome of negotiation processes will also reflect the relative bargaining power of the parties involved. In this regard, the international firm can enhance its leverage in negotiations with host governments by altering the organization and behavior of the firm in specific ways.

Fagre and Wells provide some important insights into the determinants of relative bargaining power in their study of bargains struck between host governments and investors in Latin America.[18] They find, for example, that the bargaining power of host governments is likely to be weak when negotiating with high-technology firms. This relationship is explicable, at least in part, by the fact that skilled scientific and technical resources are in scarce supply in most countries. As a result, host governments are often in a take-it-or-leave-it position if they want to develop a domestic technological infrastructure.

Fagre and Wells also find that firms with well-known brand-name products that enjoy success in export markets also possess strong bargaining positions in negotiating with foreign governments. This result is quite plausible given the objective of virtually all governments to increase domestic exports. In a related vein, Fagre and Wells find that firms that produce a wide range of products realize above-average success in international negotiations. They explain this result, in part, by the possibility that multiproduct firms fit into governments' import-substitution strategies.

One other important influence on negotiating outcomes is the opportunity that each party enjoys to substitute an agreement with another party for the benefits being sought in the relevant negotiations. Thus, Fagre and Wells find that the greater the number of firms competing in an industry, the weaker the bargaining power of any individual firm in that industry.

Just as international firms can enhance their bargaining power, at a cost, by developing certain unique skills and attributes that are in demand in the world market, so can national governments strengthen their positions vis-à-vis private firms. For example, control over market access confers bargaining power on host governments. Doz and Prahalad cite the example of the Spanish government, which was able to attract Ford's new auto plant to Valencia, Spain, by letting Ford sell just enough cars in Spain to make the greenfield site at Valencia a better alternative than expansion of its existing plants in Germany or the United Kingdom. In this case, Spain was able to restrict imports since it was not a member of the Common Market.[19]

Host governments may also increase the attractiveness of their local economies by offering subsidies and grants to those firms that are willing to abide by specific conditions for doing business. For example, ITT's European

[18]Nathan Fagre and Louis T. Wells, Jr., "Bargaining Power of Multinationals and Host Governments," *Journal of International Business Studies* Vol. 13 (Fall 1982), 9–23.

[19]Yves L. Doz, and C. K. Prahalad, "How MNC's Cope with Host Government Intervention," *Harvard Business Review* Vol. 58 (March–April 1980), 155.

telecommunications-equipment subsidiaries have received large research contracts and subsidies from host governments on the condition that they develop equipment well suited to local needs.[20]

Once management has negotiated what it believes are the best terms obtainable at that time, it must decide whether to adapt to the terms of the agreement or withdraw from the activities involved. In this respect, international firms have exhibited varying patterns of behavior. For example, Japanese companies have shown an increased willingness to set up parts and components factories in foreign markets to keep those markets open for sales of final consumer products, such as autos and video tape recorders. On the other hand, IBM has consistently avoided businesses where management would need to accept substantial restrictions on IBM's autonomy, such as the public sector of the telecommunications industry.

EXTORTION VERSUS BRIBERY
IN INTERNATIONAL BUSINESS

An important concern of international managers involved in negotiations with foreign politicians is the conflict that arises when the observance of local negotiating conventions becomes illegal bribery under home-country legislation. This issue has become especially relevant to U.S. firms since the imposition of legislated standards of ethics by the U.S. government on U.S. corporations. The particular problem is that multinational companies are often approached for payment by local politicians and bureaucrats. Beeman and Timmins label these approaches extortion, as the money is solicited in return for vague commitments to abstain from harassing or discriminating against the multinational's subsidiaries. In other cases high-ranking government officials have demanded secret "commissions" on sales made to the local government.[21]

Beeman and Timmins report the results of a survey of U.S. business leaders which found that 75 percent of them had received demands from foreign officials for "unusual" payments. The demands were greatest in industries that sold directly to governments or were heavily regulated by host governments. Nevertheless, almost half of the firms surveyed indicated that extortion was so common in most nations that it could only be considered a normal cost of doing business.

The point to stress here is that if management wants to avoid extortionary pressures from foreign government officials, it must ensure that its firm has a unique product or skill set to offer host governments. This is because the leverage to make monetary demands of international management comes from a capacity to play one multinational company off against another. Unfortunately, the highly competitive international business environment frequently confers this capacity

---

[20]Ibid.

[21]Don R. Beeman and Sherman A. Timmins, "Who Are the Villains in International Business?" *Business Horizons* Vol. 25 (September–October 1982).

on host governments; however, management can blunt the leverage exerted by host-government officials, to some extent, by anticipating changes in bargaining power and taking steps to minimize its vulnerability to extortion. These steps might include expanding the available markets for the firm's exports (or imports) and taking in local investors.

LIFE-CYCLE CHARACTERISTICS OF NEGOTIATING

In attempting to minimize vulnerability to extortion, one noteworthy characteristic of business-government negotiating that managers should keep in mind is the tendency for bargaining power to change over the life of the international business activity. For example, once a company has made substantial direct or indirect investments in doing business in a country, it is—to some extent—a hostage to host-government authorities. That is, the assets dedicated to the activity in question may be largely unsuitable for any other use. Knowing the "captive" nature of the assets involved, host governments may be tempted to change the terms of existing agreements unilaterally on the premise that the international firm would accept a modest reduction in profitability, in preference to a large write-down of its assets.

The fact that international companies must often make nonsalvageable investments to undertake specific overseas economic activities underlies a life-cycle bargaining process whereby foreign governments initially offer quite favorable terms to foreign firms but then change the terms over time to the disadvantage of these firms. Knowing the potential for this pattern in advance, management should try to negotiate an initial agreement that embodies a safety margin for the firm's profits in the event of future unilateral unfavorable decisions by governments. Management might also consider actions designed to reduce the risk of opportunistic behavior on the part of foreign governments. For example, including local investors in the international activity may encourage the host government to maintain a favorable attitude toward the initial agreement. Establishing and nurturing an infrastructure of local suppliers may also enhance the company's long-term relationship with host governments. These and other tactics can be seen as ways to manage political risk, above and beyond negotiation strategies, over the life of an international business venture.

Occasionally, management may try to renegotiate its contracts with foreign governments when it feels the original terms are too onerous to allow profitable business activity. Frequently, an excessively optimistic assessment of the economic potential of an activity leads to losses under negotiated terms that seemed reasonable at the time. A case in point is the initial bidding for oil-drilling rights in the South China Sea. Approximately twenty-seven oil companies from nine countries signed initial exploration agreements with the Chinese government. While the terms of the agreements are confidential, industry sources believe that the Chinese government drove hard bargains with all the companies—to the point where early and strong discoveries became particularly important to the economics of the ventures. One firm—Compagnie Française des Petroles of France—began to withdraw its personnel from the region after drilling fourteen wells, about four of which are believed to have produced oil. Several Chinese oil officials believe that the French company's action was a tactic to renegotiate its contract with the Chinese. However, as long as the other companies drilling in the area are relatively satisfied with their arrangements, it is unlikely that Compagnie Française will be able to extract any significant concessions from Chinese officials.

BREAKDOWNS IN AGREEMENTS

By and large, most issues that arise between business and government involve formal or informal negotiations between the two parties. Presumably, if management has incorporated the elements listed in table 11.4 into its negotiating behavior, it will be reasonably satisfied with the outcome of its interactions with government. Nevertheless, it is certainly relevant to consider the options available to management when negotiations with foreign government officials break down.

One option, of course, is for the company to simply abandon the international activity and absorb the associated losses. Another is to seek the intermediation of some third party, including one of the several organizations available for international arbitration, such as the Geneva Arbitration Tribunal. Frequently, the home-country government plays an intermediating role, either by applying informal pressure on the host government or by challenging host-government policies in international courts.

An example of the informal approach to intermediation is provided by suggestions made by the Japanese government to Canadian government officials that if Canada increased its quotas on Japanese cars, Japan would establish trade barriers to Canadian raw materials and fabricated products like newsprint. An example of a formal intergovernmental protest is provided by the activities of Canada's Foreign Investment Review Agency (FIRA), now Investment Canada. In the late 1970s and early 1980s, FIRA began to require foreign-owned companies to make a commitment to undertake more exporting from Canada and more domestic sourcing of supplies and components as a condition for obtaining approval to establish in Canada. For example, as a precondition to setting up its own distributorship in Canada, Apple Computer agreed that at least 80 percent of its sales and repair work would be performed by independent Canadian-owned firms. As a result of complaints by companies such as Apple, the U.S. government challenged the preconditions established by FIRA as being in violation of multilateral trade treaties, specifically, GATT. Both countries agreed to submit the dispute to an international arbitration panel, which ultimately supported the U.S. position.

While arbitration and the application of pressure by home governments (and other third parties) are sometimes effective, it is more typically the case that when voluntary negotiations break down, the outcome is a costly and prolonged stalemate. Suing foreign nationals, including national governments, is a difficult proposition. Even when there is agreement between parties to resolve disputes in a given domestic or international court of law, one or the other party may fail to honor the court's decision. As a general principle, therefore, companies should not place great reliance on the courts to enforce international agreements. The most reliable enforcement mechanism any international business can possess is the other party's continuing desire to do business.

CASE STUDY: *ALGERIAN LIQUIFIED NATURAL GAS—A NEGOTIATION DEADLOCK*

An ongoing billion-dollar dispute between Algeria and Spain illustrates how commercial relations can unravel over international business conflicts. The initial parties to the dispute were the Algerian state oil company, Sonatrach, and the Spanish state gas company, Enagas. Sonatrach is claiming more than $1 billion U.S. in compensation for failure by Spain to take delivery of agreed quantities of Algerian liquified natural gas.

After eighteen months of talks on the appropriate amount of compensation that Spain should pay, the dispute was brought for hearing in front of the Geneva Arbitration Tribunal. In the meantime, the dispute seriously disrupted trade relations between the two countries. For example, almost all new contracts between Algeria and Spain were frozen beginning in October 1983. Spanish sales of cement and agricultural products, worth more than $145 million in 1983, virtually shrank to nothing. Exports of plastics, timber, steel, and textiles were also drastically reduced.

As a further consequence of the conflict, Algeria suspended a contract for Spanish construction of a dam worth $68 million, and in the summer of 1983, Sonatrach suspended repayment of a $150 million loan it received from Enagas in 1975. A casual observer of this interaction between Spain and Algeria might be inclined to conclude that the consequences of the dispute have been far more costly than the initial amount in contention.

Source: This description is taken from ''Algeria Takes Row with Spain over Gas Contract to Tribunal,'' *The Globe and Mail,* October 3, 1984, B11. Adapted by permission of Reuters.

OUTLOOK FOR THE FUTURE

It is extremely difficult to predict future directions that international business-government relations will take in the future; however, it seems safe to say that the underlying issues of domestic job creation, currency stability, tax revenues, and national sovereignty will not disappear. If anything, high levels of unemployment in most parts of the world along with exceptionally large government deficits will ensure that host and home governments alike will seek to extract a maximum share of economic benefits from international business. With this attitude goes the threat of increased government involvement in international business.

At the same time, a scarcity of investment capital, as evidenced by historically high (inflation-adjusted) interest rates, suggests that national governments will be actively seeking to encourage inflows of foreign capital. While wholly owned foreign subsidiaries are likely to remain a less favored form of foreign participation in host economies, opportunities should increase for overseas ventures that allow for participation by local investors and managers. Creative joint-venturing and licensing agreements should become increasingly prominent forms of international business, especially as less developed countries seek to modernize their industries through the acquisition of Western technology.

That the future is difficult to predict does not, of course, imply that companies should not try to anticipate government actions. Companies should also be involved in shaping the forthcoming public-policy agenda by making their views known on issues affecting international business.

SUMMARY AND CONCLUSIONS

The relations that an international firm enjoys with governments, especially host governments, are a potentially critical influence on the firm's success in the international business arena. The achievement of satisfactory business-government relations requires firms to dedicate skilled management and other resources to a broad set of continuing tasks. These tasks are more complex and difficult to execute, the greater the variety of political environments in which a firm operates.

The objective of personnel assigned to government-relations work should be to provide answers to the following questions: (1) On what issues should the company focus? (2) What kinds of responses are necessary? (3) What specific tasks are appropriate? (4) What resources and systems are needed?[22] The precise strategies chosen for interacting with governments will depend upon a number of things, among them the nature of the firm's business activities and whether it is a headquarters division or a foreign subsidiary of a multinational firm.

Notwithstanding that strategies for managing government relations will be fine-tuned to fit the specific features of any given issue, elements of an effective approach to government relations have been identified in the literature. In particular, management should understand the priorities of governments as well as how the political decision-making process is structured in different countries. The use of structured "issues-management" techniques can assist international managers to identify and understand emerging business-government issues.

Much of the interaction between international managers and government authorities takes the form of formal or informal negotiating. The outcome of negotiating will depend upon the international firm's preparedness and its relative bargaining strength. Among the factors that will contribute to a company's bargaining position are its technological progressivity, the diversity of its product line, and the number of competitor firms producing essentially the same products

[22]See Kapoor and Boddewyn, *International Business-Government Relations.*

and/or services. The success that a company enjoys in specific negotiations with host and home governments will also depend upon the negotiation tactics adopted by the company. In this regard, there are certain rules of thumb that contribute to a greater likelihood of successful negotiations. One such rule is that management should identify the important objectives of the government bargainers and determine the minimal concessions that will break the negotiation bottleneck. Another is to give government officials some leeway in establishing tradeoffs between different concessions. A third is to involve senior management in the negotiation process. The importance of concluding successful negotiations is underscored by the fact that efforts to mediate or arbitrate international disputes are frequently prolonged and ineffective. The use of courts to settle disputes is also fraught with complications, and (in the last analysis) the courts often have no formal way of enforcing their judgments.

DISCUSSION QUESTIONS

1. List and discuss some issues that tend to be ongoing sources of business-government interaction.

2. Some international companies deliberately assume a "low-profile" position in host countries rather than proclaiming the benefits they confer as foreign companies in the host economy. A good example of the former approach is provided by Schlumberger, the giant French-owned oil-drilling company. Schlumberger's management consciously attempts to obscure the company's image as a large multinational. Do you believe that, as a general rule, international firms should attempt to downplay their foreign-owned status when operating abroad?

3. As a senior negotiator for a company seeking to obtain oil-drilling rights in a less developed country, how would you structure your negotiating strategy? That is, what information would you find especially useful? Would you see any advantage in coordinating your negotiations with other oil companies? What leverage might you bring to the negotiations?

4. From what you know about the company—including your personal gastronomic experiences—how would you account for the remarkable and virtually worldwide acceptance of the McDonald's Corporation? Do you think that the nature of the company's activities give it some special bargaining leverage with host governments?

5. Certain multinational companies have voluntarily adopted codes of conduct that define their specific commitments to being "good corporate citizens" in the host economies in which they do business. What benefits do you think an international firm might realize from publicly committing itself to behave in specific ways, for instance, to operate a nonpolluting plant and to be an equal-opportunity employer? What disadvantages might be present?

6. If you were asked to outline an approach to managing government rela-

tions that was likely to prove successful for the "typical" international business, what factors would you stress?

REFERENCES

BEHRMAN, JACK, *U. S. International Business and Governments.* New York: McGraw-Hill Book Co., 1971.

BRADLEY, DAVID G., "Managing Against Expropriation." *Harvard Business Review* Vol. 55 (July-August 1977).

HEWITT, GARTH, "Whose Law Rules?" *International Management* Vol. 37 (April 1982), 35–38.

LECRAW, DONALD, "Bargaining Power, Ownership, and Profitability of Subsidiaries of Transnational Corporations in Developing Countries." *Journal of International Business Studies* 15 (Spring/Summer 1984), 119–30.

SINGER, STUART R., and MICHAEL KARLIN, "Multinationals and New Customs Law Will Have Broad Impact on Intercompany Pricing." *Journal of Taxation* 58 (April 1983), 226–31.

SMITH, DAVID N., and L. T. WELLS, JR., *Negotiating Third World Mineral Agreements.* (Cambridge, Mass.: Ballinger Books, 1975).

TOWNSEND, JAMES B., *Extraterritorial Antitrust: The Sherman Antitrust Act and U.S. Business Abroad.* (Boulder, Colo.: Westview Press, 1980).

VERNON, RAYMOND, "Conflict and Resolution Between Foreign Direct Investors and Less Developed Countries." *Public Policy* Vol. 17 (Fall 1968).

CHAPTER TWELVE

Marketing
in the
International Firm

Every organization must be concerned with the fundamental strategic issues: What specific products should be brought to the market by the firm, and how should the products be made available to potential buyers in various markets? These issues constitute the focus of corporate marketing activities, which one expert defines as "the performance of business activities that direct the flow of a company's goods and services to consumers and users."[1]

More specifically, marketing strategy encompasses the determination of a firm's product portfolio as well as the prices to be charged, the nature and extent of product advertising, type of packaging, and other aspects of product promotion and method(s) of distribution. In this respect the issues addressed by international marketing managers are identical to those confronting their purely domestic counterparts. The unique attributes of international marketing derive from the more heterogeneous environment in which the international firm operates compared to the purely domestic firm. This greater heterogeneity ordinarily obliges international firms to modify components of their marketing strategy, in some cases substantially, to better "fit" the conditions surrounding specific markets. In contrast, purely domestic firms can more easily implement highly standardized approaches to marketing without suffering any loss in effectiveness.

[1]Phillip R. Cateora, *International Marketing*, 5th ed. (Homewood, Ill.: Richard D. Irwin, 1983), p. 4.

The critical overriding issues facing international marketing managers are, therefore, whether and how the firm's core marketing strategy should be modified for specific geographic markets. Since differentiated marketing approaches imply higher costs than a standardized marketing strategy, the international manager faces a difficult tradeoff between higher costs and (presumably) greater marketing effectiveness. The objective of this chapter is to examine the nature of this tradeoff as well as the techniques available to improve the international firm's effectiveness in marketing.

OVERVIEW OF THE MARKETING FUNCTION

A number of experts have argued that, ultimately, the whole field of marketing revolves around a single key issue: how to adapt marketing strategy to the prevailing marketing conditions.[2] The distinction between marketing strategy and marketing conditions is conveyed in figure 12.1. The outer ring identifies the main features of the environment that influence the likely success or failure of specific marketing plans. That is, it summarizes the dimensions of a firm's marketing conditions. These broad elements of the firm's marketing environment were considered in chapters 4 through 6.

The inner ring in figure 12.1 summarizes the major elements of a firm's marketing strategy. In marketing goods and services, managers must establish the prices to be charged. They must also determine important attributes of the firm's product portfolio including the range of products offered, the degree to which the firm differentiates its products from those of its competitors, and the packaging and other physical characteristics of products offered. Product promotion encompasses issues such as when to launch new products, whether the firm should emphasize the use of brand names and different trademarks or whether it should standardize its product offerings, and which advertising media to employ in making its products known to consumers. Finally, establishing channels of distribution essentially encompasses (1) choosing the structure of intracompany units and the extracompany agents and dealers, both wholesalers and retailers, through which goods and services are marketed, and (2) deciding on the methods for making physical delivery.

All firms (both international and purely domestic) must establish operating strategies along the dimensions of price, product offerings, product promotion, and channels of distribution in a way that is consistent with the environmental features summarized in the outer ring of figure 12.1. We might embark on our analysis of how ''going international'' complicates the formulation of marketing strategy by reveiwing some basic concepts of product-portfolio analysis.

---

[2]See, for example, Hans Thorelli and Helmut Becker, *International Marketing Strategy*, rev. ed. (Oxford, England: Pergamon Press, 1982).

Figure 12.1 Overview of the Marketing Activity
Adapted from Philip R. Cateora and John M. Hess, *Interantional Marketing*, 4th edition
(Homewood, Illinois: Richard D. Irwin, 1979), P. 7.

PRODUCT-PORTFOLIO ANALYSIS

One integrative marketing-planning technique used by multiproduct firms is product-portfolio analysis. This approach is associated with the Boston Consulting Group, which initially suggested its usefulness for strategic planning. In this approach, strategic roles for a firm's products are assigned on the basis of the product's expected market growth rate and market share relative to competition. The differences in growth potential and relative market size effectively establish differences in long-run cash-flow potential across products. The latter, in turn, determines which products represent investment opportunities, which should be sources of investment funds, and which should be candidates for elimination from the firm's product portfolio.[3]

The cash-flow implications of product growth and market share are captured in the product-portfolio chart described in figure 12.2. As shown in the diagram, product growth is usually separated into "high" and "low" growth areas by some growth line fixed by the perceptions of management. For example, depending upon the specific industrial sector in which the firm participates, as well as management's growth objectives, a discrete division between high and low growth might be made at 10 percent per annum for some firms and 20 percent for other firms. Similarly, relative market share is usually divided in some discrete fashion according to management's assessment of what would constitute relatively high and relatively low market shares.

[3]The following description of product-portfolio analysis is taken from Derek F. Abell and John S. Hammond, *Strategic Market Planning* (Englewood Cliffs, N.J.: Prentice-Hall, 1979), chap. 4.

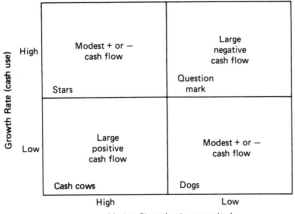

Figure 12.2 Product Categories in the Product-Portfolio Chart
Adapted from The Product Portfolio Matrix, © 1970, The Boston Consulting Group, Inc.

While there is nothing sacred about any specific division of the horizontal and vertical axes in figure 12.2, a meaningful division would define most products in the lower left corner as being cash generators, those in the upper right as cash users, and those in the upper-left and lower-right quadrants as roughly in cash balance. This distribution follows from a number of assumed relationships:

1. Profit margins and cash generated increase with a product's relative market share owing to cost reductions related to economies of scale and learning by doing.
2. Sales growth requires cash input to finance added capacity and working capital. Thus, holding market share constant, cash-input requirements increase with market growth rate.
3. In order to hold market growth constant, an increase in market share usually requires cash input to support increased advertising expenditures, lower prices, and other share-gaining tactics. On the other hand, a decrease in market share may make cash available.
4. Growth in each market will ultimately slow as the product approaches maturity. Without losing market position, the cash generated as growth slows can be reinvested in other products that are still growing.

The foregoing assumptions lead to a classification of products into four categories based on their cash flow characteristics:

1. *Cash Cows* (located in the lower-left quadrant) are products that characteristically generate far more cash than they absorb. Typically they have a dominant share of a mature, slow-growing market.
2. *Dogs* (located in the lower-right quadrant) are products with low shares of slowly growing markets. They neither generate nor require significant amounts of cash.

3. *Question Marks* (located in the upper-right quadrant) are products with low shares of fast-growing markets. These products have attractive market potential because they are in rapidly growing markets, but they require large amounts of cash if they are to gain a substantial share of the market.

4. *Stars* (located in the upper-left quadrant) are high-growth, high-share products that may or may not be self-sufficient in cash-flow depending upon whether their strong cash flow from operations is sufficient to finance rapid growth. These products will presumably become large net generators of cash in the future when the growth rates of their markets slow.

Marketing strategists contend that the foundation of a sound long-term strategy is to use cash generated by cash cows to finance market-share increases for question-mark products in which the company has a strong competitive potential. If successful, this strategy should produce stars, which in turn become the cash cows of the future. On the other hand, question-mark products with weak competitive positions are candidates for elimination from the firm's product portfolio, as are dogs with negative cash flows.

Even within the purely domestic firm, application of the Boston Consulting Group's product-portfolio technique requires a good deal of managerial judgment. The task of choosing an "optimal" product portfolio in the international firm is complicated by the fact that market-share data may be exceptionally difficult to obtain in some countries or that the designation given a product in one national market may be inappropriate when considering other markets. For example, differences across markets in characteristics such as the rate of market growth, market share held by the product, and competitive conditions might mean that a product designated a cash cow in one national market is more accurately designated as a question mark, a dog, or a star in other markets. As an illustration, at the same time as the Apple II Plus personal computer was rapidly becoming a cash cow in North American markets, it was just being introduced in South American markets, where its acceptance was very much in question. Consequently, it is often necessary to define a product-portfolio chart such as the one in figure 12.2 for each major foreign market in which the firm has an interest.

Regardless of the market potential of any individual product, the international manager may have preferences for specific markets based on their broad economic, political, and social characteristics. The product-portfolio analysis must therefore take country attractiveness explicitly into account. In effect, the marketing strategist must analyze potential product portfolios with respect to three attributes: country attractiveness, anticipated growth rate, and market share. The general nature of this analysis can be described with reference to figure 12.3.

In looking at figure 12.3, the reader should imagine that the surface represents a scatter of points in three-dimensional space that positions product opportunities according to the three relevant attributes. The higher up and farther out along the surface the product is positioned, the more desirable the particular product opportunity is. For example, point A represents a more desirable position than

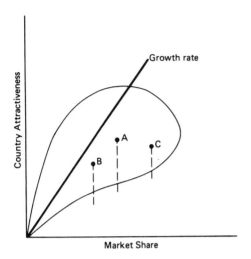

Figure 12.3   Product Categories in Three-Dimensional Product-Portfolio Space

point B, in that it represents a product positioned in a faster growing, more attractive national market, for which the firm enjoys a larger market share.[4] On the other hand, the comparison between A and C is more complicated. Specifically, point C represents a product positioned in a faster-growing market, and for which the firm enjoys a larger actual (or projected) market share, compared to the product represented by point A. However, the product at point A is positioned in a more favorable overall national market.[5] Whether A or C is a more desirable marketing prospect for the firm depends upon management's priorities with respect to the three relevant attributes. As a general decision rule, we might say that product opportunities closer to point A represent attractive opportunities to finance, while those farther away represent products that should either be ''milked'' or eliminated from the product portfolio.

Returning to figure 12.1, the growth potential of different markets can be viewed as a function largely of the environmental factors summarized in the outer ring. The success the firm enjoys in achieving a high market share of a fast-growing market or in retaining a high market share of a slow-growing market is largely a function of its marketing strategy as defined by the elements specified in the inner circle. Of course, successful products are typically those that are compatible with important features of the marketing environment. The critical distinction between international marketing and marketing in the purely domestic

---

[4]Perpendiculars drawn from points A and B from the surface to the horizontal plane would conceptually fix the positions of these points along the growth-rate/market-share axes.

[5]The reader should note that the products represented at points A and C might be physically identical products, for example, a popular brand of toothpaste. As noted earlier, a given product need not enjoy the same growth prospects and market share in every national market.

CASE STUDY: *PLANNING MARKETING PRIORITIES AT STANDARD BRANDS*

At Standard Brands Inc., a New York-based multinational manufacturer and distributor of foods and beverages, management has introduced a "grid" form of planning in which each of the firm's products is reevaluated each year. Each product is evaluated and positioned within a nine-box grid (three squares wide by three squares deep). The evaluation involves two sets of factors: the external environment in which the product must compete and the product as a self-contained entity.

To facilitate some common basic assumptions about the environment, Standard Brands compiles a "data package" with projections for inflation, economic growth, and shifts in population. Each product manager must also supply answers to specific questions including the size and profitability of the relevant industry, the status of the competition, and whether current or potential legislation could affect the industry. On the basis of such factors, each manager rates the attractiveness of his particular industry.

The manager, in a separate process, next answers questions about the product itself. What were its sales and market share in the previous year? How does it compare qualitatively with its two leading competitors? What are the probable costs for the product in the next year? Guided by his answers to such questions, the manager gives each of his products a rating. Then the two separate scores are consolidated, and the product is entered into one of the nine boxes in the grid according to predetermined criteria.

For action purposes, there are three broad product categories. Boxes 1, 2, and 3 indicate a product with great potential, in which the firm is prepared to invest capital for long-term growth. In company jargon, this is the invest/growth category. Boxes 4, 5, and 6 comprise the selectivity/earnings category, in which the products are managed primarily for their short-term earnings. Boxes 7, 8, and 9 constitute the harvest/divest category, in which the products are viewed as relatively weak and the industry as having only marginal interest. The products in this last category are managed for immediate cash generation, to finance the invest/grow products.

One senior executive at Standard Brands notes the potential danger of an attempt by each individual product manager to make a case for getting his or her product into grid position 1 and making it an invest/grow business. To prevent such mismatches or overstriving by ambitious young managers, the company has developed a "performance management system" in which an individual manager's performance is measured directly against his strategic plan. For example, an invest/grow business gives higher weighting to improving market share than to current profits. Conversely, profitability is the major performance measure for a harvest business.

Source: Sandra Salmans, "Zero Base Helps Rationalize Product Strategy," *International Management* vol. 34 (February 1979), 38–41. Reprinted by special permission from *International Management*. Copyright © 1979. McGraw-Hill Publications Co. All rights reserved.

economy is perhaps the fact that the differentiated international marketing environment makes it likely that heterogeneous strategies will be required to achieve and hold substantial market shares in international markets.

BARRIERS TO STANDARDIZED
INTERNATIONAL MARKETING

Some barriers to identifying and implementing a standardized international marketing strategy are summarized in table 12.1. The obstacles to uniformity can be categorized as being economic, cultural, competitive, and legal in nature.

Among the economic factors influencing marketing strategy, the likelihood of a product offering's success will be influenced by the current income level of a country in conjunction with the income-elasticity coefficient for the product. For example, the demand for "luxury" products such as high-performance sports cars can be expected to increase with higher aggregate income levels only after the per capita income level in a region has reached a fairly substantial critical level. Below that level, demand for such luxury products will remain quite limited. This relationship helps explain why the sewing machines that the Singer Company sells in Africa are simple, basic, and inexpensive and handpowered.[6]

Differences in consumer tastes and preferences often have an important influence on the need to "customize" products for specific markets. As an example, the Nestlé Company sells literally dozens of blends of their Nescafé coffee around the world. The local formulations were determined according to taste tests in different national markets. Another example is provided by the challenge facing Canadians trying to sell lumber in South Korea, where homes are usually made of concrete. Koreans sit and sleep on the floor, which is the warmest part of a room because increasingly Korean houses are being heated by running hot water through pipes under the floors. The challenge for Canadian lumber sellers is to design a house sturdy enough to support such a water system.[7]

In other cases, competitive or legal factors may oblige the international firm to differentiate its product offerings across countries. For example, nations tend to differ in the kinds and amounts of preservatives legally allowed in cereals and other packaged foods. In some instances, products are banned entirely from sale, as is the case with citizens' band radios in Europe. The latter restriction obliged Radio Shack Corporation, a leading seller of consumer electronic equipment in the U.S., to concentrate on other products in its European outlets.[8]

The influence of price on the demand for a product will also depend upon

---

[6] As noted in Vern Terpstra, *International Dimensions of Marketing* (Boston: Kent Publishing Co., 1982), p. 90.

[7] See Hall Lenen, "Lumber Sellers Set to Crack South Korean Home Market," *Toronto Globe and Mail*, May 7, 1984, IB8.

[8] See Cateora, *International Marketing*, p. 370.

TABLE 12.1   Barriers to Standardized International Marketing

	MARKETING INGREDIENTS			
SOURCES OF VARIATION	PRODUCT	PRICE	DISTRIBUTION	PROMOTION
Economic factors	Varied income levels	Varied income levels	Different retail structures	Media availability
Cultural factors	Consumer tastes and habits	Price-negotiating habits	Shopping habits	Language-attitude differences
Competitive factors	Nature of existing products	Competitors' costs and prices	Competitors' monopoly of channels	Competitors' budgets and appeals
Legal factors	Product regulations (including tariffs)	Price controls	Restrictions on distribution	Advertising and media restrictions

Source: Vern Terpstra, *International Dimensions of Marketing* (Boston: Kent Publishing Co., 1982), p. 10, © 1982 by Wadsworth, Inc. Reprinted by permission of Kent Publishing Co., a division of Wadsworth, Inc.

economic factors, especially the income level of a country. All other things constant, lower-income consumers will typically be more price sensitive than higher-income consumers. An illustration of this relationship is provided by the difficulty that multinational tobacco companies have experienced in selling filter-tipped cigarettes in the less developed countries. Sales of imported cigarettes are limited in poorer countries primarily because most people are unwilling (given their low-income levels) to pay the extra cost of filtered cigarettes.[9] Different price elasticities of demand mitigate against setting standardized international prices for a product.

In other cases, the ability of the international firm to set "standardized" prices will be restricted by a propensity on the part of local shoppers to haggle over prices rather than accept the price marked on a good and (or) by differential buying power among consumers. Where the government in a region is the largest (or only) customer for a product, the firm's pricing discretion may be especially limited in comparison to cases where there are a number of firms that are prepared to bid for the international firm's product offerings. The case of the Singaporean Mass Rapid Transit System offers a case in point. The competition among international firms for a piece of the $5 billion project was described by one international banker as "vicious." It included a last-minute move by one company to

[9]See "Third World Smokers Are Tough Market," *Toronto Globe and Mail*, December 27, 1983, B4.

throw in free spare parts for ten years and knock $250,000 off the tender price the day before a contract decision.[10]

The pricing discretion of the international firm is further limited by the presence of competitors and (sometimes) by formal price controls. With respect to the latter consideration, many countries have restrictions on the prices—(usually the maximum prices)—that can be charged for different goods and services. In the majority of cases, price controls exist for basic foodstuffs, although the scope of these controls can be much broader in developing and Eastern European countries.

Distribution techniques may also need to be modified to reflect international differences in economic, cultural, competitive, and legal factors. For example, the state of a country's economic development will strongly affect the extent to which wholesaling and retailing activities are centralized in large chains or are dispersed among many small shops. In this respect, the relatively large percentage of multiple-car families in North America facilitated the spread of the shopping-center concept in which major supermarkets and department stores serve large numbers of customers, thereby benefiting from economies of mass marketing. By contrast, since British homemakers are less likely to own a car and, therefore, more likely to shop on foot in the neighborhood, British stores typically are small compared to North American stores.[11]

Cultural factors may also be important determinants of more or less successful distribution channels. For example, there is evidence that shoppers in highly developed economies rely less on shopping activities as a social outlet than do their counterparts in less developed countries.[12] Cultural influences may, in turn, be augmented by legal influences, as in the case of Japan, where the competitive advantage of small retail shops is promoted not only by the propensity of the Japanese to do daily shopping but also by government laws that penalize the operations of mass merchandisers.

Finally, the likely success or failure of different promotional techniques will also reflect international differences in broad environmental factors. In particular, economic and legal factors may severely restrict the media available to advertise and promote products. Obviously, where literacy rates are low, newspapers and magazines are not viable advertising outlets, and radio and television may be preferable media; however, in certain countries, among them Belgium and the Scandinavian countries, radio and television commercials are not allowed. Perhaps the most important source of differentiated promotion is culture. An obvious example is the use of sexual imagery to promote a wide array of products in North

---

[10]This case is discussed in Chris Sherwell, "Singapore Transit Bidders Go for Broke," *Toronto Globe and Mail*, February 6, 1984, 1B10.

[11]See Jac Goldstuckor, "The Influence of Culture on Channels of Distribution," in S. K. Sethi and J. N. Sheth, *Multinational Business Operations*, vol. 3 (Pacific Palisades, Calif.: Goodyear Publishing Co., 1973), p. 235.

[12]Ibid., p. 234.

America. This approach would be totally unacceptable, not to say illegal, in Moslem countries.

It is useful, at this point, to emphasize a familiar theme of this book: differences between international and domestic management complexities are a matter of degree. For example, economic, cultural, competitive, and legal conditions will vary across regions within a country as well as across countries, thereby jeopardizing the success of standardized domestic as well as international marketing strategies. An obvious example is provided in the case of the large black and Hispanic populations in the United States. Many American companies have adopted specific marketing strategies targeted for these relatively large numbers of minority-group consumers, not the least of which strategies involves the widespread use of Spanish-language advertising in the southwestern states and California. Even in such a small country as Belgium, income differentials within the country promote the existence of luxurious department stores side by side with small retail shops that carry relatively restricted lines of goods. The distinction between the international marketing environment and the purely domestic marketing environment is therefore one of degree. The former tends to be substantially more differentiated than the latter. And as a consequence, many companies have come to grief by transplanting domestic marketing strategies into the more heterogeneous international marketing environment.

Numerous examples of international marketing mishaps can be cited, but we will restrict ourselves to a few that illustrate the main point; namely, ignoring important differences across countries in the broad marketing environment will lead to costly and ineffective marketing strategies.[13]

SOME EXAMPLES
OF INTERNATIONAL MARKETING MISTAKES

Most classic international marketing mistakes arise because a marketing strategy that proved to be successful in one country was transplanted intact to another country. In some cases the product being marketed was grossly unsuited for the targeted customers. For example, General Motors of Canada experienced major problems in fulfilling an order placed by the government of Iraq for more than thirteen thousand Chevrolet Malibu autos. A large number of the cars ordered were shipped to Iraq, where it was discovered that the cars were mechanically unfit for Iraq's hot and dusty climate. By the time GM figured out that supplementary air filters and different clutches would eliminate the mechanical failures, Iraq had canceled its order.[14]

---

[13]These examples are taken from David A. Ricks, *Big Business Blunders*: (Homewood, Ill.: Dow Jones-Irwin, 1983). Ricks provides an exhaustive and often hilarious catalogue of international marketing fiascoes.

[14]bid., p. 26.

In other cases something as seemingly innocuous as the name of a product has led to embarrassment and additional costs for the international firm. Again General Motors provides an example—this time related to marketing its Chevrolet Nova. The name *Nova* means "star" when translated into Spanish. However, when spoken, it sounds like "no va," which in Spanish means "it doesn't go." To remedy the situation, GM changed the automobile's name to Caribe.[15]

Ricks argues that in the field of international marketing, product promotion has caused the most corporate headaches. In some cases, the problems are related to language colloquialism that is not appreciated by the international marketer. For example, marketers of Pepsi Cola in Germany did not intend the slogan "Come alive with Pepsi" to mean "Come out of the grave with Pepsi," as it was interpreted. Examples also abound of companies whose products have legally been denied entry into a country because of contentious promotional practices (for example, mail-order catalogues that referred to North Korea instead of the People's Republic of Korea). In other cases, the promotional approach taken ignored relevant market conditions. An example is a foreign beer company that tried to enter the American market by portraying its product as locally brewed. This strategy proved unwise, since foreign beers were perceived as being "premium" brews, while the American market was saturated with local beers.

The types of marketing mistakes cited above were all avoidable, in some cases with a fairly trivial effort on the part of management. For example, many translation errors can be avoided by using "back translations," that is, having material translated from one language into another language and then have a third party translate it back into the original. In this way, potential misinterpretations and misunderstandings are often identified before they become public. Needless to say, translation and retranslation efforts should be undertaken by individuals who are not only fluent in the relevant foreign language but also extremely familiar with the local culture, so that they understand idiomatic constructions. Another obvious procedure to avoid marketing mistakes is to undertake market research or contract with an outside organization to undertake such research.

INTERNATIONAL MARKET RESEARCH

Marketing research is concerned with gathering, recording, and analyzing data and other information useful to making marketing decisions. While the objectives of marketing research are the same for international and purely domestic com-

---

[15]Ibid., pp. 38–39. Since we do not wish to imply that G.M. is the only, or even the most frequent, participant in international marketing fiascoes, we offer the example of an anonymous firm doing business in Quebec that advertised its product as "lavement d'auto" ("car enema") instead of the correct "lavage d'auto" ("car wash"). See Ricks, p. 78.

panies, the international marketing manager often requires different kinds of information and faces more stringent limitations on the availability of information and the applicability of research techniques.

Cateora notes that research can be divided into three types based on a firm's information needs: (1) general information about the country, area, and/or market; (2) specific information used to solve problems arising in advertising, pricing, distribution, and product development; and (3) information useful for anticipating social, economic, and consumer trends within specific markets.[16] The market researcher is expected to provide accurate and useful data within the limits imposed by available resources.

Broadly speaking, the market researcher can utilize primary and/or secondary data. The former represents data and other information collected directly by the researcher. The latter represents data collected by other researchers and made available in published or unpublished form. Secondary data tend to be cheaper to collect than primary data but sometimes have the disadvantage of not focusing specifically enough on the issues facing any individual company. Nevertheless, secondary data represent an appropriate starting point for the international market researcher. The problem here is that reliable and timely secondary data tend to be limited to the highly developed countries.

Sources of Secondary Data

Government departments and statistical agencies are a major source of secondary data. For example, the U.S. Department of Commerce publishes a wide range of data related to U.S. exports and imports, international economic conditions, and opportunities in foreign markets. Comparable data for Canada are published by Statistics Canada. As well, the Organization for Economic Cooperation and Development, the European Economic Community, and other regional organizations publish statistics and studies related to the economies of their respective regions; however, the latter tend to encompass the developed economies, by and large. For the less developed economies, the United Nations tends to be the major consistently accurate source of information, particularly the U.N. *Statistical Yearbook*. The market researcher can also occasionally glean useful information from embassies and consulates of foreign countries.

Private sources of market information are quite diverse. They include Chambers of Commerce, international and domestic banks, foreign trade associations, market research and international advertising agencies, export/import agents, and magazines and periodicals. Each of these sources can provide useful background information on general economic and political conditions in a given region. However, the aggregated information provided often lacks the detail required for product-portfolio analyses.

---

[16]Cateora, p. 252.

Primary Data Sources

Where secondary data are inadequate, the researcher should consider implementing original surveys. The important point to stress is that the design and implementation of surveys should be appropriate for the region in question. As an obvious example, there is little point in designing a broad telephone survey of household purchasing patterns where relatively large segments of the population do not have access to telephones. In other cases, problems of dialects and different languages can make nationwide questionnaire surveys impractical. Obviously, firms that have limited experience in survey research work should consider employing the services of experienced consultants, not only to collect the required information but to help interpret the data collected.

Whether the firm relies upon primary or secondary data, a proper evaluation of the information collected requires some basic familiarity with the markets being considered. All data are subject to biases of one sort or another. In particular, governments are prone to paint a rosier picture of their national economies than is perhaps appropriate. In countries where a substantial portion of economic activity is carried on in the "underground economy" to avoid the clutches of the tax collector or foreign-exchange authorities, published statistics on economic activity may be very misleading. Furthermore, primary surveys will also be misleading unless the propensity of individual respondents to hide their true incomes is taken into account. In short, the use of both primary and secondary data must be tempered by a judicious appreciation of their biases and shortcomings.

If properly executed, the market research carried out by the firm should identify specific limitations to implementing a standardized marketing strategy in different national markets. Management must then evaluate tradeoffs between the benefits associated with "customizing" strategies for individual markets and the costs of foregoing economies of standardization.

THE ADVANTAGES
OF STANDARDIZING MARKETING STRATEGY

Notwithstanding customary differences in economic, cultural, competitive, and legal factors across national markets, there may be cases where the benefits of standardization are sufficient to outweigh the costs of essentially ignoring the heterogeneity of the international marketing environment or attempting to "homogenize" it. In this regard there are four main cost savings associated with standardization: (1) common product design, (2) mass-production economies, (3) savings in packaging costs and promotional material, and (4) avoiding risk of confusion that may result from reaching audiences with different brand names and promotional appeals.[17]

---

[17]See Robert D. Buzzell, "Can You Standardize Multinational Marketing?" in Thorelli and Becker, *International Marketing Strategy.*

Mass-production economies arise from a number of sources including the ability to achieve long lengths of run for a limited variety of products. Long run lengths, in turn, contribute to the firm's ability to use specialized capital equipment and to take full advantage of learning by doing. In addition, product standardization can assist the firm to obtain discounts on input purchases by enabling management to aggregate its orders for a limited range of intermediary inputs and capital-equipment purchases.

There may also be important direct and indirect cost savings associated with standardizing marketing channels on an international basis. Such cost savings may arise from the fact that developing international trade requires a critical mass of expertise in international legal and financial institutions, as well as in the logistics of international transportation and communications. The relevant knowledge requirements will likely vary with the trade channels chosen. Thus, by choosing a limited number of distribution channels, the international firm can effectively reduce the burden of these overhead "transactions" costs.

In other cases, a firm can indirectly pool overhead costs with other international firms by employing the services of trading companies. The preeminent trading companies in the world today are the Japanese "Sogo Shosha." These general trading companies provide services in finance, engineering, construction, communications, transportation, marketing, and other areas to both small and large companies.[18] Indeed, a small firm can employ the services of a trading company to devise and implement a comprehensive international marketing strategy. In taking this approach, the firm can realize some of the economies of standardization, since its export (or import) activities will be pooled with those of other firms also using the services of the trading company. At the same time the trading company will seek to identify and implement a marketing strategy that offers strong prospects for success in the markets selected.

Several U.S.-based trading companies have emerged recently. The largest is Sears World Trade, Inc., a unit of Sears, Roebuck and Company. Besides carrying out exporting and importing activities for its parent, Sears World Trade offers its services as a trading company to third parties in five main areas: consumer goods; agribusiness, for instance, livestock deals and pulp and timber trading; health care, particularly services such as setting up clinics; high technology, with an emphasis on personal computers and telecommunications; and light industrial products such as oil and gas equipment.[19]

COUNTERTRADE

One development in international business that is enhancing the advantages of using trading companies is the growing importance of countertrade. A recent U.S.

---

[18]A prospective exporter need not be exclusively interested in the Japanese market to utilize the services of Japanese trading companies.

[19]For a description of Sears World Trade, see "Sears' Export Unit Winning Respect," *Toronto Globe and Mail*, May 7, 1984, B4.

congressional study suggested that U.S. trade would increase substantially if American exporters were more willing to enter into bartering arrangements. In barter trade, companies and countries swap goods rather than making payments in convertible currencies. The various types of barterlike exchange are known as countertrade. One expert estimates that as many as thirty countries, from Argentina and Australia to Yugoslavia and Zambia, have made countertrade an important, if not a critical, consideration in their international purchases.[20]

Many countries attempt to ration their scarce foreign exchange by tying imports directly to exports. Countertrade can also be a form of hidden discounting. That is, while a seller might want to expand volume, openly cutting prices could antagonize relations with existing customers or lead to charges of ''unfair'' competition from rival sellers. Through countertrading, the exporter can implicitly cut prices by paying above market price for countertraded imports. Oil-exporting countries belonging to the OPEC cartel are especially inclined to use countertrade as a way to ''shave'' their quotes below OPEC's official price. Among U.S. companies, those engaged in the aerospace and electronics industries are most heavily involved in countertrade commitments.

While most international companies prefer cash deals, a willingness to engage in countertrade is increasingly crucial to commercial success in a number of international markets. Large companies, such as General Electric, enjoy an advantage in undertaking countertrade since they can use counter-traded goods in-house more easily than most other companies. Smaller companies with less international trading expertise often must turn for help to independent trading companies or to large companies such as Sears World Trading. The latter can not only help smaller companies find outlets for the goods acquired through countertrading, they can also help in evaluating the implied terms of exchange. That is, they can help the smaller company evaluate the profitability of a proposed countertrade. Trading companies typically assume countertrade obligations for a fee. That is, they will undertake to place the goods acquired by the exporter for a fee that varies with the difficulty of the task.

STANDARDIZATION OR DIFFERENTIATION?

In a literal sense, multinational standardization would mean the offering of identical product lines at identical prices through identical distribution systems, supported by identical promotional programs, in several different countries. At the other extreme, completely ''localized'' marketing strategies would contain no common elements whatsoever. Since typically neither of these extremes is either feasible or desirable, the practical question is, Which elements of marketing strategy can or should be standardized and to what degree?

---

[20]See David B. Yoffie, ''Profiting from Countertrade,'' *Harvard Business Review* vol. 62 (May-June 1984), 8–16. This discussion of countertrade draws heavily on the Yoffie article.

In fact, the answer to this question will depend upon the characteristics of the international firm as well as the characteristics of the markets to be served. Specific features of the firm that influence the standardization-differentiation tradeoff include its size, the nature of its main products, and its competitive objectives. More specifically, large firms have the ability to marshal massive financial and other resources to homogenize market demand. In some cases, large firms may be such dominant forces in their industries that foreign customers have few alternatives but to accept the "standardized" models produced by the dominant firms. A good example of this phenomenon is provided by the Boeing Corporation, which is far and away the world's major producer of commercial aircraft. Since designing and developing jet aircraft is an extraordinarily expensive proposition, and since so few firms have the technical and financial capacity to undertake such work, national airlines around the world accommodate their individual corporate strategies to Boeing's assessment of the industry's "needs," rather than vice versa.

In other cases, large firms can help standardize international demand patterns through extensive advertising and "educational" campaigns. This is an especially promising strategy where the product in question has no strong direct or indirect substitutes and no long history of use in foreign markets. One such educational campaign was undertaken by the Japanese company Kikkoman. This manufacturer of soy sauce, rather than modify its product to correspond to the Chinese soy sauces that Americans were familiar with, ran extensive TV ads that emphasized how Kikkoman soy sauce is specially brewed and aged, like beer. The success of this educational campaign enabled Kikkoman to successfully market a significantly more expensive, as well as different tasting, soy sauce. But it should be noted that Kikkoman's campaign was long and extended. For example, it took twelve years before the product was moved out of its San Francisco test market area.[21]

Theodore Levitt, a well-known marketing expert, has argued that new forms of telecommunications technology have produced markets for standardized consumer products on a previously unimagined scale of magnitude.[22] In effect, widespread electronic access to potential consumer markets has made it extremely feasible to market any "good-value" product around the world with very little accommodation to unique local conditions. Some marketing professionals stop well short of accepting Levitt's hypothesis but do acknowledge that human nature and the motives of people are more or less universal. Thus, although the ways in which needs are satisfied may vary across cultures, products that can tie their appeal to a "basic" human motive can more successfully implement standardized international marketing strategies.

[21]A discussion of the Kikkoman case is contained in Hans Thorelli, "International Marketing: An Ecological View," in Thorelli and Becker, *International Marketing Strategies.*

[22]See Theodore Levitt, "The Globalization of Markets," *Harvard Business Review* vol. 61 (May–June 1983), 92–102.

The preeminent example of a ''standardized'' world product is Coca-Cola. Advertising experts agree that Coca-Cola has a universal thirst-quenching appeal that permits it to achieve a similarity of messages, visual appearance, taste, and media selection in virtually all national markets.[23] However, there are very few companies that have approached Coca-Cola's success in tying their products to the obvious fulfillment of basic human needs. Moreover, even in Coca-Cola's case, acknowledgment of unique cultural features is sometimes required. For example, signs advising Japanese to ''drink Coke'' were considered an impolite form of command and were subsequently changed to ''let us drink Coke.''

Finally, basic differences in corporate strategy can influence the standardization/differentiation tradeoffs made by management. For example, North American companies are reputed to be more concerned with short-term accounting profits than are Japanese companies. The latter are reputed to be oriented more toward long-term growth and profitability. One suggested manifestation of this longer-term orientation is the widespread use of so-called market-share pricing; that is, Japanese companies deliberately use a low entry price to build up market share and to establish a dominant market position.

Characteristics of foreign markets that influence the trade-off between standardization and diversification of product offerings are summarized in table 12.2. The table suggests that pressures to diversify a firm's product portfolio include a slow rate of growth in foreign markets, market-share instability (as a proxy for competitiveness) in each foreign market, and strong competitive advantages to a firm that first introduces a product. Conversely, the relative benefits of standardization are promoted by the need for a concentrated sales effort (that is, a need to educate consumers about the benefits of a particular product), the need for product adaptation (or local conditions that necessitate unique product characteristics), and economies of scale in distribution.

In the following sections we discuss how various elements of a firm's overall marketing strategy can be customized to better fit the unique characteristics of individual national markets. We start by considering pricing.

INTERNATIONAL PRICING

International pricing can be done on an export basis or an intra-subsidiary basis. There are four broad examples of different export price quotations.

1. Ex (named point or origin): the buyer takes possession of the merchandise at the factory of the seller and bears all risks and expenses from there on.

---

[23]The ubiquity of Coca-Cola's appeal was made stunningly obvious to the author of this book on a trip to a fairly remote Greek island. A guided three-hour trip by mule up the side of a mountain brought me to a cloister which was very infrequently visited by tourists. The first thing that caught my eye upon dismounting the burro was a dozen or so Cokes cooling in the shallow well at the entrance to the cloister.

TABLE 12.2   Factors Influencing Standardization of Product Offering

FACTORS	IMPLICATION
1. Growth rate of each foreign market.	Lower growth implies greater pressure to diversify.
2. Sales stability in each foreign market.	Less stability suggests greater pressure to diversify.
3. Competitive lead time.	Pressure to diversify where there is strong first-mover advantage.
4. Need for concentrated sales effort.	Pressure for standardization.
5. Need for product adaptation.	Reduces benefits of diversification.
6. Economies of scale in distribution.	Increases benefits of standardization.

Source: Igal Ayal and Jehiel Zif, "Market Expansion Strategies in Multinational Marketing," *Journal of Marketing*, Vol. 43 (Spring 1979), 84–94.

2. F.A.S. (named port of shipment): the exporter maintains ownership of the goods and responsibility for their handling until they are placed alongside the ship at the port of embarkation. F.A.S. stands for free alongside ship.

3. F.O.B. (loaded at named port of shipment): the seller sees that the merchandise is loaded onto the ship. F.O.B. stands for free on board. Similar quotations for other transportation channels are: F.O.T. (free on truck) and F.O.R. (free on rail).

4. C.I.F. (named point of destination): transfers title to the buyer once the merchandise is loaded aboard the transport vehicle; however, the exporter assumes responsibility for transportation and insurance to the foreign port. C.I.F. stands for cost, insurance, and freight.

As a general rule, the exporter's risks and responsibilities increase as one moves from quotation method 1 through quotation method 4. As a result, buyers will prefer C.I.F. (named point of destination) quotes when they are relatively small and, therefore, would find arranging for merchandise loading services and shipping insurance relatively expensive. In effect, the buyer will prefer more comprehensive forms of quoting when the additional activities can be provided more cheaply by the seller. On the other hand, where buyers are large and knowledgeable international traders, they may prefer to arrange themselves for handling, transporting, and insuring the goods purchased from the time at which those goods leave the premises of the seller.

Export price quotations will be employed when selling to independent foreign buyers. When the firm is exporting to its own subsidiaries abroad, internal (transfer) prices will be used. Different transfer prices may be set in different markets for essentially the same product. Terpstra cites three reasons why a multinational firm might sell to some of its affiliates at relatively low prices: (1) to lessen the impact of high tariff duties, (2) to enter a market against tough competition, and (3) to source income in specific countries if tax rates are relatively low in those countries.[24]

While low transfer prices to affiliates may occasionally be a desirable strategy, foreign customs officials can deem the prices charged to be inappropriate and use what they believe is closer to a fair market price to value the product for purposes of charging import duties. The U.S. Internal Revenue Service also has authority to look at a firm's transfer prices and to challenge those it thinks are too low.

There are also situations in which a multinational company might want to transfer goods or services to a foreign affiliate at above-average prices. One such situation is where the affiliate is located in a country with relatively high corporate income tax rates. A second is when the host-country government has imposed restrictions on dividend repatriation and where the embargoed funds have a higher expected rate-of-return if invested in another country. In the latter case, high transfer prices are an indirect way of siphoning dividends out of the affiliate. Of course, foreign tax authorities will be monitoring the transfer prices charged quite closely and may take action against companies that are perceived as avoiding their local tax burden by charging unrealistically high transfer prices.

The degree of standardization of international pricing will therefore depend upon the nature of the distribution channels employed (for example, arms-length versus foreign affiliates), the degree of competition in foreign markets, and the tax and tariff conditions in those markets. Pricing behavior will also be influenced by company goals in different markets. For example, in growth economies the international firm may be more likely to stress maintenance or growth of market share, a goal that argues for lower prices. Conversely, in stagnant or slow-growing markets, high prices may be more appropriate. Similarly, an emphasis on high quality—with commensurate prices—may be appropriate in some markets, while a low-price, low-quality package is more appropriate elsewhere.

It is worth emphasizing that consumers will differ in their willingness to pay higher prices for better quality. Some of these differences are related to the nature of the product itself. For example, industrial purchasers, especially buyers of high-technology products, tend to be especially concerned with quality and reliability, and they are ordinarily more willing to pay a premium to ensure that the expected quality is forthcoming. However, differences are also reputed to exist across national markets. As an illustration, market researchers conclude that European consumers are more ''quality conscious'' than North Americans when it comes to buying durables, such as autos and clothing, but less concerned about quality when it comes to nondurables, such as toilet tissue.[25]

Other influences that are relevant to the international pricing decision in-

---

[24]See Terpstra, *International Dimensions of Marketing*, pp. 145–46.

[25]For a fuller discussion of such national differences, see Ernest Dichter, ''The World Customer,'' in Howard A. Thompson, ed., *The Great Writings in Marketing* (Plymouth, Mich.: Commerce Press, 1976), pp. 527–41.

TABLE 12.3   Factors Influencing
International Pricing Policies

1. Distribution channels
2. Taxes and tariffs
3. Competition and demand conditions
4. Government regulations
5. Inflation

Source: Vern Terpstra, *International Dimensions of Marketing* (Boston: Kent Publishing Co., 1982), p. 148, © 1982 by Wadsworth, Inc. Reprinted by permission of Kent Publishing Co., a division of Wadsworth, Inc.

clude differences in government regulations surrounding ''allowable'' prices and differential inflation rates. As noted earlier in this chapter, many foreign governments have price controls in varying degrees, which place differential constraints on the rates at which prices can be increased in different markets. The differential impact of price constraints will be exacerbated where underlying inflation rates also differ. A summary of the various influences on standardizing or differentiating international pricing policies is provided in table 12.3.

INTERNATIONAL PROMOTION

Standardization of the key elements of promotion, especially advertising, will be more or less viable depending upon the homogeneity of national cultures and the widespread availability of advertising media. In this regard, the wide variation across countries in economic, political, and cultural conditions often obliges the international firm to adapt its promotion strategies to local conditions. In particular, the available array of communications media typically varies from country to country. For example, Japanese papers are relatively few in number but enjoy a large circulation among a broad cross-section of readers. On the other hand, in Middle Eastern countries, there is a relative abundance of newspapers, each of which has a limited and specialized readership.

Access to advertising media will also vary across countries as a result of differences in government regulation. For example, Indonesia does not allow television advertising on the country's sole television channel. In some cases the content of the advertising message itself is constrained by legislation. Some countries, such as Canada, have very strict requirements for advertisers to provide statistical support for claims made about the advantages of their products. Other countries, such as Germany, severely restrict comparisons between rival products.

Industrial products tend to employ more standardized promotional channels than consumer products. In particular, specialized technical journals, manufacturers' catalogues, and trade fairs are convenient ways to communicate information to relatively sophisticated and concentrated industrial purchasers. Direct contact with government agents is often the most important way to promote industrial products, especially in less developed economies where government is the primary purchaser of capital equipment. But even in industrial-product markets, differences will exist in the emphasis customers place on promotable features such as service, reliability, quality, performance, and costs.

Obviously, the need to tailor promotional activities to national markets will fragment a firm's budget. Furthermore, most firms simply do not have the capacity to employ sufficient in-house expertise in international marketing. Therefore, most firms that engage extensively in international business use the services of advertising agencies. Where their business is concentrated in a few countries, domestic agencies in those countries will be used. However, if their business is spread over a wide range of countries, they are more likely to employ large international agencies. By drawing on the services of international agencies, smaller firms can gain some advantages of economies of scale in promotion, much in the same way that efficiency benefits can be gained indirectly by using trading companies.

INTERNATIONAL DISTRIBUTION

The last major aspect of marketing to consider is channels of distribution. Various broad channels of international distribution are listed in table 12.4, where a distinction is made between direct and indirect exporting. The distinction has to do with where responsibility rests for the exporting activities of the firm. Where responsibility for selling the goods to foreign buyers, preparing the relevant documentation, and arranging for shipment stays with the original seller until the goods reach their overseas market, we are considering direct methods of exporting. Indirect exporting therefore refers to situations where responsibility for one or more of these activities passes to another party, either within the home market of the exporter or within the importer's market.

Direct exporting requires a greater range of expertise and a greater commitment of time and money than indirect exporting, since the direct exporter must deal with a greater variety of factors and complications further from its home market.[26] Of the various direct exporting alternatives, selling to the final buyer is most suitable for industrial or technical products that require the manufacturer's technical service and for high-value consumer items with limited sales volume.

Foreign distributors buy products, carry stock, and sell for their own account to wholesalers or retailers at prices they set themselves. In contrast, agents work for a commission or a fixed fee and generally do not take title to goods. Both

[26]The following discussion draws heavily upon George T. Jacob, *A Manual on Export Marketing* (Ottawa: Supply and Services Canada, 1983), pp. 84–87.

TABLE 12.4   Major International Distribution Channels

---

1. Direct exporting
   - Final buyer direct from manufacturer
   - Foreign distributor who buys and sells on account
   - Foreign agent who works on commission
   - Foreign broker who handles primarily commodities
   - Foreign trade organization or government agencies of socialist countries
2. Indirect exporting
   - Trading house that buys and sells on account
   - Export agent/broker who works on commission
   - Foreign resident buyer, buying for principals abroad
   - Confirming houses that source, ship, and arrange for payment of goods
3. Licensing
4. Joint ventures
5. Wholly owned affiliates

Source: Categories 1 and 2 are taken from George T. Jacob, *A Manual on Export Marketing* (Ottawa: Minister of Supply and Services Canada, 1983), p. 84.

distributors and agents promote the exporter's product; however, a distributor usually has a more extensive sales network and the capacity to handle a broader range of products. Brokers work on straight commission and tend to focus on specialized transactions in bulk commodities. Foreign brokers essentially bring buyers and sellers together and help negotiate agreements.

As a generalization, exporters have the greatest degree of control over marketing activities when they undertake direct selling. The use of a sales force operating regularly overseas but based in the home country is a fairly common method of international marketing in Western Europe, where problems of time and distance are relatively limited. In other cases, the international firm might establish its own branch office for overseas sales employing a mixture of home-company and local-company personnel. Direct selling tends to be preferable when there are a limited number of potential agents or distributors with the ability and willingness to provide after-sales service.

Where an exporter wants to concentrate on production and avoid many of the activities associated with exporting, the use of one or more of the indirect methods indicated in table 12.4 is appropriate. Trading houses may both export and import in a defined product group. They may buy products from the supplier outright and assume all credit and financial risks in selling abroad, or they may act on a commission basis and share credit and financial risks with the supplier. Trading houses assume many of the tasks of moving products from the home country to overseas markets in the case of exporting and from overseas markets to the home country in the case of importing.

Export agents or brokers in the home country operate in a similar manner to overseas agents and brokers. Foreign resident buyers or purchasing agents act on behalf of principals abroad and buy a wide variety of industrial and consumer products. Frequently they act for foreign governments. Confirming houses also act on behalf of foreign buyers by sourcing and paying for goods bought and by arranging for shipment.

Where the firm determines that production abroad is more advantageous than production in its home market, it faces a choice in terms of how directly and extensively it wants to get involved in overseas production and marketing. One possible approach is licensing, where the firm hires out the use of its patents, trademarks, or general know-how to a local firm against payment of royalties. Another is joint venturing in which ownership of production and distribution facilities is shared with private-sector foreign investors and/or with government agencies or government-owned companies. A third approach involves ownership of wholly owned manufacturing and distribution affiliates.

The determination of when one approach is preferable to another is complex. What is important to emphasize at this point is that the international firm progressively assumes increasing control of distribution activities as it moves from licensing through joint venturing to owning affiliates abroad. But this increased control implies substantial "front-end" costs associated with making investments abroad, learning about the foreign environment, and establishing good relations with foreign governments.

Whether increased control is worth the higher front-end costs will depend (among other things) upon the nature of the product involved and the ability of the international firm to identify and collaborate with promising licensees or joint-venture partners. In particular, the advantages of employing wholly owned affiliates in international business are suggested to be particularly large in high-technology industries, where control over proprietary information is jeopardized by licensing or joint-venture arrangements.

In other cases, licensing or joint-venture arrangements may founder because cultural differences between the erstwhile partners lead to constant tension and misunderstanding. For example, Wright notes that the most critical constraints and problems for North American firms in joint ventures with Japanese companies are caused by differences between the Japanese and Western character, which in turn are reflected in differences in the business systems and in approaches to specific management practices.[27] Common areas of conflict or problems include: difference of objectives, growth versus profit orientation, language and other communication barriers, and difference in the emphasis placed on for-

[27]See Richard W. Wright, "Canadian Joint Ventures in Japan," in K. C. Dhawan, Hamid Etemad, and Richard W. Wright, *International Business: A Canadian Perspective* (Don Mills, Ontario: Addison-Wesley Publishing Co., 1981, pp. 376-394).

mal contracts and lifetime employment practices. However, an apparent strong preference on the part of Japanese companies to deal with other Japanese companies implies an urgency for foreign companies wishing to do business in Japan to take on Japanese partners.[28] It should be emphasized that firms often find it necessary to employ several distribution channels in order to gain adequate coverage of overseas markets. This is because in many cases foreign markets are highly fragmented. In particular, channels suitable for an urban area are unsuitable for a rural area and vice versa. Japanese companies, in particular, are well known for using hand-picked dealers and distributors to focus distribution efforts on carefully selected customer types in specific regions. In other cases, international firms may be forced to put their own distribution channels in place because other channels simply do not exist.

CASE STUDY: *MARKETING ROOM DEODORANTS IN BRITAIN AND THE U.S.*

Even when marketing as seemingly innocuous a product as room deodorant, sales often benefit from customizing strategies for specific markets. Consider the example of the British firm, Royds Manchester Ltd. and their Airwick's Stick Ups deodorizing product. The product was introduced successfully in the U.S. before it was introduced to Britons. Before launching the product domestically, the company did extensive research to determine whether the product would work in England and if any changes were needed.

In the end, the strength of the product's fragrance was greatly increased because British consumers demanded more fragrance than Americans. Also, instead of the normal U.S. cardboard twin-pack, the British product was sold in single blister packs. Higher cost of plastic and the additional fragrance made the U.K. product more expensive, so the blister pack and single item encouraged customer trial.

To appeal to the English preference for an unobtrusive product, the TV spots were altered. They showed the product in more inconspicuous places than did the U.S. advertising. Advertising was also adjusted to account for heavier use of print and outdoor media and less radio than in the U.S.

The marketing approach was obviously successful, as the sale of Stick Ups alone increased Airwick's market share from 29 to 43 percent.

Source: "Europeans Insist on Pretesting," *Advertising Age*, August 24, 1981, 38.

OTHER CONSIDERATIONS IN MARKETING STRATEGY

Several other considerations are relevant to developing a complete marketing strategy. One consideration relates to documentation necessary to facilitate export and import shipments. Required documents include bills of lading, invoices of

---

[28]For a discussion of this apparent preference, see Steven P. Galante, "Japanese Have Another Trade Barrier: They Favor Business with Japanese," *Wall Street Journal*, April 12, 1984, 36.

various sorts, insurance certificates, and export and import licenses. The bill of lading is the most important document. It serves as a contract for shipment between the carrier and the shipper, as a certificate of ownership, and as a receipt from the carrier for shipment.[29] Generally, the required documents are relatively straightforward; however, carelessness in their preparation can lead to shipment delays and even lost shipments.

The most frequently used payment procedure in foreign commercial transactions is the letter of credit, followed in importance by documentary drafts (or bills of exchange) drawn by the seller on the buyer. Open accounts payable are used in the case of customers enjoying high credit standing. A letter of credit represents a written undertaking by a bank, made at the request of a buyer, to make payment upon compliance by the exporter with the conditions specified in the letter of credit. The importer's bank forwards credit to the exporter's bank. In the most secure form of payment for the exporter, the bank issuing the letter of credit confirms that it will make payment even if the importer defaults. A documentary draft is simply an invoice detailing how payment should be made by the importer. Unlike a letter of credit, the seller assumes risk of nonpayment in the case of draft documents.

A second set of considerations relates to methods of shipment. As with other aspects of marketing activity, shipping between countries is more complex than shipping within a single country. In the international firm, decisions concerning the physical distribution of goods and services are tied to decisions concerning the location and configuration of production facilities. Both sets of decisions are examined in the next chapter.

SUMMARY AND CONCLUSIONS

The fundamental goal in international marketing is to shape marketing strategies so that opportunities in the international business environment can be best exploited. A critical question for management is the degree to which marketing strategies should be standardized or differentiated across markets. The relevant elements of marketing strategy include product features, price, promotional techniques, and channels of distribution. Pressures to customize one or more of these elements of marketing strategy stem from differences across countries in economic, political, cultural, or technological features of the environment. In effect, management must weigh the economies of scale associated with standardizing marketing activities across countries against the risk that specific features of marketing strategy will be seriously inappropriate for various national markets.

Typically, some degree of differentiation in marketing strategies across countries will be optimal. The nature and degree of differentiation that is optimal will vary from company to company and from one market to another. Hence, sim-

---

[29]See Cateora, *International Marketing*, p. 652.

ple generalizations are quite risky. However, several guiding principles seem appropriate to emphasize. One is that careful marketing research underlies successful marketing. One of the worst strategic errors a company can make is the failure to determine if a market exists for its products and services prior to market entry. A thorough and efficient screening of the environment will go a long way toward minimizing this and other strategic marketing errors.

A second principle is that the international firm should make judicious use of trading houses, international advertising agencies, and other organizations that can provide expertise and resources that the international firm is lacking. By doing so, small and medium-sized firms can share indirectly in the economies of scale captured by these organizations while benefiting, to some extent, from the targeted marketing activities implemented by trading companies and the like. In some cases, however, end-to-end control over marketing activity may be highly desirable. This may be true, for example, in the case of high-technology companies, where quality control and reliable after-service are of overwhelming competitive importance. Once again, management must evaluate a difficult tradeoff: in this case, internalizing some or all of the firm's marketing activities versus contracting out those activities. For most firms, the ''optimal'' solution requires some degree of both.

DISCUSSION QUESTIONS

1. What are the main elements of any firm's marketing strategy? What broad marketing objectives do most firms attempt to meet by employing these elements of strategy?

2. What is the critical distinction between international marketing and marketing in the purely domestic firm? Illustrate your answer with respect to each element of strategy summarized in figure 12.1.

3. In broad terms, which of the following types of firms would you expect to be employing more standardized international marketing strategies, and which would you expect to be characterized by differentiated strategies? Explain your answer in each case.
   (a) Manufacturers of firearms for police forces
   (b) Manufacturers of toothpaste
   (c) Construction engineering firms
   (d) International banks
   (e) Makers of candies and other sweets

4. Describe various conditions that might encourage an international firm to try to charge different prices in different markets for essentially the same product. What limitations exist on the international firm's ability to differentiate its prices by market?

5. As the manufacturer of a new cordless telephone, you are interested in the possibility of selling the product in overseas markets, particularly in the rapidly growing markets of Southeast Asia. You recognize the need

for doing some research before you embark on a major marketing program. List and describe the steps you would follow to develop a marketing strategy for your cordless telephone.

6. Would you agree with the assertion that it is much easier to carry out a standardized importing program than a standardized exporting program? Explain your answer and give some illustrations of where standardized importing would work well and where it wouldn't.

REFERENCES

KEEGAN, WARREN J., *Multinational Marketing Management*, 2nd ed. Englewood Cliffs, N.J.: Prentice-Hall, 1980.

LITVAK, I.A., *Canadian Cases in International Business.* Toronto: McGraw-Hill Ryerson Limited, 1984, chap. 1.

LIVINGSTONE, JAMES M., *International Marketing Management.* London: Macmillan and Co., 1976.

MAYER, CHARLES, "Multinational Marketing Research: Methodological Problems," *European Research* vol. 6 (March 1978), 77–83.

McGUINESS, NORMAN, AND BLAIR LITTLE, "The Influence of Product Characteristics on the Export Performance of New Industrial Products." *Journal of Marketing* (Spring 1981), 110–22.

SHANKLIN, WILLIAM L., AND JOHN K. RYANS, JR., "Is the International Cash Cow Really a Prize Heifer?" *Business Horizons* vol. 24 (March 1981), 10–16.

CHAPTER THIRTEEN

Production
in the
International Firm

In the previous chapter we considered various issues related to the international firm's marketing strategy, including pricing, promotion, design, and distribution. We emphasized the fundamental tradeoff between standardization and accommodation of local market differences that the international marketer faces. Ideally, a compromise is struck so that—on the margin—the cost savings from a standardized marketing approach compensate for any competitive disadvantages associated with ignoring salient differences across the markets served.

Of course, to fully exploit the benefits of a well-designed marketing strategy, the chosen output must be produced to acceptable quality standards and then transported efficiently to the marketplace. This is as true for the purely domestic firm as for the international firm. However, as with other functions we have considered, relevant distinctions do exist between international production management and production management within the purely domestic firm. In particular, production conditions are usually more heterogeneous across countries than within individual countries. As a result, firms engaged in international production face a more complex tradeoff between the benefits and costs of standardized production strategies than do purely domestic firms.

The more heterogeneous international environment also makes the entire task of coordinating production and transportation more complex. In particular, haphazard delays in receiving necessary parts, components, and finished goods are far more common within international transportation networks than within domestic transportation systems. In the next chapter we refer to the experience of Canada Wire and Cable in its effort to install an underground power-transmission cable in Cairo. Most of the material and vehicles used on the project were shipped from Canada. At one stage a shipment was held up for two weeks on the Mediterranean when the vessel carrying it was hijacked and held for ransom because of a dispute between the shipowners and the transport company. To resolve the standoff Canada Wire paid the ransom. The goods reached Cairo just hours before work would have ground to a halt.[1] While hijackings are hardly typical of the disruptions encountered by international managers, physical hazards are not, as shippers who take goods through the Persian Gulf can attest.

International managers must try to anticipate idiosyncracies—such as disruptions to supply channels—and respond quickly to unforeseen contingencies when they arise.

The purpose of this chapter is to explore the standardization-differentiation tradeoff in international production and to identify specific operating principles that will promote efficient production management.

THE NATURE OF THE
PRODUCTION-MANAGEMENT FUNCTION

To better appreciate the differences between international production and production within the domestic economy, it is useful to describe the broad nature of the production-management function. Production management encompasses several critical decisions. One relates to whether specific components—or specific assembly operations—should be contracted out to other firms or carried out in production facilities owned and operated by the firm. This is often identified as the make-or-buy decision.

A second—and related decision—is concerned with the location of the firm's various production activities. The basic consideration here is to balance the advantages of producing in lower-cost sites against any disadvantages of having to transport the output produced over greater distances to the markets served. That is, management must strive to optimize the firm's "logistical network," which encompasses the joint costs of producing and transporting output to markets.

A third set of decisions relates to the configuration of the firm's production facilities. Among other considerations, management must decide whether to standardize production facilities with respect to size or employ production facilities of varying sizes. It must also determine whether the firm will employ specialized production facilities that offer lowest unit-cost production or more flexible facilities that can accommodate changes in underlying demand conditions.

[1] See Marian Stinson, "Canada Wire Lights Up Cairo's Street Jungle," *Toronto Globe and Mail*, October 9, 1984, B17.

In reviewing these basic issues associated with production management, it is obvious that they must be dealt with in both purely domestic and international firms. But since the international firm faces a much wider array of cost conditions and underlying production practices, its choice set is at once richer and more complex than that of the purely domestic firm. To elaborate on this point: many firms in the United States have relocated their production facilities to the Sunbelt region and the southeastern states in order to take advantage of lower wage rates in those regions. However, differences in wage rates across regions of the U.S. pale in comparison to differences between, say, Hong Kong and the southeastern states. A manufacturer of video games committed to producing entirely in the U.S. might therefore find relatively little to distinguish one region of the country from another, other than greater proximity to major markets. On the other hand, Atari—the video game affiliate of Warner Communication—was prepared to relocate its production facilities offshore. In ultimately relocating to Hong Kong, Atari dramatically reduced its labor costs. At the same time, however, it expanded the geographic scope of its production network, thereby offsetting some of the benefits of lower wage costs with higher transportation costs.

Decisions to relocate production facilities abroad will impose more pressing obligations on management to change the way the firm operates than will decisions to relocate within the domestic economy. For example, allowable labor practices may differ across countries such that production scheduling can be quite flexible in some countries but fairly rigid in others. As a result, factories in some regions of the world can be economically designed to produce "peak-load" output, while in other regions factories must be designed for a steady throughput if they are to be used at all. To illustrate this point: Rutenberg notes that in Finland, in contrast to many other countries, seasonal employment is socially and economically acceptable. Thus, a firm facing seasonal peaks in demand for its products might well consider establishing a plant in Finland designed to be operated only a few months of the year, possibly using rented equipment, presuming that higher transportation costs from Finland to the main markets served do not make this option uneconomic.[2]

The more varied production opportunities confronting the international firm are related not only to differences in labor conditions but also to such other factors as differences in the availability of natural resources and access to new technology across countries. An important implication is that the international firm can potentially realize significant competitive advantages by locating and designing production facilities to match the unique needs of specific product divisions. Thus, where a division produces a labor-intensive product of standard design, the international firm can locate production facilities in a less developed country where wage rates are low. On the other hand, where a division produces a highly engineered product in short "batches," production might be centered in job-shop-type factories located in a highly industrialized country.

---

[2] David P. Rutenberg, *Multinational Management* (Boston: Little, Brown & Co., 1982), p. 194.

COMPARATIVE ADVANTAGE
AND LOCATIONAL ADVANTAGE

The various theories that economists have developed to explain why production costs for specific products vary across countries are all concerned—in one way or another—with the concept of comparative advantage. As explained in chapter 3, all countries have a comparative advantage in specific economic activities. That is, there are certain activities that each country is particularly well suited to undertake. The comparative-advantage concept is a relative one. That is, a country may have absolutely higher costs of production for all economic activities compared to other countries. Yet there will be at least one activity in which the country is least disadvantaged in a relative context. A country's comparative advantage will reside in that activity in which its costs relative to the costs of its potential trading partners are lowest.

An implication of the comparative-advantage principle is that under free trade, production activities will be distributed geographically according to relative cost differentials. The latter, in turn, will depend upon the relative availability of different factors of production and other characteristics of national markets, including size and technological sophistication. An implication for international managers is that production of goods that utilize specific skills or national attributes intensively should be located in countries that are relatively rich in those skills or characteristics, all other things constant.

In the early stages of a product's life cycle, "non-conventional" factors of production, such as scientists and engineers engaged in research and development, industrial designers, and quality-control experts, will often be the inputs that are in critically short supply. Countries that are relatively well endowed with these inputs will therefore enjoy a comparative advantage in technology-intensive activities. As products become older and their production technologies become more widely understood, conventional costs of production—for instance, for land and for unskilled and semiskilled labor—become increasingly important factors in determining the best production location for any given set of products.

The various input factors whose costs influence locational decisions are listed in table 13.1.[3] Requirements for land may reflect a need for more than ground on which to construct factories and storage and distribution facilities. For many companies, sites with specific physical attributes may be desired. For example, access to water may be required to support special cooling and effluent-removal processes. Notwithstanding the significant impact that land costs may have on specific activities, the land input is not usually a critical locational determinant in international business, especially since an increasing proportion of international business is taking the form of services.

Another conventional input—financial capital—is also a relatively unim-

---

[3] The following discussion of conventional input factors draws heavily upon David Smith. *Industrial Location: An Economic Geographical Analysis* (New York: John Wiley & Sons, 1971), chap. 3.

TABLE 13.1   Major Inputs Required In the Production Process

1. Land
2. Financial capital
3. Fixed capital equipment
4. Materials and components
5. Sources of power
6. Labor
7. Government services (state and local taxes)
8. Enterprise
9. Technology

portant locational determinant of economic activity, since financial capital tends to be quite mobile internationally. Therefore, most large, credit-worthy companies can obtain financial capital on a worldwide basis. But for small, less well-established companies, local sources of financing may be very important, in the case of both debt and equity capital. For these companies one location may be preferred to another for financial reasons. For example, it has been suggested that many high-technology businesses locate in the U.S. in part because "venture capital" is much easier to obtain in the U.S. than elsewhere.

Physical capital, materials, and components should, in principle, be available anywhere in the world, either through local production or through imports. In practice, however, restrictions on imports may in certain countries limit a company's access to important pieces of capital equipment. Even more important, the capacity to maintain complex pieces of capital equipment might well vary across countries. For obvious reasons the availability of raw materials is a major determinant of plant location in resource extraction and primary manufacturing industries, such as wood products and metal smelting. So is access to economical sources of power. Electricity is the main source of motive power in most industries today. With an appropriate grid system, electricity can be transmitted over relatively long distances. Nevertheless, the availability of large supplies of cheap water power can confer important advantages on specific locations, especially in energy-intensive activities such as aluminum and copper processing. Indeed, a decreasing availability of low-cost energy sources is primarily responsible for Japan's decision to phase out its domestic aluminum industry.

Differences in the availability of different categories of labor are among the most important single determinants of industrial location. Specifically, the distinctive labor requirements of individual industries make some geographic locations more suitable than others for given activities. For example, a business requiring a large labor force with a wide range of skills would probably locate in one of the larger, developed countries. On the other hand, firms operating production processes that require primarily unskilled labor will probably locate in low-wage countries, all other things the same.

Wherever a company locates, it is generally subject to some form of taxation on its profits and its property. These taxes represent costs of doing business. Presumably the company receives public services in return, such as sewage facilities and road maintenance. Often the international business has a choice to locate in developed areas where both taxes and levels of government service are relatively high or in areas where both are relatively low. Given the ability of some organizations to provide their own infrastructure services (such as fire protection and road construction) high taxes can, on the margin, influence the locational decisions of international businesses. While most empirical studies conclude that tax policy has only a small effect on corporate location decisions (unless carried to extremes), there is also evidence that business managers may view taxes as indicative of hostile attitudes toward industry. Such subjective attitudes may have a greater influence on choice of location than taxation levels per se.

The efficiency with which inputs are combined to produce output depends heavily on the technical and entrepreneurial abilities of management. Given barriers to the free flow of labor, superior managers and technical personnel are easier to obtain in some places than others, even among developed economies. For example, above-average concentrations of software engineers are found along the east and west coasts of the U.S. and in southern England. Often the availability of skilled managerial and technical personnel is related to the presence of prestigious universities and the existence of government-sponsored programs in research and development.

OTHER FACTORS INFLUENCING INTERNATIONAL COMPETITIVENESS

As Magee notes, the competitive production of specific goods in specific locations will often fail to correspond to expectations based on comparative-advantage principles.[4] This is especially true when considering the international competitiveness of individual companies. Specifically, companies based in countries enjoying certain locational advantages can still be unsuccessful in the international marketplace if they dissipate those advantages through inefficient management. By the same token, individual organizations can offset country-specific disadvantages with unique proprietary skills that provide a competitive advantage in world markets. To the extent that these firm-specific advantages outweigh country-specific disadvantages, production location decisions may depart from patterns predicted by an expanded Heckscher-Ohlin model. That is, production may be carried out in relatively high-cost (for the specific activity) countries, although the companies carrying out the activity may be extremely competitive on an international basis.

[4] Stephen Magee, ''Theories of Comparative Advantage,'' in K. C. Dhawan, Hamid Etemad, and Richard W. Wright, *International Business: A Canadian Perspective* (Reading, Mass.: Addison-Wesley Publishing Co., 1981).

A case in point is CAE Electronics, a Canadian manufacturer of aircraft simulators and power-station control systems. Producing in the Canadian market puts CAE at an initial competitive disadvantage in several respects. One is that comparable European and U.S. companies produce for domestic markets that are many times the size of the domestic Canadian market. Thus, CAE's rivals enjoy more direct access to economies of scale than does CAE. For another, American manufacturers have large military contracts, which help defray development costs for commercial aviation equipment. How did CAE manage to capture approximately 30 percent of the world civil aviation market in flight simulators while exporting 75 percent of its production in 1982? By being more technically advanced than its larger-country rivals and by stressing personal contact with customers. Indeed, the president of CAE is personally responsible for a substantial portion of the company's sales and oversees most other contracts. These competitive advantages are largely transportable from one geographic region to another.[5]

A number of researchers have noted that entrepreneurial skills can enable a firm to operate in otherwise relatively high-cost locations.[6] Leaving aside the question of why entrepreneurs would eschew lower-cost locations, another issue arises. Namely, why do firms not rent or sell their specific proprietary skills to other firms that are located in areas enjoying lowest conventional costs of production?

Professor John Dunning of the University of Reading, among others, has written extensively on this issue. Dunning suggests that ownership advantages largely take the form of intangible assets, such as technical knowledge and marketing expertise. The firm chooses to exploit these intangible assets itself rather than rent or sell them to other firms, because of imperfections in the markets for such assets. Imperfections may be related to difficulties in establishing a selling price for the assets or in monitoring and enforcing terms of the exchange agreement.[7] In some cases relevant expertise may be so embedded in the organization of a firm that it cannot be effectively transferred without merging the firm with the organization seeking to acquire that expertise. The process of exploiting competitive advantages internal to the firm through self-production rather than by renting or selling the underlying intangible assets has been identified in the literature as the ''internalization'' process.[8]

Another point worth briefly noting is that patterns of comparative advantage are not fixed for all time. For example, new ways of producing a product may be developed that emphasize the use of certain factors of production to a greater

[5] This description of CAE is taken from Mark Budgen, ''Breadth of a Salesman,'' *Financial Post Magazine*, September 1, 1983, 18.

[6] See, for example, Smith, *Industrial Location*. Smith suggests that certain entrepreneurs may have strong locational preferences owing to nonpecuniary factors, such as climate, topography, and cultural amenities.

[7] See John H. Dunning, *International Production and the Multinational Enterprise* (London: George Allen & Unwin, 1981), chap. 1–4.

[8] An extensive discussion of the motives for internalizing firm-level advantages can be found in Alan Rugman, ''Internalization as a General Theory of Foreign Direct Investment: A Re-Appraisal of the Literature,'' *Weltwirtschaftliches Archiv.* 116 (1980), 365–79.

extent than do more traditional methods of production. In this case, the locational advantage of producing in a given geographic region may change. Furthermore, there are usually a number of ways in which a given product or service can be produced, e.g., more capital and less labor, more energy and less labor. Hence, there is often no single "most preferred" location for an activity. Rather, a given product can often be economically produced in a number of locations, presuming that the production activity is carried out efficiently.

This qualification—efficient production—is a relevant one. Frequently, companies locate production facilities abroad in order to gain access to a low-cost factor of production that is used intensively in a specific production activity. At the same time, however, they use a production technology that is more appropriate for the home country. For example, multinational companies from developed countries allegedly automate their overseas plants more than is appropriate to the economics of the foreign (low-wage) markets in which their plants are located. Such inappropriate behavior can largely dissipate the cost advantages associated with locating in specific regions.

Government Intervention

Government intervention can also affect the underlying economics of producing in one region versus another. In particular, tariffs and quotas on imports may oblige the international company to establish production facilities in the host country if it hopes to sell into that market. Tariffs are taxes on imports levied by the government of the importing country. The tax can be a flat rate or, more typically, a percentage of the value of the imported goods, that is, an ad valorum tariff. The tax—when passed on in part or in full to host-country consumers—raises the price of foreign goods relative to their domestically produced alternatives, thereby encouraging a shift away from foreign-produced goods. Quotas are a more direct trade barrier in that the host government restricts the quantity of foreign-made goods of a specific type that can be imported regardless of price.

Sometimes even the threatened imposition of tariffs or quotas can influence a decision by an international business about where to locate production facilities. A good case in point is Hyundai Motor Company of South Korea. In February 1985, the company announced it would build a plant near Toronto to produce automotive parts. Ostensibly, the decision was made to expand the company's auto-parts infrastructure. But the need for this additional capacity was far from urgent in the view of several industry observers. It has therefore been suggested that the decision to establish an auto-parts plant in Toronto was, at least partly, an attempt to gain favor with the Canadian government to ensure that auto import quotas were not placed on South Korean cars.

Government subsidies and other public-sector grants can also have an important influence on the locational decisions of firms. The typical dichotomy here is between—on the one hand—subsidies and tax incentives granted by govern-

CASE STUDY: *"VOLUNTARY" QUOTAS AND TOYO KOGYO COMPANY*

In the spring of 1984, the managers of Toyo Kogyo Company (now Mazda Company), Japan's third-largest auto maker, whose major product is the Mazda passenger car, faced a critical decision about whether to build cars in the U.S. The company's ability to export to the U.S. was seriously impaired by a 1981 agreement between the Japanese and United States governments to limit Japanese auto exports to the U.S. The agreement was ostensibly voluntary on the part of Japanese auto makers, although it was clear to all observers that the quota was accepted under the threat that less flexible and possibly harsher measures would otherwise be imposed by the U.S. government.

Toyo Kogyo suffered a series of setbacks in the U.S. market over the 1970s. The company was hit particularly hard by the energy crunch of the 1970s as Americans turned away from its gas-guzzling rotary-engine Mazdas. As a result, the company's unit sales in the U.S. plunged from 105,000 in 1973 to as low as 35,000 in 1976. One consequence of the company's market-share decline was that it held a relatively low allowable quota compared to other Japanese manufacturers since each company's allotted share of the allowable 1.85 million cars that could be exported during the 1983–1984 selling season was based on the company's share of exports during the late 1970s. Hence, Toyo Kogyo's quota was only 174,000 cars, compared with 552,000 for industry leader Toyota Motor Company.

The relatively low quota held by the company was felt by management to be a real constraint given a belief that Toyo Kogyo's competitiveness had increased substantially since the 1970s. In particular, the company drastically cut back on its work force, automated its production lines, and reduced its reliance on the relatively inefficient Wankel engine. As evidence of the impact of the quota, company officials noted that sales of Mazda minipickups, which were unaffected by import restrictions, nearly doubled between 1982 and 1983.

Yoshiki Yamasaki, president of the company, acknowledged that the location decision was complicated by many factors, including cost differences between the U.S. and Japan, the ability to control quality, and the availability of locally sourced components. Notwithstanding these complications, the company expressed a strong leaning toward joining its rivals—Toyota, Nissan, and Honda—that were already producing or planning to build vehicles in the U.S. As Yamasaki put it: "We feel it's not possible to export in a large volume from Japan to the U.S. forever. It's wiser to have a production base in the U.S."*

Source: Adapted from "Why Mazda May Be Forced to Build in the U.S.," *Business Week*, April 9, 1984, 43.

*As of May 1, 1984, the company's name was officially changed to Mazda Corporation. The reader should note that approximately one year later, Mazda anounced its decision to go ahead with construction of a $450 million U.S. car assembly plant in Flat Rock, Michigan.

ments to encourage domestic firms to continue to produce locally and export to foreign markets and—on the other hand—similar incentives offered by foreign governments to firms willing to relocate their production facilities abroad.

One general form of subsidy that is causing increasing concern among international trade officials is the use of export-financing credit. In the past, governments promoted exports of domestic goods by subsidizing interest rates on loans granted to finance the exports. When this practice was blocked by an agreement among OECD countries to limit the use of subsidized interest rates, a number of countries resorted to mixing aid funds with export financing in order to reduce the effective cost of the goods to importers. This use of mixed (aid and trade) credits, so-called "credit mixte," is especially important in the case of large capital goods.

The important point about government subsidies and incentives as well as about tariffs and quotas is that they can make it economically rational for a company to choose to produce in a given country, usually to service the local market, even though that country would be a relatively high-cost location in the absence of specific government programs. But management must also recognize that it is running a significant risk in emphasizing government-induced distortions in its locational decision making, since government policies can be more easily reversed than long-standing patterns of comparative advantage.

LOGISTICAL CONSIDERATIONS

Transportation is often considered to be the most important single determinant of plant location. Where an international firm locates production facilities outside the markets in which it sells output, it obviously accepts higher transportation costs as the quid pro quo for production-cost advantages. In this case the firm must choose both its route and its method of transport.

The overall cost of transporting goods from a central factory to a foreign consumer or sales affiliate is the sum of the fairly lengthy list of items noted in table 13.2.

Several of the items listed in table 13.2 have been mentioned in earlier sections of this chapter; however, most are new concepts. Item 1 refers to the fact that often the shipping factory has to carry inventory to meet unexpected deviations from planned shipments or has to accumulate enough product to fill a shipping container. Financial capital is tied up in this inventory, which represents a cost in terms of foregone interest.

Most cargo is packed into metal containers to reduce the costs of breakage, spoilage, or theft. Since shipping charges are usually based on volume rather than weight, firms have a strong incentive to squeeze the largest number of units into a container. International firms also try to reduce the amount of unnecessary product packaging since packaging materials can account for almost 40 percent of the weight of the products shipped. For example, ITT Europe now packs ten circuit boards in one polystyrene container instead of packing them individually. By do-

TABLE 13.2 Costs of Logistics between Two Points

1. Extra inventory at the factory
2. + Packing
3. + Transport to dock and loading fees
4. + Paperwork
5. + Transportation charge of ocean liner or airline
6. + Inventory en route and waiting to clear customs
7. + Customs broker charge and other paper work
8. + Import duty
9. + Repackaging if necessary
10. + Inspection at the sales outlet
11. + Delivered inventory
12. − Export incentives
13. − Duty drawbacks
14. + Quotas
15. + Customer uneasiness about imported products

Source: David Rutenberg, *Multinational Management* (Boston: Little, Brown, 1982), pp. 153–54. Copyright © 1982 by Little, Brown and Company. Reprinted by permission.

ing so, the company reduced the unit packaging cost from $3.33 to 88¢.[9] A company can reduce inland transportation charges by locating its distribution facilities adjacent to container ports or airports.

The list of forms required to document exports can impose a formidable burden of paperwork on an international firm, especially when the firm must maneuver liquid assets from one foreign affiliate to another for purposes of exchange-rate hedging or working-capital management (discussed in the next chapter). The burden of documentation can be eased through computerization and by using intermediaries, such as export brokers or trading companies.

Overseas transportation most typically involves shipping by ocean-going vessels. Ocean-liner charges are set by price cartels called conferences. These conferences are exempt from antitrust laws, and in many nations include government-owned liners. All conferences have rules that set uniform rates for various classes of cargo and limits on internal competition. Cargo classifications proliferate because shippers differ in bargaining power. Large shippers with transportation alternatives can often negotiate effectively lower rates by obtaining a unique (and lower-priced) classification for their cargoes.

Goods in transit also tie up financial capital since the shipper is ordinarily not paid until delivery is taken. Besides the relatively slow travel time, foreign goods are sometimes deliberately delayed on arrival by customs officials. For example, French customs inspectors were taking months to inspect Japanese video

[9] See Gerard Tavernier, "Putting the Brakes on Transport Costs," *Industrial Management* (May 1979), 27–30.

tape recorders while the French government tried to persuade Japanese officials to cut back on their exports of that product to Europe.

An unloaded cargo accumulates storage fees until all necessary paperwork is complete. Ordinarily companies hire customs brokers to expedite this paperwork. The broker's fees (item 7) are usually charged as a percentage of the value of the cargo.'All products will have an assigned customs classification, which may oblige the payment of import duty. As noted above, there are ad valorem and specific tariffs. The tariff codes of different countries are not uniform for the most part, so that a shipper can find it quite onerous to keep track of the precise tariffs assigned to specific goods in various countries. In addition, some goods may be eligible for duty drawbacks or other favored treatment owing to some special tariff treaty with the shipping country or to local content requirements. While payment of the import duty is the direct responsibility of the importer, the exporter may indirectly bear some—or all—of the tax in the form of a lower price, depending upon the competition the latter faces in world markets.

Repackaging to ship inland to the importer's site, inspection at that site, and the value of lost and damaged goods (items 9 and 10) represent costs that are borne directly by the importer. But again, where there is strong local competition to imports, foreign sellers may need to absorb some or all of these additional costs implicitly by charging lower FOB (free-on-board) prices. The same consideration is relevant in the case of inventories held by the importer to smooth out fluctuations in incoming shipments.

Export incentives, such as the credit mixtes described above, can reduce the logistical costs of serving foreign markets from a central base. So can duty drawbacks such as those that allow U.S. components to be exported to Taiwan for assembly and then reexported to the U.S. with duty charged only on the value added. On the other hand, import quotas—such as those described in our discussion of Mazda—and other more explicit laws that require local production to offset imports can impose indirect costs on the exporter if they force the latter to modify an already efficient production system.

Finally, there are sometimes prejudices for or against products from specific countries. For example, it has been alleged that Europeans do not think highly of the quality of many consumer goods produced in North America. On the other hand, North Americans tend to think quite highly of the average quality of German goods. An implication is that North American exporters of consumer goods may realize a price ''penalty'' on their shipments to Europe, while German sellers may enjoy a price ''premium'' on goods shipped to North America.[10]

All of the costs identified in table 13.2 are potentially relevant when exploring the economics of establishing production facilities in alternative geographic regions to serve specific markets. And all other things equal, the higher the logistic costs, the greater the incentive to locate production facilities close to major markets for the products sold.

---

[10] The foregoing discussion of the logistical cost elements listed in table 13.2 is based largely on the analysis found in Rutenberg, *Multinational Management*, pp. 153–62.

OTHER LOCATIONAL DETERMINANTS

Risk-diversification considerations as well as comparative cost factors will often weigh in a firm's decision about where to locate production facilities. In particular, by locating production facilities in a number of different countries, a firm can hedge against production disruptions that occur at any one production site. Of course, there are other ways to mitigate the risks of production disruptions, including carrying larger inventories of parts and finished products. The net costs of diversifying through multiplant operations must be carefully weighed against the net costs of other viable alternatives.

The least-cost approach to determining location may also be misleading when demand is itself a direct function of location. For example, local competitors may be inclined to cut prices to prevent imports from gaining a toehold in the domestic market, whereas they may be inclined to adopt a live-and-let-live attitude if new competition takes the form of domestic production. In a related vein, cutting prices on goods shipped from outside the country may lead to charges of unfair competition or ''dumping'' from local producers. The latter charge may be especially difficult for exporters to counter, since it is often unclear when dumping has taken place.[11]

The perception of being a local company may also enable the international firm to increase demand for its products in specific foreign markets. For example, a local plant may be perceived by customers and especially by local dealers as a commitment to permanence. This perceived commitment may make local buyers more willing to attach themselves to the firm's products. Governments may also respond more favorably to a firm that sets up local production facilities. Besides import protection and investment incentives referred to above, some governments have encouraged the establishment of local plants by delaying the permits of other entrants for a specified number of years.

EVIDENCE ON LOCATIONAL ADVANTAGE

Economists have devoted a great deal of attention to examining patterns of locational advantage across countries, at least as revealed by traditional indicators of comparative advantage. In one major study, Balassa calculated the comparative advantage for a group of seventy-three manufactured products as ''revealed'' in the export patterns of thirteen industrial countries. Revealed comparative advantage (rca) was calculated by dividing a country's share in the exports of a given commodity category by its share in the combined exports of manufactured goods of the sample countries.[12]

---

[11] Dumping is a practice whereby foreign producers price their exports below their costs of production. It is illegal under GATT, and importing countries can take measures to block such imports from entering their markets.

[12] See Bela Balassa, ''Revealed Comparative Advantage Revisited: An Analysis of Relative Export Shares of the Industrial Countries, 1953–1971,'' *Manchester School*, no. 4, December 1977, 327–39. The rest of this discussion is based on data from this source.

As suggested in our preceding discussion, Balassa found that the United States has a comparative advantage in research-intensive industries, where research intensity was defined in terms of the share of research and development expenditures in total sales or the ratio of research-and-development scientists and engineers to all employees. Among individual industries, aircraft manufacture occupied first place in the U.S. comparative-advantage scale over the entire period 1953–1971. Other prominent research-intensive industries in which the U.S. enjoyed a comparative advantage include office machinery, electrical-power equipment, organic and inorganic chemicals, and scientific and professional instruments.

By contrast, the U.S. had a comparative disadvantage in nondurable goods that have low-research intensity, most notably woolen yarn, synthetic yarn, textile fabrics, blankets, furniture, clothing, and footwear.

Within the manufacturing sector Balassa found that Canada's comparative advantage lies in the processing of its abundant raw materials. Paper enjoyed the highest (rca) value over the entire sample period. The next highest (rca) values in 1971 were for fertilizer and fur clothing. Canada also enjoyed a comparative advantage in fabricated metals. After placing low on the (rca) index in earlier years, autos and auto parts ranked high in 1971 as a result of Canada's duty-free access to the U.S. market following the Canada-U.S. Auto Pact.

The U.S. comparative disadvantage in nondurable consumer goods contrasts with the comparative advantage in these products enjoyed in France, Italy, and Japan. Balassa found that Germany's comparative advantage appeared to lie in machinery and metal products while, apart from processed nonferrous metals, the comparative advantage of the United Kingdom showed no clear-cut pattern. The comparative advantage of Austria, Norway, and Sweden, as with Canada, lies in resource-based products.

THE "MAKE-OR-BUY" DECISION

As noted earlier, one fundamental decision that must be made by all firms is whether it would be cheaper to subcontract out specific production and assembly operations to other firms or internalize those operations within the firm; that is, produce and assemble entirely within the firm. There are significant advantages to the subcontracting option. The greatest advantage derives from the economies of scale that can be realized by the firm acting as the subcontractee and that will presumably be shared with the firm doing the subcontracting. That is, the subcontracting firm might be able to realize lower costs on specific production and assembly operations by ''buying'' rather than ''making.''

How might subcontracting facilitate the capture of economies of scale? If there are a number of different potential users of components, each using relatively small quantities, production lengths of run would be relatively short if each individual user produced the components internally. However, if each user subcontracted the production of the components to a small number of common suppliers, the latter could justify operating much longer production runs.

In turn, there are a number of economic advantages to operating with longer lengths of run. One is that production ''downtime'' associated with switching over machines and workers is reduced. A second is that more specialized equipment, better suited to the operations required, can be employed rather than general-purpose machinery. The third and perhaps most impertant advantage is that both workers and managers gain experience with specific production activities more quickly and more intensively. This ''learning by doing'' leads to improvements in methods of production that reduce costs over time.

The phenomenon whereby costs fall with cumulative production is called the experience effect. This relationship has been observed in various industries, including automobiles, semiconductors, petrochemicals, synthetic fibers, and airline transportation, among others.[13]

The basic experience-curve relationship is captured in figure 13.1. The cost curve shown in figure 13.1 captures the basic mathematical relationship associated with the experience effect: each time cumulative volume of a product doubles, total value-added costs, including administration, sales, marketing, distribution, and so forth, plus manufacturing costs, fall by a constant and predictable percentage. In figure 13.1, an 85 percent experience curve is shown. This means that every time cumulative units of production doubles, costs per unit drop to 85 percent of the original level. Stated differently, costs per unit decrease 15

Figure 13.1 A Typical Experience Curve
Derek F. Abell and John S. Hammond, *Strategic Market Planning: Problems and Analytical Approaches,* © 1979, pp. 176–70. Adapted by permission of Prentice-Hall, Englewood Cliffs, N.J.

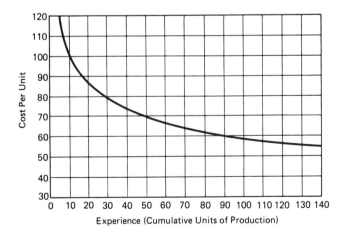

[13] For a discussion of the experience effect, see Derek F. Abell and John S. Hammond, *Strategic Market Planning: Problems and Analytical Approaches* (Englewood Cliffs, N.J.: Prentice-Hall, 1979), pp. 106–8.

percent for every doubling of cumulative production. Many observed experience relationships follow this specific pattern.[14] As noted in the preceding chapter, Japanese companies have relied upon volume-related scale economies (including learning economies) to improve the competitiveness of their products in international markets.

Given the advantages of concentrating production in order to achieve longer product lengths of run, there would have to be substantial offsetting benefits to justify internalizing the production of specific components and assembly operations. One such offsetting benefit is enhanced quality control. With the internalization of production, management has more direct control over the quality and supply reliability of critical components. This advantage would be especially

CASE STUDY: *AMERICAN PRODUCTION AND MEXICAN MAQUILADORAS*

Increasing foreign competition in world markets encouraged many American firms in the 1960s to begin production-sharing operations overseas. By locating firms abroad to assemble U.S.-made components, American manufacturers were able to take advantage of cheaper foreign labor and other sources of lower cost. Special tariff concessions were enacted by the U.S. government to facilitate international subcontracting. Specifically, U.S. tariff duty was assessed on the value of the products imported into the United States minus the value of the American components.

Some of the most successful production-sharing operations involve integrating Mexican assembly operations with more sophisticated stages of production undertaken in the U.S. While the cost of Mexican labor is higher than in the Far East, dramatically lower transportation and management costs more than compensate for wage differentials. By 1980 almost 6 percent of all U.S. imports entered duty free under production-sharing arrangements, with Mexico being the largest offshore assembler of U.S. components for reexport. Mexican assembly operations (called *maquiladoras*) are important in a variety of industries, including the manufacture of television receivers and parts, textiles, motor-vehicle parts, electrical-equipment circuits, electric motors and generators, and semiconductors and parts.

Location of assembly operations in Mexico offers significant advantages to U.S. firms, including sharply lower labor costs and more managerial control than in production-sharing facilities in Asia. Mexico allows raw materials to be imported to the country duty free if the product will not be sold in Mexico. Under Mexican law, American ownership of *maquiladora* operations is legal. This feature, along with the fact that U.S. managers can easily move back and forth across the border, makes *maquiladoras* an attractive organizational approach to production sharing.

Source: Marc Scheinman, ''Production Sharing: Mexico and the United States Join Forces on the Border,'' in Erdener Kaymak, ed., *Proceedings of the First Annual Marketing Conference Devoted to International Marketing Management,* Mount Saint Vincent University, Halifax, 1983.

[14] Ibid., p. 108.

relevant when it is difficult to establish the quality of a component prior to its use and when failure of a component can lead to widespread breakdowns in production acitvities. Another benefit is the enhanced protection of proprietory technology.

While all firms must weigh carefully the pros and cons of a make-versus-buy decision, there are certain things that a firm can do to mitigate the potential for supply and quality-control problems among subcontractors. One approach is to use a variety of subcontractors, essentially spreading one's risk among a number of alternatives. This tends to be an approach favored by North American firms. On the other hand, Japanese companies tend to rely on one—or at most two— main suppliers for specific components. Japanese managers limit the risk of dealing with unreliable suppliers by rigorous inspection of suppliers' plants.

Schoenberger notes that Japanese customers ordinarily want to inspect suppliers' plants and will demand that suppliers implement easy-to-see, measurable standards of quality. He offers the example of Webco Lumber Company, a small California company that was in danger of succumbing to the recession of the early 1980s. A team of Webco managers went to Japan to try to drum up business. Representatives from two dozen Japanese companies descended on Webco's mill to see if the mill could meet their exacting quality standards. "They did everything from measuring the thickness of our saw to measuring the ring counts of our logs," Barbara Webb, the president of Webco, recalled. "They're real tire-kickers," another Webco official added. Incidentally, Webco was successful in getter Japanese orders.[15]

THE NATURE OF PRODUCTION FACILITIES

Following preliminary decisions about what to produce internally as opposed to subcontracting, management must determine the design of the firm's production facilities. The point here is that output can ordinarily be produced in a variety of ways. For example, it can be produced in factories with specialized equipment designed for long product lengths of run. Alternatively, it can be produced in facilities that are equipped with multipurpose machines best suited for producing groups of products in batches. Production facilities can also differ in terms of their optimal capital-labor ratios. That is, facilities can be designed to substitute automated equipment (such as robots) for skilled craftspersons. Alternatively, plants can be designed with an emphasis on cheaper electromechanical equipment to be used by a greater number of workers.

In designing its production facilities, the international firm faces a tradeoff

---

[15] See Richard J. Schoenberger, *Japanese Manufacturing Techniques* (New York: Free Press, 1982), p. 59.

between benefits and costs associated with standardization. The advantages of standardization include:

1. Economies with respect to support personnel such as technicians, engineers, and designers. That is because a common set of design and engineering plants can be used worldwide.
2. Improved logistics of supply since components are interchangeable across plants. Also production loads can be shifted from plant to plant more easily.
3. Improved quality control since the periodic reports submitted by the various production units can be easily compared. Deviations from the norm can therefore be more quickly spotted and the cause of the deviation corrected.
4. Economies in production and maintenance control. The experience gathered in one plant related to the required frequency of overhauls and the stock of spare parts needed is directly useful to the efficient operation of other identical plants.
5. Simplification of planning and design work since it is essentially repetition of work that has already been done. The savings in planning and design work can be substantial. As an example, Teece found that the cost to chemical and petroleum companies associated with transferring production technology to their foreign affiliates dropped by 34 percent for the second factory start up, and by a further 19 percent for the third start-up.[16]

The benefits of standardization can be more than outweighed in certain cases by the associated costs. One set of costs can arise because the firm uses an inefficient mix of factors of production given the relative prices of those factors. For example, in developing countries where labor is quite cheap relative to imported capital equipment, a factory identical to one in a high-wage country that is designed to substitute capital for labor could prove uneconomic, notwithstanding the aforementioned benefits of standardization. As another example, in countries such as Canada, where oil and gas prices were maintained for years below world prices by the federal government, it made sense to use plants that were relatively energy intensive. Conversely, oil and gas prices were not subsidized in Japan. Hence, firms sought to design plants that would be among the most energy efficient in the world.

Political factors might also dictate a movement away from standardization. For example, where host governments have great concern about unemployment problems in the local economy, a firm that installs a highly automated plant could face reprisals from the government. More directly, governments might offer subsidies to firms that construct labor-intensive plants in high-unemployment regions.

Cultural factors can also make it disadvantageous for firms to standardize production facilities. To use a prior example, where labor-force-participation rates are highly seasonal, it makes sense to design a plant to be operated only a few

[16] See David J. Teece, ''Technology Transfer by Multinational Firms,'' *Economic Journal*, June 1977, 242-61. The list of benefits of standardization is taken from D. A. Ball and W. H. McCulloch, *International Business: Introduction and Essentials* (Plano, Texas: Business Publications, 1982), pp. 428-30.

months of the year rather than one designed to produce at full capacity on a year-round basis. As another example, where workers are able and willing to shift job responsibilities on a short-term basis, it is feasible to implement a flexible factory that operates in a "job-shop" fashion. On the other hand, where union policies or historical labor-relations patterns codify worker responsibilities fairly rigidly, the flexible factory concept simply won't work.

An important area in which the issue of cultural differences, as they pertain to the design of production facilities, has become especially prominent relates to Japanese production techniques. Specifically, the striking success of Japanese firms in the world market has led many firms to consider adopting attributes of Japanese management practices. A reservation expressed is that cultural differences make it difficult to impossible to transplant Japanese practices to other countries. Of course, this is also a direct concern of Japanese firms, which are increasingly establishing production facilities abroad.

JAPANESE PRODUCTION TECHNIQUES

Given the strong interest in Japanese management practices, it is worth briefly reviewing the main characteristics of what management experts consider the primary advantages of Japanese factories, namely, the use of so-called just-in-time production systems and the total quality-control concept.

The essence of the just-in-time (JIT) system is simple: produce and deliver finished goods just in time to be sold, subassemblies just in time to be assembled into finished goods, fabricated parts just in time to go into subassemblies, and purchased materials just in time to be transformed into fabricated parts.[17] The overriding objective of the JIT system is to minimize the costs of inventory at all stages of the production process. Thus, all materials are intended to be in active use as elements of work in process, never at rest and thereby tying up working capital—or requiring borrowing—to finance the inventory.

The focus on minimizing carried inventory also means that Japanese manufacturers utilize production-line schedules that closely match market demand. This implies that there are frequent starts and stops in the production process for specific product models. In an earlier section of this chapter, we discussed the advantages of long product lengths of run. Japanese JIT practices would therefore seem to impose severe penalties associated with frequent production-line switchovers to accommodate short lengths of run.

In fact, Japanese companies have attempted to minimize this problem by successfully cutting down setup costs. Schoenberger describes the case of Toyota, which began a campaign in 1971 to cut setup times. In that year, it took an hour to set up 800-ton presses used in forming auto hoods and fenders. After about five

[17] This description of the JIT system is taken from Schoenberger, *Japanese Manufacturing Techniques*, p. 16.

years of intensive engineering work, the setup time was down to twelve minutes. This compared with six hours for a U.S. competitor; and Toyota was running lot sizes of just one day's worth of output per setup versus a reported ten days' worth for the U.S. competitor. Schoenberger reports that Toyota has often been able to reduce setup time to less than one minute.[18]

The just-in-time production system is one way by which major Japanese companies minimize inventory levels. A related approach involves the extensive use of subcontracting. Specifically, small companies are utilized more or less intensively, depending upon business-cycle conditions, either to overcome short-term capacity constraints faced by the large companies or to absorb the impact of slowdowns in general economic conditions. The smaller companies, in turn, make extensive use of part-time labor and homemakers to gain the flexibility needed to respond to changes in demand from their large corporate customers.

The essentials of Japanese total quality control (TQC) programs are summarized in table 13.3.

Most of the items listed in table 13.3 are self-explanatory. Item 1 identifies an important distinction between Japanese and North American factories. In the former, personnel directly involved in the production process are responsible for quality control, while in the latter, primary responsibility rests with quality-control departments. The second item refers to an explicit objective of many Japanese companies to strive for continuous improvement in the production process. Items 3 and 4 denote that every process is to be controlled by checking the quality during production using measurable standards of quality. Item 5 identifies the readiness of Japanese managers to enforce compliance with quality-control

TABLE 13.3 Essentials of Total Quality Control

1. Production people have primary responsibility
2. Instill goal of perfection
3. Total process control
4. Make quality measures apparent
5. Insist on compliance
6. Principle of rework
7. 100% check
8. Small lot sizes

Source: Richard J. Schoenberger, *Japanese Manufacturing Techniques* (New York: The Free Press, a Division of Macmillan, Inc., 1982), p. 61.

[18] Ibid., p. 21. In Toyota's case, setup time for the presses was reduced by modifying the presses to allow the old dies to slide quickly out of the press onto a waiting table while new dies are pushed in from the other side.

standards, which includes line stops until the problem is located and corrected. Generally, the worker or work group that made the bad parts performs the necessary rework (item 6). Whereas North American plants inspect production on a sampling basis, item 7 indicates that the Japanese believe in checking all output produced. Finally, item 8 recognizes that small lot sizes are vital for assuring that defectives are caught early.

There is little doubt that companies around the world are paying increasingly close attention to Japanese production techniques not only with respect to new techniques in the mass production of high-quality products but also for the Japanese influence on design. In particular, Japanese packaging design is thought to be of particularly high quality. This is not to suggest that other areas of the world do not contribute useful ideas for improving production. On the contrary, some experts argue that most successful recent functional packaging innovations have come from Europe.[19] Furthermore, a number of observers have expressed strong reservations about both the desirability and the feasibility of transferring Japanese production techniques to other parts of the world, notwithstanding the fact that many of the techniques employed by Japanese companies were orginally adopted from the United States and Western Europe.

So far, there is relatively little experience to draw on to evaluate the ease or difficulty of transferring production techniques from one region of the world (say Japan) to other areas. However, it is becoming clear that the widespread adoption of even relatively simple Japanese production practices can often improve efficiency. For example, neatness is an important characteristic of the Japanese factory. Schoenberger relates a story involving Sanyo's TV-manufacturing plant in Arkansas, which had faltered to the point of failure under U.S. ownership. One of the first actions taken by the new Japanese managers was to clear out the plant over a weekend, clean it, and polyurethane the floors. Not only did the plant look cleaner and brighter but dust in the air, which sometimes caused the failure of equipment and electronic parts, was reduced.[20]

Whatever the influence of Japanese techniques, it should be stressed that a firm's choice of production technique will be related to its chosen scale of operation. The latter, in turn, will be related to the location of the firm's production facility. Indeed, these three attributes of a firm's production activities are usually closely linked. For example, firms choosing to operate at relatively large scales of production will tend to choose capital-intensive production techniques since automation becomes increasingly economical at larger scales of output. At the same time, firms producing large volumes of output tend to locate near major population centers in order to economize on logistical costs.

---

[19] See Peggy McCallum, "Foreign Marketing Trends Grow," *Toronto Globe and Mail*, October 10, 1984, B10.

[20] Schoenberger, *Japanese Manufacturing Techniques*, p. 67.

CASE STUDY: *THE PRODUCTION STRATEGY OF CATERPILLAR TRACTOR*

Caterpillar Tractor has achieved global dominance in the heavy, large-scale construction-equipment market. One key hurdle to achieving this dominance was the need to produce relatively low-cost, quality products while meeting the widely varied specifications for construction equipment across countries. At the same time, the company faced the logistical burdens of overcoming high transportation costs and satisfying demanding field distribution requirements, including user financing, spare parts, and repair facilities.

For the construction equipment produced by Caterpillar, two-thirds of the total product cost is in heavy components, that is, engines, axles, transmissions, and hydraulics. These manufacturing costs are highly capital intensive and very sensitive to economies of scale. As a result, Caterpillar designed its product lines to use identical heavy components and manufactures these in a few centralized large-scale, state-of-the-art production centers.

The company then augments the centralized production system with assembly plants in its major markets. At these plants they add local product features and thus avoid costs associated with transporting end products. Caterpillar also achieves lower costs without sacrificing product flexibility and without forcing a "world model" on local customers.

Recently, a strong U.S. dollar has encouraged Caterpillar Tractor to move some domestic production facilities offshore. It is also doing more offshore sourcing of components from a variety of suppliers.

Source: Thomas Hout, Michael Porter, and Eileen Rudden, "How Global Companies Win Out," *Harvard Business Review* vol. 60 (September–October 1982), 98–108.

WORLD PRODUCT MANDATES

A growing influence on the decision of firms to standardize or differentiate production facilities is the increasing demands of host governments on multinational firms to grant their foreign affiliates world product mandates. In its most direct form, a world product mandate (wpm) is obtained by a subsidiary from its parent firm to manufacture a product for the world market. This mandate encompasses not only the assignment of production responsibility but also the assignment of important complementary activities such as research design-and-development work, as well as export marketing.

The assignment of wpms generally implies that overseas plants must be designed to produce efficiently for world markets rather than operating as "branch plants" to service the local economy. It also implies some decentralization of research and development and other overhead functions of the firm. While at first glance, the wpm concept would seem to dissipate the benefits of standardization, it could represent an effective way to exploit subtle differences in comparative advantage across countries and to accelerate experience-curve effects for individual classes of products.

Rutenberg notes that world product mandating is actually an old practice. He discusses the case of Exxon as an example. In the 1950s, Exxon management

CASE STUDY: *LITTON SYSTEMS CANADA: WORLD PRODUCT MANDATING*

In the early 1970s, Litton Systems Canada Ltd. was in desperate straits. When the demand for North American military hardware plummeted in the late 1960s, manufacturing at the Canadian subsidiary virtually ceased and employment dropped from 3,000 in 1968 to 670 in 1970. During the 1960s the U.S. parent—Litton Industries, Inc., had developed inertial navigation systems (INS) for military and commercial aircraft. While the U.S. divisions still enjoyed a large amount of military work, it had become convinced that the commercial product lacked potential.

Canadian management had a different view of the potential for commercial navigation systems. In 1967 it proposed an R&D project aimed at developing a second generation commercial system that would cut production cost by one-third. The total cost of the project was $9 million, of which the Canadian government funded half. By 1970, Litton Canada had developed greater technical expertise in commercial INS than its parent. The U.S. parent agreed to transfer the charter for commercial navigation systems to its Canadian affiliate, preferring itself to remain in the military avionics market. In 1971, Litton Canada introduced the finished product to the commercial market. The product was a substantial success with sales rising from $22 million to $100 million over the 1970s.

Today commercial INS are the principal product line for Litton Canada, which has more than 2,000 employees. It controls about 65 percent of the world market for commercial INS. Its systems, which are not dependent upon contact with ground facilities, are used primarily on commercial aircraft on transoceanic routes, military transports, and maritime patrol aircraft.

Sales from commercial INS have provided Litton Canada with the product base and cash flow to support R&D programs that have led to the development of many new product lines, including special-purpose simulators, automated test equipment for entire navigation systems, gyrocompasses, and airborne search and tactical radar systems. It has the exclusive wpms for all these lines. Indeed, more than 90 percent of the company's sales are generated by world-mandated products. In commenting on why there are not more Canadian subsidiaries aggressively pursuing wpms, Litton Canada's president, Ron Keating, stated: ''The biggest difficulty is getting the Canadian companies to move their asses and be prepared to challenge the parent corporation. You've got to tell your corporation that if you're going to survive in Canada, it's got to give you a world charter. And you have to prove that it's cost effective to do the work in Canada.''

Source: The details of this case study are taken from Mark Witten, ''Branch Plants Bear New Fruit,'' in K. C. Dhawan, Hamid Etemad, and Richard W. Wright, eds., *International Business: A Canadian Perspective* (Don Mills: Addison-Wesley Publishers, 1981), pp. 602–604.

decided that each of its foreign affiliates would assume worldwide responsibility for a particular technical problem in addition to routine technical service and product tailoring. Thus, Esso France became the center for process-control electronics and Imperial Oil in Canada the center for mercaptan chemistry. What is relatively new is the pressure of certain foreign governments for more widespread implementation of the wpm concept.

Obviously, when assigning wpms is in the multinational firm's self-interest, host-government pressure to do so presents no conflict for management. But it may not always be in the interest of the firm to grant wpms. In this regard, Rutenberg outlines a "life-cycle" process for assigning wpms. Specifically, in the early stages of launching a new product family, a flexible management and production structure is desirable so that unpromising new products can be quickly cut from the firm's product portfolio. Rutenberg argues that this flexibility is incompatible with global product mandating. However, as the rate of product design improvements slows and as manufacturing processes stabilize, there is less to gain from centralized coordination and direction and more to gain from decentralizing production to low-cost sites around the world.[21]

A challenge for international managers is posed by the fact that foreign governments value not only the production activity but also the innovation activity. This implies that international managers must learn to shorten the wpm life cycle. Specifically, they must become adept at quickly determining which emerging new products are likely to be successful so that further design-and-development work can be spun off to foreign affiliates with the appropriate production capabilities.

SUMMARY

An important component of any international strategy is decisions related to where and how to produce the firm's chosen product portfolio. In this context management is faced with the task of designing an "optimal" network that minimizes the joint costs of producing and distributing output on a worldwide basis.

The basis for the decision on where to locate production facilities is rooted in what economists call the theory of comparative advantage. This theory suggests that certain regions of the world will be endowed with resources and other production characteristics that make them relatively low-cost producers of specific goods and services. Production facilities located in comparative-advantaged regions should therefore enjoy a competitive advantage in world markets, other things being constant. In reality, other considerations—primarily related to government

---

[21] David P. Rutenberg, "Global Product Mandating," in Dhawan et al., *International Business*, pp. 590–91.

policy—may alter the siting of production facilities that would be dictated strictly by patterns of comparative advantage. In particular, tariffs and quotas imposed against the imports of foreign goods frequently encourage the establishment of production facilities in relatively high-cost countries.

Prevailing patterns of comparative advantage do not necessarily prevent firms from competing successfully even though they are based in relatively high-cost countries. The example of the Canadian company, CAE Electronics, was cited to demonstrate that firm-specific advantages can sometimes offset country-specific disadvantages. Furthermore, for certain goods and services, transportation costs and other logistical factors may have a predominant influence on the geographical distribution of production capacity.

Besides deciding where to locate its production facilities, a firm must also determine how much of its required production and assembly operations should be subcontracted to other firms rather than internalized. There are pros and cons associated with each option, with the imperative for tight quality control being an important motive for internalization. In recent years, North American managers have become impressed with the ability of large Japanese companies to utilize the subcontracting option while retaining control over the quality of output. This ability is apparently due to the concerted effort of Japanese companies to ensure that their suppliers subscribe to strict and readily observable quality-control standards. By using subcontractors judiciously, companies such as Nippon Steel have been able to produce as much output as the largest U.S. steel companies with approximately half as many employees.

The widely recognized success of Japanese production techniques underscores another issue related to international production management, namely, whether management should standardize its production facilities on a worldwide basis or whether it should tailor its facilities to the specific background conditions of a region. While the resolution of this issue will vary from case to case, it is probably true that certain production practices are fairly transportable across cultures. Indeed, the Japanese are apparently enjoying success in transplanting certain production procedures into their North American factories. For example, just-in-time sourcing of parts has been successively instituted in Nissan Motor Company's giant new truck factory in Tennessee. There is also substantial rotation of production-line workers at the Nissan plant.[22]

A concept that has become increasingly prominent among multinational companies in recent years, partly due to the influence of host governments, is world product mandating. Under this arrangement individual affiliates are given the responsibility to produce one or more products for the global market rather than a range of products solely for the domestic market. The wpm concept takes advantage of economies of scale and specialization. At the same time it involves

[22] For a description of the Nissan plant, see Margaret Wente, "Opening Lines," *Canadian Business*, May 1984, 11.

some decentralization of overhead functions such as research and development and export marketing. The goal of management should be to take optimum advantage of opportunities to establish specialized world-scale plants while avoiding ''excessive'' decentralization of activities that can be efficiently centralized at headquarters level. Some multinational companies may have been unduly reluctant to grant their affiliates charters to perform R&D and export promotion, as suggested by the success of their foreign affiliates once the latter obtained full wpms.

DISCUSSION QUESTIONS

1. Imagine that you are a management consultant hired by Mazda to advise on its decision as to whether to build cars in the United States. What factors would you advise Mazda's management to consider in making its decision? How much weight would you place on the possible resumption of the "voluntary" export quotas on Japanese cars? (Note: in April of 1985, the Reagan Administration announced its intention to discontinue voluntary quotas on Japanese cars. At the same time, however, Congress was taking steps toward restricting a wide range of Japanese exports to the United States.)

2. Do you think it would be easier for management to standardize petroleum-refining production techniques than to standardize the manufacturing of clothing? Explain your answer.

3. In the nineteenth century Great Britain was the world's major exporter of finished textile products. Today the major exporting center for clothing and many other textile products is the Far East—Hong Kong, Malaysia, China, and so forth. Is this pattern inconsistent with the principle of comparative advantage?

4. Centralizing production in a small number of plants provides the benefits of economies of scale and associated experience-curve benefits. What disadvantages might such centralization entail?

5. Imagine that you are a manager of a multinational firm that produces telecommunications equipment and has affiliates in Europe and South America. The management of your Dutch affiliate approaches you with the request for a world product mandate to produce a small interoffice telephone-switching machine. What factors would you consider in evaluating the affiliate's request?

6. A firm is considering establishing production facilities in a foreign country. It comes to management's attention that a rival firm in that country is considering selling off some of its local production facilities. What are the advantages (and disadvantages) of buying the rival's facilities rather than constructing an entirely new production plant?

REFERENCES

ANDERSON, WILLIAM S., "Meeting the Japanese Economic Challenge." ITT Key Issues Lecture Series, University of Notre Dame, September 25, 1980.

BALASSA, BELA, "The Changing Pattern of Comparative Advantage in Manufactured Goods." *Review of Economics and Statistics*, 61, (May 1979), 259–66.

HAYES, ROBERT H., "Why Japanese Factories Work." *Harvard Business Review* vol. 59 (July–August 1981), 57–66.

SCHONBERGER, RICHARD J., "The Transfer of Japanese Manufacturing Management Approaches to U.S. Industry." *Academy of Management Review* vol. 7 (July 1982), 479–87.

SCIENCE COUNCIL OF CANADA, "Multinationals and Industrial Strategy: The Role of World Product Mandates." In K. C. Dhawan, Hamid Etemad, and Richard W. Wright, *International Business: A Canadian Perspective*. Don Mills, Ont.: Addison-Wesley Publishing Co., 1981, pp. 583–87.

SKINNER, C. WICKHAM, "Management of International Production." In Douglas N. Dickson, ed., *Managing Effectively in the World Marketplace*. New York: John Wiley & Sons, 1983, pp. 225–43.

CHAPTER FOURTEEN

Asset Management in the International Firm

In chapter 7 we considered a number of issues related to the financing of international business activities. In effect, chapter 7 can be viewed as a focus on managing the liability side of the international firm's balance sheet. In this chapter we are concerned with the implications of "going international" for the management of short-term and long-term assets and with capital-budgeting techniques in the international firm.

The nature of asset-management activities can be made more explicit by examining the balance sheet of a large international firm, the Colgate-Palmolive Company, in table 14.1. The asset side of the balance sheet is described in greater detail than the portion dealing with liabilities and shareholders' equity, as it is the management of assets that especially concerns us here.

As seen in table 14.1, the two main asset categories encompass current assets, including cash, short-term investments, accounts receivable, and inventories, and long-term investments, which primarily encompass property, plant, and equipment. The administration of current assets is usually described as working-capital management, while the administration of long-term assets is considered to fall within the realm of capital budgeting. By accounting definition, cur-

TABLE 14.1   Consolidated Balance Sheet of Colgate-Palmolive Company ($ thousands) December 31, 1983

Assets	Current assets		
	Cash	$ 13,195	
	Short-term investments	513,298	
	Net receivables	524,228	
	Inventories	676,425	
	Other	76,467	
	Total current assets		$1,803,613
	Property, plant, and equipment		
	Land	32,578	
	Buildings	258,971	
	Machinery and equipment	1,070,739	
	Less: depreciation	601,073	
	Total fixed assets		761,215
	Other assets		99,137
	Total assets		$2,663,965
Liabilities and shareholders' equity	Current liabilities		826,605
	Noncurrent liabilities		495,692
	Shareholders' equity		1,341,668
	Total liabilities and shareholders' equity		$2,663,965

Source: Colgate-Palmolive 1983 annual report.

rent assets are assets normally converted into cash within one year, and long-term (or fixed) assets are assets that are ordinarily held for more than one year.[1]

While some financial economists argue that it does not make sense to separate the components of working-capital management from fundamental decisions of investing and financing, in actual practice most firms tend to segment the management of current and long-term assets. And, indeed, most finance textbooks tend to separate into distinct chapters their discussion of working-capital management from their treatment of capital-budgeting issues. The convention we adopt in this chapter is to include working-capital management and capital budgeting as self-enclosed segments of a common chapter. This procedure reflects our limited treatment of the two topics, compared to standard finance textbooks. It also reflects our emphasis on the financial implications of internationalization. To a significant extent the important implications are similar when considering the management of short-term and long-term assets.

The primary purpose of this chapter is to identify the main issues associated with working-capital management and capital budgeting in the international firm. As we concluded with respect to other functional activities, the basic objec-

[1] These standard definitions of current and long-term (or fixed) assets can be found in virtually any finance textbook. See, for example, James C. Van Horne, Cecil R. Dipchand, and J. Robert Hanrahan, *Financial Management and Policy,* Canadian 4th ed. (Scarborough, Ont.: Prentice-Hall of Canada, 1977), p. 333.

tives and techniques of asset management are similar for both international and purely domestic firms. However, international financial managers confront certain unique complexities that must be acknowledged in the financial procedures followed.

OVERVIEW OF WORKING-CAPITAL MANAGEMENT

The management of working capital is an ever-present component of tactical planning and decision making in any organization. The basic objectives of international working-capital management are similar to those of domestic working-capital management:

1. Bring the company's cash resources within control as quickly and efficiently as possible.
2. Achieve the optimum conservation and utilization of the company's available funds.

The first objective is facilitated by improving the organization's collection and disbursement of cash and decreasing the cost of moving funds among divisions and affiliates of the firm. The second objective is promoted by economizing on the level of cash balances used to support the firm's business activities, by making money available to different units of the firm when it is needed, and by increasing the risk-adjusted return on those funds available for investment.

This description of objectives emphasizes the importance of cash management as a component of working-capital management. While the principles of domestic and international cash management are identical, the latter is a more complicated exercise. Shapiro suggests three important factors that support this assertion:

1. International firms often face restrictions that impede the free flow of money into and out of countries.
2. Firms doing business in different countries must cope with multiple tax jurisdictions and multiple currencies.
3. There is a relative absence of internationally integrated interexchange facilities like those available in the U.S. and other Western nations for moving cash swiftly from one location to another.[2]

While the task of working-capital management is more complex in the international firm, it enjoys certain advantages that are not available to the purely domestic firm. For example, the international firm can often achieve higher returns overseas on short-term investments that are unavailable to purely domestic companies. Frequently, it can also take advantage of various international tax laws and treaties to keep a higher proportion of its investment income after taxes.

[2] See Alan C. Shapiro, *Multinational Financial Management* (Boston: Allyn & Bacon, 1982), pp. 235–36.

MANAGING FUNDS WITHIN THE INTERNATIONAL FIRM

The positioning of funds within the global organization is the main task of international working-capital management. This task involves the choice of location and currency of denomination for all liquid funds. The growing volatility of currency and interest-rate markets along with increasing complexity of international trade patterns within the multinational firm has mandated the centralization of working-capital management. Centralization denotes a concentration of decision making at a high organizational level within the company, usually at head-quarters, so that all relevant information is available to the decision maker in order to "optimize" the firm's working-capital position.

The ultimate goal of management is to maximize the after-tax, risk-adjusted returns on the assets held by the firm while ensuring that each foreign affiliate is provided its liquidity requirements in a timely and efficient manner. This essentially obliges management to address two interrelated questions:

1. What mix of assets should the firm hold?
2. In which affiliates should the asset position be built up and in which should it be reduced?

CASH MANAGEMENT

With regard to the issue of asset mix, a question arises as to why an international company, or indeed any company, should hold cash—primarily in the form of demand-deposit accounts—in any of its affiliates or divisions since checking accounts represent a noninterest-bearing asset. The primary motive relates to the need for a means of payment that arises because of a lack of perfect synchronization between receipts and disbursements. Where the firm stores all its wealth in the form of interest-bearing assets, it will need to liquidate some portion of those assets periodically in order to pay its bills. The transactions costs associated with liquidating interest-bearing assets and moving the requisite funds into demand-deposit accounts may outweigh the foregone interest associated with keeping a minimum cash balance in demand-deposit accounts at all times. In addition, delays in liquidating interest-bearing assets may result in the firm's failing to meet required payments in a timely manner, with explicit costs in the form, say, of interest penalties, or with implicit costs, such as damages to the firm's credit rating with suppliers.

Another motive for holding cash relates to the need for a cushion or buffer against unexpected contingencies. While a firm may have a reasonably good forecast of payments it will be required to make over the foreseeable future, there is always a chance that it will meet with some unanticipated expenses that necessitate further disbursements of cash. In theory, it could meet such contingencies by liquidating some interest-bearing assets. And, indeed, many firms do draw upon such assets to meet financial emergencies. But since a quick liquidation of assets may inflict capital losses upon a firm, it is usually advisable to maintain some portion of this emergency buffer in the form of cash. In that way the firm is less likely to find itself in the position of having to "firesale" assets in order to meet unexpected financial emergencies.

The third motive for holding cash is also related to uncertainty about asset prices. Specifically, firms may hold cash in order to take advantage of anticipated changes in asset prices. For example, management may believe that interest rates will decline substantially in the near future after first rising a bit more. Thus, they may view an optimal strategy as holding cash for a short period of time and then buying bonds or other long-term financial assets once interest rates have hit their peak. In such circumstances firms may choose to invest in short-term interest-bearing assets and liquidate those assets when they believe that it is an opportune time to invest in bonds. But if the time horizon for such a conversion is relatively short, and if there are financial penalties associated with liquidating short-term assets before they mature, firms may choose to hold some so-called speculative cash balances.

Notwithstanding these motives for holding cash, the fact that demand deposits do not ordinarily pay interest places a premium on satisfying these motives efficiently. That is, companies should not hold excessive cash balances through inefficient management. This caveat is especially relevant when international affiliates are located in countries with high rates of inflation. As an illustration, interest rates in some South American countries have gone above 50 percent per annum, reflecting hyperinflation in those countries. The logic of holding minimal balances in noninterest-bearing checking accounts is obvious in such cases. The imperative to minimize noninterest-bearing deposits has in turn led to the development of a variety of techniques and procedures designed to improve the efficiency of the cash-management process.

Minimizing Intracompany Transfers

One way to improve the efficiency of an international cash-management system is to speed up intrasystem flows by setting up an internal clearing center. The idea here is to "net out" interaffiliate flows to the greatest extent possible, so that payments are offset against each other through bookkeeping entries rather than through actual transfers of checks and other payment instruments.

Robbins and Stobaugh offer as an illustration the case of a U.S. oil company that loans $500,000 to an affiliate producing oil in North Africa. The affiliate then spends the funds on operations producing oil. The oil is sold for $600,000 to a European refining subsidiary. The refining subsidiary, in turn, forwards the refined product to a European marketing subsidiary (for $700,000), which sells the product at $800,000 to the public and remits the full amount to the U.S. All these transactions would be recorded in the company's New York clearing center, where they would be simply offset against each other with a final balance of $100,000 applicable to each affiliate but kept in New York.[3]

The oil companies, with a considerable experience in managing systems of international payments and receipts, have been pioneers in the formulation of internal clearing systems for intracorporate payments. However, other large multinational firms have also implemented such systems with beneficial results. For example, Monsanto, the large multinational chemical company, estimates it is saving $2.25 million annually by using a multilateral netting system that reduces interaffiliate payments from $300 million gross to $150 million net.[4] These savings arise from reduced transactions costs associated with check-handling fees and other processing charges as well as from the bid-ask spread in the foreign-exchange markets.

Given the obvious advantages of interaffiliate netting, it is somewhat surprising that most international firms do not use one or another such system. For example, surveys by the consulting company Business International reveal that well less than half of surveyed U.S.- and European-based multinationals have a multilateral netting system. Part of the reason for the relatively limited use of multilateral netting may be the detailed information requirements attached to such systems. These requirements include the amounts and currency denominations of interaffiliate flows, the origins, destinations, and timing of the flows, and the per unit costs involved in sending funds between any two points.

The essence of the information system outlined in the preceding paragraph is captured by the hypothetical intracorporate payments matrix shown in table 14.2. The matrix is a table of interaffiliate payables and receivables for a specified time interval. Table 14.2 shows, for example, that the U.S., West German, and Swiss affiliates are net receivers of intracorporate payments, while the other affiliates are net payers. The interaffiliate payment process can be expedited by simply having the net payers remit their respective balances to the clearing center to be credited to the respective accounts of the receiving affiliates. Thus, the U.S. affiliate would be credited with a deposit of $7 million, the German affiliate with a deposit of $5 million, and the Swiss affiliate with a deposit of $16 million. Through this process of interaffiliate netting, the actual dollar value of payment flows is reduced from a potential $350 million to, at most, $28 million.[5]

The minimum costs and information requirements associated with operating a multilateral netting system are not trivial, especially when a firm has numerous subsidiaries in different parts of the world. Where interaffiliate transactions are fairly limited, the additional management time and added costs

[3] Sidney M. Robbins and Robert B. Stobaugh, *Money in the Multi-National Enterprise* (New York: Basic Books, 1973), pp. 102–3.

[4] Shapiro, *Multinational Financial Management,* p. 241.

[5] Note that the U.K. affiliate would need to remit $12 million; the French affiliate, $10 million; the Swedish affiliate, $2 million; and the Belgian affiliate, $4 million. But if these affiliates have sufficient surpluses on deposit at the clearing center, no physical transfer of funds need take place.

TABLE 14.2   Intracorporate Payments Matrix ($ millions U.S.)

	PAYING AFFILIATES							
RECEIVING AFFILIATES	U.S.	U.K.	GERMANY	FRANCE	SWITZERLAND	SWEDEN	BELGIUM	TOTAL
U.S.	X	21	18	0	7	10	17	73
U.K.	25	X	16	10	2	8	5	66
Germany	13	10	X	18	6	9	7	63
France	9	15	0	X	1	0	15	40
Switzerland	6	0	12	7	X	5	4	34
Sweden	5	14	11	0	0	X	0	30
Belgium	8	18	1	15	2	0	X	44
Total	66	78	58	50	18	32	48	350

Source: Alan C. Shapiro, *Multinational Financial Management* (Boston: Allyn & Bacon, 1982), exhibit 9.2, p. 242.

associated with a multilateral netting system may be greater than the anticipated savings in transactions cash balances. However, most multinational companies can probably cost justify operating a multilateral netting system.

Accelerating Collections

Another key element of cash management involves accelerating the collection of payments owed by affiliates or from independent companies. Typically, there can be delays of as much as ten business days from the time a foreign purchaser pays a bill until the funds are available for use by the seller. The goal of corporate management is to reduce this transit time (or float) in order to reduce the average cash balances needed to fund accounts receivable.

There are a variety of techniques used by international companies to speed the receipt of payments.[6] One technique involves establishing mobilization centers in overseas regions characterized by large sales volumes, where funds flows within that region can be managed centrally. In effect, the international company might establish regional clearing centers. For example, a company doing a large volume of business in Southeast Asia might establish a mobilization center in Singapore. Receipts from Asian customers might then be made to the firm's financial office in Singapore rather than to its office in North America. These receipts could then be invested in the Asian money market, remitted to head office, or used to fund expenditures in the Asian area. The point is, by locating the receiving facility closer to the sources of payment, the firm will effectively reduce the net amount of receivables outstanding and (relatedly) economize on its required working cash balances.

[6] Many of the techniques outlined here are discussed in Shapiro, *Multinational Financial Management*, pp. 237–40.

Another technique to speed the conversion of receivables into cash is the lock box. In this case, a lock box is actually a postal box to which a local bank or a branch of a multinational bank has access. Mail sent to the international company at the postal box address is actually collected by the bank, and credit for the funds received is usually given to the company on the same day. In this way, the period in which payment is in transit can be cut to one or two days.

An effective technique for speeding cash collection, but one that requires the cooperation of a firm's customers, is equivalent to postdating checks. Specifically, a customer allows its account to be debited periodically by the supplier's bank up to some maximum amount. With this method there is no delay in customer payment, nor are there mail delays. Delays associated with clearing the check for deposit to the supplier's account can also be reduced by initiating the debiting before the bill's due date.

With the emergence of electronic fund transfers, rapid transfers of funds can be accomplished within a given banking network. For example, multinational banks can transfer funds between branches of different countries and usually credit their customers' accounts that same day. This rapid funds transfer constitutes an important benefit of utilizing a given banking network, since funds transferred from other local banks may not be accorded same-day credit; however, this is often a matter for negotiation between company management and bank officials.

Using Futures Contracts and Currency Options

International firms can economize on the cash balances held to facilitate payments denominated in different currencies by using futures contracts and currency options. For example, if a firm perceives a significant probability of a required payment in a foreign currency, it can hold short-term negotiable assets denominated in that currency. Alternatively, the firm might buy a forward contract or call options in the amount of its anticipated requirement. In this way, disbursements can be ''covered'' without hoarding unwanted cash (or near-cash) balances denominated in specific currencies.

INTERAFFILIATE FUNDS-TRANSFER TECHNIQUES

To this point, we have discussed how management can economize on holdings of cash balances through interaffiliate netting practices and by implementing various techniques to speed the conversion of receivables into cash. In this section, we consider the mechanics of how the multinational company actually transfers funds from one affiliate to another. Given differences in tax rates across countries, as well as government intervention into the transfer process, the transfer activity is not as straightforward as one might imagine.

Dividend Payments

Dividend payments are probably the most common method by which corporations effect a transfer of funds from affiliates to the parent company. Formulating a dividend policy for the entire multinational system that takes into account all of the organization's relevant objectives has usually proven too complicated for most companies to implement. Hence, most large companies use a rule of thumb as a guide to determining dividend remission policies. Nevertheless, there are a number of important influences on dividend policy that should be noted.

One such influence is the tax structure in different countries. For example, parent-country taxes may be higher than taxes in the host country. In this case, the after-tax income of the global organization would be maximized by retaining more income in the foreign affiliate and distributing less to the parent in the form of dividends, all other things constant. Dividend policies may also be influenced by different effective tax rates in various host countries. Shapiro describes the example of a company that has a German affiliate and an Irish affiliate. The former faces a tax rate of 51 percent on retained earnings and a withholding tax on dividends remitted to the parent of 25 percent. The latter, on the other hand, pays no tax on retained earnings, since all of its earnings come from exports, and export earnings are untaxed. Furthermore, there is no Irish withholding tax on dividends. Both affiliates earn $2 million per year.[7]

If the parent wishes to withdraw $1 million from abroad in the form of dividends, it is clear that the funds should be withdrawn from the German affiliate from the perspective of overall tax consequences. To elaborate, note that if the parent withdraws the $1 million from the Irish subsidiary, it implicitly accepts a tax loss of $510,000, since the $1 million left in the German affiliate will be taxed at a rate of 51 percent. Alternatively, if the $1 million is withdrawn from the German affiliate, that affiliate will have to pay a withholding tax of $250,000. The tax consequences to parent-company shareholders of remitting $1 million from abroad are therefore more favorable when the German affiliate remits the full amount of the required dividend payment. The presumption here is that parent-country shareholders want this repatriation of foreign income, even though it will increase their tax liability in the home country.

Of course, tax consequences may be only one consideration bearing on the firm's dividend policy. In particular, dividend policies lead to shifts in liquidity. In the foregoing example, when dividends are remitted from the German affiliate, corporate liquidity is implicitly moved from Germany to Ireland. The overall benefits to the company from this implicit reallocation of funds will depend upon the rates of return obtainable on retained earnings in the two countries. It is possible that higher rates of return in Germany may more than offset the tax savings realized by remitting dividends from the German affiliate.

[7]Ibid., p. 300.

Another factor influencing dividend policy in the multinational company is the risk that access to the retained earnings of an affiliate will be blocked because the host government makes the local currency nonconvertible or requires central bank approval of any fund transfers to nonresidents. Where a company is concerned about the threat of blockage, it might be inclined to remit dividends at a faster rate from the threatened subsidiary. Of course, such an accelerated dividend policy might be the very factor that triggers a hostile host-government reaction. Where ownership of the affiliate is shared with local investors, an accelerated remittance of dividends might also antagonize the local investment community. For example, in countries with high income taxes but low (or no) capital-gains taxes, local investors may very much prefer a policy of reinvesting most corporate earnings. Hence, the parent might wish to employ more subtle tactics for hastening the withdrawal of funds from threatened areas. We shall discuss some of these alternative withdrawal techniques in a later section.

The problem of blocked earnings is severe in a number of industries. One example is the airline industry. A 1984 estimate placed the total owed to the world's biggest airlines in blocked earnings—ticket sale receipts that national governments, especially in the Middle East, Africa, and South America, refuse to allow to be transferred—at around $864 million U.S. That figure is more than three times the size of the world airline industry's estimated net profit for 1984.[8]

Foreign-exchange risk is the risk that host-country currencies may depreciate in value against the home-country currency, so that retained earnings remitted in the form of dividends are worth less (in home-currency terms) than in prior periods. Among the hedging techniques available to reduce this risk, international companies might consider accelerating the payment of dividends from affiliates in weak-currency countries. Again, however, it is precisely in weak-currency countries that host governments will be concerned about the exchange-rate impacts of massive repatriation of funds by multinational subsidiaries. In some cases, governments (such as the Mexican government) have frozen the domestic bank accounts of foreign companies and personal investors to prevent them from remitting funds out of the country.

Other influences on dividend policy in the international firm include the age and size of affiliates, the availability of funds, and the presence of joint-venture partners. With respect to age and size of affiliates, it has been noted that older affiliates remit a greater share of their earnings to the parent in the form of dividends. This presumably reflects the fact that reinvestment opportunities are more limited in mature subsidiaries whose products are in the later stages of their life cycles.

Dividend payout ratios tend to be more stable in large firms, where rules of thumb are adopted both to minimize complexity and in recognition of the generally smoother pattern of earnings. In a related vein, dividend payout policies will

---

[8] See Michael Donne, "Blocked Airline Earnings Top Sector's Net Profit," *Toronto Globe and Mail*, June 11, 1984, IB. 7.

reflect the availability of funds. Specifically, when affiliates must borrow to continue a dividend payout pattern, remittances will ordinarily be cut back, since borrowing rates are generally higher than the reinvestment rate the parent can expect to earn on the remitted funds. In addition, local stock ownership leads to a more stable dividend policy.[9]

A number of experts in the area have argued that a consistent dividend disbursement policy reduces the danger of host-government intervention in the form of currency blockages, since historical consistency makes more credible a firm's claim that it is not trying to flee from a weak currency. Nevertheless, in view of the scrutiny that dividend remittances are sometimes accorded, firms may find it advantageous to "unbundle" their transfer of funds from foreign affiliates to parent into explicit and separate payments for inputs and services. This unbundling may allow a multinational company to recover funds from its various foreign operations without antagonizing host-country sensitivities with large "dividend drains." Unbundling may also provide greater flexibility in terms of matching each type of fund transfer with the tax position of each affiliate.

Royalty and Management Fees

Royalty and management fees may often facilitate payment of funds to the parent when payment of dividends is blocked or restricted. They may also have certain tax advantages relative to dividends, especially when the host-country tax rate is above the parent's tax rate. The basic reason is that while the parent can take a tax credit for the local income and withholding taxes paid, it can claim only up to its own maximum tax rate. On the other hand, royalties and management fees are usually fully deductible from host-country income after being paid to the parent.

An example of how the overall tax burden of an international company can be lowered by switching from "bundled" remittances—that is, dividends—to unbundle remittances, in this case in the form of royalties and management fees, is provided by Eiteman and Stonehill in table 14.3.[10] It is assumed that a foreign affiliate earns $5,000 before payment of any return to the parent and before income taxes. The parent wants to receive $2,000 before parent-country taxes from its foreign affiliate. In the "bundled" column, this is paid entirely as dividends, while in the "unbundled" column it is paid as $1,200 as royalties and fees and $800 as dividends. The host-government income tax rate is assumed to be 50 percent, while the parent-government income tax rate is 40 percent. For simplicity, Eiteman and Stonehill assume that the host government imposes no dividend withholding tax, and that the parent country "grosses up" in determining taxable income: it adds local income taxes paid on the earnings from which the dividends were paid back to taxable income and then allows credit for local income taxes.

---

[9] For discussion of these points, see David Eiteman and Arthur Stonehill, *Multinational Business Finance,* 2nd ed. (Reading, Mass.: Addison-Wesley Publishing Co., 1979), pp. 393-95.

[10] This example is described in detail in ibid., pp. 399-400.

TABLE 14.3   Tax Effect, Bundled versus Unbundled Compensation to Parent

AFFILIATE STATEMENT	BUNDLED	UNBUNDLED
1. Net income before taxes and compensation to parent	$5,000	$5,000
2. Less royalties and fees	—	1,200
3. Taxable income	5,000	3,800
4. Less local income taxes	2,500	1,900
5. Available for dividends	2,500	1,900
6. Cash dividends to parent	2,000	800
7. Reinvested locally	500	1,100
PARENT STATEMENT		
8. Royalties and fees received	—	1,200
9. Dividends received	2,000	800
10. Total received from affiliate	2,000	2,000
11. Credit for foreign income taxes	2,000	800
12. Taxable income in parent country	4,000	2,800
13. Parent tax liability (40%)	1,600	1,120
14. Less credit for foreign taxes	2,000	800
15. Income tax payable by parent	—	320
16. Lost income tax credit	400	—
TOTAL TAXES PAID		
17. Taxes paid to host government	2,500	1,900
18. Taxes paid to parent government	—	320
19. Total taxes paid	2,500	2,220
TOTAL FUNDS REINVESTED		
20. Reinvested in host country	500	1,100
21. Reinvested in parent country	2,000	1,680
22. Total reinvested	2,500	2,780

Source: David Eiteman and Arthur Stonehill, *Multinational Business Finance*, 2nd ed., © 1979, Addison-Wesley, Reading, Mass., p. 400, Figure 11.2. Reprinted with permission.

In the affiliate's statement shown in table 14.3, under the bundled assumption, the affiliate pays no royalties or fees but pays income taxes of $2,500 and dividends of $2,000 and reinvests the remaining $500. Under the unbundled assumption, the affiliate pays $1,200 of royalties and fees, thereby lowering local taxes to $1,900. After a dividend of $800, the affiliate has $1,100 to reinvest locally. From the affiliate's point of view, therefore, a tax savings is derived when the parent is compensated via royalties and fees rather than via dividends.

In the parent's statement, $2,000 of cash is received under both the bundled and unbundled procedures. Because the local income tax rate is 50 percent, a sum equal to the cash dividend is added back to determine taxable income in the parent country. The parent tax liability is 40 percent of this total—$1,600 in the bundled case and $1,120 in the unbundled case. However, the company may take credit for income taxes already paid in the foreign country. In the bundled example, this credit, $2,000, exceeds the tax liability, $1,600, and no income taxes are paid. Thus, some $400 of potential tax credit goes unused. In the unbundled case, the parent applies a tax credit of $800 against the liability of $1,120 and pays the difference, $320. The net result is that the total funds available for reinvestment equal $2,500 in the bundled case and $2,780 in the unbundled case.

While the distinction is not watertight, royalties are typically paid for use of trade names and patents. Management fees typically are paid for services such as marketing expertise or technical advice provided by headquarters. The U.S. Internal Revenue Code, as in the case of tax codes for most developed countries, prescribes certain acceptable practices in setting royalty and management fees. In particular, it requires that prices charged to an affiliate be no higher than those charged to unaffiliated parties, that is, so-called arms-length prices. However, since the services in question are often unique, thereby making comparisons to arms-length prices difficult, multinational companies, in practice, have substantial leeway in setting royalties and management fees.

Transfer Prices

The prices charged for interaffiliate transfers of more conventional goods and services are identified as transfer prices. As in the case of royalty and management fees, transfer prices are frequently established with an eye toward reducing the global corporation's tax bill. In some cases, income taxes are the critical consideration. Hence, firms may charge affiliates in high-tax jurisdictions artificially high prices on goods shipped from other affiliates in order to reduce the reported profits of the highly taxed affiliates. In other cases, import taxes in the form of tariffs may be an especially onerous burden. In highly tariffed markets the multinational might seek to reduce its tax burden by charging affiliates prices substantially below arms-length prices charged for the same or similar goods shipped elsewhere.

Actual or threatened restrictions on the remittance of profits are another inducement for firms to charge artificially high transfer prices on intracorporate sales to certain affiliates. Thus, studies have found that prices charged to multinational affiliates in less developed countries, such as India and Columbia, for imports from other affiliates are usually substantially above arms-length prices for comparable goods.[11] This pattern reflects the fact that political uncertainties and prospects for exchange-rate devaluations make less developed countries more risky places to store retained earnings.

As in the case of royalties and management fees, transfer pricing is often a

---

[11] For a discussion of some relevant evidence on transfer-pricing practices in less developed countries, see Sanjaya Lall, ''Transfer-Pricing by Multinational Manufacturing Firms,'' *Oxford Bulletin of Economics and Statistics* Vol. 35 (August 1973), 173–95.

more flexible way to transfer funds among affiliates than are dividend policies, since departures from established practices are less likely to be noted by host-government officials. However, there are certain constraints on transfer-pricing behavior. One is the need for management to avoid creating inefficiencies by improper pricing. For example, affiliates charged artificially high transfer prices may in turn report below-average profits. But it would be a mistake for headquarters management to cut back corporate investment by those affiliates if a more appropriate set of transfer prices would show those affiliates earning above-average profit rates. The potential problems associated with utilizing noneconomic transfer prices can be eliminated to a large extent by adhering to the ancient business bromide: keep two sets of accounts, one for the tax man and one for running the business.

Tax and customs authorities constitute another, less easily circumvented restriction on the scope that multinationals enjoy in setting transfer prices. International firms sometimes find to their chagrin that—like the police inspector in English mystery stories—customs officials can ferret out wrong doers through dogged investigation. One recent example that transfer-pricing abuses do not always pay is provided by the Amway Company.

In 1983 Amway, the giant direct-selling company, received the heaviest fine in Canadian history—$25 million—for a sophisticated fifteen-year effort to avoid paying taxes and duties on goods imported into Canada. Amway was charged with faking invoices and price lists to mislead the Department of National Revenue and with creating a bogus company in Hawaii to generate authentic-looking documents to show customs officials. In effect, the company made it appear that the artificially low prices it was charging its Canadian affiliate were actually arms-length prices. A tip from the company's custom brokers to the Canadian government initiated the investigation that led to the company's conviction.

In relating the Amway experience, we wish to avoid any implication that international managers are generally a cut-throat and untrustworthy lot. Indeed, we hasten to note that most large companies tend to establish uniform transfer-pricing policies that involve standard markups.

MANAGING SHORT-TERM INVESTMENTS

Given that firms will ordinarily wish to store some portion of their retained earnings in a liquid but interest-bearing form, an important task of international working-capital management is to determine the levels and currency denominations of the international company's global investment in short-term assets, that is, assets of less than one year's maturity. There are two polar approaches to this task. One involves centralizing all cash management at corporate headquarters while minimizing investible funds held by foreign affiliates. The second is associated with attempts to maximize investment returns worldwide without excluding any foreign securities from consideration. In general, most international firms pursue an intermediate strategy. Specifically, while some "surplus" cash may be used to pay down local debt and/or to make investments in the home country, foreign affiliates are usually allowed to place some portion of their excess funds in local short-term investments.

Treasury bills constitute one popular instrument for short-term corporate investments. Such bills are issued by central governments in developed countries and, as such, represent the safest and most liquid investment. They are typically issued for three- and six-month maturity. Other comparatively safe and liquid short-term investment opportunities exist in the form of money-market deposits or time deposits placed with financial institutions. These represent funds placed on deposit with a stated interest rate for a stated maturity, usually less than one year. Early withdrawal typically involves some penalty in the form of a lower than stated interest rate. Since deposits in chartered financial institutions are often government insured, and since depositors have firm claims on the capital of the deposit taker, money-market and time deposits are only slightly less secure than Treasury bills. Eurodollar banks offer an especially large outlet for short-term deposits. Rates quoted on June 25, 1984, for Eurodollar deposits of different maturities are reported in table 14.4, along with rates for other short-term investments as a basis of comparison.

Several other short-term investments shown in table 14.4 include commercial paper and bankers' acceptances. The former represent IOU's issued by large corporations that typically enjoy high credit ratings. The usual maturities for commercial paper range from 30 to 270 days. Since commercial paper represents a promissory note on the part of the issuing corporation, it carries some risk of default. As a concomitant of this higher risk, commercial paper usually offers a

TABLE 14.4   Money Market Instruments

INSTRUMENT	TERM TO MATURITY	EFFECTIVE ANNUAL YIELD
1. Canadian government Treasury bills	91 Days	11.75%
2. Commercial paper in Canada	30 Days	11.35%
	60 Days	11.70%
	90 Days	11.90%
3. Bankers' acceptances in Canada	30 Days	11.30%
	60 Days	11.65%
	90 Days	11.85%
4. Eurodollar deposits	Overnight	10.63–10.75%
	1 Month	11.87–12%
	3 Months	12.12–12.37%
	6 Months	12.50–12.68%
	1 Year	13.50–13.68%

Source: *The Globe and Mail*, June 26, 1984, B10.

higher yield than Treasury bills of a similar maturity. Bankers' acceptances represent promissory notes (that is, promises to pay a stipulated amount) issued by private-sector businesses that are in turn guaranteed by a commercial bank. With this guarantee, most bankers' acceptances represent a lower risk to investors than commercial paper. The former therefore bear a lower yield for comparable maturities, as seen in table 14.4.

Managing an investment portfolio is a complicated activity for which there are no shortcuts to success; however, there are certain common-sense guidelines suggested by Shapiro:

1. The instruments in the portfolio should be diversified to maximize the yield for a given level of risk.
2. The portfolio must be reviewed daily to decide which securities should be deleted and which added.
3. In revising the portfolio, care should be taken to ensure that the incremental interest earned more than compensates for added costs, including transaction costs.
4. The maturity of the investment should be tailored to the firm's projected cash needs, or a secondary market with high liquidity should exist.
5. Opportunities for covered and uncovered interest arbitrage should be carefully considered.[12]

The last point is relevant in light of our discussion of the interest-arbitrage model in chapter 3. An important implication of that model is that if investments denominated in one currency offer a higher yield than investments of similar risk and maturity denominated in some other currency, the yield differential should approximate the anticipated depreciation of the former currency relative to the latter currency. In this case portfolio switching will not provide higher returns adjusted for currency changes. But when there are imperfections in currency or capital markets, there are also opportunities for arbitrage; that is, the potential exists to increase the yield on the firm's investment portfolio denominated in a common currency.

ACCOUNTS RECEIVABLE

Another major short-term asset carried on the balance sheets of corporations are accounts receivable. This asset category essentially represents trade credit extended to customers in order to promote sales of the company's products. In this context, the "return" on accounts receivable may be viewed as the profit margin on the additional sales (net of any additional inventory costs) that are stimulated by extending trade credit to customers.[13] This return should be compared to the interest charge that firms must pay on funds borrowed in order to extend trade

---

[12] Shapiro, *Multinational Financial Management*, p. 254.

[13] Most firms also levy an interest charge on overdue accounts.

credit to customers, or, alternatively, to the yield foregone by investing retained earnings in receivables rather than in direct interest-bearing assets. Where the profit margin on the additional sales stimulated by trade credit exceeds the cost of extending trade credit, building up accounts receivable may be an appropriate use of the firm's net working capital.

Unfortunately, it is very difficult to estimate the true impact on sales from the more liberal extension of trade credit to customers. This difficulty is compounded in the international firm by currency changes, which affect the propensity of both foreign and domestic consumers to buy the firm's products as well as the value (in home-currency units) of international accounts receivable. As well, both domestic and international firms must be concerned about the possibility of default on their outstanding accounts. Again, the management of default risk is more complex in the international firm, since formal and informal methods of rating the credit worthiness of corporate borrowers are both less accessible and less reliable outside of North America, especially in less developed countries.

An important potential tool for managing accounts receivable is the practice of factoring. Firms with a substantial export business and companies too small to afford foreign credit and collections departments can turn to factoring companies for help in collecting payment on their invoices. Factoring companies make an immediate payment of a proportion of the value of invoices they take over, thereby accelerating the conversion of accounts receivable into cash. For these services, factoring organizations charge a fee that varies from 0.5 percent to 2.5 percent of sales turnover. They may also charge an interest rate of around 3 percent above local interest rates for cash advanced.

Perhaps the most important development in this area in recent years is the spread of international factoring and, in particular, of export factoring. In this form of factoring, the provision of service is as prominent as the provision of finance. For a U.S. exporter, for example, an international factoring organization will check out the ultimate customer, purchase the invoice with a guarantee of payment by a certain date, and put a notice on the goods saying that payment must be made to the factoring company. It is then up to the factoring firm's local affiliate to collect payment.[14]

Three main organizations are involved in international factoring. One is the U.S.-headquartered Heller group of companies. This is the largest single factoring organization in the world, with affiliates in twenty-one foreign countries. Second is a loose collection of factoring companies known as Factors Chain International. This is a group of forty-five independent factoring companies throughout the world with a secretariat in the Netherlands. The third is International Factors Ltd., a company 75 percent owned by U.K.-based Lloyds & Scottish Finance Company, which has associate companies in most developed parts of the world.

One major advantage of using a factor is the "muscle" that international

---

[14] This description of international factoring is taken from Simon Proctor, "Time to Turn Debts into Cash," *International Management* Vol. 34 (December 1979), 25–28.

CASE STUDY: *HOW FIAT MANAGES ITS SHORT-TERM MONETARY ASSETS*

The following brief description provides some background on how one major multinational company, Fiat, manages its cash and short-term financial-asset portfolio. In 1983 a total of $54 billion in cash payments, receivables, and other items flowed through Fiat's Italian operations. Tight financial controls and centralized management enabled Fiat to make new investments at a rate of about $1 billion a year while reducing its debt by $1.5 billion over the period 1980–1984. Indeed, the managing director of Milan-based investment bank Euromobiliare has praised Fiat's cash-management system for being as sophisticated as any worldwide.

To keep a tight rein on the short-term asset positions of its 421 affiliates in 55 countries, Fiat has opted for a high degree of centralized financial control. Executives at company headquarters in Turin set financial strategy and manage operations for the worldwide group. The head office also does most of the negotiating for new lines of credit and international loans, and it oversees all Fiat's foreign-exchange operations.

To keep track of everything, Fiat has put in place a complicated reporting system that allows it to check the exact income and outflow positions of its companies over successive ten-day periods and to estimate the company's financial position over the following four months. That allows the central finance operation in Turin to exploit expected cash surpluses by investing the money or to cover potential shortfalls.

Because Fiat's home currency—the Italian lira—is prone to devaluation, Fiat generally bills all exports in the buyer's currency, and the company tries to minimize its exchange risk by borrowing in local currencies. Long and short positions in different currencies are netted out at financial headquarters, and exposed positions are hedged. Fiat management believes that its close attention to foreign-exchange exposure and local cash management can translate into significant savings. For example, when Fiat recently decided to transform some short-term debt into medium term, it elected to borrow in dollars to cover simultaneously a long dollar position it held in the foreign-exchange market. By issuing $100 million in variable-rate notes priced at 1.4 percent over the London interbank offered rate (LIBOR), Fiat solved two problems at the same time.

In another example, Fiat found that its U.S. operation had an excess of $10 million and that its Swiss-based company, International Holding Fiat (IHF), had a $10 million debt for which it was paying 1.4 percent over LIBOR. If the U.S. affiliate had put its money on deposit, it would have earned LIBOR minus 1.8 percent. So headquarters had the U.S. operation lend its excess cash to IHF at LIBOR. The American company earned more than it would have from a bank, and IHF had its interest payments cut. In all, the company saved 3.8 percent on the deal. Ultimately, it is Fiat's efficient cash-management system that enables management to identify opportunities to match short-term cash surplus and deficit positions in the organization.

Source: "Clever Cash Management Revs Fiat's Finances," *Business Week,* April 30, 1984, 60.

factoring companies carry in export credit markets. As one international factoring company puts it: "A local importer has to pay us because otherwise he won't get credit. We can cut off all his credit from his other customers here who are our clients."[15] Since the debtor does not know the identity of the supplier for whom the factor is acting, there is less chance of a disruption to established customer relations.

Debt-collection agencies are distinct from factoring companies in that they focus strictly on the collection of debt on behalf of their clients. The largest—Dun & Bradstreet—also operates a credit-rating service. Debtors who want to maintain their credit rating might therefore be receptive to the blandishments of the Dun & Bradstreet bill collectors. They may also wish to avoid the "subtle" ways that Dun & Bradstreet collectors announce the existence of slow payers. In Spain, for example, the Dun & Bradstreet collectors wear far from discreet red jackets as they go about their business. The company also resorts to sending an open telegram to a debtor, knowing that his failure to meet a debt on time will soon become open knowledge.[16]

INVENTORY MANAGEMENT

Both international and purely domestic firms hold inventory in the form of raw materials, work in process, and finished goods, both to facilitate uninterrupted production and to ensure that goods are available for delivery at time of sale. While inventory items are not financial assets, they are conventionally considered a part of working capital. Upon reflection, one can see that inventories serve much the same purpose as accounts receivable; they enable the firm to make a greater quantity of sales at the cost of income foregone from tying up capital in a noninterest-bearing asset.

It will not surprise the reader by now to see a claim that inventory management is more complex and often more costly in the international firm than in the purely domestic firm. In particular, international shipments over water routes are subject to delays and variability compared to overland rail and truck shipments. Attacks by Iran and Iraq on oil tankers in the Strait of Hormuz during the spring and summer of 1984 provided an extreme example of the vagaries to which international shipping is sometimes subject. Another somewhat extreme example is provided by Canada Wire and Cable's experience in shipping material and vehicles from Canada to be used on a project in Egypt. One shipment was held up for two weeks on the Mediterranean when the vessel carrying it was hijacked and held for ransom.[17]

---

[15] Ibid., p. 27.

[16] Ibid., p. 28.

[17] See Marian Stinson, "Canada Wire Lights Up Cairo's Street Jungle," *Toronto Globe and Mail*, October 9, 1984, B17.

Host-government policies, especially restrictions on imports, can also create havoc with low-cost inventory management in the international firm. Finally, the limited availability of reliable suppliers, especially in less developed countries, can impose a need for foreign affiliates to hold above-average (by home-country standards) levels of inventory.

As noted above, the basic tradeoff in the inventory-management decision involves profit losses on foregone sales against carrying costs in the form of foregone interest income. Therefore, as the probability of supply disruption (of either critical inputs or finished goods) increases or as carrying costs go down (say because of lower interest rates), it will pay to hold more inventory. Similarly, if the profit margin on foregone sales increases, or if future input supplies are expected to be more expensive, larger inventory holdings will be more desirable than previously. Optimization of the inventory tradeoff, given the relevant environmental parameters, involves the solution of a fairly well-known mathematical model called the economic-order quantity (EOQ) model.[18]

BARRIERS TO INTERNATIONAL
WORKING-CAPITAL MANAGEMENT

In *Moby Dick,* the classic novel by Herman Melville, the bane of Captain Ahab's existence is the great white whale. In international business, the financial manager's great white whale takes the form of blocked funds. When funds become blocked, they are effectively frozen in the host-country currency, thereby seriously limiting management's ability to shift those funds into higher yielding alternative uses.

There are two main ways in which funds held by foreign affiliates may be blocked. In one case the host government may make its currency nonconvertible, meaning that domestic residents cannot legally sell the host currency for other currencies. The currencies of Communist-bloc countries are typically nonconvertible for private (as opposed to government) transactions, as are the currencies of many less developed countries. In another, less extreme case, governments may require central bank approval of any fund transfers to nonresidents. Some may be approved, some rejected. In fact, a number of developed countries, including Great Britain, have at various times required multinational companies to obtain approval for large dividend payments to their parents or to undertake other financial transactions that might put downward pressure on host currencies. Hence, barriers to international working-capital management may sometimes be the rule rather than the exception.

Ideally, the international firm should see the blockage coming and use one

---

[18]The interested student can find a description of this model in most management-science or managerial-economics textbooks.

or more of the funds-transfer techniques described earlier to circumvent its effect; however, if the firm is caught by the blockage, it can:

1. Continue to try to get funds out of the country where desirable
2. Reinvest the blocked funds locally in the next most desirable form

We earlier described the use of management and royalty fees and transfer prices to accomplish interaffiliate funds transfers. These techniques would presumably be pursued in the case of blocked funds as well. But host governments concerned about the siphoning of funds out of their countries may pay particular attention to the internal fees and prices set. Other funds-transfer techniques might therefore be implemented.

One approach to dealing with blocked funds is the use of fronting loans. In the most typical case the parent deposits money in a private bank, and that bank lends the same amount of money to the borrowing affiliate. The interest paid to the parent is usually slightly lower than the interest paid by the affiliate. But since government authorities are more likely to allow the local affiliate to repay a loan to an international bank than to its parent, the fronting loan serves to mobilize blocked funds, as the parent will draw down its deposit as the loan is repaid. A fronting loan can also have tax advantages where the interest received is taxed in a low-tax jurisdiction, while the interest paid on the loan is deductible from income earned in a high-tax jurisdiction.[19]

Another alternative approach to dealing with blocked funds is to ''create exports.'' In this approach, affiliates in the country whose currency is blocked export to other affiliates and bill them in the blocked currency. This approach is viable when blocked currencies can be purchased in outside markets at prices approximating their international purchasing parities. In effect, the affiliate whose currency is blocked can continue to produce while the parent avoids feeding it with additional ''hard'' currency. It might be pointed out, however, that the affiliate runs the risk of government reprisal by billing in the local currency, since the host government's interest is in bringing hard currencies into the country.

Where it is either too difficult or too politically risky to implement fronting loans or to create more exports billed in the local currency, the affiliate should seek to invest its retained earnings in the highest risk-adjusted local alternative available. In low-inflation countries, this will often involve investing in short-term money-market instruments, such as those listed in table 14.4. But it is more typically the case that funds are blocked in countries that are suffering rampant inflation and are not characterized by well-developed short-term money markets. In these cases it often makes sense for affiliates to invest in additional production facilities or in other real assets, such as land, since real assets are generally a better

---

[19] This description of fronting loans is taken from Eiteman and Stonehill, *Multinational Business Finance,* chap. 11.

inflation hedge than financial assets in countries characterized by highly imperfect capital markets.

The discussion to this point in the chapter suggests the complex nature of working-capital management and the extensive amount of information required if corporate headquarters attempts to allocate its worldwide pool of funds in accordance with global profit-maximization objectives. It is therefore not surprising that most international firms pursue more limited objectives—in particular, finding higher yield uses of the company's internal financial assets, on the margin. But this objective is not limited just to short-term assets. Hence, we must consider the management of long-term assets.

CAPITAL BUDGETING

The management of long-term assets is usually subsumed under the activity known as capital budgeting. As defined by Van Horne, capital budgeting involves the generation of investment proposals, the evaluation of cash flows, the selection of projects based upon an acceptance criterion, and the continual reevaluation of investment projects after their acceptance. Long-term investment proposals can emanate from a variety of sources, but they most typically comprise proposals for new products or expansion of existing products, for replacement or expansion of physical plant and equipment, and for natural-resource exploration.

The heart of the capital-budgeting exercise is to estimate the cash-flow implications of an investment adjusted for various risks. Since it is cash receipts that are reinvested in the firm or paid out to shareholders as dividends, cash, rather than income, is what is important in capital budgeting. To illustrate approaches toward capital budgeting, we adopt the stylized example presented in Van Horne.[20] The example involves the replacement of an old machine by a new one. The total cost of the new machine is assumed to be $20,000. Implementation of the new machine is expected to cut labor and maintenance costs and effect other cash savings totaling $7,600 a year before taxes for the next five years, after which it is not expected to provide any savings, nor is it expected to have any salvage value.

The cash-flow implications of replacing the old machine by the new one can be evaluated by setting up a table comparable to that in table 14.5. This table shows the reported effects upon income in the column headed "Book Account," and the impact on cash flow in the other column. To understand the entries in the table, it is important to recognize that machines with useful lives of more than one year must be depreciated for tax purposes. If our sample firm employs straight-line depreciation, the annual depreciation charge is 20 percent: 100 percent divided by the five-year estimated life of the machine. The annual depreciation charge is, therefore, $4,000. If we assume that the old machine has a remaining

---

[20] Van Horne et al., *Financial Management*, p. 77.

TABLE 14.5   Estimating the Cash-Flow Impacts of an Investment

	BOOK ACCOUNT	CASH-FLOW ACCOUNT
1. Annual cash savings	$7,600	$7,600
2. Depreciation on new machine	4,000	
3. Less depreciation on old machine	400	
4. Additional depreciation charge	3,600	
5. Additional income before taxes	4,000	
6. Income tax (50%)	2,000	2,000
7. Additional income after taxes	2,000	
8. Annual net cash flow		5,600

Source: James C. Van Horne et al., *Financial Management and Policy*, Canadian 4th ed. (Scarborough, Ont.: Prentice-Hall of Canada, 1977), p. 81.

depreciable life of five years and that its estimated book value is $2,000, the annual straight-line depreciation charge is $400. Because we are interested in the incremental impact of the project, we must subtract depreciation charges on the old machine from depreciation charges on the new one to obtain the incremental depreciation charges associated with the project.

In calculating the net cash flow, we simply deduct the additional cash outlay for federal income taxes from the annual cash savings. Assuming a 50 percent federal income tax rate, the expected annual net cash inflow for this replacement proposal is $5,600 for each of the next five years compared with additional income after taxes of $2,000 per year. For an initial cash outlay of $18,000—equal to the purchase price of the new machine minus the salvage value of the old machine (assumed to be equal to its book value)—the firm anticipates a net cash savings of $5,600 per year over the next five years.[21]

Once this cash-flow estimate is obtained, the attractiveness of the investment can be calculated according to various criteria.

Investment Criteria

One investment criterion is the payback method. The payback period of an investment is calculated as the ratio of the initial fixed investment to the annual cash inflows over the recovery period. Given the hypothetical case described in the preceding paragraphs, the payback period would be calculated as in equation 14.1:

$$(14.1) \quad \text{Payback period} = \$18,000/\$5,600 = 3.2 \text{ years}$$

If the annual cash flows are not equal, the calculation is somewhat more difficult, but it essentially follows the same format as 14.1. If the payback period calculated

[21] Ibid., pp. 80–81.

falls below the company's maximum acceptable payback period, the proposal is accepted; if not, it is rejected.

The payback-period criterion has several major shortcomings. One is that it fails to consider cash flow after payback is realized. Hence it can give a very misleading indication of the long-run cash-flow benefits of a project. A second shortcoming is that it does not consider the timing of cash flows received over the payback period. It therefore values a dollar received today as equal to a dollar received at the end of the payback period. While we would all be thankful if our creditors showed such magnificent indifference to when we paid them back, most firms are not predisposed to forgo interest that can be earned on reinvested cash flow. The payback-period method implicitly fails to incorporate a rate of interest into the investment analysis over the relevant life of the project, that is, the period to payback.

The internal-rate-of-return method takes account of both the magnitude and timing of expected cash flows in each period of a project's life. The internal rate of return (r) is the discount rate that equates the present values of the expected cash inflows and outflows. It is determined as the solution to equation 14.2:

$$(14.2) \quad A_0 = A_1/(1+r) + A_2/(1+r)^2 + \ldots + A_n/(1+r)^n$$

In our hypothetical example, A would equal 18,000 and each of the right-hand side As would equal 5,600. The solution value for r is 16.8 percent.

The acceptance criterion for this method is to compare the internal rate of return with a required rate of return, sometimes called a hurdle rate. If the internal rate of return is greater than the required rate, the project proposal is acceptable; if it is not, the project should be rejected.

A third approach to capital budgeting is the net-present-value method. In this approach, all cash flows are discounted by the firm's required rate of return (k). This approach is illustrated in equation 14.3:

$$(14.3) \quad NPV = A_0 + A_1/(1+k) + A_2/(1+k)^2 + \ldots A_n/(1+k)^n$$

In the net-present-value approach, the required rate of return is an input to the equation. The right-hand side of the equation, when evaluated, gives the net present value (NPV) of the proposed investment. If the required rate of return is assumed equal to 10 percent, the NPV would be valued by solving equation 14.4:

$$(14.4) \quad NPV = -18,000 + 5,600/(1.10) + 5,600/(1.10)^2 + 5,600/(1.10)^3 + 5,600/(1.10)^4 + 5,600/(1.10)^5$$

Given the numbers in the example, NPV = \$3,228.48.

The decision criterion for the net-present-value method involves accepting investment proposals with positive NPVs and rejecting those with negative NPVs. While the internal-rate-of-return and present-value methods generally lead to the same acceptance or rejection decisions, that is not always the case, for reasons beyond our concern here. The business student will also learn in his or her finance course why the net-present-value method is generally preferred by financial theorists. Our purpose here is merely to identify the major approaches to capital budgeting before considering aspects of that activity of particular interest to international managers.

COMPLEXITIES OF INTERNATIONAL CAPITAL BUDGETING

There are two general issues associated with capital budgeting that are of special concern to the international firm:

1. The choice of viewpoint from which to measure rates of return, that is, the project or parent viewpoint
2. Whether to adjust cash flows or the cost of capital for additional risks that are uniquely foreign

The Budgeting Viewpoint

Conceptually, since headquarters is presumably interested in maximizing the global value of the organization, the relevant impact of a foreign investment is on the consolidated cash-flow or long-run profit position of the multinational firm. Hence, foreign projects should presumably be evaluated from the parent's perspective; however, in some cases a firm may feel itself constrained to reinvest some portion of its affiliate's retained earnings in the host economy. For example, it may encounter explicit or implicit constraints imposed by the host government against repatriating all of an affiliate's earnings in the form of dividends or other transfers. In this case, it is necessary to evaluate the return on a proposed project against the potential returns on competing projects in the same geographic region.

In fact, survey results show that the greatest percentage of U.S. multinationals evalute foreign investments from the perspective of the project.

In one study based on a survey of the top financial executives of the 306 largest U.S.-based multinationals, Bavishi found that 42 percent of respondents looked at cash flow from the foreign subsidiary's viewpoint in evaluating overseas investments, while cash flow from the U.S. parent's viewpoint was preferred by 21 percent. The remaining 37 percent of respondents looked at cash flow from both the foreign subsidiary's and U.S. parent's viewpoint.[22] Comparable results were obtained by Stanley and Block in their survey of financial officers in 121 large U.S. multinationals. Forty-eight percent of their respondents reported that

[22] See Vinod Bavishi, "Capital Budgeting Practices at Multinationals," *Management Accounting* (August 1981), 33.

foreign projects are evaluated on the basis of subsidiary cash flow, 36 percent on the basis of parent cash flow, and 16 percent on both.[23]

ADJUSTING FOR FOREIGN RISKS

The additional risks that stem from a project's foreign location can be handled in at least two ways:

1. Increase the discount (or hurdle) rate used to deflate cash flows in equation 14.3 or to compare to the internal rate of return calculated in equation 14.2.
2. Adjust cash flows to incorporate potential monetary losses (or gains) associated with specific foreign contingencies, and employ the same discount (or hurdle) rate as that used in evaluating domestic projects.

Eiteman and Stonehill offer several compelling arguments for choosing the second method of incorporating foreign project risk into an investment evaluation. In essence, their reasons boil down to the fact that simply adjusting the firm's hurdle rate up or down will likely fail to match the actual amounts of money at risk or the time pattern of the uncertainties. For example, changes in exchange rates may have an impact on cash flows because of economic exposure. The direction of the effect may be up or down depending upon a variety of factors discussed in an earlier chapter. Neither the pattern nor the magnitude of the potential changes is likely to be accurately captured by simple adjustments (up or down) of the firm's hurdle rate.[24]

In fact, survey results suggest that multinational managers use the two methods of risk adjustment about equally in international capital budgeting. For example, Stanley and Block found that 62 percent of their respondents reported the use of some risk-adjustment technique, with risk-adjusted discount rates and risk-adjusted cash flows used with similar frequency.[25] Bavishi reports that 70 percent of his respondents incorporate foreign risk into their investment evaluation either by shortening the minimum required payback period or raising the hurdle rate of adjusting project cash flows subjectively.[26]

Evaluation Technique

Notwithstanding the preference of finance textbooks for the use of the net-present-value approach, most multinational managers use some other invest-ment-appraisal technique. For example, 65 percent of respondents to Stanley and

---

[23] See M. Stanley and S. Block, "An Empirical Study of Management and Financial Variables Influencing Capital Budgeting Decisions for Multinational Corporations in the 1980s," *Management International Review* 23 (1983), 69.

[24] Eiteman and Stonehill, *Multinational Business Finance,* p. 268.

[25] Stanley and Block, "Empirical Study of Management," p. 66.

[26] Bavishi, "Capital Budgeting Practices," p. 35.

Block's survey reported that the internal-rate-of-return approach was their primary method of evaluating investment projects. The net-present-value approach was favored by only 17 percent of respondents. Bavishi reports that 76 percent of his respondents reported using the payback-period method in combination with either the internal-rate-of-return (two-thirds of the time) or the net-present-value approach (one-third of the time).

Cost of Capital

Finally, financial economists argue that the appropriate hurdle rate to use in investment evaluation is the firm's overall cost of capital, presuming that the project in question does not change the firm's optimal financing structure, and that any project-specific risks have been incorporated in adjustments to expected cash flows. In fact, less than half of the financial managers surveyed by Bavishi use the firm's weighted average cost of capital for worldwide financing in their capital-budgeting activities. Thirty percent report that they apply subjectively determined hurdle rates to specific investment projects, while 27 percent use the firm's overseas financing costs exclusively.

In summary, there tends to be a gap between what international finance theorists preach as "best practice" and what international managers implement in their actual practice. To some extent this may reflect a lag between theory and practice when moving from the relatively neat and contemplative world of academia to the messy and harried world of the corporate manager; however, it is interesting to note that surveys have shown that international managers have (over time) increasingly incorporated the suggestions of academics in their capital-budgeting practices.

International Divestment

Most studies of capital budgeting presume that the firm is undertaking capital investments or adding to its stock of physical assets. But management must also be prepared to liquidate physical capital investments that are not paying off. That is, management must be prepared to divest foreign assets, when more profitable, risk-adjusted opportunities present themselves. In recent years, there has been an upswing in divestment by American multinational companies. To some extent, an accelerated repatriation of capital by U.S. multinationals was stimulated by the rapid growth of the American economy in the first half of the 1980s. The more rapid growth of the U.S. economy, especially in comparison to European economies, created profitable investment opportunities in the parent affiliate's market.

In principle, the divestment decision is analogous to the investment decision. That is, the net present value of the foreign assets in question should be estimated. If the calculated net present value is less than zero, or if the assets in question can be sold to some third party for more than their net present value to the firm, divestment of those assets is called for.

While in theory investment and divestment (or disinvestment) decisions are financially analogous, in practice the latter are fraught with hazards and ambiguities not present to the same degree in the former. In particular, shutting down production facilities abroad can lead to retaliation by the home government against other activities carried on by the international firm in that country. Other foreign governments may perceive the firm's willingness to shut down production facilities as an expression of "poor corporate citizenship," and this perception may lead them to favor rival multinational firms by offering them subsidies and other incentives to do business in their countries.

Repercussions from severe legal restrictions on employee layoffs may also arise. For example, in Belgium all companies are required by law to inform and consult with employee representatives (in principle, before decisions are taken) in order to examine how dismissals can be avoided or limited and to find ways to alleviate the consequences. Furthermore, layoffs are costly and complex. The minimum length of notice for a white-collar employee can range from three months to two years.[27] These formal and informal restrictions on the freedom of firms to dismiss workers severely constrain the multinational firm's divestment policies.

It may also be difficult to find a buyer for the foreign business. In some countries, there may be no well-developed stock market in which to sell shares in the business. There may also be no large private interests willing to buy the assets involved.

In sum, narrow financial calculations of the consequences of divestment decisions may be incomplete and even misleading. Decisions to shut down overseas facilities must ordinarily consider a wide range of political as well as financial factors.

SUMMARY AND CONCLUSIONS

This chapter was concerned with how international companies manage the asset side of their balance sheets. The two main asset categories encompass current assets, including cash, short-term financial investments, accounts receivable, and inventories, and long-term assets, which encompass primarily property, plant, and equipment. The administration of current assets is usually described as "working-capital management," while the administration of long-term assets chiefly involves the capital-budgeting process.

The basic objectives of working-capital management are similar in both international and purely domestic companies:

1. To bring the company's cash resources within control as quickly and efficiently as possible
2. To achieve the optimum conservation and utilization of the company's available funds

[27] See Hern C. Jain, "Disinvestment and the Multinational Employer—A Case History from Belgium," *Personnel Journal* Vol. 59 (March 1980), 201–5.

However, international working-capital management is complicated by certain unique factors, including political restrictions that impede the free flow of money into and out of countries. In managing working capital, managers must determine the mix of short-term assets held by the firm as well as the distribution of the firm's retained earnings across its various affiliates. One short-term asset that all firms must hold is cash. Since firms do not ordinarily earn interest on cash balances, there is a strong incentive to implement techniques that improve the efficiency of cash management. One technique involves interaffiliate netting of receivables and payables. A second involves accelerating the collection of accounts receivable from either affiliates or independent companies.

The movement of funds from one affiliate to another can be accomplished in various ways. The most common method involves dividend payments. Funds are also transferred through payment of royalty and management fees, and through transfer prices for interaffiliate sales of goods. The choice of transfer technique will be influenced by a number of considerations, including the tax consequences of each technique.

In general, multinational firms allow their foreign affiliates to use some portion of their surplus cash to make investments in short-term assets. These assets include accounts receivable, inventory, and short-term financial instruments such as Treasury bills. The composition of a firm's short-term asset portfolio will ordinarily reflect the balancing of opportunities for higher returns against greater financial risks, including the risk of default or of currency blockage imposed by a sovereign government. The latter risk is a unique concern of international companies. While there are often ways for the international company to get around the problem of blocked funds, in many cases the firm's only option is to reinvest the funds in the host economy.

Capital budgeting is concerned with the management of long-term assets. The heart of the capital-budgeting exercise is the estimation of the cash-flow implications of an investment. These estimated cash-flow implications must then be evaluated using one or another investment criterion. Financial theorists argue for the use of the net-present-value criterion, although most international firms, in practice, use more than one evaluation technique. Again, there are unique complications attached to the capital-budgeting exercise in the international firm, including the choice of viewpoint from which to measure rates of return.

DISCUSSION QUESTIONS

1. Japanese companies are renowned for their "just-in-time" production methods. An essential component of this approach is to hold virtually no inventories but to rely upon on-time delivery of necessary parts and materials. A growing number of North American companies are giving serious thought to adopting Japanese-style inventory-management systems. What potential differences between the Japanese and North

American business environments should North American managers consider before implementing their own just-in-time inventory systems?

2. Suppose that the Canadian subsidiary of International Harvester sells 1,500 tractors monthly to the company's French affiliate at a per unit transfer price of $27,000. The Canadian and French marginal tax rates on corporate income are assumed to equal 45 percent and 50 percent respectively.

   (a) Suppose the transfer price can be set at any level between $25,000 and $30,000. At what transfer price will corporate taxes be minimized?

   (b) Suppose the French government imposes an ad valorem tariff of 15 percent on imported tractors. How would this affect the firm's transfer-pricing strategy, assuming it wishes to minimize taxes?

   (c) If the transfer price of $27,000 is set in French francs, and the French franc revalues by 5 percent, what will happen to the firm's overall tax bill? Consider the tax consequences both with and without the 15 percent tariff.

   [This question is taken from Alan Shapiro, *Multinational Financial Management* (Boston: Allyn & Bacon, 1982), p. 325.]

3. Discuss the alternatives available to the international firm faced with blocked funds in one or more overseas affiliates.

4. Is it likely that headquarters management of a multinational company will adopt the same policy toward accounts receivable in all of the company's foreign affiliates? Explain your answer.

5. What are the major objectives of transfer-pricing policies in the international firm? What restrictions exist on management's choice of inter-affiliate transfer prices?

6. In what ways might the capital investment (and disinvestment) decisions in the international firm differ from those in the purely domestic firm?

REFERENCES

BODDEWYN, J. J., "Foreign Disinvestment Theory: Is It the Reverse of FDI Theory?" *Weltwertschaftliches Archiv* 119 (1983), 345–55.

BOOTH, LAWRENCE, "Capital Budgeting Frameworks for the Multinational Corporation." *Journal of International Business Studies* Vol. 13 (Fall 1982), 113–23.

OBLAK, D. J., and R. J. HELM, "Survey and Analysis of Capital Budgeting Methods Used by Multinationals," *Financial Management* (Winter 1980), 37–41.

RUGMAN, ALAN, ED., *Multinationals and Transfer Pricing*. Beckenham Kent, England: Croom Helm, 1984.

SHAPIRO, A. C., "Capital Budgeting for the Multinational Corporation," *Financial Management* Vol. 7 (Spring 1978), 7–16.

——, "Payments Netting in International Cash Management," *Journal of International Business Studies* Vol. 9 (Fall 1978), 51–58.

STONEHILL, ARTHUR, and L. NATHANSON, "Capital Budgeting and the Multinational Corporation," *California Management Review* Vol. 10 (Summer 1968), 39–54.

CHAPTER FIFTEEN

Structuring and Controlling the International Firm

In the preceding chapters we emphasized that management should strive to evolve business strategies that match organizational strengths with opportunities in the international business environment. In analogous fashion, management should avoid strategies that require skills and resources the firm does not possess in relative abundance. However, identification of strategies consistent with organizational strengths and opportunities in the environment does not guarantee a firm success in realizing its objectives. In particular, promising strategies can fail to produce their anticipated results if they are poorly implemented and improperly monitored.

There are several possible reasons why a conceptually appropriate set of business plans might prove unsuccessful. One is that relevant aspects of the environment may change in the interim between the formulation and implementation of strategy so that an initial set of business plans is no longer appropriate. This observation merely underscores the caveat that strategies must be reevaluated regularly to ensure that they are appropriate to achieving the firm's objectives.

It is also possible that appropriate strategies may simply be mismanaged in the implementation stage. The greatest threat in this regard is that managers and other personnel may promote their own interests at the expense of overall organizational goals. As a result, global organizational strategies may be subverted by managers at the individual division or subsidiary level, leading to reduced profitability of the global corporation. A key to effective international management is an ability to coordinate the pursuit of worldwide corporate objectives without stifling management initiative in local operations. In effect, international management confronts a critical issue of centralizing versus decentralizing organizational decision making. This is an important issue for managers of large, purely domestic firms as well; however, it is widely conceded that the decision is far more complex in the international firm for reasons discussed below.

The primary purpose of this chapter is to describe how the structure of an international organization can be designed to guide the international company toward the achievement of worldwide objectives without stifling the initiative of local affiliates. A company's organizational structure establishes the distribution of decision-making power through formal and informal lines of authority and responsibility. Organizational structure, along with data-management systems, constitutes the basis of a firm's control system, where control (in this context) may be thought of as the monitoring and coordinating of actions undertaken by managers in international divisions and affiliates.

THE CONTROL PROBLEM
IN INTERNATIONAL COMPANIES

While present to a greater or lesser extent in all companies, the potential for managers and other personnel to (wittingly or unwittingly) subvert the goals of the overall organization is stronger in the international firm than in the purely domestic firm, primarily because of the diversity of environments in which the former ordinarily operates. For example, language differences can distort communications between headquarters management and management in overseas affiliates, thereby hampering the ability of headquarters to motivate and monitor the performance of overseas personnel. In addition, cultural differences can contribute to the dismal failure in some countries of programs that have successfully motivated employees in other countries.

Political differences across geographic regions can also complicate the task of harmonizing the behavior of affiliate managers and other personnel with the corporation's global objectives. In particular, pressures exerted by host governments on subsidiary managers to act in the perceived best interests of the local economy can lead to decisions by affiliate managers that may reduce overall corporate profitability. One frequent manifestation of this problem is the demand by host governments that multinational affiliates buy from local suppliers, even though cheaper sourcing might be done through home-country or third-country suppliers. Of course, failure to comply with the host government's local purchasing initiatives might lead to consequences far more damaging both to the local affiliate and to the overall international company. The problem facing headquarters management is to determine when seemingly inefficient behavior on the part of affiliate management is actually an appropriate reaction to host-government pressures and when it represents opportunistic behavior on the latter's part.

This problem of interpretation arises because affiliate managers may use the rationale of host-government pressure against importing to justify, for example, a decision to integrate vertically through acquisitions of local suppliers. The incentive to integrate vertically might, in turn, be rooted in a desire on the part of affiliate managers to expand the size of their own organizations. This growth incentive can be especially acute in companies where executive salaries are tied to measures of organizational size, such as the number of employees.

The basic point is that headquarters management will ordinarily be less familiar with the overseas political and economic environments than with its own domestic environment. As a result, it may be poorly equipped to evaluate the basic motives of its overseas managers as well as the causal link between decisions taken by the latter and the performance of overseas affiliates. This inherent complexity puts a great premium on designing an organizational structure that facilitates effective communication between headquarters and local decision makers and encourages a sharing of common objectives throughout the organization. It also puts a premium on a rational decentralization of decision making whereby managers best equipped to implement an activity have responsibility for that activity. In effect, coordination and control require that relevant information from all parts of the global organization flows to decision makers who are capable of initiating action effectively.

BROAD FORMS OF ORGANIZATION

Modern organization theory recognizes two fundamentally different aspects of business organizations: formal organization and informal organization. Formal organization encompasses the division of work and the allocation of personnel, functions, and resources. It includes the communication system and the chain of command required for the coordination and control of the different parts of the organization.

Informal organization primarily refers to the interrelationships between members of an organization that result from decision-making processes going on in the company. Temporary coalitions, such as task forces and senior management conferences to which staff and line managers are invited, are examples of informal coordination vehicles. The informal organization is the social structure that develops more or less spontaneously in every company.[1] An important component of this structure has been identified as a corporation's "culture." This consists of a value system that governs positions and relationships in the organization. The corporate culture represents an unofficial code of behavior based on a set of shared values, norms, and beliefs. Ideally, a widely accepted organizational culture will delineate roles and modes of behavior without the need for a formal

---

[1]Endel-Jakob Kolde, *Environment of International Business* (Boston: Kent Publishing Co., a division of Wadsworth, 1982), chap. 12, pp. 217–18.

organizational structure or other explicit forms of control over employee behavior. In practice, the exercise of managerial control in a hierarchy will depend upon both formal structure and reporting systems as well as upon personalities, shared values, and so forth. This point is underscored in the following comment by an IBM manager on the role of socialization within his company: "Socialization acts as a fine-tuning device; it helps us make sense out of the procedures and quantitative measures. Any number of times I've been faced with a situation where the right thing for IBM was Y. I've always been counseled to tilt toward what was right for IBM in the long term and what was right for our people. They pay us a lot to do that. Formal controls without coherent values and culture are too crude a compass to steer by."[2]

ORGANIZATIONAL STRUCTURES

A company's formal bureaucratic structure is concerned primarily with the design of decision making and reporting relationships in the firm. These relationships are, in turn, concerned with where responsibility for decisions bearing on specific corporate activities should be located in the corporate hierarchy and what approval and "checking" routines should be put in place for those decisions. A company's bureaucratic structure therefore consists of an explicit hierarchy accompanied by rules and procedures that delineate desired behavior. Codified standards of performance exist for many of the positions in the hierarchy, and monitoring involves comparing an individual's performance to the standards of performance anticipated.

The objective in designing a formal organizational structure is to decentralize decision making so that responsibility for specific decisions is vested in those individuals who, for reasons of better access to information or superior ability, are best able to make those decisions while at the same time ensuring that decisions are taken in the best interests of the global organization. As noted by Herbert, the organizational structure of an international firm should be consistent with the firm's operations or "technical core." That is, organizational structure should be congruent with an organization's business strategy, including (among other things) the characteristics of products sold and markets served and the degree to which production processes are standardized or differentiated.[3]

While there are many variations on the theme, it is possible to group the various organizational structures of international companies into four basic types: (1) the international-division structure, (2) the geographic structure, (3) the prod-

[2]This quote and a surrounding discussion of corporate culture can be found in Richard Pascale, "Fitting New Employees into the Corporate Culture," *Fortune*, May 28, 1984. Also see Geert Hofstede, "Hierarchical Power Distance in Forty Countries," in Cornelius J. Lammers and David J. Hickson, eds., *Organizations Alike and Unlike* (London: Routledge & Keegan Paul, 1979), pp. 42–60.

[3]Theodore Herbert, "Strategy and Multinational Organization Structure: An Interorganizational Relationship Perspective," *Academy of Management Review*, 9 (1984), 259–71.

uct structure, and (4) the matrix structure. Each provides a separate solution to the issue of how decentralization of decision making should proceed in the international firm.

The International Division

This organizational model tends to be implemented by companies that are in the relatively early stages of developing international business activities. As a result, management has limited experience in operating under foreign conditions. The pronounced scarcity of international management expertise in the early stages of a firm's international expansion makes it advisable to concentrate the available expertise rather than distribute it broadly throughout the organization. In this way, available skills can be concentrated in their most effective uses.

The essential characteristics of the international-division structure are summarized in figure 15.1. As shown in the figure, all of the company's foreign operations are grouped into one separate unit and assigned to a senior executive at the corporate headquarters. The company's overall business activities are thereby effectively segregated into a domestic component and a nondomestic component. The executive in charge of the international division generally has line authority over the company's foreign operations and is held responsible for the profits from those operations. Thus, responsibility for implementing tactical strategies in functional areas like marketing, finance, and production is essentially duplicated within one or more domestic management units and an international management unit.

In another version of the international-division structure, international management's input is concentrated at the staff level rather than at the line management level. In this organizational model, the international division functions as a service division to other managers in the global organization. Its typical function in this role is to provide information about foreign markets to other staff and line management units. In other cases, it may play a more active role in

Figure 15.1   International-Division Structure
Arvind Phatak, *Managing Multinational Corporations* (New York: Praeger Publishers, 1974), p. 174.

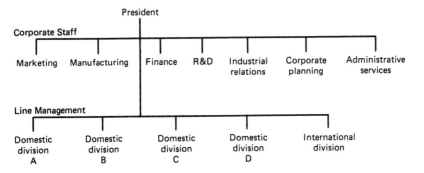

establishing overall corporate strategy in the broad functional areas of marketing, production, finance, and so forth. Whether concentrated at the staff level or at the line management level, the major functions of the international division are to look after the growth and development of the company's nondomestic business and to provide an effective liaison between domestic and nondomestic operations. With a separate international division, differences between the international and domestic environments can be more easily recognized and translated into unique operating strategies. Furthermore, if all international activities are grouped into a common division, economies can be achieved in the size of requisite management and staff. General Foods, Campbell Soup, and Scott Paper are among the well-known companies that, at one time or another, have employed an international-division structure.

The separation of domestic and international divisions also raises several potential problems. One is conflict between management in each division, since they are at the same organizational level. Conflicts could arise over issues of objectives and broad strategy or over specific tactical issues such as the prices that the international division should charge for products produced by the domestic division and distributed abroad. For example, the domestic division may view demand as being more price sensitive than the international division does. As a result, domestic managers may favor charging lower prices than those proposed by managers in the international division. Of course, a diligent and strong senior management should be able to nip most such interdivisional disputes in the bud.

Of greater concern, perhaps, is the lack of exposure and experience in foreign countries on the part of the technical staff in the international division. The centralization of international operations in corporate headquarters may often result in staff decisions that are inconsistent with the realities of specific foreign markets. The relevant requirement then becomes to shift operational decision making closer to the environment in which management decisions are implemented. This concern becomes increasingly relevant as the firm's international operations become more mature and more heterogeneous.

The Geographic Structure

The heterogeneity of different geographical regions can be acknowledged within the international division (headquarters) structure by disaggregating international management resources into regional units, as shown in figure 15.2. In this organizational structure, responsibility for operational decision making within specific regions is assigned to area managers within corporate headquarters. The disaggregation into regional units should be based on characteristics that distinguish geographic markets in a significant way. In some cases, the critical characteristic may be differences in customer requirements. In others it may be differences in the cost and availability of critical inputs.[4]

---

[4]The foregoing discussion of the international division structure drew heavily upon the relevant discussion in Arvind Phatak, *Managing Multinational Corporations* (New York: Praeger Publishers), 1974.

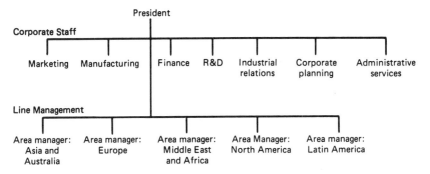

Figure 15.2   Worldwide Geographic Structure
Arvind Phatak, *Managing Multinational Corporations* (New York: Praeger Publishers, 1974), p. 176.

As the international activities of a firm increase in importance, the need to integrate the contribution of international managers into the overall corporate-planning exercise also increases. A danger in centralizing international management within corporate headquarters is that the international division(s) will be regarded purely as an entity for handling technical tasks—translating foreign documents, arranging for letters of credit, and so forth. The input of international managers to the formulation of business strategies may be minimal in this case. A way to increase the influence of international management in the formulation and implementation of overall corporate business plans is to establish separate subsidiary management structures outside of the home economy.

Worldwide Product Structure

In cases where a company produces and/or distributes a wide range of products but product differentiation by geographic region is not a dominant concern, the company might adopt a worldwide product structure. As illustrated in figure 15.3, in the case of a worldwide product structure, managers are assigned responsibility for the worldwide management of all functional activities related to specific products or product lines. Each product division acts as a profit center operating within the framework of the corporate headquarters strategic plan. During the 1970s, a large number of multinational companies switched from a structure built around an international division to a worldwide (or global) product structure.

An example of a company organized along worldwide product lines is Colgate-Palmolive. While headquartered in the United States, the company operates in over fifty countries around the world. In 1983 more than half the company's sales were made outside the United States. Colgate's many products are grouped into the following core categories for purposes of global product management: oral care, soap, laundry products, liquid and hard surface cleaners, health-care products, food, and specialty consumer products.

A worldwide product structure affords the advantage of linking manage-

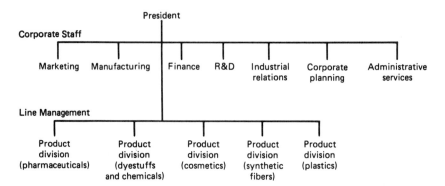

Figure 15.3   Worldwide Product Structure
Arvind Phatak, *Managing Multinational Corporations* (New York: Praeger Publishers, 1974), p. 182.

ment decisions closer to the marketplace since the life cycle of individual products can be more closely monitored. Also, closer links to the customer can assist in product design and differentiation. Indeed, it is precisely in the case of firms that produce differentiated products for a broad number of geographic markets that a global product structure is suitable. Colgate is one such firm since the company produces a variety of different types of soaps, toothpastes, detergents, and other household goods that are marketed in essentially the same way all over the world.

There are several dangers in adopting a global product structure. Since the product divisions have their own sets of functional staff groups, there is a danger of excessive staffing of functional managers. There is also a danger of coordination breakdowns between various product divisions. For example, some of the company's products may be marketed in a way that conflicts with the brand image that is being created for other products sold by the firm. But the main potential problem with a global product structure is that it can result in overlooking important differences among countries in economic, political, and cultural conditions.

When both product categories and geographic regions are relevant ways to segment operational management decision making, either the simple geographic structure or the product structure might be unsatisfactory. A focus on managing product lines might lead to unduly homogeneous treatments of different markets, whereas a strict regional structure might lead to a failure to properly match product characteristics with market needs.

The Matrix Organization

To some extent, regional distinctions can be accommodated within the product structure model by investing responsibility for product line management in separate regional headquarters; however, this approach invites substantial duplication of staffing requirements. A related solution to the problem of coordinating product-oriented and geographically oriented management is the so-

CASE STUDY: *ORGANIZING THE STRUCTURE OF CLUB MED*

For twenty years, Club Méditerranée's headquarters in Paris had much of the flavor of one of the club's free-wheeling holiday villages. The informal management structure, whereby executives in jeans dropped in and out of the office of the firm's chief executive, recently gave way to a more strait-laced corporate structure with four regional operational centers covering the globe.

According to chief executive Gilbert Trigano, the change in management style was dictated in part by the club's continuing spread around the world—a network of resorts that totals ninety installations in twenty-six countries. Another factor pushing the club to reorganize was the brief danger that Trigano might leave Club Med to assist French President, François Mitterrand, in determining whether Paris should be the site of the 1989 World's Fair. In the old structure, decisions seemed to be made on an ad hoc basis, reflecting Trigano's personal-management style. Centralization was the rule, to the point where such things as commercial policies to be pursued in the Japanese market or how to run a holiday village in Tahiti were dictated from Paris. An "animator" would fly from Paris to Agadir, Morocco, just to discuss evening entertainment at the company's Agadir resort.

The need for quick financial decisions in different parts of the globe, the need to adapt rapidly to changing market conditions and to maintain close links between marketing staff and operating personnel at the firm's resort villages all argued in favor of decentralization. Given the basic uniformity of the company's resort villages around the world, a geographic divisional structure made more sense than a product-based organizational structure. Under the current structure, the regional directors fly into Paris once a month to review world strategy and to discuss the financing of new villages and problems with tour operators, exchange controls, and the like.

Source: "Club Med Management Gives Up Some of Its Free-Wheeling Style," *International Management* Vol. 39 (May 1984), 27. Reprinted with special permission from *International Management*, © McGraw-Hill Publications Co. All rights reserved.

called matrix organizational structure in which operational responsibility for a company's international production and marketing activities is assigned to both area and product managers. In effect, the company is organized along both product and geographic lines, with both sets of managers enjoying comparable levels of authority within the organization. The purpose of this hybrid structure is to ensure that both geographic and product considerations receive appropriate weight in tactical decision making.

The basic nature of the matrix structure is illustrated in figure 15.4. In this organizational model, responsibilities for product lines and regions are shared by separate but equal managerial units. An obvious concern here is that product and area managers at the same hierarchy levels in the organization will be at loggerheads over policies that cut across the two organizational dimensions. Such conflict might be anticipated where managers' perceptions of the "relevant en-

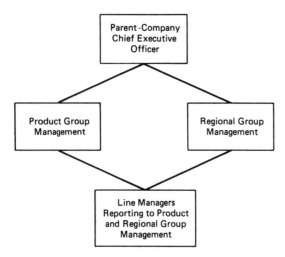

Figure 15.4   Matrix Organizational Structure

vironment'' differed depending upon whether management had area, product, or functional responsibility. In this context, the goal of headquarters management should be to promote a healthy exchange of ideas and opinions among managers charged with different lines of responsibility while preserving a strong shared sense of the organization's identity and overall objectives.

Achieving an environment of ''harmonious competition'' for scarce resources within a matrix organization is no easy task, and line managers often find themselves faced with conflicting demands of product and regional group managers. What is required, among other things, is a mechanism for conflict resolution that is perceived to be fair to all managers and a program for managing managers that promotes a balanced view of the needs of all divisions of the organization, as well as a commitment to the welfare of the global organization. This frequently entails setting up a formal superstructure at parent company headquarters to resolve disputes between product and regional group management.

Market-Oriented Organizations

Although the basic organizing dimensions for international businesses are functions, products, and geographic areas, some firms have begun to base their global structures on differences in prospective markets. Markets are grouped on the basis of homogeneity in patterns of purchasing power and buying behavior. In this context, physical proximity is a much less important criterion for globally oriented structures.[5]

[5]For a discussion of market-oriented structures, see Stanley M. Davis, ''Organization Design,'' in Ingo Walter and Tracy Murray, eds., *Handbook of International Business* (New York: John Wiley & Sons, 1982), pp. 39.3–39.20.

To elaborate, a simple geographical dichotomy is frequently drawn between developed and less developed economies. But a more valid categorization would recognize important differences among countries, even at comparable levels of economic development. For example, countries may enjoy different prospective growth rates.

An example of a market-oriented structure is provided by Richardson-Merrill, a multinational pharmaceutical company. The company reorganized its geographic groupings (within its Latin America/Far East unit) to reflect the following market differentiation:

Group 1 Andean Group, Southeast Asia, the Philippines, and the Caribbean represent small, noncomplex, and underdeveloped markets for their products in places they have chosen to operate.

Group 2 India, Indonesia, and Iran represent large, noncomplex, and high-potential growth markets.

Group 3 Mexico, Brazil, and Australia represent large, complex markets with proven records as well as satellite markets in neighboring countries.

Group 4 Japan stands by itself as a large, complex, and mature market that requires specialized attention.[6]

STRATEGIC CONTROL

A firm's formal organizational structure should be characterized by established reporting relationships and information channels that contribute to informed and consistent decision making across the global organization. While an appropriate formal structure is clearly important if the international firm is to evolve and implement an integrated global strategy, the orientation and characteristics of management are also relevant. For example, head-office managers who are enterprising, strong willed, or skillful at eliciting personal loyalties and commitments are likely to move their organizations toward a pattern of increased headquarters influence over subsidiary decision making. At the same time, if subsidiary managers are also strong willed and entrepreneurial, there is the danger that a power struggle will develop between headquarters management and managers in overseas branches and affiliates. Doz and Prahalad suggest that two entrepreneurial personalities pitched one against the other would probably be unable to develop jointly a consistent resource allocation focus or manage a clear implementation process.[7]

There is no implication that a compliant subsidiary management that passively follows the marching orders of headquarters management is appropriate

---

[6]Ibid., pp. 39.14–39.15. It might be noted that the Group 2 definition reported was formulated before the Islamic Revolution in Iran.

[7]See Yves L. Doz and C. K. Prahalad, "Headquarters Influence and Strategic Control in MNC's," *Sloan Management Review* Vol. 23 (Fall 1981), 15–21.

or desirable. Some decisions are better left to overseas branches and affiliates while others are best made in a centralized fashion. A fair generalization is that strategic questions are best centralized, and operational issues are best decentralized. An example of the former is the capital-budgeting decision. An example of the latter is the hiring and firing of employees. In most cases, however, effective representation of regional perspectives is desirable, even when the decision-making sovereignty of headquarters is a corporate imperative.

In cases where a substantial degree of subsidiary autonomy is appropriate, there is a premium placed on having effective conflict-resolution mechanisms in place since disputes over the regional allocation of scarce resources are bound to arise. One such mechanism involves elaborate decision-making grids in which the respective powers of headquarters and subsidiaries are spelled out according to the type of decision involved. It is important that the grid be adaptable to changing circumstances, however, or the international organization may find itself unable to respond flexibly to changing demands on its global business operations.

Other conflict-resolution mechanisms involve the use of intersubsidiary coordinating committees, teams, and task forces, which may meet on a regular or irregular basis to address points of conflict between affiliate managers. As Doz and Prahalad note, appointing senior executives to coordinating roles enhances the prestige of coordinating units and signals management's commitment to worldwide product line coordination.[8] Furthermore, by deciding the agenda of the conflict-resolution mechanism and influencing the direction of analysis, senior management can ensure that specific issues are dealt with from a multiaffiliate perspective.

Perhaps the most effective way to avoid dysfunctional conflict in the long run is to infuse a strong organizational culture in the various affiliates of the international company. The prototype model of "conflict-free" organizations is the Japanese company, in which lifelong employees are alleged to be very loyal to their organizations, and behave in accordance with the company "way."[9] Organizational control in Japanese businesses stresses a shared set of values throughout the organization. These shared values provide what Jaeger calls "recipes" for members' behavior. The values are reinforced through interpersonal interactions. This strong corporate culture may explain why Japanese multinationals tend to delegate more decisions to their affiliates than do American multinationals.

For the international organization, significant costs (as well as benefits) may be associated with control systems based upon shared cultural perspectives. For example, such systems ordinarily require extensive personal contact between head

[8]Ibid., p. 17. Doz and Prahalad offer a list of conflict-resolution mechanisms.

[9]A discussion of informal control mechanisms in Japanese firms is found in Alfred Jaeger, "The Transfer of Organizational Culture Overseas: An Approach to Control in the Multinational Corporation," *Journal of International Business Studies* 14 (Fall 1983), 91–114. For some contrary evidence to this view of Japanese organizations, see Fred Luthans, Harriette McCaul, and Nancy Dodd. "Organizational Commitment: A Comparison of American, Japanese and Korean Employees," *Academy of Management Journal* 28 (March 1985), 213–18.

office and affiliate personnel, where less expensive written communications might be used in bureaucratic control systems. They may also require duplicating employee facilities in all international affiliates, even when such duplication is undesirable on grounds of production and marketing efficiency. Nevertheless, an increasing number of North American companies are beginning to merge bureaucratic-formal control systems with corporate control systems.

How Much Control?

The desired magnitude and nature of strategic control exercised by headquarters over subsidiaries will vary with the location and nature of the firm's inter-

CASE STUDY: *CHANGING THE MANAGEMENT STRUCTURE
OF THE EAST ASIATIC COMPANY*

An illustration of a broad-based approach to changing management structure (including an attempt to alter the company's culture) is provided by the example of the East Asiatic Company. The company is Denmark's largest publicly owned company and one of the world's oldest trading firms. East Asiatic Company (EAC) is a conglomerate with interests ranging from timber to motor scooter manufacturing and operates in about fifty countries.

After several years of losses in the early 1980s, top management concluded that a major corporate shakeup was required. Among the changes implemented was a commitment to identify strategic objectives and to shed business units that were not consistent with the firm's overall strategic business thrust. Furthermore, the organization's structure was shifted from one based on geographic regions to a product-based divisional organization. Traditionally, branch managers around the world ran their own operations and reported directly to the managing directors in Copenhagen. Under the new structure, there are four main product divisions: timber, shipping, graphic-arts equipment, and "informatics." The hope is that by bringing related activities together within divisions, decision making will become more market oriented.

Perhaps the most substantial changes implemented relate to long-standing personnel policies that constituted an important part of EAC's corporate culture. They included practices such as recruiting virtually all personnel straight from Danish high schools, not appointing outsiders to middle-management positions, and refusing to fire employees or hire women managers. EAC's anachronistic labor policies included a provision that young male employees required corporate permission to marry.

Management now says that its policy is to hire the best person for the job, regardless of sex or background, and that managers will have to justify their continuing place on the payroll. Indeed, the head office staff was reduced by almost 50 percent in a recent three-year period. But one practice that remains in force is the requirement that apprentices remain unmarried during their first few years with the company.

Source: Roy Hill, "East Asiatic Charts a New Course," *International Management* Vol. 39 (February 1984), 12–15.

national business activities. For example, where foreign politicians are worried about the degree to which decisions of subsidiaries operating on their soil are controlled by the headquarters of multinational firms, a greater degree of decentralized decision making may be appropriate.

The stage of development of the international firm may also influence the nature of strategic control. In particular, as subsidiaries mature and become autonomous with respect to strategic resources, such as technology, capital, management, and access to markets, the ability of headquarters to control the strategies of subsidiaries by regulating the access by subsidiaries to scarce resources is significantly reduced. Headquarters must then place greater emphasis on creating a sophisticated organizational context—a blending of organizational structure, information systems, measurement and reward systems, and a fostering of a common organizational culture.[10]

The International Subsidiary Company Model

An extension of the international division structure that has been implemented by many companies involves establishing separate headquarters for the firm's foreign activities.[11] International subsidiary companies are frequently created by removing the international division from the domestic corporate structure and elevating it to the status of a legally independent company.

The international subsidiary is typically the central headquarters of a variety of operating companies located in foreign markets. While international subsidiary headquarters may or may not be directly involved in operational activities, it clearly does not exist simply as a routine service unit for domestic divisions. As suggested by figure 15.5, international subsidiary headquarters shares an equal status with domestic operations. The two structures are linked on top in the office of the chief executive officer, who heads both companies. Domestic and international operations are further synchronized by centralized staff managers who report to the chief executive officer and by operations specialists who interact with both domestic and international line managers.

As international operations become larger and more geographically diverse, several international subsidiaries may be created, with separate headquarters management reporting to the chief executive officer. For example, Exxon has foreign subsidiaries separately headquartered in Toronto, London, Caracas, Tokyo, and several other foreign centers. Its domestic divisions are headquartered in Houston. All regional headquarters report to the parent headquarters located in New York. The key notion underlying the international subsidiary model adopted by Exxon and other companies is that relevant and important distinctions exist

[10]See C. K. Prahalad and Yves L. Doz, "An Approach to Strategic Control in MNC's," *Sloan Management Review* Vol. 22 (Summer 1981), 5–29.

[11]This description of the international subsidiary company model is taken from Kolde, *International Business,* pp. 230–32.

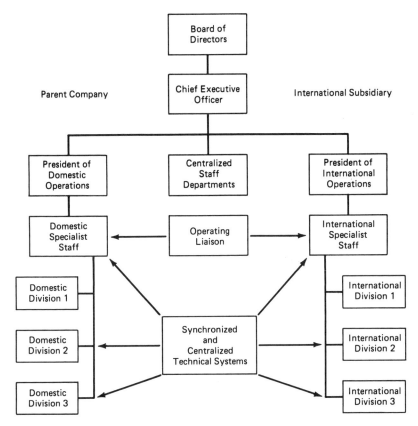

Figure 15.5 International Subsidiary Model
Endel-Jakob Kolde, *Environment of International Business* (Boston: Kent Publishing Co., A Division of Wadsworth, Inc., 1982), p. 231 (Figure 12.4).

between geographic markets, and the overall organization should be structured to recognize those geographic distinctions.

Companies favoring a geographic structure tend to produce a variety of products that must be adapted to local consumer needs or conditions of use but can be marketed through similar channels of distribution. The Swiss confectionary and food company, Nestlé, is organized according to geographic structure. Another example is CPC International, an international distributor of many brand-name food products, headquartered in the United States. CPC certainly fits the description of a firm that would benefit from a geographic structure. Management believes strongly in the necessity to adapt food products to local tastes and preferences. An illustration of this market-oriented approach is provided by the bouillon cubes distributed by the company. Bouillon cubes serve a number of needs, mostly as a flavor contributor to soups and the like. The company sells chicken and beef flavor in the U.S., Germany, and Switzerland. But in

Mexico, in addition to these two flavors, it also sells tomato and shrimp varieties. In Argentina, the major product is corn bouillon; in Kenya, a chili variety; in Ireland, mutton; in Thailand, pork.[12]

The primary advantage of the geographic structure is that it places tactical decision-making responsibility in the hands of managers who are presumably best acquainted with those markets. It is also an excellent way to coordinate the activities of two or more affiliates within a given geographic region. A potential shortcoming is that production and marketing of individual products may suffer because there is no single executive responsible for all activities related to specific products.

There is no doubt that managers believe organizational structure matters to the performance of their firms. However, the discussion to this point is a caution that formal organizational structure is only one element of a firm's control system. Furthermore, experience indicates that there is no "ideal" organizational structure for the international firm. Companies like Westinghouse have (at various times) employed global product, area-based, or matrix structures. In this regard, one expert recently argued that companies ideally should be able to adapt to complex demands without necessarily changing their formal organization structures.[13] The key requirement is flexible managers who are free from the limitations of representing organizations in strict accordance with organizational design charts.

DATA-MANAGEMENT MECHANISMS

Besides the formal and informal organizational structure, two other key elements of a firm's control mechanisms are management information and measurement systems. The latter consist of accounting, financial, marketing, and personnel reporting systems that provide headquarters management with information about the actual state of the organization compared with the desired state. Significant differences may signal the need for central management intervention.

There are two broad foci of management information and measurement systems: personal performance and economic performance. The former is concerned with how well individual managers or groups of managers are doing. The latter is concerned with how well any given profit center is doing as an economic entity.[14] These two concerns are not necessarily identical. For example, an overseas affiliate in a thriving macroeconomic climate may enjoy a satisfactory profit performance notwithstanding the fact that it is operating in an inefficient manner. Conversely, a foreign affiliate's profit performance may be adversely af-

---

[12]See Eric Haueter, "Organizing for International Marketing: Youth and Misconception," *Vital Speeches of the Day,* 49 (August 1, 1983), 620–24.

[13]See Christopher Bartlett, "MNC's: Get Off the Reorganization Merry-Go-Round," *Harvard Business Review* Vol. 61 (March–April 1983), 138–46.

[14]Daniel Shapiro, *Foreign and Domestic Firms in Canada* (Toronto: Butterworths, 1980).

fected by unfavorable currency trends, although its management is highly effective in developing and implementing tactical strategies. A proper data-management system should ideally be able to identify the causal factors associated with the performance of an international division or subsidiary.

Budget Systems

Studies of U.S. multinational corporations show that most use operating budgets to evaluate the performance of foreign operations. Operating budgets encompass both pro forma income statements and cash-flow projections. In effect, managers of foreign divisions and affiliates, in conjunction with headquarters management, establish targets for revenue and cost streams over time. Performance is then evaluated relative to those targets.

A budget system of evaluation has several advantages in international business. Specifically, by establishing the size of tolerable variation, it permits the application of the "management-by-exception" procedure, particularly by headquarters management. Hence, the latter can minimize day-to-day scrutiny of the decisions of affiliate managers and concentrate their time and energy on solving organizational problems and formulating broad corporate strategy. Further, a budget motivates subsidiary managers to put all their efforts into achieving planned goals rather than into manipulating certain variables that make their own affiliates' performance look better.[15]

Comparisons of actual results to budgeted outcomes must proceed quite cautiously in the international firm. In particular, differences across geographic regions may render specific information systems inoperable for some affiliates. For example, if local managers do not fully understand the various managerial decision and control techniques in place, a sophisticated managerial accounting system will lose its usefulness. The likelihood that this problem will emerge is increased by the fact that the international firm must keep accounting records in several languages—making misunderstandings more likely—and also by the fact that a shortage of qualified managerial accountants exists in many countries.[16]

The presence of intercompany transactions can also obscure the relevance of deviations between actual and planned results unless care is taken to acknowledge interdependencies among subsidiaries. For example, unanticipated delays in receiving payments from other affiliates for intercompany sales may saddle an affiliate with "excessive" accounts receivable; however, rather than being evidence of poor financial management in the latter, the excessive receivable position might be the result of a headquarters decision to delay payment from other affiliates located in strong-currency countries. It would be misleading not to take into ac-

---

[15]For a comprehensive discussion of budgeting and other managerial accounting techniques in the international context, see F. P. Kollaritsch, "Managerial Accounting Problems of Multinational Corporations," in H. Peter Holzer, *International Accounting* (New York: Harper & Row Publishers, 1984), pp. 173–204.

[16]Ibid., 175–76.

count the earnings of the rest of the enterprise system that can be attributed to the operations of the affiliate being evaluated.

Other intercountry differences should also be taken into account in evaluating the actual performance of subsidiaries. Prominent among these are tax laws and employment laws. Unanticipated changes in tax laws can dramatically influence (for better or worse) the accounting performance of an overseas affiliate. For example, a change from first in-first out (FIFO) to last in-first out (LIFO) inventory accounting will reduce reported profitability below anticipated profitability in an inflationary economy. Changes in tariffs and customs procedures can also affect affiliate performance.

Perhaps the most significant "uncontrollable" influences on affiliate performance are economic and political in nature. In particular, the timing of the business cycle is not identical from country to country. Hence, a faster than anticipated economic recovery in one country will likely improve the performance of affiliates located there relative to their targeted performance. A principal objective of any management information system, in this case or in related cases, should be to ensure that a manager's performance is judged on the basis of results in those areas over which he or she has control.

Kollaritsch suggests that international firms modify their budget-control systems to acknowledge the complexities induced by a diverse external environment. Specifically, he argues that the unstable environment of certain countries requires that high priority be given to cutting the time horizon for planning. This type of environment also requires that plans be reviewed and revised more frequently. He further suggests that language barriers can be overcome, to a significant extent, by numerical coding of budgetary accounts. A broad-based understanding of accounting-control systems can also be promoted by the exchange of personnel between host and parent countries as well as between affiliates. Kollaritsch stresses that any control system is probably doomed to failure unless affiliate managers understand the objectives, policies, and expectations of headquarters management.[17]

Next to budgets, rate-of-return measures are the most frequently used performance criteria in the international firm. Such measures typically relate income (usually net before taxes) to assets or to equity.[18] These measures may be appropriate where affiliate managers have fairly complete financial and operational independence. In certain countries broader nonfinancial measures of performance may require monitoring. For example, in France since 1978 all companies employing more than 250 people have been required to produce an annual "social report" that details such matters as pay, conditions of health and safety, absenteeism, training, industrial relations, and hours worked.[19]

[17]Ibid., 182–83.

[18]See Sidney Robbins and Robert Stobaugh, *Money in the Multinational Enterprise* (New York: Basic Books, 1973), pp. 143–44.

[19]See Kollaritsch, "Managerial Accounting Problems," p. 180.

Evaluation of these financial and nonfinancial indices of performance also becomes more complex as interdependence between foreign affiliates increases. In most cases, interpretation of performance involves a good deal of subjective judgment on the part of headquarters management.

Computerized Information Systems

It should be apparent that management information systems in the international firm involve the transfer and processing of a great deal of information. Delays in receiving information at headquarters or errors in the information transmitted can be quite costly to the international firm. In this regard, the widespread computerization of management information systems is considered by most experts to have substantially enhanced the capacity of accounting-based and other control systems.

The importance of computerized management information systems has progressively increased over the past twenty-five years. Specifically, there is increasingly greater use of management information systems in international firms for applications in marketing, manufacturing, logistics, and finance functions. The demand for multinational computer systems is being stimulated by increased competition and complexity in international business along with economies of scale in sharing on-line software and information data bases.[20]

Nanus suggests that the multinational use of computers will result in fundamental changes in three critical areas:

1. Decision making: more accurate and timely information will be available to management as a result of the network of libraries, data banks, and research centers in different countries that can be tied together through computer networks.
2. Organizational design: computer systems will facilitate decentralized decision making in the international firm. It will also encourage new supervisory practices and (possibly) significant changes in the characteristics of jobs.
3. Entrepreneurship: multinational computer systems can alert managers to new opportunities (worldwide). They can also promote new approaches to corporate planning—for example, simulation models and polling techniques that can be used to detect changes in the international marketplace. Computers will also enable managers to better tailor products and services to local tastes and preferences.[21]

To be sure, the management of computer systems has become a major activity in both international and purely domestic firms. As in the case of other functional activities we have discussed to this point, the management of computer operations is rendered more complex by a firm's international business activities. It is particularly difficult to coordinate the computerization of affiliates within an integrated management information system.

[20]For a full discussion of these forces, see Burt Nanus, "Business, Government and the Multinational Computer," *Columbia Journal of World Business* Vol. 13 (Spring 1978), 19–26.
[21]Ibid.

Differences across countries often make it difficult to implement corporatewide standards for data processing. For example, regional offices may be at different stages of maturity in their information-systems operations. Furthermore, diverse products and markets in various countries may create a need for different types of information systems. The cost and availability of hardware and applied software may also differ across countries in which the international firm is operating.[22]

Since local help in the form of systems-and-support engineers is likely to be less available in international sites than within the domestic U.S., ease of use for overseas computer installations is frequently stressed by international firms headquartered in the U.S. The poor quality of telephone lines in certain countries can also create data-transmission problems. And while some European countries offer high-quality computer-networking facilities, national telephone companies are government bureaucracies. Requests for services relating to telephone lines may therefore take a long time to be filled.

RESTRICTIONS ON MULTINATIONAL COMPUTER SYSTEMS

One especially important feature of the international data-processing environment is the growing number of legal and regulatory restrictions on the transmission of information across national boundaries. It has been estimated that over sixty countries are either considering or have passed legislation that directly or indirectly affects transnational data flows.[23] A variety of reasons have been offered for the growth of obstacles to the flow of information across borders. Ostensibly, the most important concern is related to the protection of personal data transmitted to and stored in other countries that are considered to have relatively weak privacy-protection laws. These data encompass employment history, family background, salary, and so forth. A somewhat related concern pertains to the protection of "national sovereignty." The flavor of this concern is conveyed by the following statement of Joubert de Oliveira Brizida, executive secretary of Brazil's Special Informatics Secretariat: "It is fundamental that a country have control over the information resources essential to its sovereignty and development."[24]

A more practical and perhaps more important worry is that multinational information systems will lead to jobs lost, or not created, in the data-exporting countries. In this regard, governments are increasingly using legislation to enhance the competitiveness of domestic data-processing companies and equipment producers relative to their foreign counterparts. An example is provided in

[22]For a discussion of these points, see Martin D. J. Buss, "Managing International Information Systems," *Harvard Business Review* Vol. 60 (September–October 1982), 153–62.

[23]Saeed Samiee, "Transnational Data Flow Constraints: A New Challenge For Multinational Firms," *Journal of International Business Studies* 15 (Spring/Summer 1984), 141–50.

[24]See Victor Block, "Barriers to the Free Flow of Information," *Infosystems*, 28 (September 1981), 108ff.

the case of the 1980 Canadian Banking Act, which obliges banks doing business in Canada to carry out the data processing of its customer records in Canada. The act also empowers the Canadian Minister of Finance to suspend processing outside the country if he deems that "such processing is not in the national interest." The Brazilian government turned down an application from the Chase Manhattan Bank to import a computer from a U.S. vendor because the computer was not produced locally, and most foreign processing of Brazilian data is prohibited.[25]

The frustration created by government restrictions on international data transfers has led to actions by management that are—at times—both humorous and bizarre. For example, a high official of an international bank, facing resistance to the movement of computer tapes out of an African country, took a chance on smuggling them across the border. Another example is provided by a diversified consumer-products company, which in seeking to avoid restrictions imposed by two European countries, rented a house straddling their common border so that it could store computer tapes in the environment found to be the more friendly at any given time.[26]

Government laws limiting the ability of international companies to transfer information across borders can impose a variety of costs on these businesses. In particular, they can contribute to poor management decisions. They can also be an obstacle to hiring qualified personnel. In some cases companies may need to duplicate costly data-processing facilities in a number of countries.

Two basic types of information are typically required at corporate headquarters: internal data relating to operations and external data concerning the overseas business environment. The precise type and amount of data required by headquarter affiliates of multinational companies will depend upon the nature of the company's business, including the industries and geographic locations in which they operate.

In this regard, restrictions on the flow of computerized information are especially disruptive to the activities of international financial companies and other service organizations, such as airlines, which need virtually instant consolidation of information. Unfortunately, a lack of uniformity in national privacy laws has compounded the difficulties in gaining an international agreement to moderate the proliferating number of restrictions. Currently, the U.S. government is promoting OECD's 1980 voluntary guidelines on privacy as a means of harmonizing the privacy laws of the OECD member countries. The guidelines include eight principles that corporations would agree to follow when handling personal data.

As in other activities undertaken by the international firm, management must determine the appropriate extent to which responsibility for data-processing activities is centralized in headquarters. Some firms' businesses demand that key

---

[25]See Martin D. J. Buss, "Legislative Threat to Transborder Data Flow," *Harvard Business Review* Vol. 62 (May–June 1984), 111–18.

[26]See Block, "Barriers to the Free Flow of Information," p. 110.

TABLE 15.1   Guidelines for Organizing International Data Processing

1. Determine international data-processing priorities.
2. Create a task force to recommend approaches to be followed.
3. Ensure that broader issues are considered, including:
   (a) The nature of the business in each country
   (b) Corporate structure and style
   (c) Personalities and cultural characteristics of key executives
   (d) The information policy of host governments on issues such as privacy
   (e) Sophistication of technology and its availability in various countries
4. Evaluate proposals with particular emphasis on ease of implementation:
   (a) Ability of proposal to generate support from country managers
   (b) Legality of proposal

Source: Adapted from a discussion in Martin D. J. Buss, "Managing International Information Systems," *Harvard Business Review* Vol. 6 (September–October 1982), 153–162.

data files be managed centrally in order to be accessible to all units of the firm around the globe immediately or on a short delayed-access basis. Airline reservation files for international air carriers require such access. Other firms require integration and on-line updating of only some of their files in specific areas, such as production and logistics, while accounting and other data are essentially processed on a country-by-country basis. Still other firms (typically highly diversified conglomerates) require essentially no integration of data processing across countries.[27]

Companies will also differ in their capacities to integrate data-processing activities within a common system designed by the corporate head office. However, the process in any given organization can potentially be improved by following certain guidelines. A set of guidelines suggested by Buss is summarized in table 15.1. In many ways they resemble our outline of the broad strategic-planning process as discussed in chapter 1. Specifically, the guidelines emphasize the need to establish priorities (or objectives) to consider the international data-processing environment, along with the internal strengths and weaknesses of the organization, and to evaluate proposed data-processing strategies in light of the foregoing. International companies must also develop contacts with government data-protection agencies and understand both the relevant laws and unwritten priorities governing transnational data flows in various countries.

SUMMARY AND CONCLUSIONS

If corporate business plans are to be implemented successfully, managers of a firm's various divisions and affiliates should be clear about the basic objectives of the firm's strategies, since they will be responsible for developing tactics in specific

[27]James Icash, Jr., F. Warren McFarlane, and James L. McKinney, *Corporate Information Systems Management: Texts and Cases* (Homewood, Ill.: Richard D. Irwin, 1983), pp. 457–74.

business activities designed to implement broad business strategies. Headquarters management must also be able to monitor decisions taken by managers in divisions and affiliates, in order to reward behavior that promotes attainment of the firm's global objectives and curtail behavior that is inconsistent with the organization's overall welfare.

While all firms need to have effective and efficient reporting and information systems in place, the requirement is ordinarily more difficult to fulfill in the international firm than in the purely domestic firm, given the heterogeneous environment surrounding the former's business activities. Relevant differences in the economic, political, and even social environments across countries oblige international management to implement formal and informal control systems that recognize the unique aspects of the firm's international business environment.

The formal structure of the international firm constitutes one element of the firm's control system. It is generally agreed that no single structure is ideal or necessarily appropriate at all times. Indeed, a firm may find it advisable to alter its formal structure as its international business activities change and grow over time. Typically, the initial step involves establishing a separate international division located at corporate headquarters. As international business activities grow, regional divisions may be established and eventually "spun off" as separate subsidiaries. A potential problem with this geographically based structure is that it does not sufficiently emphasize product-specific features of the firm's business plans. When both product characteristics and geographic territories are relevant determinants of corporate strategy, a matrix structure may be advisable.

Informal structure encompasses the dimensions of what organizational theorists have come to call an organization's "culture." This refers to the underlying values and mores of senior management that define the boundary between acceptable and unacceptable behavior in the organization. The belief is growing that a firm's culture may be a more effective control mechanism than its formal organizational structure.

Regardless of the formal and informal organizational structures implemented by the firm, management information systems must also be put in place to provide headquarters management with the information needed to monitor the performance of affiliates and their managers. The basis of the international firm's information systems is the capital and operating budgets of divisions and affiliates. Specifically, budgets provide the benchmarks against which actual performance is compared. Deviations from budgeted outcomes provide the basis for "managing by exception." In this respect, it is critical that headquarters management acknowledge the contributions of affiliates to the global organization's performance, even when those contributions do not have a direct impact on an affiliate's measured performance. It is equally important that affiliate management be held accountable only for those determinants of performance over which it has a strong measure of control.

The computer revolution has had its impact upon international business as well as on all other dimensions of society. In particular, it has enhanced the capacity of headquarters management to coordinate a more geographically dispersed set of business activities. At the same time, it has brought to the fore a new set of issues for home-country managers to deal with, including conflicts with host-country governments over the right to transfer computerized information across national boundaries.[28] The growing prominence of data-processing issues in international business underscores the point that business management is a dynamic process—especially in the international context. There are no simple formulas for success. Rather, managing in an international organization represents a commitment to adaptation and personal flexibility. Harkening back to the desired educational characteristics of international managers discussed in chapter 1, it is also apparent that international management represents a commitment to a lifelong education process.

DISCUSSION QUESTIONS

1. In what ways does the organizational-control problem differ between international and purely domestic firms?

2. From what you know about the nature of the fast-foods business, what type of organizational structure do you think would best suit the McDonald's Corporation? What about the Hilton Hotel Company?

3. Now consider General Foods Corporation, which produces a multitude of consumer goods for the international marketplace. Do you think that (ideally) General Foods should have the same organizational structure as the McDonald's Corporation? Explain your answer.

4. What attributes do you think are most desirable in a set of criteria designed to measure the performance of affiliate management? Do you agree that a comparison between actual and planned performance best serves the function of monitoring the performance of affiliates?

5. In what ways might a firm's performance-evaluation procedures for affiliates located in developed countries differ from those for affiliates in less developed countries?

6. What major issues arise in establishing a management information system for the international firm that do not arise (at least to the same extent) in the purely domestic firm?

REFERENCES

CATEORA, PHILLIP, *International Marketing,* 5th ed. Homewood, Ill.: Richard D. Irwin, 1983, chap. 22.

DAVIDSON, WILLIAM H., and PHILLIPE HASPESLAGH, "Shaping a Global Product Organization." *Harvard Business Review* Vol. 60 (July–August 1982), 125–32.

[28]For a comprehensive overview of the relevant transnational issues, see Robert P. Burton, "Transnational Data Flows: International Status, Impact and Accommodation," *Data Management* Vol. 18 (June 1980), 27–33.

Davis, S. M., "Creating a Global Organization." *Columbia Journal of World Business* 7 (1976), 35–47.

Drake, Rodman L., and Lee M. Caudill, "Management of the Large Multinational: Trends and Future Challenges." *Business Horizons* Vol. 24 (May/June 1981), 83–91.

Kelley, Neil D., "Checkpoints for International Data Systems." *Infosystems,* 27, (1980), p. 44.

Kluckas, William, "Planning for International Data Processing." *Datamation* Vol. 24 (November 15, 1978), 56.

Otterbeck, Lars, ed., *The Management of Headquarters—Subsidiary Relationships in Multinational Corporations.* Hampshire, England: Gower Publishing Co., 1981.

Index